MW00352987

Soviet Workers and Late Stalinism

Soviet Workers and Late Stalinism is the first study of labour and labour policy during the critical period of the Soviet Union's postwar recovery and the last years of Stalin. It is also the first detailed social history of the Soviet Union in these years available to non-Russian readers. Using previously inaccessible archival sources, Donald Filtzer describes for the first time the tragic hardships faced by workers and their families right after the war; conditions in housing and health care; the special problems of young workers; working conditions within industry; and the tremendous strains which regime policy placed not just on the mass of the population, but on the cohesion and commitment of key institutions within the Stalinist political system, most notably the trade unions and the procuracy. Donald Filtzer's subtle and compelling book will interest all historians of the Soviet Union and of socialism.

DONALD FILTZER is Professor of Russian History at the University of East London. In addition to many other publications on Russian history, he has written three studies of Soviet labour: *Soviet Workers and Stalinist Industrialization* (London, 1986); *Soviet Workers and De-Stalinization* (Cambridge, 1992); and *Soviet Workers and the Collapse of Perestroika* (Cambridge, 1994).

Soviet Workers and Late Stalinism

Labour and the Restoration of the Stalinist System after World War II

Donald Filtzer

University of East London

CAMBRIDGE
UNIVERSITY PRESS

PUBLISHED BY THE PRESS SYNDICATE OF THE UNIVERSITY OF CAMBRIDGE
The Pitt Building, Trumpington Street, Cambridge, United Kingdom

CAMBRIDGE UNIVERSITY PRESS
The Edinburgh Building, Cambridge CB2 2RU, UK
40 West 20th Street, New York, NY 10011-4211, USA
477 Williamstown Road, Port Melbourne, VIC 3207, Australia
Ruiz de Alarcón 13, 28014 Madrid, Spain
Dock House, The Waterfront, Cape Town 8001, South Africa

http://www.cambridge.org

First published 2002

Printed in the United Kingdom at the University Press, Cambridge

Typeface Plantin 10/12 pt   *System* LaTeX 2$_\varepsilon$ [TB]

A catalogue record for this book is available from the British Library

ISBN 0 521 81503 7 hardback

To Mick, Sue, and Natasha

Contents

Tables

Preface and acknowledgements

Every idea for a book has a particular genesis, and the genesis of this one lies in a monumental stupidity. When I first began to teach Soviet history, and for quite a few years thereafter, I was somehow possessed of the insane notion that the USSR's experience during World War II was essentially of military importance, and that the political and social history of the period were relatively uninteresting. I therefore used to race through this part of the syllabus as quickly as possible. I knew from standard texts, of course, that the war had seen a number of changes in state policy, for example, a tacit toleration of semi-private trade in agriculture and a rapprochement with the Orthodox Church, but I nevertheless managed to keep such inconvenient pieces of information from challenging my basic prejudices. Yet deep down inside I knew there was something not quite right with this interpretation. When I had read K. S. Karol's autobiography, *Solik*, I remember marvelling at his descriptions of the way in which soldiers separated from their units or whose companies had been destroyed or dispersed in battle wandered more or less freely around the country seeking another military unit to which they could attach themselves. Films about the war made in the Khrushchev and Brezhnev years painted a similar picture of a population over which the state – the Stalinist police state – was exercising surprisingly little control during a time of dire national emergency. The scales finally fell from my eyes when I read John Barber's and Mark Harrison's social history of the USSR during the war, *The Soviet Home Front*, in which they described how the regime intensified the centralization of some key areas of decision-making and social life (primarily economic and military planning and internal discipline within the factories), but at the same time radically decentralized others, most notably the delegation of a great deal of independence down to local Party and state bodies which needed such discretion and flexibility in order successfully to prosecute the war.

This process of intellectual self-reform, however, posed another dilemma. During the 1930s the Stalinist regime and the emerging Soviet elite had waged a bloody confrontation with the majority of their own society, and partially with themselves, in order to put in place a stable and reproducible social and economic system from which they could extract their privileges. To ensure the perpetuation of this system and their domination over it they had also erected a strong police state. Yet in the wake of the Nazi invasion the regime had been forced to relax many of its controls over the population. But if this was the case, how after the war did the regime put the genie back in the bottle, so to speak, that is, how did it restore the system of power relations that it had struggled to erect prior to 1941? This was going to be my Big Idea. I soon, discovered, however, that it was not my idea at all. When discussing it with my former colleague, Robert Service, he immediately directed me to a newspaper interview on precisely this theme given during *perestroika* by the Soviet historian, Gennadii Bordyugov, and to a series of articles by another Russian historian, Elena Zubkova. Zubkova's articles proved to be a revelation, for as I discuss in the introduction, she had identified a more or less similar problematic and begun to work towards an answer. It was from these articles, and the monograph, *Obshchestvo i reformy*, into which she developed them, that I went on to construct the detailed study of labour and industry that is the subject of the present book. The approach I have adopted therefore owes much to her early analysis and in many ways extends it.

The successful completion of the research and the production of a hopefully successful monograph owe a great deal to an inordinately large number of people and institutions. Starting first with collective entities, pride of place should probably go to the archivists and staff at the many archives listed in the bibliography. The archives in Russia struggle under almost unimaginable resource constraints, yet without exception everywhere I worked I encountered supreme professionalism and warmth, an immeasurable amount of indispensable advice, and some very excellent senses of humour.

The second collective thanks are to the Department of Sociology and Anthropology at the University of East London. The department's research committee financed all of my visits to the archives plus attendance at a number of international conferences, at which I was able to present preliminary drafts of most of the book's chapters as papers. Our research committee is a model of how a working-class institution with very little money can manage a research budget in a way that allows hard-pressed staff to find time to develop their research and produce publications. I speak not just for myself, but for everyone in my department, when I say that other British universities might wish to emulate our system. I am grateful, too, to colleagues who never complained when I took off as soon as summer teaching had ended and left them to sit through the tedium of end-of-year examiners' meetings (I did, however, always have my marking done before I left). As the work was nearing completion the department generously gave me a sabbatical during the academic year of 2000/1, which, in combination with a Research Leave Award from the Arts and Humanities Research Board, allowed me to finish off the research and write the book.

The third collective thanks are to the Arts and Humanities Research Board and the British Academy for their financial support. As already mentioned, the AHRB funded the first half of my sabbatical leave, during which I completed the final tranche of research prior to writing the manuscript. The British Academy kindly gave me an international conference grant, which allowed me to present a draft of the conclusion to the American Association for the Advancement of Slavic Studies conference in November 2000.

The final collective thanks go to the former Soviet citizens in Baltimore and Samara who allowed me to interview them about their experiences after the war. The relatively small number of direct quotations or references to these interviews in the book may give the impression that they were of peripheral importance, but this is quite misleading. Their accounts played a profound role in shaping my understanding of this period, not the least by showing the pitfalls of document-based histories. The tiniest points of detail dropped into the middle of a conversation could prove decisive to explaining the larger context of a topic or to compelling me to rethink an erroneous or overly presumptuous interpretation.

As for the many individuals who helped me, it is simply impossible to say that one person's contribution was greater than another's. They all were important in different ways, and so I shall just cite people in alphabetical order.

Chris Burton read through the section of chapter 3 which deals with public health, offered many corrections and comments, and, most importantly of all, directed me to additional archival sources without which I could not have worked the material into a form which warranted inclusion in the final manuscript.

Tim Butler, in addition to his role as chair of our departmental research committee, has given me a tremendous amount of moral encouragement over the years, including at some very key moments in the early 1990s when I was beginning to think I'd never again complete another piece of serious research. It was largely thanks to Tim that I began this project in the first place.

Bob Davies and I spent quite a few lunch times in the archives in Moscow discussing my work and, as always, he gave me more insights than I can count into what it all might mean.

Sarah Davies invited me to give a paper at the 1999 conference of the British Association of Slavonic and East European Studies, which served as an early draft of chapter 4. Our discussions of her own work on postwar Stalinism played no small role in helping me to work out my larger analysis of the period.

Sheila Fitzpatrick acted as discussant at this panel and posed for me a number of key questions to which I would need to find the answers before turning the paper into a publication. As it turned out, it was the search for these answers which led me on to the material which became chapter 5.

Juliane Fürst discussed with me her dissertation research on the Komsomol after the war and helped me to understand my material on young workers in its broader perspective. She also kindly took time off from her own work to find, read, and copy key documents for me in the Komsomol archive when I could not get to Moscow to do this myself.

Ina Giller, formerly of the Jewish Community Center in Baltimore, arranged for me an exhaustive programme of interviews there in January 1997.

Lena Gordeeva transcribed all of my interview tapes and offered valuable advice on how to interpret the experiences which my interviewees reported.

Yoram Gorlizki invited me to participate in a panel he organized at the 1999 conference of the American Association for the Advancement of Slavic Studies; the paper I presented there became a draft outline of the final book.

Barbara Harrison, Chair of the Department of Sociology and Anthropology at the University of East London, has given me a great deal of moral and administrative support over the course of my research, and authorized my sabbatical during the academic year 2000/1.

Mark Harrison generously read the manuscript draft, offered very extensive and detailed comments and suggestions, and gave advice on how to interpret the economic data.

Julie Hessler spent many, many hours reading through the chapters on the standard of living, suggested corrections and additional sources, and engaged in ongoing correspondence and debate which played a very large part in helping me to clarify my ideas and to present the material more accurately.

Sylvia Hudson handled the paperwork for all my trips to Russia, kept me (sometimes reluctantly on my part) in touch with real-world events while I was in Moscow, and together with Diane Ball, Susan Fitzgerald, and Iris Stevens, proves what I believe to be a general law of British higher education: that the brains, as well as the soul, behind any successful academic department reside in the office staff.

Natasha Kurashova has over the years discussed with me every single aspect of the research and how to interpret it – not to mention giving the odd bit of help with tricky linguistic issues and rather large amounts of support and encouragement.

Vera Kurashova helped me to track down urgently needed references which I could not find in the UK.

Hiroaki Kuromiya read a draft of the manuscript, made a number of important corrections, and offered key suggestions for revision. His strong support of the project has been warmly appreciated.

Kevin Murphy also read the manuscript, suggested some very substantial corrections, directed me to the archive documents I needed to make these changes, and shared with me the findings of his own work in local archives in this period.

Stefan Plaggenborg invited me to contribute a lengthy chapter on the Soviet economy and society during the postwar period to a volume of the *Handbuch der Geschichte Rußlands* under his editorship, which provided me with an early opportunity to systematize my ideas and work out what eventually became a final plan for the book.

Pavel Romanov organized a programme of interviews for me in Samara during the summer of 1998.

Bob Service was instrumental (and not for the first time in my career) in the early stages of the work helping me to formulate the issues and advising me on key sources to help me to get started.

Peter Solomon arranged for me to present a summary of my research to a conference of the University of Toronto's Stalin Era Research and Archive Project, and invited me to participate in the panel he organized at the VI World Congress for Central and East European Studies in Tampere, Finland, in the summer of 2000. The paper I presented there turned out to be a near-final draft of chapter 5 of the book, and benefited greatly from Peter's comments. Peter also gave me advice on sources to use for my research into the procuracy, and provided me with photocopies of relevant material which he had found in the files of the procuracy and the Ministry of Justice.

Isabel Tirado helped me to learn my way around the Komsomol archive and devoted a lot of time to discussing with me what I had found there.

Steve Wheatcroft gave advice on how to interpret family budget data, and directed me to additional files I needed to complete that part of the manuscript.

Elena Zubkova gave me priceless – and that is far too mild a word – help in the early stages of my research. She instructed me about the various sources I would need to use, helped me to define the topic more precisely, referred me to key Russian secondary sources, and gave a lot of useful information on the significance of specific items I was finding in the archives.

Finally, some of the material in chapters 2 and 3 appeared originally in the article, 'The Standard of Living of Soviet Industrial Workers in the Immediate Postwar Period, 1945–1948', published in *Europe-Asia Studies*, vol. 51, no. 6, 1999, pp. 1013–38, and is used here with the kind permission of the journal.

As readers will gather from this list, I have been extremely fortunate. Colleagues have shown tremendous generosity reading and commenting on conference papers and draft chapters, engaging in lengthy and time-consuming correspondence, agreeing to informal meetings so that I could ask for advice and help, sharing information about which archives and which documents I should use, and sharing copies of documents which they had found themselves. The spirit of solidarity and cooperation they have shown has been a paragon of what academic research should be about. I hope that in some small way I have been able to repay their favours. For all their input, however, none of them carries any blame or responsibility for the mistakes and shortcomings that almost certainly are still there. For those only I can take full credit.

Terms and abbreviations

FZO (pl., FZO)	factory training school (*shkola fabrichno-zavodskogo obucheniya*), a three- or six-month training school for 'mass' trades
glavk (pl., *glavki*)	chief administration, a subdivision of a ministry
Gosplan	State Planning Commission (Gosudarstvennaya planovaya komissiya)
Gulag	Chief Administration of Camps, more generally used as the name for the system of MVD labour camps
ispolkom	executive committee (*ispolnitel'nyi komitet*)
ITR	engineering and technical personnel (*inzhenerno-tekhnicheskie rabotniki*)
kolkhoz	collective farm (*kollektivnoe khozyaistvo*)
kolkhoznik (pl., *kolkhozniki*)	collective farmer or collective farm member
komandirovka	temporary posting or assignment to work in another locality
Komsomol	Communist Youth League, formally known as the All-Union Leninist Communist Union of Youth, or VLKSM
kulaks	prosperous peasants deported into internal exile or sent to labour camps during collectivization of the 1930s
militia	police (*militsiya*) – the regular police force, as distinct from the secret police

Mintyazhstroi	Ministry of Construction of Enterprises in Heavy Industry (Ministerstvo stroitel′stva predpriyatii tyazheloi promyshlennosti)
MPS	Ministry of Railways (Ministerstvo putei soobshcheniya)
MTS	machine-tractor station
MVD	Ministry of Internal Affairs (Ministerstvo vnutrennikh del), in charge of the system of labour camps (Gulag) and police (militia)
norms	individual output quotas for workers on piece rates
obkom	oblast′ committee (*oblastnoi komitet*) of Communist Party, trade union, or other organization
oblast′ (pl., oblasti)	region, roughly equivalent to a province
orgnabor	organized recruitment of workers
ORS (pl., ORSy)	Department of Workers' Supply (Otdel rabochego snabzheniya)
Procuracy	Public Prosecutor's Office
procurator	public prosecutor
progul	unauthorized absenteeism from work
raikom	district committee (*raionnyi komitet*) of Communist Party, trade union, or other organization
raion (pl., raiony)	district (administrative subdivision of a city, oblast′, or other larger territorial unit)
RSFSR	Russian Soviet Federative Socialist Republic (Rossiiskaya Sovetskaya Federativnaya Sotsialisticheskaya Respublika)
RU (pl., RU)	trade school (*remeslennoe uchilishche*) under the Ministry of Labour Reserves, a two-year training school in skilled trades
sovkhoz	state farm (*sovetskoe khozyaistvo*)
sovkhoznik (pl., *sovkhozniki*)	state farm worker
SSSR	Union of Soviet Socialist Republics (Soyuz Sovetskikh Sotsialisticheskikh Respublik)

Stakhanovites	model workers rewarded for achieving high output targets or, especially in the postwar period, adopting allegedly advanced production methods
TsSU	Central Statistical Administration (Tsentral'noe statisticheskoe upravlenie)
VLKSM	All-Union Leninist Communist Union of Youth (Vsesoyuznyi Leninskii Kommunisticheskii Soyuz Molodezhi) – see Komsomol
VTsSPS	All-Union Central Council of Trade Unions (Vsesoyuznyi Tsentral'nyi Sovet Professional'nykh Soyuzov)
ZhU (pl., ZhU)	trade school (*zheleznodorozhnoe uchilishche*) to train skilled workers for the railways; equivalent to an RU

The notes use standard abbreviations for Russian archive references, which consist of five elements:

1. The abbreviation of the archive name (the full names of the archives are given in the bibliography).
2. f. = *fond*, or fund. These generally correspond to a particular institution or major subdivision of an institution, for example, the USSR Procuracy, an industrial ministry, or a specific trade union.
3. op. = *opis'*, or inventory. The *opisi* are the primary subdivisions of a *fond*. Sometimes the *opisi* represent subdivisions or departments within an organization; some *fondy* simply divide the *opisi* chronologically.
4. d. = *delo*, or file. These are the actual folders containing the documents.
5. l. = *list(y)*, or sheet(s). Russian archives give files sheet numbers, rather than page numbers, since a file almost always contains many different documents, each of which had its own separate pagination when it was originally written.

Thus a typical reference will be something like this: GARF, f. 8131, op. 29, d. 476, l. 259–60. The document will be in GARF (State Archive of the Russian Federation), *fond* 8131 (Procuracy of the USSR), *opis'* 29, *delo* 476, *listy* 259–60.

Introduction: the political imperatives of the postwar recovery

In early May 1990, just before the traditional 9 May Victory Day celebrations marking the 45th anniversary of the end of World War II in Europe, *Komsomol'skaya pravda* published a lengthy interview with the Soviet historian Gennadii Bordyugov, under the title 'The Stolen Victory'.[1] In it Bordyugov advanced the idea that, far from the Stalinist government and the Soviet people having forged an unbreakable unity to defeat the Nazi aggressors, there were serious conflicts and divergences between them. Basing his argument on recently uncovered documents which attested to significant popular discontent both during and after the war, he argued that what he called 'the people' and the Stalinist regime had fought the war with different sets of objectives. The people's aim had been the liberation of their country, and having accomplished that goal they believed that they would be able to create a freer (if not totally free) society. In part they were reacting against what they saw as the incompetence of the national government in the early days of the war, and the open corruption of local officials throughout its duration; in part they based their expectations on various relaxations in regime policy which Stalin had introduced in order to forge a stronger national unity, and which they believed would continue. Stalin and the leadership, however, had other war aims, namely the survival of their system of power. From this point of view the changes Stalin made, such as the relaxation of state control over the collective farms, the rapprochement with the Russian Orthodox Church, the modicum of intellectual freedom granted to the intelligentsia, and the displacement of revolutionary rhetoric by appeals to national pride and open nationalism, were not reforms of the system, but tactical manoeuvres made in the interests of victory. In Bordyugov's view, the regime and the population had emerged from the war with different agendas, and it was Stalin's that prevailed.

---

[1] Interview between Gennadii Bordyugov and Aleksandr Afanas'ev, *Komsomol'skaya pravda*, 5 May 1990.

This interpretation directly challenged an assumption commonly held in both the former USSR and the West, that the Soviet Union's victory had won for Stalin and his regime massive and unquestioning popular support. This assumption, however, had always sat alongside another one which at first view would seem to be in direct contradiction to the first, namely that the postwar period marked the apex of what Western historians labelled 'High Stalinism'. Until relatively recently most studies of these years concentrated on high politics and the waves of repression that Stalin and the leadership meted out against suspect groups within the population and even against the elite's own members. We know, for instance, that national minorities were subjected to sustained persecution during the war and afterwards – they made up the vast bulk of those sent into internal exile as 'special settlers'. We also know that many Soviet soldiers and civilians who had been captured by the Nazis or deported into the Reich as forced labourers were sent to labour camps upon their repatriation.[2] In 1948 Andrei Zhdanov, the member of the inner circle who was responsible for ideological matters, launched a vicious campaign to stifle any semblance of independent thinking within the intelligentsia, a campaign which to this day carries his name, the *zhdanovshchina*. Its attack on all things Western and, more importantly, on anyone accused of sympathy with Western ideas or cultural trends meshed closely with the openly anti-Semitic campaign against so-called cosmopolitans, which at its low point saw the persecution and execution of leaders of the Soviet Jewish Anti-Fascist Committee. If softness towards the West or Jewishness did not provide sufficient pretext for persecution, it was always possible to be branded a 'Titoist', in the wake of Stalin's humiliation at the hands of the leader of the Yugoslav Communist Party, who had had the temerity to assert his independence from Moscow. Following Zhdanov's death in late 1948, a wave of intrigue gripped the leadership itself, as Georgii Malenkov, a rival of Zhdanov's, reasserted his ascendancy within the Party Secretariat and the Council of Ministers by purging – and executing – many of Zhdanov's former allies (some on charges of 'Titoism'). And when it must have seemed that the blood-letting was finally coming to an end, a few months before Stalin died we had the infamous 'Doctors' Plot', where a group of mainly Jewish Kremlin doctors were arrested and accused of plotting to murder Stalin and the rest of the Kremlin leadership. Taken together it all adds up to a grim picture of what in reality was a very grim time.[3]

---

[2] Davies, *Soviet History in the Yeltsin Era*, p. 167.
[3] On the politics of this period, see Carrère d'Encausse; Conquest; Dunmore, *The Stalinist Command Economy* and *Soviet Politics, 1945–1953*; Gorlizki, 'Party Revivalism' and 'Stalin's Cabinet'; Hahn; Kostyrchenko; McCagg; and Rapoport.

The obvious question here is, if there had been such close identification between populace and regime after the war, why such extensive terror was necessary. The account given by Bordyugov suggests a resolution of the contradiction by challenging the essential premise: the identification did not exist or, if it did, it was sufficiently tenuous that the regime could not take for granted that its political domination was secure. On this interpretation, the leadership needed to resort to terror in order to reestablish its political preeminence and control over society. Bordyugov was not, in fact, the first to pose this possibility. Back in the 1970s, Vera Dunham, who was not a historian but a literary specialist, had produced a highly insightful and provocative analysis of the social relations of late Stalinist society based on the evidence provided by Soviet fiction.[4] Her book has subsequently become a classic text in the methodology of social and literary analysis, but what perhaps escaped the attention of most historians was the book's introduction, in which she set out her underpinning interpretation of what she saw as a conflict between leadership and populace immediately after World War II. The causes for that conflict were not, in her view, difficult to trace, nor were the Stalinist regime's reactions. The war, she argued, had unleashed 'obstreperous elements' within the population, whose aspirations and behaviour provoked widespread fear of dissent within the regime, which responded by 'swelling the size of the concentration camp population'. Dunham's main argument was that force alone was not sufficient to restore the regime to a position of unchallenged authority. It needed to go further and create a social base for itself within what she called the new 'middle class', similar, in fact, to what the regime had done during the industrialization of the 1930s when it promoted hundreds of thousands of young people from working-class and peasant backgrounds into the ranks of management and the technical intelligentsia. In the postwar period the regime would accomplish this task through what Dunham called 'The Big Deal', that is, the promise of 'middle-class' lifestyles to this stratum, in the midst of general deprivation.[5]

Given that Dunham had constructed this argument without access to any historical documentation, but strictly on the basis of personal observation and a close analysis of Soviet fiction, it is remarkable how accurate it turned out to be. She may have overestimated the extent of popular discontent after the war, the homogeneity of the demands and aspirations which different sections of the populace articulated, and even perhaps the size of the repression, but in its general contours she was, in my view, correct.[6]

[4] Dunham.   [5] *Ibid.*, pp. 12–13.
[6] Dunham's thesis has recently been taken up and approached from an entirely different standpoint in the book by J. Eric Duskin, *Stalinist Reconstruction*. Duskin seeks to show

It was left to a later Soviet/Russian historian, Elena Zubkova, to take advantage of the limited access to archives permitted under *perestroika* and develop the idea of the 'Stolen Victory' with historiographical rigour and the necessary attention to detail. Not long after Bordyugov's *Komsomol'skaya pravda* interview, Zubkova began publishing a series of path-breaking articles in the journal *Bol'shevik* and its post-Soviet successor, *Svobodnaya mysl'*.[7] Following along the lines set out by Bordyugov, she posed the question of why the various pressures and discontents outlined by Dunham had failed to lead to a concerted movement for reform. The answer may seem obvious, given the enormous power of the Stalinist repressive apparatus, but this was not, in fact, how events unfolded. For Zubkova the main potential vehicles for change were the returning veterans, the *frontoviki* (literally, those who had served at the front). The solidarity they experienced in the trenches, their growing accustomed to taking their own decisions and to speaking amongst each other with relative freedom, the disillusion they experienced when they marched into Central Europe, and the feelings of self-confidence they enjoyed as the ones who had won the victory all made them a difficult element to integrate back into society. Moreover, they continued to mingle with one another after the war: in communal flats, in dormitories, and even in squalid beer cellars known as 'Blue Danubes'. The other side of this equation was that the Stalinist regime's mechanisms of social control were themselves less than secure. During the 1946 elections for the USSR Supreme Soviet people readily expressed dissent, including the view that the elections were a waste of time and money, since the Party would impose its own candidates anyway. Zubkova cites similar outbursts at factory meetings. Nor was the regime's army of propagandists and political educators particularly adept at explaining the leadership's position:

that after the war the leadership deliberately cultivated the technical intelligentsia as a privileged social group by abandoning what he calls the voluntarism and class-based foundations of its prewar promotion policies in favour of a new emphasis on professionalism and scientific-technical training. Thus the intelligentsia saw its social role enhanced not simply through higher consumption, but by acknowledgement of its professional status and the greater managerial authority it was given on the shop floor. The book is also worthy of interest because, although it appeared in 1999, the research for it was clearly done when access to archives was still limited. Duskin has used some archives, but extracts most of his evidence from published sources. In an era when the use of archives has become almost a fetish it is gratifying to see that it is still possible to derive an understanding of key social processes in the USSR through a careful reading and piecing together of what the censors allowed into print. More extensive use of archives might have allowed Duskin to provide additional detail and to write a longer and perhaps more interesting book, but I doubt that it would have led him to a different analysis. This analysis may indeed be flawed – I am not fully competent to judge – but if so it is not because of the sources he chose.

[7] See the list of Zubkova's publications on this theme in the bibliography.

their own political literacy was extremely rudimentary and many simply did not know what particular line they were supposed to take.[8]

If change did not come about it was not, according to Zubkova, because the regime immediately launched a wave of arrests and repression directed at the general population. In almost a mirror image of Dunham's argument, which stressed the privileges offered to an aspiring 'middle class', Zubkova identifies popular exhaustion and poverty. For ordinary people, their main hope was that the extreme hardships and strains should end, that they should be left in peace to try to rebuild something. When the harvest failure of 1946 crushed these hopes and instead sent living standards plummeting further, the result was deep popular demoralization which gave the regime additional breathing space. It was only then, essentially from 1948 onwards, that the regime felt sufficiently confident to assert its political grip and resort to the open repression which I briefly described above.[9] The significance of this repression for Zubkova was that, with the manifest popular exhaustion and dissipation of political energy, the only social group from which any pressures for reform might have come was now the intelligentsia, and it was they who were its main victims. They were not, however, its sole or even primary target for, in attacking the intelligentsia and reasserting the role of the Party leadership as the sole arbiter of what was correct and safe to think, the regime was demonstrating to all of society, not just the intellectuals, that dissent and opposition were futile. 'One should not think that everyone was ruled only by fear. Fear, of course, was there, but even stronger (or in any case, more weighty) was, in my view, the consciousness of the fact that struggle was hopeless.'[10]

It was this, in Zubkova's view, that led 'High Stalinism' into its dead end. The regime may have achieved a political victory, but the fundamental economic and social crises facing the country were not going to go away. Instead they continued to ripen. The popular energies which

---

[8] Zubkova, 'Obshchestvennaya atmosfera posle voiny (1945–1946)', p. 12; 'Obshchestvennaya atmosfera posle voiny (1948–1952)', p. 83. Amir Weiner, in his recent study, *Making Sense of War*, draws rather different conclusions from similar observations about the *frontoviki*. The book is an analysis of the postwar reconstruction of Soviet political institutions in Vinnitsa oblast' in Ukraine, and in it Weiner argues that for both returning soldiers and their families the war experience served to bind them to the Soviet system, a fact which helps explain the weakness of Ukrainian nationalism in that region. Ironically, in Vinnitsa it was the partisans who were seen as untrustworthy because of their independence and wartime exposure to anti-Soviet propaganda, although this was not necessarily true of other oblasti in that part of Ukraine. See in particular ch. 1, afterword, and pp. 305, 312, 326–8. The argument of the book is beautifully constructed but whether it has a wider relevance to anywhere else in the USSR outside Vinnitsa oblast' is open to question.
[9] Zubkova, 'Obshchestvennaya atmosfera posle voiny (1945–1946)', pp. 4–14.
[10] Zubkova, 'Obshchestvennaya atmosfera posle voiny (1948–1952)', p. 86.

might have provided the basis for solving them had been scattered and coerced into quiescence. This left the only possibility of change within the leadership itself, and this was impossible so long as Stalin remained alive.[11]

It is now over twenty years since Dunham published *In Stalin's Time* and over ten years since Zubkova's first article appeared in *Bol'shevik*. Since that time interest in the postwar reconstruction among both Western and Russian scholars has broadened considerably, although much of it is still work in progress by Ph.D students or is only now being published. But we already know that, as in the USSR in the 1930s, the society was not passive and that the institutions through which the leadership needed to transmit and enforce its policies were far from monolithic. Much of this book is devoted to demonstrating both of these points.

In their different ways both Dunham and Zubkova argue that following the war the Stalinist regime faced a political crisis. That crisis never reached a point at which it threatened to topple the elite from power, but so long as it persisted the elite could not exercise effective control over the society. The regime thus faced a political imperative not just to reassert that control, but to do so through the political institutions and hierarchies of power through which it had ruled before the war. What this book argues is that the regime faced a parallel crisis within the economy, and that the resolutions of these twin crises were intimately linked.

The process of industrialization during the early 1930s can be viewed as the period of what we might term 'primitive Stalinist accumulation'. By forcing down consumption, driving millions of peasants off the land into industry or into the slave labour sector, and by destroying the working class as an independent social and political entity, the emerging Soviet elite had been able to lay the economic foundations of a specifically Soviet system of production through which it could reproduce its control over the surplus product and the extraction of its privileges. By the end of the 1930s this system had achieved a position of relative stability, perhaps even reproducibility. It faced no organized opposition from either the working class or the peasantry, both of which had been effectively atomized. In the wake of the purges it had restored some degree of continuity and stability to industrial management. Granted, the economy faced serious structural problems. Agricultural productivity was still low in the wake of the calamity of collectivization. Production within industrial enterprises was badly organized and suffered from chronic shortages of materials, frequent breakdowns of machinery, and poor quality of both inputs and outputs. Innovation and technological modernization

---

[11] *Ibid.*, p. 88.

were haphazard, if they occurred at all. Although no one could have understood this at the time, these were permanent structural flaws within the Stalinist system, which imbedded within it a long-term tendency towards slower growth and loss of dynamic, but *within* that system the elite's privileges and those of its social support in the managerial and technical intelligentsia appeared secure.

World War II threw all of this into chaos. Economic priorities and production profiles had to be radically regeared to the war effort. The country lost large tracts of its principal agricultural and industrial regions. Wherever possible factories were physically dismantled and carted thousands of kilometres eastwards into the Ural mountains or beyond, where they were hastily reassembled. There were huge population movements, some planned, others totally spontaneous. Lines of command, both political and economic, were altered, so that greater centralization of key decision-making at the very top coexisted with greater latitude and freedom for local political officials and managers. Without such decentralization it would have been impossible to prosecute the war effort. Thus the war brought not simply massive physical destruction, the contours of which I outline at the beginning of chapter 1, but disruption to the whole political and decision-making edifice through which the elite had transmitted its decisions to lower echelons and through which it had expected those decisions to be enforced.

What this meant was that, when the war ended, the regime faced a crisis not just of acceptance and popular expectations, but of monumental physical and institutional proportions. It had to restore a shattered economy, and at the same time it had to reconstruct the institutional foundations through which it had managed that economy. This was not an administrative or organizational issue. It was highly political. The reconsolidation of the elite's political control over society required the rapid restoration of the system of production on which that control had been based. In this sense the postwar period saw a partial repetition of the process of primitive accumulation which had been effected during the first two five-year plans of 1928–37. Living standards were forced down; millions of peasants were conscripted, cajoled, or driven by economic necessity into abandoning the land for work in industry and construction; and the slave labour sector was considerably expanded – all so that 'capital' and labour power could be concentrated in core sectors of mining, iron and steel, construction, and machine-building.

To accomplish this in a society that was also in tremendous flux and whose political docility and loyalty were not entirely secure added both urgency and complexity to the task. In the regime's eyes it demanded an almost unprecedented degree of control over labour power.

To understand this we need to appreciate a fundamental change that took place in the prewar and postwar position of Soviet workers. One of the most important differences between the process of accumulation in the 1930s and that which took place after the war was the erosion of the distinction between slave and free labour. At the risk of oversimplification, until 1940, when unauthorized job-changing was made a criminal offence and the regime introduced compulsory labour conscription for rural teenagers,[12] the regime had maintained a fairly clear distinction between the two categories. Free labourers were keenly aware that they had virtually no political liberty and that if they even discussed the possibility of organizing a strike or some other form of industrial action they would either lose their lives or join the slave labour sector. But so long as they abjured activity which the regime might deem politically dangerous or escaped arbitrary denunciation during the terror of 1936–8, they were pretty much left alone. They could change jobs as often as they wished, they could violate labour discipline regulations and suffer only relatively minor, non-judicial sanctions, and they could exercise considerable control over the organization and execution of their work. The main weapons which the regime employed to try to force workers to conform to its desires and demands were economic, in particular yearly rises in output quotas ('norms' in Russian) and wage cuts through which the elite tried to increase the intensity of labour and the rate of exploitation.

During the war this distinction became blurred, as workers in all but the most peripheral industries were declared to have been mobilized and could be sent to work wherever the regime chose to direct them. In the postwar period these regulations were left in force, and in certain respects even augmented. When workers had faced a catastrophic fall in their standard of living during the First Five-Year Plan (1928–32) they had responded with a combination of strikes and mass protests and by simply quitting their jobs and seeking employment somewhere where conditions might be less intolerable. There was also a dramatic decline of discipline and order in the factories through absenteeism and insubordination. In the postwar period neither of these avenues was available. There was simply no question of strikes or mass protests – the power of the state even in the uncertain postwar situation was simply too great. Job-changing and absenteeism were not just criminal offences: industrial workers who left their employment faced a spell in a labour camp of between five and eight years; workers on rail or water transport would receive three to ten years. To this extent the regime should have found it easier to impose its control over labour power and to extract from it a greater surplus product.

---

[12] For a fuller discussion of these laws, see ch. 5.

This, as we shall see, was the main objective of regime policy. The actual implementation of this policy was far less straightforward. It provoked tremendous social strains and upheavals. Perhaps the most obvious and dramatic was the spontaneous flight from the factories which workers and industrial trainees undertook in defiance of the draconian penalties. Other stresses were less overt but probably had more long-term consequences, in particular the difficulties which the regime had in socializing the millions of young labour conscripts whom it dragged out of the village to work in its factories, mines, and construction sites.

In the end, of course, the elite did succeed in putting the Stalinist 'mode of production' back together again, but its victory came at a high cost. No less than during the 1930s, the Stalinist system was riven by polycratic tendencies not just at the level of political relations within the leadership, or between the leadership and its agents at local level, but more fundamentally in its relations with society at large. A system that aspired to near-total control over its subjects singularly failed to achieve it. Political opposition within society, and among industrial workers in particular, may have been virtually nonexistent, but the repression and material deprivation through which the elite attempted to demoralize society and thereby to render it harmless provoked millions of individuals to take spontaneous actions which undermined the economic reconstruction and which the regime proved unable to curb or control. More durably, insofar as the Soviet Union's structural, as opposed to conjunctural, economic problems emanated directly from the Stalinist political system, the victory of that system effectively rendered it permanently vulnerable to long-term decline, an issue which I analyse in more detail in the conclusion.

The plan of the book is as follows. The first chapter analyses the sources from which the regime drew most of the new workers for industry, construction, and transport, in particular the different roles played by the slave labour sector, that is, the prisoners in the labour camps run by the Ministry of Internal Affairs, and the large army of what I call indentured labourers, that is, workers who were nominally free, but who were effectively coerced into entering the workforce and who were bound to their place of work under threat of harsh criminal sanctions if they left. The two main categories of indentured labourers were so-called organized recruitment, and the network of vocational training schools under the USSR Ministry of Labour Reserves.

Chapters 2 and 3 analyse workers' living conditions. Chapter 2 examines the food crisis of 1946–7. The crisis began with the harvest failure of 1946, which led to a famine in rural regions of Ukraine and Moldavia, but its ramifications extended way beyond this to virtually every sector of the non-agricultural economy and over the entire territory of the USSR. The crisis took on the severity that it did because the regime, which very probably had the reserves of food needed to avert rural starvation and urban malnutrition, refused to tap these reserves, but instead pushed down consumption by reducing or removing altogether workers' entitlements to rations. Chapter 3 takes the story into the second half of the period, from the end of rationing in 1948 through to Stalin's death. It argues that there was a significant improvement in living standards, but that consumption of both food and consumer items remained at a very basic level. It also looks at two other aspects of living standards, namely housing conditions and health care, and concludes that the rate of improvement in these areas was significantly slower than the increase in food supplies. I therefore label this period one of 'attenuated recovery'.

Chapter 4 examines the special position of young workers. They were one of the two main sources of new labour power in this period, and they suffered intense deprivation. Moreover, their standard of living improved far more slowly than did that of other workers. Labour turnover among this group was very high, and remained so even when illegal job-changing among adult workers dropped to almost insignificant levels. Their poverty, their generally abysmal housing conditions, and the discrimination they suffered at work from factory managers created serious barriers to the regime's attempts to socialize them into what we might term model Stalinist citizens.

Chapter 5 analyses one of the least known and most intriguing aspects of the postwar period, the mass defiance of the wartime laws against job-changing. Workers in coal mining and construction, and for a time also metallurgy, fled their jobs and went back to the villages from which they had been recruited or conscripted. So, too, did the young students in the vocational training schools attached to these industries. What we shall see, however, is that few of them were ever apprehended and brought before the courts. Serious conflicts erupted between the industrial managers and vocational school commandants, on the one hand, and the village authorities, on the other. The village officials – including police, public prosecutors, and collective farm managers – hid the runaways and protected them from capture. It is an interesting story in its own right, but it also sheds a great deal of light on institutional conflicts within the structures of the Stalinist state.

Chapter 6 takes a detailed look at the industrial enterprise. It begins with an overview of working conditions, and then analyses the main features of work organization and the endemic structural problems which limited industrial efficiency. It closes by examining the arena of so-called informal bargaining, that is, the network of informal relationships which workers and line managers evolved in order to achieve a *modus operandi* on the shop floor. This system of informal relations had already reached a high degree of sophistication before the war, when the severe labour shortage more or less compelled industrial managers to grant workers various concessions over work speeds and earnings. The chapter reaches the tentative conclusion – tentative, because the evidence in the archives is not completely unambiguous – that this system of informal bargaining was substantially, albeit temporarily, eroded during late Stalinism, and that workers were far less able to protect themselves against centrally imposed speedup and downward pressures on earnings.

The conclusion examines some of the implications of this material for our understanding of late Stalinism. It argues that during the first half of the period the social strains imposed by the food crisis and the regime's attempts to regulate popular responses to that crisis through coercion caused serious cleavages within the Stalinist executive structure. The most clear-cut example of this is the procuracy, which had a very ambiguous attitude towards enforcement of the laws against theft of June 1947 and the laws against illegal job-changing. But we find similar examples of confusion and uncertain loyalties within other institutions, for example, lower-level trade union organizations. From about 1950 onwards, however, the Stalinist system consolidated itself and demonstrated greater institutional cohesion. With the improvement in the standard of living, which took place against a political backdrop of greater repression and regime self-confidence, society became more tame, but also more disillusioned. Although the Stalinist leadership appeared to have secured its unchallenged political position, the processes through which it achieved this objective stored up significant social problems for Stalin's successors.

Before proceeding to the main body of material I should comment on some important gaps in the story which this book tries to tell. It will become immediately obvious to readers that certain groups of workers dominate the narrative far more than others. Young workers and workers in industries where social unrest was greatest – coal mining, construction, iron and steel, and to a certain extent also the railways – tend to loom large in most of the discussions. Yet we know that numerically they were not the majority of the workforce, even though they predominated within the sectors which were most crucial for the reconstruction effort. Workers in other industries, most notably engineering, are less conspicuous, although they are most definitely there, particularly in the chapters on living conditions and the factory environment. If the narrative seems unbalanced, however, this was not intentional on my part, but simply because this was the information which the documentation yielded up. We find a similar blank spot in our knowledge of women workers. The sources (or at least those examined for this study) offer relatively little insight into the unique problems women faced in Soviet factories during these years, even though they were roughly half of all workers and studies of the post-Stalin years (for which a great deal of information is available) tell us that they occupied a very specific place in the political economy of Soviet industry. We can only hope that future researchers will be able to piece together the material needed to provide a comparable analysis for the postwar period.

The other glaring hole is the question of anti-Semitism. We know that anti-Semitism was a prominent feature of the late Stalin years, and that it had serious repercussions within industry. Those Jewish interviewees who worked in industry right after the war certainly confirmed its existence, mainly, however, in blocking their access to higher levels of training, promotion, or assignment to more prestigious enterprises. Yet in all the documents I have examined, including many factory committee reports and accounts of workers' medical facilities where we might expect to have found evidence of it, I have come across not a single case of either open or oblique anti-Semitism or racist slurs against Jewish managers or factory doctors. This was true even during the height of the campaign against 'cosmopolitans' or the period surrounding the Doctors' Plot. My colleague, Kevin Murphy, who has read factory committee records in the Kuibyshev (Samara) and Moscow local archives, has reported in a private communication that he, too, found no evidence of the anti-Semitic campaigns in those enterprises. I cannot explain this disjuncture between a phenomenon that we know existed and the documents. Here, too, perhaps future research will shed light on the topic. But it explains why the issue barely appears in this book; it was certainly not because I have overlooked it.

1 Rebuilding the workforce: free, slave, and indentured labour

The extent of the destruction the Soviet Union suffered in World War II is well known. Losses of plant and equipment, crops and livestock, housing stock, and population were on a truly massive scale. According to the most recent calculations by Mark Harrison, the war cost the Soviet Union some 25 per cent of its physical assets and approximately 14 per cent of its prewar population. In absolute terms, this meant the premature death of between 23.9 million and 26.6 million people, plus the emigration of 2.7 million people from the territories the USSR had seized in 1940.[1] In this sense, as many historians have noted, the Soviet Union emerged from World War II as one of the defeated powers, not one of the victors. It is obvious that the process of recovery would be truly daunting. Destroyed assets – plant, equipment, housing stock, livestock, seed, and fields – had to be restored to use or replaced. Enterprises had to be converted from military to civilian production. Dislocated populations – at least those not in exile or labour camps – had to be resettled. Returning veterans had to be reintegrated into society and, more importantly from an economic point of view, into production. All this had to be done with a productive population which was far smaller in number, malnourished, and in worse health. And it had to take place in the context of a deteriorating international environment which, among other things, deprived the USSR of the Western aid it had received during the war, including vital foods and medicines.

The demographic shock brought about by the war could not fail to have a major impact on the scope, pace, and methods of the postwar recovery. The massive mobilization for the front, the Nazi occupation of a large part of the USSR's most productive agricultural and industrial territory, and the tens of millions of working-age people killed or disabled together placed an enormous strain on the country's labour resources. During the war itself this had required a radical redistribution of labour power, in line with military priorities. As the production of armaments took precedence

---

[1] Harrison, pp. 160–2.

13

Table 1.1. *Workers in industry and construction,*
1940–1953

	Industrial workers	Industrial apprentices	Construction workers
1940	9,971,000	393,000	1,335,000
1945	8,054,000	462,000	1,312,000
1950	12,226,000	361,000	2,297,000
1951	12,998,000	382,000	2,365,000
1952	13,511,000	380,000	2,463,000
1953	14,283,000	387,000	2,521,000

Source: *Trud v SSSR* (Moscow, 1968), pp. 81, 121. Figures for construction include apprentices.

over the growth of food, the fall in the size of the industrial workforce
was minimized at the expense of the farming population. Even so, the
number of industrial workers (excluding those in small-scale industrial
cooperatives) fell by a third between 1940 and 1942, before rising back
to around 86 per cent of its prewar level by 1945.[2] This still left the
core sectors of state industry 'short' of around 1 million workers; if we
include workers in industrial cooperatives (which were incorporated into
official Soviet statistics from the mid-1960s onwards), the discrepancy
was even larger, approximately 1.9 million (see table 1.1). The postwar
reconstruction of industry was therefore constrained not just by shortages of materials, plant, and equipment, but also by a shortage of labour
power.

From where was the Stalinist regime to make good this shortfall? To
some extent it could, and did, fill the gap by directing demobilized soldiers
to jobs in industry, transport, and construction. Their number, however,
was insufficient to cover all of the demand for new workers, especially
since veterans also received preferential access to higher education. The
state would have to make up the gap by tapping other sources, mainly
from agriculture. This, too, was problematic. From an economic point
of view, the agricultural population had been so badly depleted by the
war it was hard to see how it could surrender yet more people to industry and still have enough on the farms to feed the country. From
a political point of view the regime faced the problem that the sectors
most in need of new workers, mainly coal mining, construction, and
during the very first postwar years also iron and steel, had the worst
living and working conditions, which made it very difficult to persuade

[2] *Ibid.*, p. 256.

rural residents to accept employment in them voluntarily. What emerged was what we might call a bifurcation of industrial recruitment. Industries which, by Soviet standards, were relatively 'clean' (most notably machine-building), which were centred in larger conurbations, and which could offer new workers some prospect of tolerable food supplies, housing, and vocational training could attract workers reasonably freely. So, too, could many rural-based enterprises which manufactured building materials or consumer goods – not because the conditions they offered were particularly good, but because they were at the very least a preferable alternative to the collective farms. Recruitment to coal mining, construction, and metallurgy, however, had to rely extensively on coercion. This, in turn, took two forms. First, these enterprises made heavy use of prison labour contracted to them by the Ministry of Internal Affairs (MVD). Secondly, they employed what came to be a vast army of semi-free, or indentured, labourers, drawn from disparate sections of the population: workers compulsorily mobilized during the war to work in industry or rail transport, who were refused permission to return to their native districts after the victory; Soviet citizens repatriated from Central or Eastern Europe, where they had been prisoners of war or forced labourers under the Germans; MVD labour camp prisoners given early release on condition that they work out the remainder of their sentence in designated construction or mining enterprises; some members of the 'suspect' populations deported into internal exile during the war; young workers conscripted into the network of vocational training schools run by the USSR Ministry of Labour Reserves; and workers notionally freely hired through so-called organized recruitment (*orgnabor*), but who were subject to labour contracts which greatly restricted their freedom of movement. In this way the postwar recovery became heavily dependent on an unwilling and resentful workforce, whose bitterness was both confirmed and intensified by the dreadful circumstances in which they lived and worked, and which I analyse in detail in this book's remaining chapters.

Most of the new workers came from the countryside. Of these, the overwhelming majority were workers recruited, mobilized, or conscripted through the Labour Reserve system, either through *orgnabor* or the Labour Reserve training schools. Many others were driven out of the villages by government policy. One of the regime's first political tasks after the war had been to reverse the wartime relaxation of state control over the collective farms and subordinate them once more to state authority. Rural living standards were squeezed to below subsistence levels, especially in the wake of the harvest failure of 1946, to which the regime responded by increasing exactions of grain to the point that farms were left with no seed corn. Mass famine ensued, an issue to which I return in chapter 2.

For the sake of the present discussion what is important is that millions of rural residents felt they had no choice but to pick up stakes and take their chances in the towns and newly developing workers' settlements. This had enormous political significance, because it meant that they entered industrial employment not as a *tabula rasa*, but with already formed attitudes towards the regime and their new employment which at best were highly ambiguous and at worst openly hostile.[3]

The industrial workforce: changing social composition and conjunctural labour shortage

At the beginning of this chapter I noted that World War II saw a sharp fall in the number of workers until 1942, and then a gradual recovery until 1945. This was then followed by an extraordinarily rapid expansion, so that by the time Stalin died in 1953 Soviet industry employed 75 per cent more workers than it had in 1945. Table 1.1 (p. 14) summarizes these results.[4]

The assessment of workforce expansion in individual industries is more difficult because we have data only for the years 1940 and 1950; these are presented in table 1.2. Without figures for 1945 we cannot fully appreciate how rapidly or slowly the different sectors of the economy grew during the postwar years. Table 1.2 nevertheless gives an approximate indication of how this process unfolded and which industries received highest priority. We see that the largest increases were in coal mining, construction, iron and steel, and building materials. These were the core sectors of postwar accumulation, and it was precisely they which relied most heavily on slave and indentured labour. The figures in tables 1.1 and 1.2 exclude prisoners in MVD labour camps and prisoners of war, but include those MVD prisoners who were contracted out as workers to industrial ministries, and whose position is discussed in more detail below.

Here I should make special mention of the railways: they were far and away the largest employer in the country, at least in the productive sector.

---

[3] On agriculture in this period, see Zima; Zhores Medvedev, *Soviet Agriculture*; Nove, 'Soviet Peasantry'; Popov, *Rossiiskaya derevnya*; and Fitzpatrick, 'Postwar Soviet Society'.

[4] Tables 1.1 and 1.2 are taken from the 1968 and 1988 editions of the statistical handbook, *Trud v SSSR*. These use the post-1960 definitions of employment, which include artisanal industry and members of so-called industrial cooperatives. In 1945 artisan production and cooperatives employed 1.3 million people; this rose very gradually to 1.4 million in 1946, and 1.5 million in 1950 (*Narodnoe khozyaistvo SSSR v 1967 g.*, p. 647). These 1940 figures are thus higher than those given in Harrison, pp. 256 and 258, who used the pre-1960 definition, that is, the definition actually applied at the time. Unfortunately, detailed data on the number of workers employed in each industry during the postwar years, required to construct table 1.2, exist only in the later handbooks, which use the new definition.

Table 1.2. *Workers by major sector, 1940 and 1950*

	1940	1950
All industry	9,971,000	12,226,000
Energy production	108,000	131,000
Coal	436,000	733,000
Iron and steel	405,000	605,000
Chemicals	297,000	332,000
Engineering and metalworking	2,575,000	3,332,000
Timber, woodworking, paper and cellulose	1,594,000	1,828,000
Building materials	295,000	557,000
Light industry	2,334,000	2,164,000
Food	1,161,000	1,268,000
*Construction**	1,335,000	2,297,000

*Figures for construction include apprentices, but exclude junior service personnel.
Source: *Trud v SSSR* (Moscow, 1968), pp. 84–5, 121.

The Ministry of Railways (MPS) was militarized during the war, a status which continued until the middle of 1948. Its workers were civilians, but were subject to military discipline, while the minister of railways and the heads of the regional rail networks held military rank. The ministry was a virtual empire. It had its own independent complex of construction organizations, machine-building plants, and locomotive and carriage repair factories. It also had its own network of schools and hospitals, independent of the Ministry of Education and the Ministry of Health. The vastness of its economic domain can be judged from the fact that in 1945 the Railways Ministry employed just over 3 million workers and clerical staff (the distinction between the two was often quite blurred), of whom nearly one in six (476,000) was there to provide food and services for the rest of the ministry's employees: trade and distribution, agriculture to grow food for the ministry's employees, health care, vocational training, and the education of employees' children. By 1950 the ministry had grown to 3.5 million employees.[5] By 1953 its school system alone was educating just slightly fewer than 1.3 million children, of whom 762,000 were those of ministry employees and more than 500,000 were children from

[5] Data for 1945 are from RGAE, f. 1884, op. 61, d. 283a, *Trud na zheleznodorozhnom transporte v 1945 godu: materialy po statistike zheleznodorozhnogo transporta*, Vypusk 211 (Moscow, 1947), pp. 8–9. Data for 1950 are from RGAE, f. 1562, op. 15, d. 2923, l. 18–19. The handbook for 1945 is the only comprehensive set of labour statistics available on the Railways Ministry during the postwar years. All other data compiled by MPS and the Central Statistical Administration provide only aggregate figures for workers and clerical staff combined.

rural localities for whom an MPS school was the only one accessible.[6] These figures tell only part of the story. The Soviet Union's vast size and the fact that the rail network covered the entire length and breadth of its territory meant that a very large proportion of railway workers and clerical employees lived not in large cities but in small, isolated communities. Thus in many ways their mode of life was decidedly rural, rather than urban, a fact which was to have enormous consequences during the food shortages of 1946–8. The other key feature of the railways was their strategic importance. Passenger services were perhaps the least significant of their functions: agriculture, industry, construction, the military, and the MVD's complex of labour camps all depended on the railways to deliver supplies and carry away finished output. Accidents and delays had significant knock-on effects throughout the economy and severe punishments awaited those deemed responsible for causing them. On the other hand, their strategic significance may also help explain the apparent militancy with which many rail workers responded to the food crisis and the regime's equally apparent reluctance to use force against them.[7]

Turning back to the workforce as a whole, the war clearly caused major changes in its demographic composition which were to have significant repercussions in the postwar period. Unlike Western belligerent countries, the high casualty rates among working-age males meant that the women and juveniles who entered industry after 1941 did not necessarily vacate these jobs once the war ended and men returned from the front; on the contrary, they continued to account for a large percentage of industrial workers through the entire postwar period. The percentage of women among industrial workers is shown in table 1.3. Women's share of all industrial workers increased only modestly, a somewhat surprising result given the persistent shortage of working-age men, although it is important to note that it went up strikingly in two very important industries, engineering and building materials. There are, however, various reasons which might help to explain the broader trend. First of all, during the Stalinist industrialization of the 1930s women had already begun to enter *en masse* into industries and occupations from which they had previously been excluded, and which remained more or less closed to them in capitalist countries. To this extent they already made up a large share of industrial and construction workers.[8] Secondly, during the war women had taken over certain skilled trades, such as tool-setting, from which prior to the war they had continued to be excluded, even in industries such

---

[6] RGAE, f. 1884, op. 31, d. 11195, l. 18.
[7] These issues are discussed in some detail in chapters 2 and 3. See below, p. 61 and pp. 85–8.
[8] Filtzer, *Soviet Workers and Stalinist Industrialization*, p. 64. See also Ilič, p. 185.

Table 1.3. *Women as a percentage of industrial workers,*
1940 and 1950

	1940	1950
All industry	43	46
Engineering and metalworking	32	40
Cellulose and paper	49	50
Cement	29	37
Textiles	69	73
Garments	83	86
Leather and hides	61	62
Footwear	56	63
Food	49	51
including:		
baking	58	61
confectionery	67	67

Source: *Trud v SSSR* (Moscow, 1988), p. 106. In 1950 women
were approximately one-third of construction workers (RGAE,
f. 1562, op. 15, d. 3006, l. 14–15).

as textiles in which women were the overwhelming majority of workers.
When the war ended these women were not expelled from these jobs
but, as industry expanded and new workers were trained for these occupations, the new jobs tended to go exclusively to men, thus reducing
women's overall representation in them. This trend is easy to document
during the Khrushchev period, but there is no reason to believe that it did
not begin even earlier, during late Stalinism.[9] If so, it would have partially
counteracted the growth of female industrial employment in other trades.
In this context we should note that women's representation among railway employees (that is, workers and clerical staff taken together) seems
also to have fallen dramatically after the war.[10] Finally, the precipitous fall
in the number of men working on collective farms, including the many
demobilized soldiers who refused to go back into agriculture, meant that
the supply of women available for recruitment into industry had definite
limits.

In contrast to women workers, the percentage of young and first-time
entrants into industry and construction fully reflected the demographic

[9] Filtzer, *Soviet Workers and De-Stalinization*, pp. 182–8.
[10] Data are available only for the Central Railways for the period 1944–8. This was, however,
the largest of the regional rail networks. During that time the percentage of women among
all employees (*rabotayushchie*) fell from 42.1 per cent in 1944 to 31.5 per cent in 1948
(RGAE, f. 1884, op. 31, d. 7878, l. 51).

Table 1.4. *Young workers and workers newly entering employment as a percentage of all workers, selected industries, March 1947*

Industry	Workers under age 20	Workers employed less than 1 year	Workers employed 1–2 years
Machine tools	24.1	21.8	18.6
Heavy machine-building	22.2	22.0	19.6
Electrical industry	24.0	23.0	18.0
Means of communications	22.2	25.8	16.6
Coal industry – Western Region	16.3	25.6	22.8
Coal industry – Eastern Region	16.1	26.8	24.3
Iron and steel	18.6	22.6	21.0
Construction materials – all-union enterprises	20.1	33.1	17.3
Construction materials – republican enterprises	13.2	38.1	19.4
Textiles	19.8	26.8	15.1

Note: Figures for the coal industry include workers employed in mining, mine construction, and the manufacture of mining equipment.
Source: RGAE, f. 1562, op. 15, d. 2285, l. 3–3ob., 17–17ob., 45–45ob., 61–61ob., 85–85ob., 104–104ob.; d. 2286, l. 1–2ob., 3–5, 7–10, 39–39ob., 57–57ob., 126–126 ob.

shock caused by the war. This is clear from table 1.4. The table presents two types of data. Column 2 shows the percentage of workers in key industries who were teenagers at the time of the survey, which was taken in March 1947. Columns 3 and 4 show the percentage of workers in these industries who had entered production within the previous one or two years, that is, approximately since the end of the war in Europe. These figures warrant closer examination. They show that not all new entrants into the workforce were young. The workforce was augmented by millions of peasants of all ages who came into industry and construction as demobilized soldiers, through the system of organized recruitment (*orgnabor*), or as workers hired spontaneously directly by the enterprise. It is therefore noteworthy that in a number of industries the share of new, inexperienced workers (that is, those who had been at their job for less than a year) was higher – in some cases significantly higher – than the proportion of young workers, and in no case fell below 20 per cent. In virtually all of the industries listed in table 1.4, between 40 and 50 per cent of workers had entered that industry during the two years following the end of the war.

These various statistics conceal what was in fact a complex and often dramatic social and political process. Virtually every branch of industry suffered from labour shortages, at least until the end of the 1940s. The shortages were severe enough to create major bottlenecks and jeopardize enterprise plan fulfilment, even in industries with relatively tolerable conditions like engineering.[11] Construction projects found it especially difficult to attract free workers, something not overly surprising given the harsh environment and low wages which dominated that sector. Recruiting agents from the Ministry of the Building Materials Industry, for example, reported that it had been virtually impossible to persuade about-to-be-demobilized soldiers to take jobs on their construction sites.[12] Even the iron and steel industry, which by 1951 was actually shedding labour surpluses in its industrial enterprises, continued to suffer a deficit of construction workers.[13]

There were a number of officially sponsored attempts to solve the labour shortage through persuasion and positive incentives. *Trud*, for example, ran an intensive campaign throughout 1946, in which it accused managers in coal mining and iron and steel of retaining inflated establishments of clerical and administrative staff and excessive numbers of line managers, all of whom could have been working in direct production.[14] This was tied to a more generalized campaign to convert clerical staff to production workers, although it seems that only engineering factories made any real effort to put it into practice.[15] The Railways Ministry made a more serious attempt to expand recruitment. It offered a wide range of financial incentives to recruit demobilized soldiers and to attract free workers to the Far North (the latter was partly undermined by Gosplan's refusal to allocate it the funds it had asked for); it also, in conjunction with the railway trade unions, actively recruited the wives of railway workers to clear snow off the lines, work in public catering, clean dormitories, and work as volunteers in creches and hospitals.[16] The most prominent – and promising – source of new labour power, of course, was demobilized soldiers. Local soviets were instructed to implement a number of measures to ease their integration back into the workforce, including assistance in finding housing or in repairing their prewar homes, preferential access to higher education, and accelerated vocational training for those who had entered military service before they had acquired a skill. The fact that so

---

[11] For engineering, see *Uralmash*, 1 March 1947.

[12] RGAE, f. 8248, op. 189, l. 197. This was a general trend for the industry. Data from the second quarter of 1947 showed that, while the ministry's factories were very close to planned establishments, most *glavki* had only from one-half to three-quarters the number of building workers they needed (*ibid.*, op. 21, d. 275, l. 147).

[13] RGAE, f. 8592, op. 2, d. 754, l. 84, 128, 162–3.

[14] *Trud*, 10 April, 14 April, 13 July, 23 November, 30 November, 14 December 1946.

[15] *Trud*, 30 November, 3 December, 19 December 1946, and 28 January 1947; *Za sovetskuyu malolitrazhku*, 29 October 1946; *Stalinets* (Rostsel'mash), 21 December 1946.

[16] RGAE, f. 1884, op. 31, d. 6585, l. 231–2, 247–54; d. 6588, l. 80, 86–7; d. 7878, l. 49, 51–2; d. 7882, l. 66–7; d. 8317, l. 1.

many soldiers were also Party members no doubt lent such efforts even greater urgency. It was certainly true that in Moscow – which may well have been atypical because of its privileged status – well over a quarter of a million returning soldiers had been placed in jobs between July 1945 and August 1946, some 91 per cent of all those who had returned to the city during that period.[17]

Compared to the magnitude of the problem these various efforts, including the recruitment of war veterans, proved totally inadequate. I should point out that the very industries which had suffered the worst were by 1951 and 1952 reporting labour surpluses. Even coal mining identified a number of regions, including those which had found it almost impossible to recruit or retain workers during the period 1945–9, which were now refusing to accept graduates from the Labour Reserve vocational training schools because they could not find jobs for them.[18] The postwar labour shortage was, therefore, a conjunctural crisis, quite distinct from the structural shortages which had always characterized the Soviet enterprise. The fact that this conjunctural crisis was eventually resolved must not obscure the fact that while the drive for accumulation was at its most feverish the regime could find adequate supplies of labour power only by making massive use of slave labour and, even more so, of indentured or semi-free labour. It is their position which I now analyse.

Filling the gap: prison and indentured labour

The MVD economy

Stalinist industrialization during the 1930s had been heavily dependent on prison or slave labour, and this trend continued after the war. The Ministry of Internal Affairs (MVD) controlled a vast army of workers. In addition to the labour camps themselves, the MVD contracted out prisoners to the different industrial ministries, for which it received a fee. The MVD was also responsible for German and Japanese prisoners of war, almost all of whom were set to work as labourers under the aegis of the ministries. Finally, the MVD had disposal over a large pool of workers who had been sentenced to internal exile. In the postwar years these were mainly members of ethnic minorities and prisoners who had been released from the camps but not allowed to return to civilian life.

---

[17] RGASPI, f. 17, op. 125, d. 421, l. 12–15, 73. That Moscow may have been a special case is suggested by Party complaints over the slow reintegration of returning soldiers in Stavropol' and Penza (*ibid.*, op. 116, d. 232, l. 79–80, and d. 235, l. 3–5).

[18] RGAE, f. 8875, op. 46, d. 279, l. 179, 181 (iron and steel industry); f. 8248, op. 21, d. 699, l. 145–6 (building materials); GARF, f. 9507, op. 2, d. 538, l. 11, 12, 39, 44 (coal mining).

Taken together these different groups accounted for a large percentage of the total workforce in industry and construction. At the end of 1947 the labour camps held approximately 2.2 million prisoners. Of these, slightly fewer than 1.7 million worked on MVD-run economic projects, the most important of which were in agriculture and consumer goods manufacture (717,000); timber and logging (273,000); so-called special construction projects and construction operations in the Far North (246,000); railway construction (216,000); and mining and metallurgy (179,000). In addition to the MVD enterprises themselves, the MVD rented out 500,000 prisoners to the major industrial ministries. The second category of prison labour was German and Japanese prisoners of war, who in 1947 accounted for a further 1 million workers, including 205,000 in various branches of construction, 161,000 in coal mining, 32,000 working at electric power stations, and 30,000 in iron and steel and non-ferrous metallurgy.[19] Finally, exiles (who at the end of 1948 totalled 1.8 million people, over a million of whom were Volga Germans) accounted for another 1 million employed persons. Half of them worked in agriculture, but 72,000 were in coal mining; 58,000 in the timber and paper industry; and 33,000 in metallurgy.[20] Thus if we add up all the people in these various categories who were employed outside agriculture, we see that they gave the economy somewhere in the vicinity of 3 million workers, mainly in industry and construction. If we consider that in 1947 there were probably something of the order of 12 million 'free' workers in industry and construction (extrapolated from table 1.1 above), the MVD economy was providing approximately 20 per cent of total industrial labour power. This figure did not alter appreciably even as the USSR gradually repatriated prisoners of war back to Germany and Japan: it merely replaced them with camp prisoners, especially in the key sectors of coal mining and metallurgy.[21]

In addition to prison labour the MVD and the USSR Ministry of Defence also organized the supply of two types of indentured labourers. The first category were Soviet citizens who had been repatriated back to the USSR from Central and Eastern Europe following the war. In

[19] GARF, f. 9401, op. 2, d. 199, l. 396 (labour camps), and l. 73–4 (prisoners of war).
[20] GARF, f. 9401, op. 2, d. 234, l. 8.
[21] Thus the number of POWs employed in coal mining fell from 161,000 at the end of 1947 to 120,000 at the end of 1948. The number of camp prisoners leased out to the Ministry of Coal Mining correspondingly increased from 24,000 to 64,000 over this same period (GARF, f. 9401, op. 2, d. 199, l. 73–4, 397, and d. 234, l. 76, 153). The number of camp prisoners in coal mining rose further, to 71,000 in 1949, and accounted for nearly 10 per cent of all workers in this sector. Another branch heavily reliant on contract prisoners was the oil industry, which by 1949 was employing 56,000 MVD prisoners, as against a free labour force of 124,500 (ibid., d. 269, tom 1, l. 63 (prisoners); RGAE, f. 1562, op. 321, d. 416, l. 40 (oil workers)).

the main these were either Soviet Army soldiers who had been captured and held as prisoners of war, or Soviet civilians who had been transported into the Third Reich as forced labour. The Soviet government estimated that over 6.8 million people had been captured or transported in this way, nearly a million of whom had died. By the end of 1947 just over 5.4 million of the remaining 5.8 million had been repatriated back to the Soviet Union.[22] Before access to the archives Western historians had more or less assumed that most of these repatriates were imprisoned by the NKVD/MVD. More recent evidence, however, suggests that the percentage persecuted in this way was much smaller. R. W. Davies cites 1946 figures, according to which just over 6 per cent of repatriates were sent to NKVD 'special contingents' and another 14 per cent were assigned to 'labour battalions' organized by the People's Commissariat (later Ministry) of Defence.[23] In March 1946 there were 774 such labour battalions, with 607,095 former Soviet prisoners of war and repatriated civilians.[24] Using the percentages cited by Davies, this implies that another 260,000 repatriates were in 'special contingents', so that the two categories together made yet another sizeable addition to the pool of industrial and construction workers.[25] The conditions under which these repatriates lived and worked were truly tragic. In early 1946 the USSR Procuracy intervened to protest about the appalling treatment to which they were subjected in the coal mining trusts of Tula oblast', although, as we shall see in the following chapters, their crowded dormitories, inadequate food supplies, and lack of even underwear and soap differentiated them from ordinary workers only in degree. The procuracy launched another investigation at about the same time in Sverdlovsk oblast', after a group of repatriates staged a protest strike over similar abuses.[26]

The second category of indentured workers under the MVD were labour camp prisoners given early release from their sentences on condition that they accept assignment to designated enterprises and construction projects where they would work out the remainder of their sentences. The idea of granting prisoners early release and despatching them to the

[22] RGASPI, f. 17, op. 121, d. 686, l. 1.
[23] Davies, *Soviet History in the Yeltsin Era*, pp. 167–8.
[24] RGASPI, f. 17, op. 121, d. 545, l. 14.
[25] I should point out that both of these 'institutions' had existed during the war. The coal mines of the Kuzbass, in Western Siberia, for example, had drawn nearly 60 per cent of their workers from these two groups (GARF, f. 7416, op. 4, d. 109, l. 8).
[26] GARF, f. 8131, op. 37, d. 3150, l. 1–1ob., 3, 8–11. The procuracy was not alone in raising these issues. In April 1946, Golikov, of the Administration of the Plenipotentiary of the USSR Council of Ministers for Repatriation Affairs, protested against the low pay and mistreatment of repatriates in a number of industrial ministries. Of these, only the Ministry of the Iron and Steel Industry appears to have taken the complaints even somewhat seriously and made some effort to introduce improvements (RGASPI, f. 17, op. 121, d. 545, l. 19–21, 23–5, 28).

coal industry was first proposed by Kruglov, head of the MVD, in late 1946. Under the scheme 120,000 prisoners were to go to the coal mines and 55,000 to construction in the coal and oil industries, although we do not know how many prisoners were eventually involved. They were obliged to work at their assigned enterprise for at least five years; if they absconded from their job or committed any other offence they were to be returned to a labour camp, where they would serve out the unexpired period of their sentence, plus any new sentence associated with the crime they had just committed. The first contingent of these prisoners was despatched in January 1947.[27] Later the scheme was extended to major construction projects in the Far East and Lower Volga, for which it became a regular supplier of labour power right up until the end of Stalin's lifetime. As the system evolved, so, too, did the rules governing who could participate and how much remission they should receive from their sentences. Political prisoners and criminals convicted of banditry, armed robbery, or other violent crimes were excluded. Those prisoners eligible to take part received a certain number of days remission from their sentences for each month that they overfulfilled their production targets.[28] The use of early-release prisoners was not without its complications. They made up a large proportion of the workers in the Urals who illegally fled from their jobs during the famine of 1947. Procuracy reports from 1950 complain of prisoners deserting their jobs in the gold industry, and even of a sit-down strike of prisoners in transit to Dal'stroi, who were protesting at the conditions under which they were being transported.[29]

The importance of the MVD's economic empire in the overall process of accumulation is well known. According to Ivanova, in 1949 the Gulag's production accounted for approximately 10 per cent of the USSR's entire gross industrial output. It had a virtual monopoly over the mining and processing of strategic metals and minerals, such as platinum, mica, and diamonds (100 per cent); gold (90 per cent); and tin (70 per cent). It produced 40 per cent of the USSR's copper and 33 per cent of its nickel. Its logging operations provided 13 per cent of the country's timber, and its coal mines hewed nearly 4 per cent of its coal.[30] In 1950, MVD construction organizations put up well over 10 per cent of Moscow's new civilian housing.[31] But the economy's reliance on the MVD was greater than even these figures suggest, since the other economic ministries became heavily

---

[27] GARF, f. 9401, op. 2, d. 139, l. 368–71; f. 8131, op. 29, d. 476, l. 309–11.
[28] GARF, f. 8131, op. 28, d. 597, l. 54–6, 58–9, 66–71, 73; op. 29, d. 476, l. 13–16, 48, 199–200, 231–6, 309–11; d. 480, l. 197–200, 203–6.
[29] GARF, f. 8131, op. 29, d. 476, l. 259–60; d. 480, l. 149–50, 223–6. For flight from jobs in the Urals, see ch. 5, p. 172.
[30] Ivanova, p. 116. For figures from previous years and other items of output see GARF, f. 9401, op. 2, d. 168, l. 81–2; d. 234, l. 17; d. 269, tom 1, l. 1–2.
[31] Ivanova, p. 110.

dependent on prison labour to cover labour shortages and to cope with bottlenecks. During 1946 and 1947, the Ministry of Construction of Enterprises in Heavy Industry (Mintyazhstroi) incorporated into its labour plans the allocation of workers from new labour camps or the expansion of already existing camps on its building projects for the iron and steel industry. The Ministry of the Building Materials Industry, which also found it difficult to recruit free labourers to its construction organizations, made similar appeals to the MVD to provide it with labour camps. Yet this came at a price. Prisoners were notoriously inefficient, both because of their low motivation and the grotesque undermechanization of most camp production operations. The building materials industry estimated that their productivity was one-fifth to one-sixth that of their regular workers, while the railways complained that they were so unreliable that site managers had to take free workers from urgent construction jobs in order to complete the jobs the prisoners had left undone.[32] Ministries made the same complaint about the poor performance of the 'special contingents' and labour battalions. As I shall have cause to mention on other occasions in the course of this book, their unreliability prompted the iron and steel industry to adopt a conscious policy of replacing them with free workers.[33]

At a macro-economic level there is the very real possibility that the MVD economy was actually a net drain on accumulation rather than one of its major sources. Over and above the low motivation of prison workers, the Gulag economy was inordinately wasteful, as MVD enterprises rarely were subjected to any kind of budget or cost constraints.[34] Ivanova, for example, notes that the production costs of building materials made by prison labour were two to three times what it cost neighbouring civilian enterprises to produce them, even though the cost of labour power for the Gulag was virtually free.[35] Insofar as we can take this as a general trend, it suggests that it would have been far cheaper to have released the prisoners and employed them as free workers in local industries. We also need to take account of the huge volume of resources which the camps sucked out of the non-camp economy in the form of food for the prisoners, raw and semi-finished materials, motor vehicles, fuel, lubricants, machinery, and construction materials, not to mention the vast size of the camp administrative and security apparatus (the latter was set by law at 9 per cent

---

[32] RGAE, f. 8592, op. 2, d. 115, l. 131, 134, 137, 140, 143, 146, 149, 151, 153–4 (Mintyazhstroi); f. 8248, op. 21, d. 184, l. 91, 97, 106, 267; d. 275, l. 105 (building materials); f. 1884, op. 31, d. 7199, l. 393–4 (railways).
[33] The 'special contingents' and labour battalions accounted for 18 per cent of iron and steel workers in April 1946. By September 1947 this had already fallen to 11 per cent (RGAE, f. 8875, op. 46, d. 222, l. 50, 52).
[34] Ivanova, pp. 104, 108.   [35] Ibid., p. 118.

of the number of prisoners, but in fact was perpetually below that level
due to difficulties with recruitment).[36] Thus that proportion of the production of non-Gulag enterprises which went to supply the Gulag was
to a large extent simply wasted: if the inputs which they supplied to the
MVD economy had gone to the civilian economy instead, the end result
in finished output would have been several times higher. Moreover, in
many areas this extra burden caused labour shortages in the non-Gulag
economy which, as just noted, could be made up only by prisoners, who
worked at a fraction of the productivity of free workers, thus extending
this invidious downward spiral into the non-MVD economy itself. To
this extent the Gulag and that part of the non-Gulag economy which
supported it partially negated the process of accumulation, slowed the
pace of recovery, and further depressed popular consumption.

This, of course, is only part of the story. The MVD economy had other
reasons for its existence. The MVD was a powerful ministry, and it justified its own overblown existence by constantly expanding the volume
of economic tasks for which it was responsible. The MVD empire also
acted as a political deterrent. Its very presence served to intimidate and
coerce the population into a state of political submissiveness. Moreover,
the mentality of the Stalinist regime was such that it simply did not trust
its own population voluntarily to carry out those tasks which it had identified as essential to the country's and its own survival. This led it to
try to exert unprecedented control over people's behaviour. What this
meant was that, with so much ordinary activity criminalized, the regime
converted a large minority of its population into criminals – and criminals had to be put to work. In the regime's eyes the interests of political
domination dovetailed neatly with the interests of accumulation. It was
only after Stalin died that the new Soviet leadership realized the futility
of this philosophy. What concerns us here, however, is that the attitude to
labour power which the MVD economy embodied extended far beyond
the camps to even greater numbers of notionally free workers.

This leads us to one further aspect of the MVD labour force which
deserves special attention. In a very important sense the use of repression
after the war differed quite fundamentally from the terror of the 1930s.
The latter, while containing a large random element, was primarily directed against former Oppositionists, the Party and bureaucratic apparatus, and suspect social groups (most notably ex-kulaks). Many of these
people were executed, but they also made up a substantial proportion
of the additions to the Gulag in these years. The repression of the postwar period was far more democratic. Its victims were overwhelmingly

[36] GARF, f. 9401, op. 2, d. 199, l. 392; Ivanova, p. 107.

workers and peasants, and it was effected mainly through the application of criminal law.

During the seven-year period 1946–52, slightly fewer than 495,000 people were convicted of political crimes, 461,000 of whom (93 per cent) went to a labour camp. However, approximately 4.8 million people were sent to prison or labour camps for criminal convictions.[37] These are convictions only in civil courts. We need to add to this figure the roughly 200,000 people sent to labour camps between 1946 and 1948 by military tribunals for violation of the laws against illegally quitting jobs in military enterprises or transport.[38] Taking the two together we see that during the late Stalin years additions to the Gulag for violations of criminal law exceeded overtly political prisoners by a factor of 10 to 1. Moreover, from 1947 onwards the length of sentences increased sharply. Prior to the imposition of the anti-theft laws of June 1947, *relatively* short sentences for criminal convictions had been the norm. In 1937, at the height of the Terror, nearly a quarter of criminal (as opposed to political) convictions earned sentences of less than one year, and there were no sentences longer than ten years. In 1946, the pattern was even more marked: 38 per cent of all criminal convictions received sentences of under a year; the number sentenced to more than ten years was so small as to be statistically insignificant. With the 1947 anti-theft laws, however, the picture changed dramatically, with roughly half of all convictions resulting in labour camp sentences of six years or longer, not to mention the fact that with the repeal of the death penalty maximum sentences were increased to twenty-five years.[39]

The two edicts of June 1947 – one against theft of state property, the other against theft of personal property – were part of the arsenal of measures, both economic and political, through which the regime tried to limit consumption after the 1946 harvest failure and the resulting famine.[40] Theft of state property, no matter how small the amount, earned a minimum sentence of seven years in a labour camp, with a

---

[37] Convictions for 'counterrevolutionary' crimes are from Popov, 'Gosudarstvennyi terror', p. 28; those for criminal convictions are from GARF, f. 9492, op. 6s, d. 14, l. 17, 29.

[38] Zemskov, 'Ukaz ot 26 iyunya 1940 goda', p. 45. The data on criminal convictions exclude the 1.4 million people – mainly workers – who received short jail terms of between two and four months during 1946–52 for illegally abandoning their jobs in non-military employment.

[39] GARF, f. 9492, op. 6s, d. 14, l. 17. For the repeal of the death penalty, see Edict of the Presidium of the USSR Supreme Soviet, 26 May 1947, 'Ob otmene smertnoi kazni', *Trud*, 27 May 1947.

[40] Edicts of the Presidium of the USSR Supreme Soviet, 4 June 1947, 'Ob ugolovnoi otvetstvennosti za khishcheniya gosudarstvennogo i obshchestvennogo imushchestva', and 'Ob usilenii okhrany lichnoi sobstvennosti grazhdan', *Pravda*, 5 June 1947. For a detailed discussion of the penalties imposed by the new laws and the deliberations that preceded their promulgation, see Solomon, pp. 409–13.

maximum sentence of twenty-five years. Punishment of petty theft from industrial enterprises was now increased from one year's imprisonment to seven. Together, these two laws accounted for nearly half of all those incarcerated after their promulgation, that is, around 2 million people.[41] Their victims were primarily workers and peasants. Although at first glance we might intuitively assume that the laws had been introduced primarily as a weapon against the peasantry, this was not strictly so. Looking first at the law against theft of state property, only in 1947, the actual famine year, did collective farmers outnumber workers among its victims. Thereafter the number of workers represented a larger share of convictions, although after the end of rationing in 1948 and the growing importance of graft and embezzlement, clerical employees became even more prominent than workers. As for theft of personal property, workers were about 45 per cent of all those convicted, but this is understandable, given that such crimes were more likely to take place in the towns.[42] Yet this merely reflects a much broader trend. Looking at all crimes in this period, workers and their families consistently made up between 32 and 40 per cent of convictions; collective farmers were about 25 per cent.[43] To a certain extent the rise in crime reflected the breakdown of social norms during the war and the desperation of an impoverished population struggling by any means to survive. But it also reflected a larger reality of the Stalinist system in this period: by criminalizing so many aspects of ordinary existence the regime effectively made criminals of a large minority of its population. Here, too, the distinction between the prison labour of the Gulag and the indentured status of millions of 'free' labourers had been effaced.

Organized recruitment (orgnabor)

Whatever the strategic and conjunctural significance of prison and semi-prison labour, they proved less important than two other forms of indentured labour, namely workers recruited through so-called organized recruitment (*orgnabor*) and the teenagers mobilized into the vocational

---

[41] Between 1946 and 1952, nearly 1.7 million people were convicted for theft of state property – 1.4 million of them after 1946. Another 785,000 were convicted for stealing personal property (650,000 after 1946) (Solomon, p. 435). Solomon notes that over half of those convicted under the June 1947 laws were tried and sentenced during the first eighteen months the laws were in force. However, the real number of convictions almost certainly exceeded 2 million: first, because the returns in the Ministry of Justice files were only 90 to 95 per cent complete; and secondly, because these data cover convictions only in civil courts, and therefore exclude the large number of cases of theft on the railways, which up until March 1948 (when the rail network was demilitarized) were tried by military tribunals. See GARF, f. 9492, op. 6s, d. 14, l. 30–1.
[42] GARF, f. 9492, op. 6s, d. 14, l. 14.   [43] Popov, 'Gosudarstvennyi terror', p. 25.

training schools run by the Ministry of Labour Reserves. From a strictly numerical point of view these two sources together provided the economy with three times as many workers as all the categories of prison and semi-prison labour combined. But their importance in the regime's eyes went far beyond this, for the authorities assumed that workers brought into industry and construction via *orgnabor* or the Labour Reserve schools would become stable 'cadre' workers and evince none of the problems of poor motivation and productivity associated with prisoners.

Organized recruitment, which also came under the auspices of the Ministry of Labour Reserves, recruited both for the large non-seasonal industries, such as metallurgy, coal mining, and construction, and for such seasonal branches as building materials and peat.

Table 1.5 presents summary data showing the annual plans for *orgnabor* of non-seasonal workers and the numbers actually recruited.[44] The table reveals certain important trends. First, the large number of workers recruited during 1946 reflects the pool of demobilized soldiers who had to be reabsorbed back into the economy. One of the curious aspects of this process was that *orgnabor* in that year badly underfulfilled its plan for recruiting from the rural population (772,779 versus a plan of 1,425,600), but recruited nearly 70 per cent more than its target for urban residents and demobilized soldiers (1,393,300 versus 829,300).[45] This to a significant extent reflects the unwillingness of demobilized peasants to return to the countryside, and instead to take advantage of their status as veterans in order to find jobs in industry. This also helps account for the very serious inability to recruit enough construction workers during 1946; veterans, having priority for placement in industry and educational institutions, were able to avoid going into construction, which offered low pay and hard conditions. Secondly, with the exception of 1949, the recruitment plans were systematically underfulfilled. Taking the entire period

[44] To the best of my knowledge these figures do not include the tens of thousands of North Korean workers recruited to work in the Soviet Far East. If anything their plight was even more horrendous than that faced by Soviet recruits. They were transported in appallingly overcrowded and filthy boats. When they arrived at their jobs they were badly housed, inadequately fed, and paid extremely low wages. In fact, they suffered the same indignities as the mass of young Soviet workers whom I discuss in chapters 2 and 4: they were given no bed linen, had no underwear, and ran up massive debts to their enterprises, which the latter attempted to redeem by deducting large sums out of their already meagre earnings. In short, theirs was the typical fate of superexploited migrant workers everywhere. Their situation is detailed in a file of the RSFSR Ministry of Health, which had the task of trying to ensure that the importation of these workers from North Korea, where typhus, smallpox, and cholera were rife and difficult to contain, did not exacerbate the Soviet Far East's own, already serious public health problems. This is clearly a story which needs more detailed investigation. See GARF-RSFSR, f. A-482, op. 52s, d. 231, in particular, l. 4–5, 63–4, 77–8, 111–63.
[45] GARF, f. 9507, op. 2, d. 828, l. 1.

Table 1.5. *Workers recruited through organized recruitment, USSR and major industries, 1946–1952*

Ministry	1946 Plan	1946 Actual	1947 Plan	1947 Actual	1948 Plan	1948 Actual	1949 Plan	1949 Actual	1950 Plan	1950 Actual	1951 Plan	1951 Actual	1952* Plan	1952* Actual
USSR total	2,255,152	2,166,075	921,725	577,202	689,022	596,863	599,950	616,183	673,145	647,685	691,850	669,220	687,054	542,337
Iron and steel**	130,400	120,598	37,700	13,228	69,500	52,201	57,800	55,164	59,380	44,581	14,570	13,139	12,175	10,741
Non-ferrous metallurgy**	63,500	62,823	25,000	18,631							27,960	28,768	22,960	14,958
Coal	300,780	366,138	195,900	123,768	81,000	49,862	175,950	161,507	96,460	101,167	90,200	91,934	77,625	67,188
Oil	27,000	30,526	14,400	8,467	17,200	12,675	46,950	58,075	63,145	62,337	58,800	59,316	36,340	32,105
Electric power stations	67,780	47,495	28,595	13,928	37,000	31,167	48,850	39,592	70,113	65,903	47,935	48,337	50,355	50,929
Timber	156,040	155,267	146,450	122,074	107,575	89,247	84,150	82,830	80,210	82,886	140,125	134,737	198,070	129,086
Construction – industrial and military***	517,795	222,499	226,475	129,677	314,700	257,406	136,400	154,099	164,210	168,810	191,710	186,237	166,795	141,823
Textiles****	193,950	259,730	40,000	33,430	—	—	—	—	—	—	—	—	—	—
Railways****	146,500	52,271	25,000	24,443	—	—	—	—	19,000	7,214	400	101	—	—

Notes: *1952 data through 15 November 1952.

**During 1948–50 iron and steel and non-ferrous metallurgy were amalgamated into one ministry – the Ministry of the Metallurgical Industry.

***For 1946–8 includes the Ministry of Construction of Enterprises in Heavy Industry; Ministry of the Construction of Enterprises in Fuel Enterprises; construction for the oil industry; the Chief Administration of the Construction of Engineering Enterprises; and military and naval construction. For 1949–52 it includes only the Ministry of Construction of Enterprises in Heavy Industry and the Chief Administration for Construction of Engineering Enterprises.

****Blank cells indicate no data or an insignificant number of recruited workers.

Sources: GARF, f. 9507, op. 2: 1946 – d. 828, l. 7–8; 1947 – d. 835, l. 4; 1948–50 – d. 842, l. 3, 25, 195; 1951 – d. 855, l. 2–3; 1952 – d. 863, l. 1–2.

1946–52, *orgnabor* was expected to hire over 6.5 million workers, but managed only 5.8 million. The gap was most dramatic during the food crisis years of 1947 and 1948: in 1947 recruiters met barely 63 per cent of their plan, and in 1948 only 87 per cent. This inability to persuade sufficient numbers of free workers to sign labour contracts, especially in the metallurgical, coal, and timber industries, explains why the regime made such heavy reliance on prison and indentured labour. It could not fill the gaps in the labour force through persuasion and voluntary hiring.

In theory the people who signed labour contracts with recruiting agents were free workers, and it might seem tendentious to include them in the category of indentured labour. There were, however, quite severe limitations on their freedom of movement. The practice was for them to sign labour contracts for specified periods, usually five years. If they left their job before the contract was up they would be prosecuted as labour 'deserters' on the same basis as all other workers – in some cases even if they were working without a formal written agreement. Moreover, whilst from a legal point of view they had entered into their contracts voluntarily, in many cases they were the victims of deliberate deception and fraud by recruiting agents or enterprise managements, who apparently were able to extend expired contracts without workers' formal permission.[46] Such abuses of the system were nothing new: they had been common during the 1930s, when the regime also tried to use *orgnabor* to cover a severe labour shortage.[47] Recruiters were under intense pressure to meet or exceed targets. To do this they made all kinds of promises concerning housing, wages, and the trades for which the workers would be trained or employed. When enterprises could or would not meet these conditions, especially during the most difficult early postwar years, recruits became resentful. Not surprisingly many of them quit their jobs, even though this was a violation of the criminal law.[48] Of course it was not just recruits whom the *orgnabor* agents defrauded. The enterprises themselves were often the victims. Just as Soviet factories would meet their plans by turning out heavy or defective products, *orgnabor* recruiters would sign up and despatch to the enterprises people who were clearly unfit to carry out the work for which they were being hired. This was succinctly summed up by the procurator of Rostov oblast' in late 1947:

---

[46] A group of construction workers recruited from Bashkiriya cited their fear of this practice as the reason for illegally quitting their jobs several weeks before the official end of their contracts (GARF, f. 8131, op. 37, d. 3747, l. 158). I cite this case in another context in chapter 5, p. 172.

[47] Filtzer, *Soviet Workers and Stalinist Industrialization*, pp. 60–1.

[48] See the report of the Chelyabinsk oblast' procurator, 2 August 1947, in GARF, f. 8131, op. 37, d. 3747, l. 243–5.

We have noted cases in which, out of a drive for quantity, labour power is recruited without any account being taken of the specific conditions of work in the coal industry. They recruit workers who are sick, who are invalids, or who have large families. There are cases in which the organized recruitment of labour power is replaced by recruitment at [railway] stations, bazaars, and other places, [or by recruitment] of people who have no fixed place of residence and who have taken an unserious approach to the question of concluding a labour contract. These people, upon arriving to work in the coal industry, come face to face with the heavy labour and the inadequacies of the housing and living regime, abandon their jobs after two or three weeks, and desert.[49]

The recruiters' rough-and-ready attitude at times spilled over into overt criminal activity, sometimes with tragic consequences. In one particularly gruesome case from early 1947, 300 workers enlisted for work in the mines of Kemerovo oblast' were made to suffer a railway journey of two and a half weeks with almost no food or heating. The agents who had recruited them and organized their rail journey made off with all of the provisions, as well as the money the workers were to have received to buy food while *en route*. No one died, but thirty workers were arrested for stealing food and several had to be hospitalized, including a mother and baby both of whom had their legs amputated due to frostbite. The agents, it should be said, were caught and received lengthy labour camp sentences.[50] While this must have been one of the more extreme examples, the fact was that such shady practices did not abate as the decade wore on, although workers gradually became more emboldened to stage small-scale protests and to refuse to report for work at their new employment until the conditions promised to them had been met.[51]

One of the more interesting byproducts of these various ruses was to overstate the number of workers actually recruited via *orgnabor*. A Ministry of State Control report on *orgnabor* drawn up in early 1950 claimed that agents and enterprise managers routinely colluded to inflate

[49] GARF, f. 8131, op. 37, d. 3750, l. 52. This was by no means an isolated example. In late 1949 a dispute broke out between the procurator for Sakhalin island and the Ministry of Labour Reserves over the behaviour of recruiters, who had recruited workers from all over the USSR to come to Sakhalin and work as navvies at the ports. Many of them were clearly unfit for heavy physical labour and had to be sent home virtually as soon as they arrived, including women in late pregnancy and people with skull injuries. The ministry, in turn, blamed the problem on the carelessness of the doctors who had carried out the medical examinations on the new recruits. Yet nearly a year later the procurator was still complaining that the abuses were continuing (*ibid.*, op. 28, d. 286, l. 2–7, 9–10, 13, 15–16, 19).

[50] GARF, f. 8131, op. 37, d. 3028, l. 3–3ob., 4–41 (the pages in this file are incorrectly numbered; the report actually goes up to l. 47). At least some of the workers arrested for theft had their convictions challenged by the procuracy, although we do not learn what ultimately happened to them.

[51] GARF, f. 8131, op. 28, d. 286, l. 13, 15; op. 29, d. 218, l. 4–5, 7–11.

the number of recruits because they received a payment for each worker who signed up and eventually started a job.[52] A whistle-blowing letter from an *orgnabor* official inside the Ministry of Labour Reserves claimed that the falsification of results was even more systematic, and placed the blame squarely on the minister himself, V. Pronin, whose fixation with daily progress reports encouraged local officials to massage the data in order to produce the figures Pronin needed.[53] As discussed in this chapter's conclusion, there were other ways in which the *orgnabor* data may be misleading and which we need to take into account when assessing its overall contribution to the renewal of the workforce.

The Labour Reserve schools

After *orgnabor* far and away the largest group of indentured workers were those marshalled through the training schools of the Ministry of Labour Reserves. In October 1940 the Stalinist regime introduced a system of *de facto* labour conscription for teenagers aged fourteen to seventeen. The original plan was for a yearly call-up of between 800,000 and 1 million youth who would enter either a two-year trade school (*remeslennoe uchilishche*, or RU) or a six-month factory training school (*shkola fabrichno-zavodskogo obucheniya*, or FZO). The RU took male youths aged fourteen and fifteen; FZO students were older, sixteen or seventeen. The RU – and their counterparts for the railways, the *zheleznodorozhnye uchilishcha* (ZhU) – would provide skilled workers for the metal, iron and steel, chemical, mining, and oil industries, communications, and rail, sea, and river transport. The FZO schools would turn out workers of so-called mass trades for coal and ore mining, iron and steel, oil, and construction. Students would be wards of the state: they would receive no pay for their labour service, but the state would provide for their upkeep. Once completing their course, the newly formed Chief Administration of Labour Reserves (which after the war became the Ministry of Labour Reserves) would assign graduates to state enterprises, where they would work for a period of four years. The original conception was that most of the labour conscripts would come from the countryside. Collective farms had to provide two male youths of the appropriate age groups for every 100 kolkhoz members of both sexes between the ages of fourteen and fifteen; under prewar conditions this would mean surrendering each year 4 per cent of a farm's working-age male population.[54]

[52] GARF, f. 9507, op. 2, d. 852, l. 2–6.   [53] RGASPI, f. 17, op. 121, d. 644, l. 75.
[54] Edict of the USSR Supreme Soviet, 2 October 1940, 'O gosudarstvennykh trudovykh rezervakh SSSR', *Pravda* and other newspapers, 3 October 1940.

During the war the legal freedom of Labour Reserve students was restricted still further. Avoiding mobilization for a school was made equivalent to avoiding military conscription. Running away from a school while still a student made the latter subject to one year's imprisonment. Those who fled their jobs during their period of indenture at an enterprise were made subject to the same draconian penalties as other workers, that is, three to ten years in a labour camp until 1948 (when the wartime laws were repealed), and two to four months in jail after that date.[55]

Table 1.6 shows the number of students enrolled into the Labour Reserve schools from 1940 through 1952, the last full year before Stalin's death. The data are official returns as reported by the Ministry of Labour Reserves, and cannot be taken as strictly accurate. School records of the numbers of students on their rolls were extremely imprecise: they were sloppily kept and many directors deliberately falsified the size of their student body in order to conceal high levels of turnover.[56] The other necessary clarification is that these figures are for students who entered the system. This was a considerably higher number than those who graduated from it and took up jobs in the industries to which their schools were attached.

I have disaggregated the table to show the impact of Labour Reserve conscription during the war and postwar periods. The Labour Reserve system had been introduced some seven months before the Nazi invasion of the Soviet Union on 22 June 1941. Once the USSR entered World War II compulsory labour service became the norm for everybody. With more and more men conscripted to fight at the front, their places were taken by women and by teenagers of both sexes who were too young to go into combat. The Labour Reserve system played a major role in this process. Given the huge losses of territory during the first years of the war, the large-scale and often uncontrolled population movements, and the massive loss of life, it is somewhat remarkable that the Labour Reserve system was able to come very close to its yearly conscription targets up through 1943. When the war ended, the system bore a major responsibility for rounding up, training, and directing young workers into the priority sectors of coal mining, iron and steel, and construction, in which conditions made it very difficult to recruit free labour. Of the 1,084,000 students enrolled into the schools during 1947, some 55 per cent were in the schools attached to just five industries: coal mining (18.5 per cent); construction (12.5 per cent); the railways (11.3 per cent); iron and steel

---

[55] For a detailed account of these laws, see below, ch. 5, pp. 159–65.
[56] RGASPI, f. 17, op. 121, d. 644, l. 18; GARF, f. 8131, op. 37, d. 4160, l. 46–7. For a more detailed discussion of this point, see ch. 4, pp. 126–7.

Table 1.6. *Labour Reserve students by type of school and student origin, 1940–1952*

	Total enrolments	Of which from agriculture	FZO enrolled	Of which from agriculture	RU/ZhU enrolled	Of which from agriculture
1940	602,014	288,305	257,005	206,337	345,009	81,968
1941	688,034	403,840	380,614	334,717	307,420	69,123
1942	814,609	559,806	588,095	445,886	226,514	113,920
1943	711,718	492,744	481,429	374,730	230,289	118,014
1944	440,125	319,292	313,968	252,305	126,157	66,987
1945	446,644	323,622	277,114	240,806	169,530	82,816
Subtotal, 1940–5	3,703,144	2,387,609	2,298,225	1,854,781	1,404,919	532,828
1946	638,708	462,889	384,685	332,173	254,023	130,716
1947	1,084,684	829,216	834,408	707,398	250,276	121,818
1948	849,339	675,214	608,938	533,074	240,401	142,140
1949	610,098	487,189	441,116	388,568	168,982	98,621
1950	385,321	299,750	236,701	206,902	148,620	92,848
1951	341,109	254,750	197,437	168,066	143,672	86,684
1952	330,289	206,289	184,705	144,029	145,584	62,260
Subtotal, 1946–52	4,239,548	3,215,297	2,887,990	2,480,210	1,351,558	735,087

Source: GARF, f. 9507, op. 2: 1940–7 – d. 418, l. 1; 1948 – d. 420, l. 1; 1949 – d. 422, l. 2; 1950 – d. 423, l. 3; 1951 – d. 424, l. 4; 1952 – d. 425, l. 8.

(7.7 per cent); and textiles (5.1 per cent).[57] This trend is even more pronounced if we look just at the FZO, which trained workers for so-called mass trades. In 1948 coal mining alone received 54.5 per cent of the entire new FZO intake; the four largest receiving ministries (coal mining, metallurgy, and industrial and military construction) together took in 76 per cent. In 1949, when the role of the FZO was starting to diminish, nearly two-thirds of all students were going into just three sectors: coal mining (40 per cent); industrial construction (13.4 per cent); and metallurgy (10.5 per cent).[58]

A second striking feature of these data is how the regime used the Labour Reserve system to drive people from agriculture into industry and construction. Overall, between 1946 and 1952, 76 per cent of enrollees were from the countryside. Again, this trend is even more marked if we differentiate between the factory training schools (FZO) and the trade schools (RU/ZhU): during this same period 86 per cent of those entering FZO schools were from the peasantry, versus 54 per cent of those going into the RU.

Thirdly, entrants into the Labour Reserve schools, be they conscripts or volunteers, were overwhelmingly male. During the war women had made up 37 per cent of all students, but once the war was over their numbers fell sharply. From mid-1945 until the end of 1952 they were just 10 per cent of all Labour Reserve students, a fact which again reflects the concentration of the schools, and the FZO in particular, on industries which, partly because of their arduous working conditions, and partly because of in-built structural gender discrimination, employed relatively few women.[59]

Finally, table 1.6 shows that the Labour Reserve system was in fact two parallel systems with quite distinct functions, conditions, and responses from its students. The two-year trade schools, which prepared students for skilled trades in relatively 'clean' industries, offered far better living conditions and instruction, and wilful flight from these schools was low. By contrast, the FZO schools were a way of herding hundreds of thousands of young people into trades and sectors for which the regime simply could not recruit free workers and for which the slave labour sector was inadequate and too inefficient to cover the shortage. Living and working conditions were truly appalling, and the number of students who ran away from these schools was high, especially in the coal mining districts of the Donbass, Urals, Western Siberia, and Kazakhstan. Not surprisingly, the RU could recruit voluntarily, whereas the FZO schools relied

[57] GARF, f. 9507, op. 2, d. 418, l. 9–11.
[58] GARF, f. 9507, op. 2, d. 420, l. 9 (1948), and d. 422, l. 32–3 (1949).
[59] GARF, f. 9507, op. 2, d. 425, l. 2–3.

overwhelmingly on coercion to fill their ranks. In 1947, the year of highest FZO intake, 73 per cent of their students had come through involuntary mobilization, versus just 20 per cent of the intake into the RU. In 1952, when the system was much smaller and conditions had substantially improved (and hence resistance to entering the schools was far less), the FZO, too, had become less reliant on the call-up, at 56 per cent; but this must be set against the fact that in this same year the RU drew 98 per cent of their students as volunteers.[60] But by 1952 the demand for semi-skilled labour had abated sufficiently that not only had the overall number of Labour Reserve trainees shrunk to about a third of what it was in 1947, but the balance between the FZO schools and the RU had shifted dramatically: the RU now accounted for 44 per cent of all Labour Reserve students, as opposed to just 23 per cent in 1947.

The system's dependence on conscription and coercion had a number of consequences, the most important being consistently high turnover among young workers through most of the postwar period. Chapters 4 and 5 discuss in some detail how these young conscripts reacted to their experiences. It is worth noting here that when the Labour Reserve schools proved unable to provide the coal, metallurgical, and construction industries with a stable workforce, the regime responded by casting the net of labour conscription even wider. Laws of June and September 1947 extended the call-up for Labour Reserve schools to young men and women aged sixteen to eighteen, and to young men aged between nineteen and twenty-three who had not yet been drafted into the Soviet Army. Those in this older age group were to be trained specifically for underground work in coal and ore mining and in mine construction. Upon completing their training they were required to work in coal mining for three years, and avoidance of mobilization or abandoning their jobs before the three-year period of indenture was up would be prosecuted on the same basis as avoiding military service.[61] We do not have exact figures for the total number of young men mobilized specifically through this military call-up during the two-plus years it remained in force (it was abandoned

---

[60] GARF, f. 9507, op. 2, d. 418, l. 3 (1947); d. 425, l. 8 (1952).
[61] The levy was authorized by a series of laws, beginning with an Edict of the Presidium of the USSR Supreme Soviet, 19 June 1947, which ordered the drafting of young men aged nineteen directly into coal and ore mining. The extension of the levy to include men in the older age group who had not been conscripted into military service was laid down in an Edict of the Presidium of the USSR Supreme Soviet, 10 September 1947. I have not found the text of these laws, but they are described in detail in procuracy reports contained in GARF, f. 8131, op. 37, d. 4160, l. 16, and op. 29, d. 519, l. 70–1. The text of the comparable call-up for 1948 (Edict of the Presidium of the USSR Supreme Soviet, 4 October 1948) can be found in GARF, f. 7523, op. 65, d. 110, l. 1–8. For a more detailed discussion of their ramifications on the enforcement of the laws against illegal job-changing, see ch. 5, pp. 195–6.

in 1950), but we do know that between mid-1947 and the end of 1949 the FZO took in 606,000 young men in the affected age group, most, if not all, of whom would have entered the FZO on this basis.[62] This does not include those who were drafted directly into the mines or mine construction without going first to an FZO.

Conclusion: the impact of indentured labour on industrial reconstruction

I shall discuss the Labour Reserve schools and *orgnabor* in some detail when I examine the problems of labour turnover, labour discipline, and the position of young workers. For the purposes of our present discussion, what is significant is the sheer size of the economy's dependency on them. During the period 1946–52, nearly 4,240,000 students were enrolled into the Labour Reserve schools. The Ministry of Labour Reserves' own data claimed that from 1946 to 1951 (we do not have attrition data for 1952), 351,339 students left the system, or about 9 per cent of all Labour Reserve students during that period.[63] For reasons discussed in more detail in chapters 4 and 5, we know that this was an underestimate, although the size of the error is impossible to determine. Assuming for the sake of argument, however, that between 1946 and 1952 the system lost as many as 12 per cent of enrollees, this still suggests that it provided the economy with approximately 3,730,000 new workers, the overwhelming bulk of whom went into industry and construction. During this same period *orgnabor* recruited something of the order of 5,815,000 workers, although this figure, too, somewhat exaggerates the true number, not just because of the tendency for officials to falsify their results, but because some workers renewed their labour contracts after their initial expiration and would have been counted as new recruits more than once. Allowing for these uncertainties, we can say that these two sources alone gave to industry and construction somewhere between 8 and 9 million new workers, compared to a *net* increase in the number of industrial and construction workers of just under 7 million (see above, table 1.1).

When we take into account the size of the MVD economy we see that, even allowing for the crudeness of our estimates, the postwar reconstruction relied to an extraordinary degree upon a workforce that was either totally unfree or had been mobilized into various forms of indentured

---

[62] The figures for each year are as follows: 1947 – 219,156, including 141,520 over the age of twenty; 1948 – 249,586 (113,147 over age twenty); 1949 – 137,268 (27,129 over age twenty) (GARF, f. 9507, op. 2, d. 418, l. 23 (1947); d. 420, l. 13 (1948); d. 422, l. 10 (1949)).

[63] GARF, f. 9507, op. 2, d. 446, l. 1–2 (1946–8); d. 501, l. 20 (1949); d. 520, l. 3 (1950–1).

labour. This had profound implications for workers' morale and efficiency. Where the MVD economy is concerned this is probably obvious. But it was equally true of the youngsters conscripted or mobilized into the Labour Reserve schools and of most of those recruited through *orgnabor*. In effect, each year hundreds of thousands of young people – mostly peasant youth – were rounded up and despatched into regions, industries, and enterprises where they did not wish to be. The result was massive flight from the schools, or from the enterprises to which they were assigned upon completing their training or for which they had signed a labour contract. Ostensibly those recruited under *orgnabor* should have been a more willing cohort, but this did not necessarily turn out to be so in practice, for reasons already discussed. They made up a large percentage of those who illegally quit their jobs. The majority of recruits who did not run away were bound to their new places of work for the length of their contracts, which in some branches, such as the fishing fleet, were for a minimum of five years. Irrespective of how long their contracts ran, if they left their jobs before their contract had lapsed, they faced the same criminal penalties as other workers.

This latter point is important. We need to bear in mind that even those workers who were freely recruited or who were hired directly by their enterprises under their own volition also worked under conditions of what we might call semi-indenture: all workers were governed by the laws against unauthorized job-changing, which, as already noted, imposed penalties of greater or lesser degrees of severity on those who quit their jobs without permission. The implications of this for the morale and behaviour of workers were profound, especially during the period 1946–8, when living and working conditions were at their worst.

I should stress that the application of slave and indentured labour was not universal. Many industries, including the vital machine-building sector, had relatively few such workers, and also had lower levels of labour turnover. The problem for the regime, however, was that, by embarking on a policy of virtually breakneck accumulation, it made the recovery dependent on a few core sectors, namely coal mining, metallurgy, and construction, and it was precisely these which were most dependent – in fact, vitally dependent – on unfree and semi-free labour power. In this sense the entire process of reconstruction was made hostage to the behaviour of a workforce whose experiences of recruitment, employment, and day-to-day survival made them less than enthusiastic supporters of the Stalinist project.

2   The food crisis of 1946–1947

In this and the following chapter I take a detailed look at living conditions from 1946 through to the early 1950s. I begin by looking briefly at some of the problems of interpreting the data on the USSR's postwar recovery, and then discuss the food crisis of 1946–7, the regime's response to that crisis, and its impact on the non-agricultural population. In chapter 3 I continue the story by examining the modest recovery which began after the end of rationing and the reform of the currency. I also look at the state of housing and health care, which after food had the greatest impact on the quality of life.

Postwar recovery and consumption: analytical problems

When the Soviet Union went to war with Nazi Germany it was already an extremely poor country. Industrial production had grown immeasurably during Stalinist industrialization, but this had not translated itself into a higher standard of living for the population. On the contrary, the standard of living fell during the 1930s for both rural and urban residents. It is therefore not difficult to imagine how much worse – catastrophically worse – the situation was when the war ended in 1945. Mark Harrison has recently argued that during the war available resources had been so badly constrained that the country had been unable to sustain its entire civilian population. Without substantial outside assistance, such as that eventually provided by the Allies' lend–lease programme, mass death from starvation was unavoidable, not just in Leningrad, which had been under a three-year siege, but in the hinterlands untouched by combat.[1] For those who survived, life was extraordinarily difficult. An urban worker subsisted mainly on bread, potatoes, and groats. Some had access to luxuries on the kolkhoz market, such as milk, butter, or meat, but for most workers' families these foods were too expensive. After the war many workers saw their wages actually fall, since working hours were reduced

[1] Harrison, pp. 141, 159–61.

and they lost the *in natura* payments in vodka, bread, or tobacco which during the war they had been able to convert into cash.[2]

With such a legacy, even if the country had experienced a period of stable recovery and steady growth in agriculture and light industry, conditions would have remained difficult for many years. But as argued in the introduction, from the regime's point of view such stable growth, with some degree of balance between heavy industry and the food and consumption-goods sectors, was impossible. The regime had made the restoration of heavy industry its top priority, partly due to its fears of military encirclement during the developing Cold War, but more importantly because this was the sector in which the Soviet elite's political domination over society was rooted. It followed from this that, as in the 1930s, there would continue to be constraints on popular consumption. Consumption – at least for the non-agricultural population – was planned to grow, but only modestly, sharing the scraps of investment which fell from the dinner table of heavy industry.

The overall picture for the period 1945 to 1953 displays precisely this pattern. If we look at production series for industry and agriculture, the Soviet Union by and large had completed its reconstruction effort within three or four years after the official end of World War II. Most sectors of heavy industry had reached 1940 levels by 1948. Most of light industry, food processing, and even agriculture had reached 1940 levels by 1949 or 1950.[3] Various estimates of real wages – that is, the purchasing power of the working population – point to a similar conclusion. Janet Chapman calculated that real wages in 1948 were roughly 80 per cent of their level in 1940, but by 1952 were some 25 per cent higher than before the war. She cautions, however, that 1940 was itself a difficult year, and that the standard of living then was still 25 to 40 per cent below what it had been in 1928.[4] It is also possible to adapt figures from Eugene Zaleski on the Moscow cost of living index and movements in money wages to work out a real wage index, which would place the recovery of prewar consumption somewhat earlier, in 1949.[5] There are, of course, numerous methodological uncertainties with these and other attempts to estimate purchasing power, but when taken together with the data for physical output they suggest that by 1950 the standard of living of the non-agricultural population had returned to something approaching an acceptable but austere norm.

A more detailed look at actual consumption patterns reveals a picture that is far more complex. One of the problems of looking at real wages

---

[2] Zima, p. 39.
[3] Zaleski, pp. 578–93, 603–8, 614–33; Zhores Medvedev, *Soviet Agriculture*, p. 159.
[4] Chapman, pp. 144–5.   [5] Zaleski, pp. 458–9, 535, 668–9.

and purchasing power is that they do not measure what people actually consumed, for this was constrained not only by the amount of money people had available and the prices of goods, but by physical supply. Surveys of workers' consumption carried out by the Central Statistical Administration show that the family diet in 1946 and 1947 consisted almost totally of starches (bread and potatoes).[6] There were few sources of protein and few fruits and vegetables – and the most important component of these was cabbage. As for non-food items, acquisitions of soap, shoes, galoshes, and ready-made clothing in these years were negligible: yearly purchases per family member came to half a pair of leather footwear; a third of a pair of galoshes; 1.5 kilograms of coarse industrial soap; and a third of a *bar* of toilet soap. If workers' families needed clothes the only source was loose cloth – about 3.5 metres a year per person, approximately enough to make one men's or women's outfit. In fact, in 1946 the Soviet clothing industry *produced* only one-quarter of a piece of underwear and less than one pair of socks for each of its citizens.[7] As discussed in more detail in the following chapter, even by the end of the Stalin period, production and consumption of underwear, hosiery, shoes, and cloth was extremely limited; and while the availability of food now far surpassed that of the war years and the 1947 famine, the diet was still poor in quality. This was not a society even remotely approaching a comfortable standard of living.

Within this general trend, however, the period 1946–7 showed its own special features, what we can only call a crisis of consumption, which statistical measurements of real wages (which show buying power actually rising in these years) totally obscure. This was partly because of the extreme shortage of goods, and partially because of the way in which the rationing and pricing system influenced access to them by different strata within the population. Prior to the repeal of rationing in December 1947, which is discussed in the next chapter, Soviet consumers faced three sets of prices, at least in the official economy: relatively low prices on rationed goods, which were sold in state stores, mostly those run by the Departments of Workers' Supply attached to a person's place of employment; so-called commercial prices on goods sold through state-run shops; and more or less free prices on privately traded goods sold at the kolkhoz markets. The latter in almost all cases responded to upward or downward movements in state commercial prices, with which they were in direct competition. While logic might dictate that only the more

---

[6] RGAE, f. 1562, op. 15, d. 2129, l. 79–79ob. See table 2.3., pp. 54–5, which compares consumption before and after the September price rises and rationing restrictions.
[7] Calculated from production series and population estimates given in Zaleski, pp. 614–33.

affluent families could make ready use of the private market, it turns out that virtually all workers' families in this period, irrespective of whether their earnings were high or low, tended to spend more than they were taking home in wages. According to the TsSU surveys from late 1946, wages in the average worker's family afforded each household member a *per capita* income of approximately 325 rubles each month. Outgoings per family member, however, averaged 430 rubles, that is, nearly one-third more. The difference was made up from other sources of income, such as pensions, repayment to individuals of private and state loans, but most of all through sales to private citizens – that is, some form of private trade, even if the latter involved no more than selling food grown on private plots or liquidating private possessions.[8] Although the precision of these surveys has to be treated with some caution (families were in fact likely to understate the amount of private sales, for example, lest they be forced to pay tax),[9] the pattern here is quite clear. So, too, is the reason: the quantities of food and consumer goods available through state outlets were insufficient to sustain the population.

In September 1946 the state put up ration prices in order to curb popular consumption after the harvest failure of that same autumn. As discussed in the next section, it attempted to ease public discontent by simultaneously lowering commercial prices on many items. This, in turn, brought about a fall in prices on kolkhoz markets, sufficient in fact, to offset the rise in ration prices, and show a decline in the overall price index and a consequent rise in real wages. But to a large extent this was a statistical artefact: the drop in overall price levels did not give workers greater access to food. For one thing, the workforce was highly segmented in terms of income. For the low-paid and many of those on average wages the drop in commercial and free-market prices was of little significance, since they still could not afford them. The rise in ration prices and other state measures to curb food consumption, on the other hand, genuinely deprived them of food, first, because food disappeared from the shelves, secondly, because a large number of workers and their dependants lost their ration entitlements, and, thirdly, because many could now afford less food at the new, higher prices. For workers on higher earnings the picture was less clear cut. Whether or not their buying power suffered depended on what share of their purchases they routinely made on the private market. For most workers this percentage was still considerable, and even towards the end of Stalin's lifetime it still averaged close to

---

[8] RGAE, f. 1562, op. 15, d. 2129, l. 80, 89, 100.
[9] On the role of private trade in the postwar period and the problems of taxing it, see Hessler, 'Postwar Perestroika?'

20 per cent.[10] Whether or not their real wages fell or rose after September 1946 depended on whether the savings on kolkhoz-market purchases off-set the now higher cost of buying in state stores. Although many workers continued to have enough spare cash on hand at the end of the month to make up some of the shortfall at the kolkhoz market, others earned so little that they could not afford even the meagre rations to which they were notionally entitled.

Yet even this does not tell the whole story. As we shall see in the rest of this chapter, the real problem in 1947 was the absolute physical shortage of food – a shortage which affected workers in all industries, regions, and income groups, so much so that some not only went hungry, they did not survive.

The price rises and ration cuts of September 1946

The crisis in living standards which befell the Soviet Union in late 1946 has to be analysed from the perspective of the general problems of eco-nomic reconstruction. In most localities the situation was truly dire. Just how dire we can surmise from an internal Party report on the city of Saratov in early 1946. This is significant, because Saratov had not been occupied by the Germans and no fighting took place there. Thus we are not talking about a Stalingrad or a Kiev, but about a city representative of the Soviet heartland.

Saratov's population was chronically short of food. Its local trading network had on hand reserves of basic goods like groats, meat, and salt, but had not put them into distribution. People were routinely unable to redeem their ration cards, even for potatoes and bread. The milk shortage was acute: creches and paediatric clinics were receiving milk only two or three times a month; even pregnant women and nursing mothers could not obtain any. The situation was equally severe with non-food items. Firewood – the main source of domestic fuel – was in short supply. Nor was there enough fuel to heat the city's hospitals, clinics, or children's homes. Four of the city's twelve public baths were out of service, and this was creating a serious public health problem. Drinking water came mainly from stand pipes, and over a quarter of them did not work, forc-ing affected residents to walk to other neighbourhoods to bring back water. Moreover, the drinking water was untreated. Electricity supplies were also irregular: the city's grid could not supply both industry and domestic consumers at the same time, and in fact many factories were

---

[10] GARF, f. 5451, op. 43s, d. 841, l. 173, 176, 180. The data are from VTsSPS surveys of workers' family budgets in 1950.

drawing power from low-voltage grids designed for domestic use, since they did not have their own substations. 'Many' workers had to walk 'tens of kilometres' to and from work, because no public transport was available. New consumer goods were almost impossible to buy, and to have old clothing or shoes mended in local workshops could take from one to eight months.[11]

The situation in Saratov was by no means exceptional. Some areas of the country (Tomsk and Tatariya) continued to experience extreme malnutrition or even famine, even before the disastrous harvest of autumn 1946.[12] Even where there was no malnutrition, food supplies were meagre and often inedible. The food served in dining rooms for workers rebuilding the Stalingrad tractor factory was so bad that they refused to eat it.[13] Many dining rooms, both before and after the harvest failure, served rotten food and, although the authorities blamed some of it on the negligence of the catering workers, one suspects that these enterprises simply had to use spoiled meat and vegetables because they had nothing else.[14] Housing, as the next chapter discusses, was a problem everywhere, and not just in cities which had suffered war damage. Housing conditions had been atrocious before the war, and with the war became appreciably worse, as resources were diverted away from essential maintenance and new construction, and the problems of evacuation and movement into the towns intensified pressure on what was now a much smaller housing stock.

If this was what life was like in the towns, workers and even low-level managers in rural areas endured a state of poverty which was almost beyond description. Soon after the September 1946 price rises and ration cuts, the Trade Union of Workers on the Eastern and Far Eastern Railways carried out an inspection of the living conditions of workers and station managers at small halts and stations within the network. Allegedly their reports were part of a nationwide VTsSPS survey of how the new policies were being implemented, but the poverty and desperation which they described was only tangentially affected by these changes. It seems likely that the railway union inspectors intended their submissions to serve rather a different purpose, namely to alert the higher authorities to the widespread destitution affecting their members. The manager of a halt

[11] RGASPI, f. 17, op. 121, d. 556, l. 35–49.
[12] GARF, f. 9401, op. 2, d. 145, l. 211–211a; d. 146, l. 28–9.
[13] *Stalingradskii traktorostroi*, 29 June 1946.
[14] RGASPI, f. 17, op. 125, d. 421, l. 2 (Coal Trust No. 7, Shchekinougol', Tula oblast'); *Golos Dzerzhintsa*, 4 December 1946. Conversely, the strict enforcement of the hygiene regulations could have quite serious consequences. A dining room which served both workers and Labour Reserve students in the Moscow district of Kuntsevo had to throw away 280 breakfasts one day when a mouse was found in the food (GARF, f. 8131, op. 37, d. 3529, l. 75, 77).

on the Tomsk railway – a man, the report emphasized, with a specialized technical education and eighteen years' experience on the railways – was so poor that his oldest child could not attend school for want of shoes and clothes, and the family had placed one of their younger boys in a children's home because they could not afford to keep him. At least two settlements on the same railway did not even have secure supplies of water: in one the residents had to hike 2.5 kilometres to the nearest river; the other was totally dependent on the willingness of the crews of passing locomotives to give them water out of their engines.[15]

Whatever plans the regime may have had to accelerate reconstruction and restore the standard of living were almost irreparably disrupted by the 1946 harvest failure and the ensuing famine. In 1946 the grain harvest sank to 39.6 million tons: in 1940 it had been 95.5 million and in 1945, 47.3 million; it was to rise back to 65.9 million tons in 1947. There was correspondingly a dramatic fall during 1947 in the amount of grain available for distribution to collective farmers, and in the amount of bread and flour which could be sold to those entitled to rations. In 1940 the country had milled 28.8 million tons of flour. This fell to a wartime low of 13 million tons in 1943, after which it climbed to 14.6 million in 1945 and 16.4 million in 1946. But in 1947 it sank back to 14 million tons, which now had to cover a larger urban population than in 1940.[16] The result was a famine, which began in the winter of 1946/7, and the effects of which were to extend well into 1948. According to the most recent estimates by Michael Ellman, somewhere between 1 and 1.5 million people died of starvation or famine-induced diseases.[17] Millions of people fled the affected regions, in part in an attempt to flee serious epidemics of typhus and severe gastrointestinal illnesses, such as diphtheria. And while the worst casualties were in rural areas, primarily the drought-affected regions of Moldavia and Ukraine, the famine caused widespread malnutrition almost everywhere, in agriculture and industry alike. The famine was not an unavoidable natural calamity, but the result of regime policy. The state acted to attenuate the starvation in the worst affected areas, but not to prevent it. Instead of releasing food from its emergency reserves, the regime sought to see out the crisis by curtailing consumption. It did this in September 1946, first by substantially increasing the prices of basic foods in state stores, and then by drastically cutting the non-peasant population's entitlements to bread and food rations.

It is the harvest failure and the regime's reaction to it which explain the very steep rise in ration prices which the regime decreed on 16 September 1946 and the sharp curtailment of ration privileges which followed eleven

[15] GARF, f. 5451, op. 31, d. 247, l. 9, 10ob.
[16] Zaleski, pp. 582–3, 618–19; Harrison, p. 69.   [17] Ellman, p. 615.

days later, on 27 September.[18] Let us look first, however, at the impact of the price rises, which are presented in table 2.1.. As we can see, the increases on basic food items were dramatic, especially on bread, which formed the core of the family diet. To help compensate for the price increase, workers were awarded a so-called bread supplement equal to 20 per cent of basic wage rates. Not all workers, however, were entitled to receive it. At the Urals aluminium factory, for example, only 51 per cent of workers and 41 per cent of workers and technical personnel (ITR) were covered. Among the excluded trades were maintenance fitters in key shops, and the disgruntlement this provoked amongst them was of serious concern to the plant's management.[19]

It is difficult to gauge how widespread such discontent was. Elena Zubkova, using mainly reports filed by local Party agitators, cites a number of enterprises at which workers openly expressed their alarm and dismay at the price rises, not least because they were indignant that the government was sending grain as food aid to Eastern Europe and even to France at a time of severe shortages inside the country. Many workers, while terrified of the consequences the price rises would obviously bring, nevertheless were prepared to accept that if 'Comrade Stalin' and the government had taken such a drastic step it must have been necessary.[20] Others were less charitable. The head of the Party organization at a fisheries trust in Novgorod oblast' declaimed, 'And this is what it's come to. They call it caring about the material needs of the toilers in the Fourth Stalin Five-Year Plan. Now we understand why they don't call any meetings on this question. There will be riots, risings, and workers will say, "And we fought for this?"' [21] Trade union reports from Moscow, however, present a somewhat different picture. Even high-earning Stakhanovites were profoundly worried about how they would be able to live: a woman truck driver at a small Moscow shoe factory calculated that with the new wage supplements her earnings would shoot up from 722 rubles a month to 1,121 – but her outgoings would go up by even more, so that what used to be a modest monthly surplus would now turn into a deficit. She lamented that even she, a Stakhanovite, could not provide her children with shoes, clothing, or even firewood for the winter. Another woman worker at a Moscow garment factory estimated that after the price rises she would take home about 350 to 400 rubles a month, but it would cost her 800 rubles to live.[22] The Moscow reports equally show – as do those

[18] Order of the USSR Ministry of Trade, no. 308, 'Ob ekonomii i raskhodovanii khleba', 27 September 1946.
[19] GARF, f. 7676, op. 16, d. 39, l. 93–4.
[20] Zubkova, *Russia After the War*, pp. 43–6.   [21] Zubkova, *Obshchestvo i reformy*, p. 43.
[22] GARF, f. 5451, op. 31, d. 241, l. 36, 39.

Table 2.1. *Ration and state commercial prices, before and after September 1946 price rises, in rubles and kopeks*

Item	Ration price: 15 Sep. 1946	Commercial price: 15 Sep. 1946	Ration price: 16 Sep. 1946	Commercial price: 16 Sep. 1946
Rye bread – kg	1.10	10.00	3.40	7.50
Pasta products – kg	5.00	not available (n/a)	15.50	n/a
Potatoes – kg	0.90	27.00	0.90	24.00
Beef – kg	14.00	140.00	30.00	90.00
Pork – kg	14.00	300.00	34.00	130.00
Lamb – kg	14.00	n/a	34.00	n/a
Cheese – kg	32.50	215.00	70.00	170.00
Eggs – 10	n/a	100.00	n/a	50.00
Sugar (lump) – kg	5.50	170.00	15.00	70.00
Milk – litre	3.50	40.00	8.00	20.00
Vodka – litre	120.00	130.00	n/a	120.00
Cigarettes – 25	6.00	30.00	n/a	27.00
Men's wool suit	1,130.00	3,500.00	800.00	3,000.00
Women's cotton dress	62.50	n/a	77.00	n/a
Men's winter overcoat	725.00	7,000.00	1,000.00	5,050.00
Men's leather shoes – pr	280.00	n/a	270.00	n/a
Men's cotton socks – pr	5.00	62.00	8.25	45.00
Women's cotton stockings – pr	n/a	150.00	n/a	100.00
Household soap – kg	3.10	60.00	13.00	54.00

Notes: Ration prices are all-union prices. Commercial prices are for Moscow. Kolkhoz prices are not given.
Source: Eugene Zaleski, *Stalinist Planning for Economic Growth, 1933–1952* (London, 1980), pp. 688–96.

from other localities – that many, probably most, workers saw the solution
to their problems not in a change in government policy, but in improved
management within the enterprise which would allow them to cut stoppages, improve their individual performance, and thereby earn enough
to meet the now higher cost of living.[23]

It would be a mistake to assume that these reports were simply attempts
by local officials or inspectors to tell their superiors what they wanted
to hear by playing down the extent of vocal opposition and overstating
workers' understanding (albeit in many cases a reluctant understanding)
of the situation. Few officials, for example, tried to hide from the workers
the fact that there had been a harvest failure, although I have found no
reports in which they openly admitted that this was leading to famine.
Rather the reports suggest something else about popular perceptions of
what was taking place. Almost all of them were accounts of meetings held
in the days immediately following 16 September, before workers had had
the opportunity to assess the long-term impact of the price increases and,
more importantly, before the government announced the dramatic cut in
ration entitlements. Basically, most workers, especially in large towns
and/or large enterprises, had no idea of the true extent of the hardship
that was to come. This would confront them later, after they had lost
bread rations for their dependants and the price rises began to bite.

Prior to 27 September the rationing system had provided bread for
87.5 million people, compared to 77 million in January 1945. This total
was made up of three 'contingents': an urban contingent of 58.6 million;
a rural contingent of 27.6 million; and those in 'institutions under state
supply' (that is, children's homes, infants' homes, and homes for the
disabled and elderly), who totalled 1.3 million. Members of collective
farms had never been included in the system, under the pretext that they
would feed themselves from their labour-day income and their private
plots.[24] It is important to bear in mind that these figures are for bread

---

[23] GARF, f. 5451, op. 31, d. 241, l. 1–11; RGASPI, f. 17, op. 125, d. 425, l. 45. The latter
cites a Party agitator's report from Kazan' which summarizes this view quite succinctly,
if perhaps a bit too sanguinely: 'The fact is that in Kazan', in view of the fact that a
number of enterprises are working below capacity, and that there are organizational-
technical failings [and] disruptions to the supply to workers of tools, raw materials, and
parts, many workers are not fulfilling their norms, which is causing a fall in their wages.
There are workers who are earning 150–200 rubles a month, or even 70–80 rubles.
Workers are asking for better organization of labour, a more intensive use of the working
day, the elimination of stoppages, and the creation of conditions which would allow them
to fulfil and overfulfil their norms, and thereby raise their earnings.'

[24] RGASPI, f. 17, op. 121, d. 515, l. 92. The figures are from July 1946. This is part of a
report compiled by a special Politburo Commission, set up on 2 September 1946 and
charged with 'investigating' the rationing and distribution system. Its real aim appears
to have been to supply a rationale for the impending attack on consumption. The entire
report appears on l. 87–131.

rations only. The number entitled to receive other foodstuffs via rationing was much smaller. Although we do not have all-union figures, a detailed VTsSPS survey of Ryazan' oblast' showed that between 1 January and 1 September 1946 between 35 and 38 per cent of those receiving bread rations also received ration entitlements for other foods.[25]

Of the 87.5 million people receiving rations, 26,472,000, or 30 per cent, were workers and technical personnel (ITR). Their allowances were determined by a truly baroque system of gradations, depending on the importance of the enterprise within which they worked and/or the job they performed. A full 60 per cent – just under 16 million people – received a mere 500 to 600 grams of bread per day, including 9,790,000 in the very lowest category (production workers in low-priority industries, plus workers and ITR in service or ancillary shops irrespective of their sector). Production workers in the most important defence enterprises, together with students in the Labour Reserve vocational training schools (3,798,200 in all), received 700 grams. At the pinnacle of this pyramid of 'privilege' were underground workers in ore and coal mining; production workers labouring under hazardous conditions; and workers in the fishing industry who achieved high norm fulfilment: this 'elite' of just over 2.2 million people was entitled to a daily allowance of between 1 and 1.2 kilograms of bread – more than twice the basic ration.[26]

A Politburo commission charged with devising a 'reform' of the ration system claimed that enterprises and agencies had been systematically 'abusing' this system, primarily by inflating claims for ration cards and illegally issuing additional ration cards for special entitlements – for example, additional hot meals in dining rooms.[27] However tendentious such claims may have been, there is at least an *a priori* case for believing that they may have been correct: enterprise managers were clearly going to do what they could to improve conditions for workers in key trades, both to dampen down discontent and to stem turnover. Moreover, the minute gradations by which the regime had attempted to differentiate between one group of workers and the next almost certainly made such manipulation easier.

Deeper investigation, however, suggests that these alleged 'abuses' had little to do with the decision to cut ration entitlements, and that the latter was motivated by one factor and one factor only: to curb the consumption of grain in response to the bad harvest. There are at least four reasons for arguing this. First, the issue of second hot meals to special categories of workers, for example, had always been part of the rationing system, and

[25] GARF, f. 5451, op. 31, d. 254, l. 7ob.
[26] RGASPI, f. 17, op. 121, d. 515, l. 99–100.
[27] RGASPI, f. 17, op. 121, d. 515, l. 104, 106–7, 109–10, 112–16, 118–20.

Table 2.2. *Numbers receiving bread rations, January 1945–December 1946*

	January 1945	January 1946	June 1946	July 1946	December 1946
Urban contingent	50,200,000	55,000,000	57,800,000	58,600,000	55,184,000
Rural contingent	25,500,000	27,000,000	27,100,000	27,600,000	4,000,000
Those in institutions under state supply and others	1,300,000	1,400,000	1,400,000	1,300,000	816,000
Total	77,000,000	83,400,000	86,300,000	87,500,000	60,000,000

Source: RGASPI, f. 17, op. 121, d. 515, l. 92, 147.

the removal of these – as I shall describe presently – caused enormous hardship and provoked considerable protests from managers and trade union inspectors. Secondly, the rapid growth in the rolls of those receiving bread rations was not simply due to overgenerosity by local officials: the above-cited report on Ryazan' oblast' noted that a large but unspecified proportion of new additions to its ration contingents was made up of demobilized soldiers and their families. Thirdly, the number of ration cards illegally or improperly issued was, quite simply, insignificant. In Ryazan' oblast' just two weeks prior to the ration cuts VTsSPS inspectors had identified a mere 0.6 per cent of bread ration cards and 0.4 per cent of food ration cards which had been issued in violation of regulations. In Kurgan oblast' the corresponding figures were 1.4 per cent and 0.4 per cent respectively.[28] Finally, the ration cuts came for the most part not at the expense of workers in the large industrial centres, where the alleged 'abuses' would have been most common, but of workers and their dependants living in rural areas.

The order of 27 September removed 27.5 million people from the rationing system. Those targeted were overwhelmingly workers, clerical staff, and state officials who lived in rural areas; together they totalled 23.6 million. This was 86 per cent of the entire rural contingent and 86 per cent of all those who lost their bread rations. The remaining cuts fell on just over 3.4 million from the urban contingent (mainly workers' dependants) and about half a million residents in state-run homes for children, the elderly, and the disabled. Table 2.2. gives a summary of the changes. The 55.2 million left in the urban contingent in December 1946 broke down as follows: 29.4 million employed persons; 8.9 million adult dependants; and 16.9 million children.[29]

[28] GARF, f. 5451, op. 31, d. 254, l. 15, 77.
[29] RGASPI, f. 17, op. 121, d. 515, l. 147.

In addition to those who lost their rations altogether, about 20.5 million people lost supplemental bread rations to which they had previously been entitled. The largest groups affected by this latter provision were 7.7 million school students in towns and workers' settlements, who had previously received an extra 50 grams of bread on school days. This came on top of a 100 gram per day cut in their general bread ration, so that they were now receiving 300 grams instead of 450. Other major groups hit by the reductions were 5.8 million workers, who lost 100 grams which they had received with supplemental hot meals given them at work; 1.8 million workers who had received an additional 100 grams of bread for overful-filling their norms; 513,700 coal miners who had received from 100 to 200 grams of bread each day with their breakfast; some 3 million man-agerial personnel who had been entitled to supplemental bread rations under various regulations; and (perhaps surprisingly) 580,300 oblast' and district soviet or Party officials, who had previously been given an extra 200 grams of bread with dinner.[30] The policy was applied right across the board: doctors, teachers, trade union officials, and even personnel in the MVD lost their rations and/or supplemental entitlements if they lived outside the large towns.[31]

The rationale behind this policy was allegedly straightforward. The state assumed that employed persons in rural localities had private plots or allotments and could grow their own food – even though officials knew perfectly well that this was simply not the case. If workers' families in either towns or countryside contained non-working adult dependants, the latter were now supposed to go out and find a job. The logic be-hind stripping rations from children is somewhat more obscure, even for Stalinism. If the state was calculating that, given the general shortages, children were a more expendable human resource than adult workers, their reasoning was misguided. Parents, as we shall see, tried to ensure that at least their children survived, even when this meant that they went hungry themselves.

We can partially gauge the effect on workers' consumption from the Central Statistical Administration's family budget surveys. These are pre-sented in table 2.3., which tracks changes in the average daily consump-tion of principal food items per family member in workers' households from July 1946 – that is, before the September price rises and ration restrictions – through to September 1947, when the policy had been in effect for a full year.

[30] RGASPI, f. 17, op. 121, d. 515, l. 32, 174–5. For loss of ration privileges by Party officials and even members of the secret police, see this file, l. 37, 53–5, 59.
[31] In addition to the references in the previous note, see also GARF, f. 5451, op. 31, d. 239, l. 30, 30ob. (Moldavia); f. 8131, op. 37, d. 3200, l. 6 (Vologda oblast').

Table 2.3. *Average daily consumption of basic food items, workers' families: grams per day per family member, third quarter 1946–third quarter 1947*

Article	3rd quarter 1946		4th quarter 1946		3rd quarter 1947	
	Total	From public catering	Total	From public catering	Total	From public catering
Bread and grains including:	*641.4*	*36.1*	*534.7*	*12.9*	*549.8*	*18.1*
Rye bread	286.9	5.9	285.1	3.6	241.7	4.5
Wheat bread: coarse flour	241.9	5.0	184.9	1.7	227.0	2.0
Wheat bread: top-grade flour	46.2	2.2	19.5	1.2	19.2	1.6
Rye flour	4.8	1.6	5.1	0.4	11.0	1.4
Wheat flour	20.6	3.5	11.8	1.0	13.6	1.1
Groats	28.3	12.6	17.3	2.9	27.5	5.8
Pasta products	12.5	5.3	10.9	1.9	9.8	1.7
Potatoes	*393.9*	*22.7*	*718.6*	*51.3*	*508.2*	*20.2*
Fruits and vegetables including:	*198.0*	*42.8*	*163.2*	*38.8*	*216.8*	*36.7*
Cabbage	41.5	15.2	76.1	20.7	54.7	14.1
Other vegetables	115.2	19.8	72.6	16.1	123.2	17.2
Gourds	19.6	5.0	7.6	1.2	16.5	3.4
Fruit and berries: fresh	21.0	2.5	5.7	0.5	21.0	1.5
Fruit and berries: dried	0.7	0.3	1.2	0.3	1.4	0.5
Milk products including:	*142.0*	*15.4*	*76.1*	*6.0*	*163.9*	*16.3*
Milk, fresh and fermented	128.6	11.2	68.3	4.0	149.5	12.3

Butter	6.2	1.5	3.6	0.6	8.5	1.5
Sour cream	0.8	0.4	0.3	0.1	1.0	0.6
Cheeses	0.9	0.3	0.9	0.3	0.8	0.3
Tvorog (curds)	5.5	2.0	3.0	1.0	4.1	1.6
Eggs (units)	*0.03*	*0.01*	*0.01*	*0.005*	*0.02*	*0.005*
Meat and fish including:	*47.1*	*11.1*	*61.4*	*9.5*	*49.1*	*10.2*
Meat and meat products	26.3	7.3	44.5	7.5	25.6	6.0
Fish and fish products	20.8	3.8	16.9	2.0	23.5	4.2
Margarine	*0.2*	*0.03*	*0.3*	*0.07*	*1.9*	*0.3*
Vegetable oil	*5.9*	*1.3*	*5.8*	*0.9*	*4.4*	*0.5*
Sugar	*9.0*	*2.4*	*9.0*	*1.4*	*8.0*	*1.4*
Candy	*6.3*	*1.1*	*6.1*	*0.5*	*6.8*	*0.7*
Jams, cookies, cakes	*trace*	*trace*	*trace*	*trace*	*trace*	*trace*

Note: Small deviations between the totals for the different food categories and the individual items are due to rounding to the nearest tenth of a gram.

Source: RGAE, f. 1562, op. 15: 1946, d. 2129, l. 79–79ob. (3rd quarter), l. 80–80ob. (4th quarter); 1947, d. 2475, l. 11–11ob.

In order to put these various figures into perspective, it is worth noting that even before the price rises and ration cuts *per capita* food consumption was not very much better than the official allowances which the government had decreed during the war for juvenile prisoners in its labour camps. These had prescribed 600 grams of rye bread per day, plus 75 grams of groats and pasta, 500 grams of potatoes and vegetables, 70 grams of fish and fish products, 25 grams of meat and meat products, 15 grams of sugar, and 25 grams of animal and vegetable fats.[32] I do not pretend that the young Gulag inmates actually received this amount of food, but it is nonetheless significant that in early September 1946 the average member of a worker's family was consuming barely more than what the Stalinist state had deemed sufficient to sustain the lives not of adult labour camp prisoners doing hard penal labour, but of prisoners in their very early teens. Only in their consumption of milk, fruit, and probably also vegetables did workers' families appreciably exceed this standard.

What then can we say about the changes in diet after mid-September? Bread and grain consumption fell still further, as did that of milk products, workers' main source of protein. Workers at first were able to compensate by increasing their daily consumption of potatoes, not, however, by buying potatoes on the market, but by dipping into stocks they had built up over previous months. Once they had eaten these stocks potato consumption also dropped.[33] Surprisingly, meat consumption (mainly beef and mutton) initially went up, perhaps because farms had to slaughter livestock which they could no longer feed. Despite this increase, the total amount of meat consumed was inadequate to make any measurable impact on nutrition, and in any case was not sustained. The fall in consumption of fruit and vegetables was also partially tempered, in this case by the increased consumption of cabbage. On the whole, the table suggests that workers as a group were able to moderate the effects of the food shortages by substituting less nutritious or less palatable foods for those they could no longer obtain. Total daily calorie intake, on these figures at least, would have been adequate to fend off starvation, if not hunger or a deterioration in overall health due to inferior nutrition. The table also shows that for most essential foods a modest recovery had begun by late 1947. The reason for including columns on foods purchased through public catering will become clear later in the chapter, when I discuss the difficulties workers had affording meals in factory canteens.

---

[32] *Gulag: Glavnoe upravlenie lagerei. 1918–1960*, p. 518, reproducing an order from the NKVD dated 29 May 1943. The document is from GARF, f. 9401, op. 1a, d. 141, l. 165–165ob.

[33] RGAE, f. 1562, op. 15, d. 2129, l. 79ob., 80ob.

The story table 2.3. tells is, therefore, a grim one, especially if we bear in mind that the drop in consumption was taking place in a situation in which diets were already very poor in both quantity and quality. But the figures in this table are only averages, and to this extent are lacking in detail and conceal the true extent of the cruelty and hardship which the government's measures caused.

Most severely affected were rural residents in the famine regions of Moldavia and Ukraine. Within just a few weeks of the ration cuts some 102,979 rural residents in Moldavia had lost their rations, including 42,505 workers, 35,149 children, 21,368 adult dependants, and 3,957 clerical employees. The largest groups affected were 15,522 people working or living on state farms (sovkhozy) and 9,182 adult and child dependants of workers on the Kishinev Railway. The other prominent groups were workers and workers' families engaged in small-scale production and producers' cooperatives. By December, and despite the obvious dangers now posed by the harvest failure, the ration lists had been pared still further: some 3,800 actual employees on the Kishinev Railway now lost their rations, and the number of dependants deprived of bread had almost doubled, from 9,182 to just over 16,500.[34] In Ukraine the most badly affected region was Izmail oblast' near Odessa (later incorporated into Odessa oblast'). There the authorities trimmed the urban ration lists from 89,652 workers and dependants in September 1946 to 71,800 in January 1947, a cut of 20 per cent. During the same period they cut the rural contingent by almost two-thirds, from 44,362 to just 16,900; not a single one of the 19,000 adult and juvenile dependants who had previously received bread continued to do so.[35]

The impact of the cuts was devastating and immediate, most notably on the railways. Railway workers were especially vulnerable because the nature of the sector meant that a large percentage of its employees resided in small rural or semi-rural communities, where supplies were poor and where they depended on private allotments for food. The food situation for these workers had always been precarious: in January 1946, Kovalev, the railways commissar, protested at planned cuts in the commissariat's food allocation which its network of enterprise farms and allotments would not be able to cover.[36] When the drought came later in that year the private plots in many regions failed and rural railway employees were left defenceless. Worst affected of all were the low-paid, who, without their ration cards, sank into such extreme poverty that some families could not even afford to bury their dead children.[37] On 20 January 1947 the Central

[34] GARF, f. 5451, op. 31, d. 239, l. 31, 51.
[35] GARF, f. 5451, op. 31, d. 239, l. 3.   [36] RGAE, f. 1884, op. 31, d. 6585, l. 14.
[37] GARF, f. 5451, op. 31, d. 239, l. 45–9.

Committee of the Trade Union of Workers on the Southern Railways – a large network which covered Moldavia and Southern Ukraine, that is, the regions worst affected by the bad weather – sent a report marked 'Extremely Urgent, Absolutely Secret' to the Ministry of Railways:

As a result of the fact that many of those living in rural localities are workers with large families or who are low paid, the withdrawal of ration cards has left the entire family having to feed itself on just the one ration of the basic earner. The inadequate caloric content of the food, the inadequacy of complete proteins, the pronounced impact which the cold weather has had on the organism, and, finally, vitamin deficiency, have all contributed, and are contributing at the present time, to the development of oedemas caused by protein deficiency: acute malnutrition [alimentarnaya distrofiya] and avitaminosis-related illnesses. According to our present data, such illnesses are occurring on the Kishinev, Northern Donetsk, Southern, Stalino, South-Eastern, and North Caucasus Railways. Two thousand four hundred eighty-one cases of acute malnutrition have already been registered, of which 249 people have been hospitalized. According to incomplete data, twenty-nine of these cases have resulted in death.[38]

On the Northern Donetsk Railway the report claimed that 'workers have to divide their ration [paek] between all the members of the family, as a result of which they themselves soon become physically weak and unable, or nearly unable to work. Many families are selling their possessions and even their clothing; the children have stopped going to school.' On the Southern Railway officials had registered 400 pre-school and school-age children suffering from acute malnutrition. On the South-Eastern Railway, localities as far east as Voronezh reported that experienced workers were abandoning their jobs (an act which was punishable by three to ten years in a labour camp – see chapter 5) and seeking refuge in other industries. At one railway junction a group of ten workers and their families picked up stakes and went to the nearby coal mines, which were taking people in and giving bread and food to any newcomers and their dependants. The union had on its own initiative begun issuing emergency relief to as many of the stricken families as it could, all the while trying to explain to workers 'the temporary nature of our difficulties with food products, and that the situation will improve significantly in the near future'. But it concluded on a sombre note: 'However, all the measures taken by the local [unions] and the union Central Committee are completely inadequate, and without direct assistance from higher managerial organizations cannot prevent or eliminate acute malnutrition or avitaminosis.'[39]

In fact, the regime did take limited steps to alleviate the situation, at least in Moldavia. In December 1946 the Moldavian minister of trade

[38] RGAE, f. 1884, op. 31, d. 7696, l. 2.   [39] RGAE, f. 1884, op. 31, d. 7696, l. 3–6.

announced plans to restore bread rations on an emergency basis during the winter months. Among those due to benefit were 9,500 workers and dependants in Kishinev; 23,000 children in various forms of state care or foster homes; 40,000 workers and clerical employees in rural areas; and 20,000 rural dependants.[40] We do not know if all of the promised aid was actually granted, but at least some of it was: 10,000 people had been put back on the rural contingent by January 1947. In any event, such relief was confined strictly to Moldavia. Izmail oblast' in Ukraine received no such largesse.[41]

Despite this intervention the situation for workers in Moldavia and Southern Ukraine continued to deteriorate. In February 1947 a worker on the Vinnitsa Railway in Ukraine – a war veteran and a member of the Communist Party – wrote a letter to the Party Central Committee describing the plight he was in. He earned 500 rubles a month and received nothing other than a ration of 700 grams of bread per day and a monthly allowance of 500 grams of sugar. In theory workers in his section were supposed to receive other foods on rationing through the Railways Ministry, but had seen nothing for five months: no meat, no fats, not even fuel to keep him and his family warm. 'Our ration cards', he said, 'remain just ration cards.' He then went on to outline the moral dilemma which now faced him:

Believe me, I'm ashamed to write to you but I'm writing just the same. They issued me with a uniform and I've made up my mind to sell it for food, since I've no other funds and no help, only my working hands . . . As a Communist I'm ashamed to abandon my job and resort to speculation, but I've got to do it, because death by starvation is worse than any other kind of death . . . I ask you to forgive my rudeness, but when a man is hungry he loses both his ability to work and his reason.[42]

This was no isolated case. In April 1947 the trade union for the Southern Railways again wrote to Kovalev. The union now recorded 30,000 workers, clerical staff, and their dependants suffering from acute malnutrition, plus an unspecified number in a state of 'pre-acute malnutrition' who were urgently in need of increased nutrition. 'Considering also that we have cases of acute malnutrition on the Southern Railways which have resulted in death, we must necessarily conclude that a number of our railroads are now faced with an extraordinarily serious situation.' The first priority was to provide emergency rations of 150 grams of bread a day to railway workers and employees in the Ukrainian districts. Nor was this all. The letter equally noted that the food shortages had led to a

[40] GARF, f. 5451, op. 31, d. 239, l. 33, 35–6.
[41] GARF, f. 5451, op. 31, d. 372, l. 6.   [42] RGAE, f. 1884, op. 31, d. 7198, l. 358–9.

'significant' increase in the number of orphans and children abandoned by their families, and so it was necessary to expand the network of children's homes.[43] And while railway workers were especially vulnerable for reasons already stated, they were by no means alone: a procuracy report on conditions at one of the shipyards in Nikolaev, Southern Ukraine, noted that cases of acute malnutrition had leapt from 486 in March 1947 to 739 in April, and affected nearly 15 per cent of the yard's workers. The oblast' procurator noted that despite the arrival of emergency supplies of food these were insufficient to prevent a further deterioration in workers' health.[44]

The repercussions of the ration cuts extended far beyond the immediate famine regions. According to V. Kuznetsov, the chair of the VTsSPS trade union council, the dependants of workers on the railways, coal mining, ore mining, weapons factories, and textile mills had all been cut from the ration lists because they lived in rural areas. In some cases the numbers were relatively small, for example, eighty experienced workers at the agricultural equipment factory in the Moscow suburb of Lyubertsy. But in other enterprises the suffering was on a massive scale: the Tulaugol' coal mining trust lost rations for 11,300 of its miners' children and dependants.[45] The largest number of casualties were those engaged in non-kolkhoz farming, primarily state farm workers. Many of them were workers on state livestock farms who simply had no possibility of growing their own food, and whose pay was too low to allow them to buy food on the open market. Approximately 1.5 million workers and family members had lost their ration privileges in this sector alone. The Ministry of Livestock Breeding was concerned because farmers and herdsmen were fleeing the farms to seek jobs in industry or even to go to collective farms.[46] The Ministry of the River Fleet filed a similar petition: the fleet's state and enterprise farms were unable to feed their own workers, and many were in danger of shutting down, since without food they would not be able to hold workers in their jobs.[47]

Such fears of labour shortages were expressed almost everywhere. Industries as diverse as the timber workings of Sverdlovsk oblast' to the

---

[43] RGAE, f. 1884, op. 31, d. 7696, l. 9–9ob., 10. The letter makes reference to a decree of the USSR Council of Ministers, which enumerated measures to aid railway families living in rural areas who had 'no ties to agriculture', that is, had no means to grow their own food. I have not found the text of this decree. Among the other emergency steps called for in the letter was an agreement between the Ministry of Railways and the USSR Ministry of Procurements to allow the railways to acquire vegetables and other foods in non-famine regions for distribution on the Southern Railways.

[44] GARF, f. 8131, op. 37, d. 3761, l. 10–12.

[45] RGASPI, f. 17, op. 121, d. 515, l. 31.   [46] RGASPI, f. 17, op. 121, d. 515, l. 42.

[47] RGASPI, f. 17, op. 121, d. 590, l. 60.

factories of Leningrad city complained that without ration entitlements they would not be able to recruit enough workers.[48] For other industries the problem was not recruitment, but the ability to keep the workers they already had. The flax and hemp industry claimed in October 1946 that a number of its factories had been brought to a halt because workers who had lost their bread rations had simply quit. The problem was exacerbated by the fact that overzealous local officials, anxious to show how good a job they could do at economizing grain, had cut many of the ration allowances illegally.[49]

Perhaps the central authorities felt they could afford to ignore pleas emanating from non-priority sectors such as livestock breeding or textiles, but in fact the same story was repeating itself all over the country. Workers denied rations were (illegally) quitting their jobs, in response to which local Party and soviet officials virtually inundated the centre with telegrams begging to have their ration quotas at least partially restored. In late September 100 workers walked off the Dneprostroi construction project in Ukraine.[50] In October a district procurator in Vologda oblast' wrote to Gorshenin, the USSR's procurator general, warning of mass quittings from local enterprises and institutions.[51] In May 1947, 300 workers left a major railway construction site in L'vov.[52] More ominously for the authorities, some of these actions spilled over into industrial militancy, namely the refusal to report for work. On 31 October 1946 a locomotive brigade on the Moscow – Gor'kii Railway refused to take their train out because its members had been denied ration cards.[53] In the same month, the procuracy in Rostov-on-Don oblast' reported that the oblast' had lost ration entitlements for 5,486 children and over 40,000 adult dependants, and that this had provoked not only illegal quitting, but also an 'amoral phenomenon' – people were refusing to work.[54]

Almost all the complaints from local officials concerned industrial or transport workers whose enterprises either were located in rural areas or had housed them outside the towns because of the dire housing shortage. Typical of these was a letter from the Party organizer at the Urals

---

[48] GARF, f. 7676, op. 16, d. 39, l. 38ob. (Sverdlovsk oblast'); RGASPI, f. 17, op. 121, d. 590, l. 76–7. See also Zima, pp. 42–3, 66–7.

[49] GARF, f. 5451, op. 31, d. 248, l. 17. According to Sedin, the minister of the textile industry, such officials had arbitrarily cut ration allowances for workers from the 600 grams of bread a day stipulated by law to just 300 or 400 grams, 'and in individual cases have been completely removing workers, together with their children and non-ablebodied dependants from the bread supply'.

[50] GARF, f. 5451, op. 31, d. 250, l. 26.   [51] GARF, f. 8131, op. 37, d. 3200, l. 6.

[52] RGAE, f. 1884, op. 31, d. 7204, l. 143.

[53] GARF, f. 5451, op. 31, d. 247, l. 27–27ob.

[54] GARF, f. 8131, op. 37, d. 3200, l. 1–1ob.

aluminium factory, which in October 1946 had lost 40 per cent of its bread entitlement:

At present those workers at the factory and its mines living in flats in rural areas without their own plots of land find themselves in extremely difficult circumstances, as a result of the fact that their children and dependants are deprived of ration cards for bread, and the factory has no way to rehouse them in its workers' settlements because of the severe shortage of accommodation. As a result, among the families in this group of workers illnesses (acute malnutrition) have appeared. The workers at our factory who live in rural areas do so not of their own [free] will, but were relocated there involuntarily because of the lack of housing at the factory. The majority of them are skilled workers, who have been working at the factory for three years or more.

The request for additional ration cards was refused.[55]

Party officials in Molotov oblast' made a similar case on behalf of workers on the Perm Railway, carefully rebutting the very premises of the new policy point by point. The workers and their families were in 'an exceptionally difficult situation':

Having been deprived of rations for bread and food products, the dependants and children in large families are forced to starve. The employees [*rabotniki*] themselves – the heads of the families – are dividing up their own ration with their children and are driving themselves to emaciation. In connection with this, cases of acute malnutrition, of a sharp decline in labour productivity, of quitting their jobs, etc. have become more frequent.

This 'exceptionally difficult situation' had arisen for two reasons. First, the railway workers had no agricultural holdings; the soil where they lived was of too poor a quality to allow them to grow food, and they lived too far from any collective farms to make private purchases. Secondly, few mothers with preschool-age children could go out to work, since there were no child-care facilities whatsoever in their localities.[56]

In almost all cases the requests for extra rations were either denied outright or fulfilled to an insignificant degree, even where the requests themselves were extremely modest. There were exceptions, of course, most obviously when a factory or construction project was considered strategically important. This, for example, was the case at the iron and

---

[55] RGASPI, f. 17, op. 121, d. 515, l. 83–4. The letter was dated 23 December 1946. According to a trade union report, the Sverdlovsk city department of trade eventually provided rations for about 3,500 of the 4,800 children and dependants originally stripped of their bread allowance. The rest remained uncovered. This same report also complained that factory managers were issuing ration cards to people not entitled to them (GARF, f. 7676, op. 16, d. 39, l. 98–9).

[56] RGAE, f. 1884, op. 31, d. 7199, l. 20–1.

steel works at Magnitogorsk.[57] In the main, however, the regime's policy was pursued with firmness and ruthlessness, even where it seemed to jeopardize undertakings vital to the economy. In fact, the government's strategy had a macabre subtlety to it. In order to deflect blame from Stalin and the top leadership, responsibility for carrying out the cuts was invested in the USSR Ministry of Trade. It was to the Ministry of Trade that local officials directed their appeals, and it was the ministry which took the decisions to grant or turn down their requests. Most of the time the ministry took such decisions directly. In other cases, however, it itself passed the buck, by claiming that the ultimate decision rested with its oblast' and district subdivisions. The ministry in Moscow set quotas on how many ration entitlements would go to each oblast'. But it did not make the specific decisions as to how these quotas would be allocated, for example, how many would be granted to each enterprise or district. Rather it gave the overall quota to the oblast' executive committee and the oblast' department of trade. The latter then set quotas for each city and district under its authority, and it was the city and district officials who allocated ration cards to enterprises and institutions. Thus very often when the Ministry of Trade in Moscow received a request to increase the ration allowance for a specific enterprise it referred the plaintiff back to the local executive committee and the local department of trade. The latter, however, when approached with a request to liberalize these allowances, could in turn hide behind the ministry in Moscow and claim that their hands were tied.[58] Yet we know from files of the Railways Ministry that the individual industrial ministries did have discretion to increase allocations. When needy workers wrote to the Party (sometimes addressing their appeals to Stalin or Zhdanov, sometimes simply to the Central Committee), or when railway trade unions appealed for special assistance, the requests were often granted. What is striking about these cases, however, is that the concessions were in all instances made to specific individuals or small groups within a remote locality. Thus the ruling powers were prepared to make some concessions so long as these did not appear to be a relaxation of the policy itself.[59]

[57] The authorities in Irkutsk oblast' lost rations for 134,000 of 170,000 workers, clerical employees, and their families. They had 23,000 of these restored in November 1946, but in December asked for a further 30,000. The Ministry of Trade 'supported' this request – with an additional 6,900 ration allocations. A similar but even more extreme case occurred in Arkhangel'sk oblast'. At the other end of the spectrum, in addition to Magnitogorsk, strategically important construction and fisheries projects in Murmansk also had their requests for increased rations met in full (RGASPI, f. 17, op. 121, d. 515, l. 14–15, 35–6, 39–40, 60, 74–6).
[58] These procedures are made clear in reports contained in GARF, f. 5451, op. 31, d. 250, l. 17 (Barnaul); and f. 8131, op. 37, d. 3200, l. 6 (Vologda oblast') and l. 8–9 (Crimea).
[59] For a collection of such cases, see RGAE, f. 1884, op. 31, d. 7198.

Even the procuracy proved powerless to force changes in the official line. Some local procurators responded to the ration cuts with barely concealed outrage. In October 1946 the procurator of Crimea oblast' wrote to Gorshenin that the quotas set for his oblast' by the USSR Ministry of Trade were 'illegal', and he begged Gorshenin to intercede to have it changed. The already cited district procurator in Vologda oblast' made an equally powerful protest to Gorshenin against a decision by the RSFSR Ministry of Social Security to withdraw the supplemental pensions (introduced to compensate for the higher bread prices) from those who had also lost their ration cards – that is, from precisely that group of pensioners most in need of the extra money. 'I do not know whether they have legally or illegally taken away [the rations of] children, the elderly, and pensioners who live in rural localities and have no ties to agriculture, but we now have a situation in which they have taken away the supplement to their pensions. I ask you, in respect both to my first letter and to my present one, to communicate to me, since I am receiving a mass of complaints about this issue, and indeed complaints have even gone to you.' The USSR Procuracy replied that it had checked into the situation and could only dolefully confirm that all local decisions to cut entitlements had been 'based on the corresponding decree of the Government'.[60] The local procurators were faced with a difficult dilemma. Workers were quitting the factories in violation of the criminal law. How were they to handle such cases? In some instances workers had gone to their factory management and asked for a legal discharge on the grounds that the enterprise could not give them or their dependants bread. Where managers refused, the workers were quitting anyway. And what of the cases in which managers took the workers' point of view and said yes? This, too, was a violation of the spirit of the law.[61]

As the account thus far should indicate, the workers who lost their access to rations, either for themselves or for their families, faced extraordinary hardship. They were not, however, the majority of workers. Nonetheless, for the rest the simultaneous cutback in supplies and the increase in prices caused severe distress – often as grave as that experienced by workers deprived of rations. Almost everywhere the twin curbs on consumption caused a serious deterioration in nutrition. The impact of the price rises was felt immediately in factory dining rooms, where costs shot up beyond the reach of many workers. At the Stalingrad tractor factory it now cost workers between 250 and 350 rubles a month to eat in its canteens.[62] This would have represented half the monthly wages

[60] GARF, f. 8131, op. 37, d. 3200, l. 9, 14.
[61] GARF, f. 8131, op. 37, d. 3200, l. 3ob., 8. The files give no indication of how the USSR Procuracy replied to these queries.
[62] GARF, f. 5451, op. 31, d. 249, l. 75.

of a worker on average earnings and a third of the pay of a skilled worker significantly overfulfilling his or her norms. The numbers of workers taking meals at work therefore fell dramatically, especially during the first month after the increases. Where possible, managers tried to compensate by substituting cheaper foods, such as vegetables, or by having the factory absorb the extra costs. Workers themselves dictated the trend by refraining from more expensive meat and groats dishes and giving up desserts.[63] In some enterprises the fall was either relatively modest or only temporary, as both factories and diners made adjustments in their budgets. But this was not always the case, and table 2.3. shows that there was a protracted and noticeable decline in the quantity of most foods that workers and their families acquired through public dining rooms. Indeed, a number of enterprises had to close down some of their canteens because so many workers had abandoned them.[64] It is interesting that, while the number of factory meals was declining, the better-off sections of Soviet society enjoyed something of a windfall, thanks to the fall in commercial prices. Restaurants in Sverdlovsk saw business increase dramatically because of the fall in the commercial price of meat, so much so, in fact, that at one tea room the cost of a meal was now competitive with what we may assume was a far less appetizing meal at a typical factory canteen.[65]

Probably no group of workers suffered more from the price rises than young workers, in particular those who had entered employment after completing training in a Labour Reserve school. The story of young workers in this period is a complex one, and is crucial to understanding the social history of the late Stalin years. I deal more fully with this topic in chapter 4, where I look in detail at their wages, working and living conditions, and vocational training. For purposes of the present discussion it needs to be emphasized that young workers were chronically low paid: their basic wage rates were low, and because they were inadequately trained and put on the least productive jobs they found it difficult to fulfil their production targets and take home enough pay to live on. Many fell

---

[63] See GARF, f. 7676, op. 16, d. 39, for numerous reports from the engineering and toolmaking trade union. For similar accounts in textiles, see GARF, f. 5457, op. 23, d. 604, l. 21, and d. 613, l. 22.

[64] GARF, f. 5451, op. 31, d. 243, l. 5. Even one year after the price rises, in September 1947, the housing construction trust in Stalingrad still had only eighteen workers using its dining room. Meals cost an average of 10 to 15 rubles a day, against an average daily wage for the trust's workers of only 11 or 12 rubles (GARF, f. 8131, op. 37, d. 3751, l. 194). By the same token not all of the decline in custom was due to high prices. Some less favoured enterprises received so little food for their Department of Workers' Supply that, unless they had the funds to purchase food locally in addition to their planned allocation, they could only cater for a handful of workers. See the case of the Nikolaev Construction-Erection Administration under the Ministry of the Building Materials Industry reported in RGAE, f. 8248, op. 21, d. 275, l. 108.

[65] GARF, f. 7676, op. 16, d. 39, l. 130–2.

deeply into debt at their enterprises. On taking up a new job they were given an advance to tide them over until they were bringing in regular wages, but their earnings were often so low that they could not repay what they owed; on the contrary, the debts kept on mounting.

It is not surprising, then, that the price rises dealt a devastating blow to these workers. Many industries had special provisions – held over from the war – whereby workers under eighteen could take three meals a day in the factory dining room. The food allowances were not generous – for example, in the linen industry workers on such a regime received each month only 2.3 kilograms of meat or fish and six eggs.[66] Workers could probably survive on such a ration, but even before the price rises workers in at least some sectors did not earn enough to cover the cost of these meals: at one building materials factory – an industry in which wages of all workers were relatively low in any case – young workers earned between 140 and 240 rubles a month, yet the cost of meals was between 240 and 300 rubles a month; commenting on a similar situation at another factory in the same industry, a report from the parent ministry claimed that chronically low wages were driving young workers to theft.[67] After the price rises this problem became far more widespread – young workers simply could no longer afford to take the meals made available to them. According to VTsSPS, at the time of the price rises over half of all young workers in the textile industry of Ivanovo and Yaroslavl' oblasti earned 300 rubles or less, the same as it would now cost them to eat in factory canteens.[68] This phenomenon, although perhaps most thoroughly documented in textiles, prevailed virtually everywhere. A March 1947 procuracy report on the construction of the iron and steel works in Zlatoust (Chelyabinsk oblast) found that young workers were taking home just 316 rubles a month, the same as it would cost them to take just two meals a day in the site's dining rooms.[69] Komsomol members in military construction in Sevastopol were said to be 'starving; their wages are sufficient only to buy bread'.[70] Young workers at a rail depot in Saratov lived in such desperate conditions that they resorted to stealing food from the depot's freight yard at night. Other young railway workers abandoned their jobs and headed back to their parents in search of food.[71] A trade union report on the plight of young workers at the Kuibyshev heavy engineering works in Irkutsk provided one of the more succinct summaries of the situation:

[66] GARF, f. 5457, op. 25, d. 195, l. 1.   [67] RGAE, f. 8248, op. 21, d. 274, l. 156, 161.
[68] GARF, f. 5451, op. 31, d. 243, l. 64. For more detailed accounts, see GARF, f. 5457, op. 23 (cotton textiles), d. 613 and d. 624; and op. 25 (flax and hemp), d. 173 and d. 195.
[69] GARF, f. 8131, op. 37, d. 3747, l. 148.   [70] TsKhDMO, f. 1, op. 3, d. 509, l. 106.
[71] GARF, f. 5475, op. 21, d. 746, l. 34, 47.

However, it is necessary to note that, from the end of 1946 and the beginning of 1947, a certain number of juveniles and young workers find themselves in exceptionally difficult conditions. The majority of them are living in a state of semi-starvation, do not have a change of linen or warm clothing, although they are the first in line for vouchers for clothing and linen issued by [their] production shops [*tsekha*]. This circumstance is explained by their very low wages, itself a consequence of their insufficient skills. There are frequent cases in which juveniles remain in debt to the shop [*tsekh*] even after receiving their wages. Many juveniles go days on end without seeing a hot meal, are badly exhausted, and unfit to work. Many of them do not have the bread which the shop issues them (they sell their bread ration cards and all their vouchers at the market), because they don't have the money to redeem the bread or the commodities for which they have vouchers. Recently we have found a large number of cases of acute malnutrition among juveniles and young workers.[72]

Even at the end of 1948 young construction workers in the Urals were reported to be so poor that they were selling their uniforms (*obmundiro-vanie*), issued to them as street clothing, and living in their work clothes.[73] In early 1949, the trade union committee at the Baryshnikov engineering works claimed that young workers were often so hungry that they did not have the strength to leave the dormitories and report for work.[74]

The picture I have painted thus far might suggest that malnutrition was confined to the famine areas of Moldavia and Ukraine or to the extremely low-paid. It very quickly reverberated across the entire country. Almost everywhere factories found that workers were so enervated that production was being jeopardized. According to Zima, in March 1947, over 30 per cent of Leningrad industrial workers were suffering from acute malnutrition or vitamin deficiency.[75] The physicians who serviced heavy engineering factories reported a steady rise in the number of cases of acute malnutrition over the course of 1947, and, like enterprises in the famine districts, were forced to set up special dining rooms to provide high-calorie diets to those worst affected. This was far from a simple humanitarian gesture: unlike many other forms of illness, workers suffering from malnutrition had to be signed off work for anything from two to eight weeks, thus costing their enterprises significant amounts of lost work time.[76]

The real losses from malnutrition were even greater, since they rendered workers vulnerable to a host of other diseases, in particular gastrointestinal

---

[72] GARF, f. 7676, op. 9, d. 488, l. 20.   [73] TsKhDMO, f. 1, op. 4, d. 961, l. 42–3.
[74] GARF, f. 7676, op. 16, d. 714, l. 6ob.   [75] Zima, pp. 75–6.
[76] See the various reports contained in GARF, f. 7676, op. 9, d. 674. At Uralmash (Sverdlovsk), the special dining room was feeding nearly 2,000 people by the autumn of 1947; this figure excludes the 481 suffering from acute malnutrition (*alimentarnaya dis-trofiya*) who received supplemental feeding during July and August, and the 538 workers with tuberculosis who had their own separate dining room (*ibid.*, l. 101).

ailments. According to Zima, the most serious epidemic caused by the famine was typhus. Without indicating how he arrives at his figures, he estimates that the two most prevalent strains (exanthematic and European) affected a million people, of whom from 5 to 10 per cent died. Although the epidemic's epicentre was the countryside, the large-scale and essentially uncontrolled population movements the famine provoked meant that it soon entered the towns.[77] In industrial centres dysentery was perhaps even more costly. At Uralmash in Sverdlovsk, days lost due to gastrointestinal ailments tripled between January and September of 1947.[78] Nationally, although the total number of officially reported cases of dysentery did not necessarily increase in the major towns, the number of deaths during 1947 compared to 1946 rose dramatically, in most cases from two- to five-fold, almost certainly because victims were badly weakened by hunger: 23 to 155 in Astrakhan; 19 to 118 in Barnaul; 41 to 199 in Irkutsk; 25 to 253 in Izhevsk; 232 to 788 in Khar'kov; 138 to 616 in Kiev; 1,440 to 2,226 in Leningrad; 2,128 to 3,844 in Moscow; 157 to 521 in Vologda; and 23 to 177 in Voronezh.[79]

This sharp rise in malnutrition was not solely due to the cut in rations and the shortage of bread. Even industrial workers who did not lose their rations suffered a deterioration in nutrition because of the vagaries of the food distribution system. This system was based on the principle of differential allocations. The most obvious manifestations of this were the byzantine gradations in the size of the bread ration granted to different categories of workers, clerical employees, and officials. The fact that some workers were allowed to obtain non-bread foodstuffs via rationing while others received only bread was another. In the same spirit, major enterprises in industry, construction, and transport also obtained each month a certain number of ration coupons for second meals or additional courses for distribution to favoured workers. The enterprises and their Departments of Workers' Supply (ORSy), which ran their internal shops and dining rooms, were given additional food supplies corresponding to

---

[77] Zima, pp. 173–5. According to the TsSU, the number of typhus cases in Moscow rose from 1,153 in 1946 to 3,910 in 1947; in Leningrad the number of cases jumped from 429 to 2,043; in Kiev, from 245 to 1,162; and in Khar'kov, from 121 to 3,017 (RGAE, f. 1562, op. 18, d. 361, l. 28, 31, 64–5 (1946) and d. 418, l. 32, 35, 69–70 (1947)). Even allowing for the problems of systematic underreporting by local doctors, these figures at least show the markedness of the trend.

[78] GARF, f. 7676, op. 9, d. 674, l. 100.

[79] Derived from RGAE, f. 1562, op. 18, d. 361 (1946) and d. 418 (1947) (cities are listed alphabetically). Here, too, we must treat the figures with caution. In addition to underreporting, not all those suffering from dysentery would have sought medical attention, and many cases would have been misdiagnosed, for example, some might have been wrongly classified as typhoid fever, while some cases of typhoid would have been incorrectly recorded as dysentery. Nevertheless, here, too, the general trend is clear.

the quota of supplemental meal tickets; in some cases the central allocations were less than what was required, especially if enterprises had viable factory farms or could obtain some food stocks through so-called decentralized supply, that is, by purchasing it on the private market or from other regions of the country.[80] When the government imposed its cut in bread rations it also abolished these authorizations for supplementary meals. If enterprises carried on providing them, they would have to find the food from sources outside central allocation.

The results for those workers who had received these meals could be quite serious. Some of the dining rooms which were closed down did so because they had primarily catered to workers or dependants who had been entitled to these supplemental meals but now lost them.[81] In some cases the meals had not been a privilege to strategic workers, but had been used to feed new arrivals for whom enterprises did not have ration allocations and who had no other means of providing themselves with food. In some railway enterprises the problems were compounded by a Railways Ministry policy – which in fact pre-dated the price rises – to close what it deemed to be unprofitable Departments of Workers' Supply.[82] Yet even prestigious projects, such as the construction of the Moscow Metro – Metrostroi – fell victim to the cuts. Until October 1946, Metrostroi's underground workers had received 16,000 additional hot courses when eating dinner. They also had received between them 10 tons of confectionery products each month. Both of these privileges were eliminated by the ration cuts. Ironically, intervention by the workers' trade union and the Metrostroi management managed to win agreement from the USSR Ministry of Trade to restore a third of the lost allocation, but this was blocked by Gosplan – the workers were to receive nothing. This caused a genuine food crisis within the construction organization, which it managed to surmount by relying almost solely on food supplies obtained from local soviets, grown on its own subsidiary farms, or purchased on the open market in order to feed its workers.[83] The equally prestigious Dneprostroi hydroelectric project was not so lucky. The liberal issue of extra ration cards to any workers who overfulfilled their norms

---

[80] This system was first used during the First Five-Year Plan as a privilege to shock workers (*udarniki*). Some factories set up special *udarnik* tables in the dining rooms where shock workers were quite conspicuously served larger and higher-calorie meals. The idea behind the scheme was that non-shock workers would be sufficiently envious of their privileged workmates that they, too, would aspire to break production records. In reality this and related schemes tended to deepen rank-and-file resentment against shock workers rather than to prod ordinary workers to join their ranks. See Filtzer, *Soviet Workers and Stalinist Industrialization*, pp. 96–100.
[81] GARF, f. 5451, op. 31, d. 249, l. 75–6 and d. 251, l. 143.
[82] GARF, f. 5474, op. 25, d. 341, l. 39, 66–7, 69–70, 72.
[83] GARF, f. 5451, op. 31, d. 373, l. 29–36.

had, by early 1947, entitled over 15,000 workers to claim them, yet the project's ORS, despite the good harvests from its farm, could provide supplies for less than a third of this total.[84]

The contrasting fates of Metrostroi and Dneprostroi throw into further relief the complexity and, from the workers' point of view, also the arbitrariness of the distribution system. The fate of a worker and her or his family was in the first instance dependent on how well placed her or his enterprise was to provide for its workers over and above what it received through central channels. Workers at enterprises which had some degree of bargaining power with their parent ministry or with the local soviet were likely to fare far better than workers at enterprises of lower status; it was even the case that workers in the same trade and working in the same locality for the same industrial ministry could have entirely different ration allowances, depending on whether or not their enterprise or construction organization had been placed in a priority category.[85] To this extent both Metrostroi and Dneprostroi were in a far better position than factories in light industry. But this on its own was not enough. Survival might equally depend on whether an enterprise had a solvent budget, or, most important of all, a viable factory farm and land which it could allocate to its workers for cultivation as private allotments.

The system of private allotments and factory farms had been central to state food policies since the war, and stood in rather stark contrast to the regime's attitude to the peasantry who worked on state and collective farms. Where the latter were concerned, the aim was to increase the amount of grain siphoned off into state reserves (only some of which it distributed as famine relief) by raising the procurement quotas on farm lands and on the produce of peasant private plots. What it could squeeze out of the private plots was limited, partly by the fact that the same drought that destroyed kolkhoz yields also affected private cultivation, but partly by its own policy of discouraging private production through the imposition of punitive taxation.[86] Enterprise farms and private plots held by workers, technical specialists, and clerical staff, on the other hand, received official encouragement.

The Engineering and Toolmaking Workers' trade union claimed that, during 1946, 102,385 of that sector's employees had their own plots; between them they raised 53.5 tons of food, 41 tons of which were potatoes.[87] On the Central Railways – the country's largest network of railroads – nearly 95 per cent of its employees (845,000 people) held plots

---

[84] GARF, f. 5451, op. 31, d. 372, l. 37–8.   [85] RGAE, f. 1884, op. 31, d. 7198, l. 389–90.
[86] This latter point is well described in the secondary literature. See Zaleski, pp. 476–7; Nove, *Economic History*, pp. 308–9; Zhores Medvedev, *Soviet Agriculture*, p. 141.
[87] GARF, f. 7676, op. 16, d. 51, l. 53.

in 1947, which between them cultivated nearly 2.5 million tons of food.[88] According to *Trud*, in 1948 for the economy as a whole around 19 million workers and clerical employees were growing their own food (up from 16.5 million during 1944),[89] and that each plot yielded on average 760 kilograms of vegetables and potatoes – 160 kilograms more than in 1947. This implies that the country received approximately 14.4 million tons of food from this source, a not inappreciable sum when compared to the total potato harvest that year of around 95 million tons, and a state procurement for the urban population of only 7.2 million tons.[90] Nevertheless, all was clearly not well. According to both the *Trud* article and isolated trade union reports, factory managers and trade union organizations were less than helpful in providing land and helping with ploughing.[91] The drought of 1946 also took a heavy toll. According to the Engineering and Toolmakers' union, in some regions entire crops died, and in others workers were barely able to harvest seed potatoes for next year's planting.[92] Curiously, when in April 1947 the Council of Ministers made available a small amount of money (135 million rubles) to lend to workers and clerical employees to help them buy livestock, the take-up was very low. Only workers in the rubber, chemicals, and iron and steel industries showed any kind of enthusiasm, at least during the first few months of the programme. We do not know exactly why this was so, although the difficulties of obtaining fodder, worries about repayment, and the fact that even workers had to provide the state with compulsory deliveries of meat, milk, and other produce from their plots may have played a contributing role.[93]

The network of factory and state-institution farms – of which some 10,000 had been set up by 1942[94] – is in many ways more revealing of the general strains and dysfunctions of the system in this period. The farms were beset by inordinate structural problems, over and above those caused by the drought. Because working and living conditions on the farms were so bad, it was difficult to recruit people to work on them. Like their counterparts at the parent factory, many farm workers lived in run-down buildings, often with leaky roofs, no heating, poor or non-existent sanitation, and no kitchen or dining room in which to prepare

[88] GARF, f. 5475, op. 21, d. 723, l. 34; f. 5451, op. 31, d. 421, l. 7.
[89] Zaleski, p. 336.   [90] *Trud*, 4 March 1949; Zaleski, pp. 622–5.
[91] *Trud*, 4 March 1949; GARF, f. 7416, op. 4, d. 268, l. 6–7.
[92] GARF, f. 7416, op. 16, d. 51, l. 56.
[93] GARF, f. 5451, op. 31, d. 428, l. 5; RGAE, f. 1884, op. 31, d. 7881, l. 13–14. The first of these files (l. 10) notes that even the loans that were made did not necessarily boost the amount of private livestock, since, as we would expect in a famine year, recipients used the money for personal needs instead of buying animals.
[94] Zaleski, p. 335.

or eat their meals. Their low morale was not improved when they lost their ration entitlements because of their rural employment. The farms equally struggled with lack of equipment or machinery in poor repair, shortages of seed and fertilizer, insufficient numbers of draft animals, and inadequate fodder for the ones they had. The combination of all these factors, together with the weather, produced a range of poor harvests or outright harvest failures which paralleled those affecting agriculture as a whole.[95] The position of the farms was not made any easier by the fact that at least some of them were forced to surrender dangerously high percentages of their livestock herds for slaughter, at the risk of depleting them.[96]

Adding to all of these problems was the sheer arbitrariness and inconsistency of policy at both national and local level. The fact was that in such a desperate situation people and the economic and political entities within which they worked were competing for resources, even when such competition exacerbated the situation they were trying to alleviate. A tragic example of this was the Poltava locomotive repair factory in Eastern Ukraine. Like other Ukrainian enterprises, its oblast' Department of Trade had granted it but a small fraction of the food it required. By February 1947 the factory could feed only its Labour Reserve student trainees; it could provide nothing for its 4,500 workers, or for these workers' 2,000 dependent children who had lost their bread ration. The factory had managed to organize the purchase of 100 tons of potatoes from other oblasti, but it could not take delivery of them because the Quarantine Inspectorate of the Ministry of Agriculture was taking its time issuing the required certificates. What made the situation even more desperate was the fact that the factory had its 250-hectare farm taken away because it was on kolkhoz land, and the law stated that the leasing of kolkhoz land by outsiders was illegal. Still, the situation might have been saved had it been able to distribute land to its workers for private allotments, but the oblast' and city Executive Committees claimed that they had no spare land which they could give them. While this bureaucratic nightmare was unfolding, the factory's workers were starving. The factory trade union had managed to arrange interim assistance for about 1,000 workers or dependants, but the scale of the problem was outstripping its capacity to cope. It appealed

---

[95] GARF, f. 7676, op. 11, d. 181, l. 12; op. 16, d. 258, l. 28–9ob., 37, 43–4, 47–8, 51–51ob., 104–105ob., 108–9; d. 490, l. 3–4, 6, 9, 46; TsGAIPD, f. 1224, op. 2, d. 214, l. 8, 15; *Elektrosila* (Elektrosila factory, Leningrad), 21 March 1947, 14 April 1948.

[96] Thus the farms belonging to the gigantic Dneprostroi hydroelectric project were asked to give up 763 head of cattle, pigs, and sheep, even though their stocks had declined from a combined 1,553 head in January 1947 to just 962 head in May. It is unclear how much of these losses were due to slaughter and how many animals had died because of the famine (GARF, f. 5451, op. 31, d. 372, l. 32–3).

to its parent trade union (the Union of Workers in Railway Enterprises) for help:

The number of workers with swollen bellies is going up day by day. For the most part it is the main backbone of the workforce which is suffering – the older cadre workers and those with large families who live in villages and aren't receiving any bread for their children. We have cases of people passing out at work. The factory committee has taken urgent measures, but these are inadequate, since what's now needed is assistance on a massive scale.[97]

There was, however, an even more sinister factor which added to the misery, namely the privileges, often buttressed by corruption, which went to senior managers, middle-ranking officials, and technical specialists. I am not referring here to the pilfering and embezzlement which plagued the distribution system in the wake of price rises and again after the end of rationing in late 1947 (the first of these is discussed later in this chapter; the second in chapter 3). Rather we are dealing with the fact that at least some enterprise managers and trade officials grabbed the lion's share of their institution's supply allocation for themselves or favoured personnel. It goes without saying that such preferential distribution lay at the very core of the Stalinist order and was the foundation upon which the ruling elite constructed a social base for itself. Thus, while workers were barely able to survive, their managers had few such problems, even if there were strict and very noticeable gradations between lower-level administrative staff and top officials. This was all part and parcel of the system. There was a fine line between such privileges and using one's power and authority to lay hold of scarce goods, for example, managers sending their subordinates on 'business trips' to buy up scarce consumer goods or foods for these same managers' own personal use. The regime's attitude towards such actions was highly ambiguous. We know from the files of the Railways Ministry that, when employees filed complaints about verifiable corruption, the higher authorities would feel compelled to step in, investigate, and at the very least put a halt to such practices.[98] By the same token, the Stalinist leadership was quite willing to turn a blind eye to very serious offences. A July 1947 report prepared by the Central Committee's Administration of Cadre gave a scathing account of the behaviour of top officials within the Railways Ministry. B. P. Beshchev, the deputy railways minister, was accused of 'immodesty' (that is, leading an ostentatious lifestyle) and abusing his position, including assigning

---

[97] GARF, f. 5474, op. 25, d. 341, l. 48–53.
[98] See, for example, a June 1947 internal Railways Ministry report on how the Administration of Workers' Supply allocated food and consumer goods between managers and workers on the Stalingrad Railway, RGAE, f. 1884, op. 31, d. 7201, l. 47–52.

special trains to his wife so that she could travel to Western Ukraine and buy up furniture for her own private speculation. This did not, however, prevent Beshchev's elevation to minister of railways once the ministry was demilitarized in 1948.[99] At a time of famine, however, the privileges of the elite, whether 'legally' or illegally acquired, could place the vulnerable in a perilous position. Looking again at Dneprostroi, the site's 814 technical specialists were granted a full 40 per cent of the milk produced by its farm, while the children of workers in creches or pioneer camps received almost nothing. Between them these specialists consumed more fats than all of the workers put together. Worse still, there was a superprivileged core of 288 specialists who received a special extra ration of over two kilograms a month, at a time when the project had 387 workers suffering from acute malnutrition, some of whom died.[100]

The regime's official attitude was one of cynicism and hypocrisy. Presiding over a system which drew its lifeblood from the maintenance of such hierarchy, it blamed the food crisis on the pilfering of grain by peasants and procurement officials, and on inefficiencies and low-level corruption within the supply system, in particular the shops belonging to the Ministry of Trade and the Departments of Workers' Supply (ORSy) which were in charge of trade and distribution at the enterprise. This was not entirely a question of political posturing. Kruglov, Minister of Internal Affairs, issued regular reports to Stalin, Beria, and the rest of the leadership detailing crackdowns against alleged abuses of the rationing system. Such campaigns had always been in existence, but they accelerated in fervour and intensity after the September 1946 price rises. Thus, in October 1946, 26,444 people were arrested for 'speculation', buying and selling ration cards, and other abuses. In November another 23,323 were detained, although after preliminary investigation only just over 2,000 were actually arrested.[101]

I should stress, of course, that the primary victims of such vigilance were peasants and workers, who together made up the overwhelming bulk of those convicted under the two anti-theft Edicts of 4 June 1947.[102] Although workers in industry probably made up only about half of all

---

[99] RGAE, f. 1884, op. 31, d. 7203, l. 272. The entire report, which lists similar forms of corruption among a host of top railway personnel, appears on l. 268–312.

[100] GARF, f. 5451, op. 31, d. 372, l. 24, 33–6. These resentments did not abate with the end of the food crisis. In 1950 one of the regional railway unions complained to VTsSPS that top management was siphoning off the bulk of the director's fund (a special discretionary fund which managers were to use to 'expand production', put up additional housing, and improve facilities and amenities) and allocating other bonus funds almost exclusively to themselves, with virtually none of the money going to workers or to projects from which workers would benefit (*ibid.*, op. 26, d. 1128, l. 38–40).

[101] GARF, f. 9401, op. 2, d. 139, l. 361, 576, 578.

[102] See above, ch. 1, pp. 27–9.

the workers convicted under these laws, it is clear that they were one of the main targets of the repression. The newspaper at Leningrad's Krasnyi treugol'nik rubber goods factory openly reported the cases of two women who received labour camp sentences of eight and nine years respectively for stealing four metres of calico, and of a third who was given ten years for stealing three pairs of boots and a pair of slippers. The paper made it clear that their convictions should serve as a warning to 'all those who still stand on the path of easy gain'.[103]

Conclusion

In its political consequences the food crisis of 1946–7 has a number of parallels with the collectivization of agriculture during the early 1930s. Collectivization had led to an unplanned and totally undesired collapse of food production which led ultimately to famine. The major victims were peasants, but the collapse of the food supply placed inordinate pressure on workers' living standards and provoked widespread social unrest. The harvest failure of 1946 had comparable, although less drastic, results, and led to a famine in which most casualties were peasants, but which badly depressed the supply of food to the towns.

The political outcomes of the two food crises were also very similar. The protests of the early 1930s had died down not simply because of repression, but because workers and their families were desperate for food. They were so enervated by the struggle for survival that participation in any kind of opposition, even of the most limited nature, became unthinkable. A sudden collapse in the standard of living is, after all, more likely to lead to political demoralization among workers than to revolutionary militancy, especially where workers have no independent political or even trade union organizations through which they can organize collective action. The postwar food crisis occurred against a slightly different background, but its political effect was very much the same. It struck a workforce that had already lost its internal coherence and consciousness of itself as a working class, which had been intimidated by the terror, and which had been partially galvanized to support the regime by the war against Nazism. The war and its immediate aftermath may have brought intensified expectations of political relaxation and the return of a 'normal' life, but there was no prospect of open economic, much less political, protest such as occurred during the First Five-Year Plan. Yet

---

[103] *Krasnyi treugol'nik*, 1 August 1947. According to GARF, f. 9492, op. 6s, d. 14, l. 27, only around 16 per cent of cases of theft of state property between 1946 and 1952 took place within industry; this is about half of workers' overall share of these convictions. Clearly workers in other areas – trade, services, and on collective and state farms – made up the other half.

the regime could not ignore the population's expectations or the fact that it had become used to a certain degree of freedom of action and thought. It is true that a rapid improvement in living standards might have allowed the Stalinist elite – if it had so wanted – to construct the type of unifying popular consensus that Western capitalist governments achieved largely through the astute use of anti-Communism during the onset of the Cold War. The food crisis deprived the regime of such a possibility, even if it had sought it. It did, however, cause an almost total shift of popular morale and attitudes. Dreams of a calm, even if slow, advance forward were dashed forever. The struggle to fend off starvation or somehow to survive starvation if it set in now dominated everything. In this sense the famine performed the same political service to the Stalinist elite as did the food shortages at the start of industrialization: it produced a profound feeling of demoralization within the population.

The famine was already abating by 1948, and from the end of that year living standards rose quite rapidly. However, at no time before Stalin died could people relax and consider that they were living comfortably. In addition, the morale and attitudes of the population, while mainly bound up with the issue of food, were not limited by it. Foremost among their other concerns was the problem of housing. As we shall see in chapter 5, when the spontaneous flight from the factories during 1946 and 1947 is discussed, what drove workers and young trainees to run away was not just hunger but also appalling housing. Let us therefore continue our story by looking at the recovery in the food situation after 1948, together with housing and health care, which after food had the greatest role in determining how well or how badly people lived.

3 Attenuated recovery: the end of rationing, housing, and health

The end of rationing

Nineteen forty-seven marked the highpoint of the economic crisis and the social instability which it caused. In this sense we can say that 1948 was a turning point for the regime. With the harvest of 1947 food supplies began to improve. So, too, did the production of many basic consumer goods. Social tensions began to ease. Together these developments gave the regime the confidence to announce a far-reaching reform of the currency and the simultaneous end of rationing.[1] The regime had wanted to abolish rationing as early as the end of 1946, but the harvest failure and ensuing famine had made this impossible. To move to open trade even at the close of 1947 was perhaps questionable from an economic point of view, but the regime calculated (almost certainly correctly) that such a policy would bring compensating political benefits by winning the approval of most of the non-agricultural population, at least in the largest cities. Economic liberalization did not, of course, mean that there would be accompanying steps towards political liberalization. On the contrary, 1948 saw an intensification rather than a relaxation of the political repression, which though aimed at selected groups, most notably the Jews and the intelligentsia, acted as a warning to the whole of society. The message to ordinary people – unless they belonged to suspect national minorities – was clear: if you want to stay out of trouble just worry about yourselves and get on with your life as best you can. This was difficult enough for, although the worst of the crisis had passed, life remained extremely hard in both the countryside and the towns.

The currency reform and the transfer to open trade had, in fact, two different targets. The monetary reform was aimed almost exclusively at the peasantry, and was designed to soak up the cash savings which many

---

[1] Decree of the USSR Council of Ministers and the Central Committee of the All-Union Communist Party (Bolsheviks), 'O provedenii denezhnoi reformy i otmene kartochek na prodovol'stvennye i promyshlennye tovary', 14 December 1947 (*Pravda* and other newspapers, 16 December 1947).

had accumulated during the war. Prices and wages remained the same. If a worker earned 600 rubles a month he or she continued to earn the same amount; an item of food that cost 3 rubles before would still cost 3 rubles, excepting any adjustments caused by the end of rationing. Cash notes, on the other hand, now had to be exchanged for new notes, and would be redeemed at a rate of only one to ten, that is, one new ruble for every ten rubles handed in. Small savings accounts of up to 3,000 rubles would be converted at par; larger accounts would be converted at significantly lower rates – 2:3 (new for old) for amounts between 3,000 and 10,000 rubles, and 1:2 for amounts over 10,000 rubles. Few peasants used savings accounts, and so those with cash immediately lost nine-tenths of the value of their hoards. By the same token, few workers held large sums of cash; if they had any savings at all, these would likely be small deposits in the state savings bank, or *sberkassa*, and these were protected. Anyone with large accounts would lose out, but some of these people were speculators whom the state wished to denude of their ill-gained income in any case. Insofar as members of the elite also held large savings accounts, they undoubtedly found other sources of compensation.

The abolition of rationing, by contrast, was aimed at the urban population, although in many ways it stood also to benefit those in the countryside who were excluded from the rationing system insofar as it made many goods somewhat cheaper than they had been before. In place of the existing system of two separate price structures – cheaper ration prices on bread and basic consumer goods, and far higher state commercial prices – there would now be one, unified price structure. Bread, flour, groats, and pasta products were to be priced at between 10 and 12 per cent below their ration prices; meat, fish, fats, sugar, canned goods, salt, potatoes, and vegetables were to be pegged at their current ration prices; milk, eggs, and fruits were to stay roughly at their ration-price level, with some repricing; and cloth, footwear, clothing, and knitwear were to be sold some 60 per cent below their commercial prices.

Looked at strictly from the point of view of supply-and-demand economics, the shift to open trade would appear to have some justification. Alec Nove, a historian who was by no means uncritical of the capitalist free-market economy or unsympathetic to the plight of the disadvantaged, argues in his textbook that the fact that kolkhoz-market prices fell dramatically in the wake of the reform, to levels very near to state prices, shows that the latter now brought demand more or less into line with supply.[2] The observation is certainly correct. The overall index of kolkhoz prices dropped from 2.5 times state prices in 1947 to just 1.1 times in 1948

---

[2] Nove, *Economic History*, pp. 316–17.

and even dipped below state prices in 1949.[3] Nove equally notes that the net impact of the reform on state retail prices was to make goods slightly cheaper for the general population; he calculates that the general index of state retail prices dropped by 17 per cent.[4] Unfortunately, this gives a misleading picture. The fall in the price index was mainly caused by the drop in price of expensive items like clothing and shoes, but the supply of these goods remained extremely limited and their prices were still too high for ordinary consumers. The prices of basic foods remained high. More seriously, outside the two major metropolises of Moscow and Leningrad, food continued to be scarce and most people continued to live on the knife-edge of survival.

Preparation for the reform was chaotic and bureaucratically clumsy. According to an MVD report, rumours of the reform began circulating around Moscow a full month before anything was announced. Ironically, the rumours were wildly mistaken. They assumed that prices were going to rise steeply, not fall, and that all money would depreciate in value, not just that held in cash. The result was a run on the shops and a run on the savings bank as well, as people withdrew as much cash as they could and tried to buy up everything in the markets at what they assumed would be better prices than those which would follow. By the end of November the rumours had spread, and shoppers were flooding into Moscow from outlying oblasti.[5] The first days of trading proceeded relatively normally in Moscow, but there were terrible shortages elsewhere. USSR Minister of Trade A. Lyubimov had warned in early December that the trading infrastructure in almost every major city was simply unprepared for the changeover. Only a small proportion of the additional retail outlets had been made ready and, although gross stocks of flour and groats were in excess of anticipated sales, once allowance was made for the government's plan to hold much of this back in its reserves there would be a shortage. In some cities and oblasti, such as Rostov-on-Don, Rostov oblast', Tula oblast', and Kaliningrad oblast', even gross stocks were only from two-thirds to three-quarters of requirements. Fish products were in adequate supply, but meat and fats were not, although Lyubimov calculated that what was currently in production should cover the shortfall.[6]

It is clear that local trade authorities tried to cope with the shortages by establishing priorities. In general, it appears that city centres did better

[3] Jasny, p. 274.   [4] Nove, *Economic History*, p. 317.
[5] GARF, f. 9401, op. 2, d. 171, l. 332–6, 343–7. In fact, the government had begun giving people little hints of the reform some six months before. Factory newspapers began carrying articles, quite gentle in tone, advising people to put their money into the *sberkassa* and even explained the different types of accounts available and the rates of interest offered on each (*Stalingradskii traktorostroi*, 29 May 1947).
[6] RGASPI, f. 17, op. 121, d. 587, l. 87, 89–96, 116–18.

than outlying workers' districts; cities did far better than rural areas; and major industrial regions fared far better than outlying territories or republics. Workers' districts in Kalinin were unable to buy basic necessities for several days; long queues for bread began forming early in the morning.[7] In Kostroma everything except bread was in short supply, although even the latter was a problem, since the city's bakeries were making preferential deliveries to kindergartens and public dining rooms.[8] Even in Khar'kov, a heavy industrial centre which should have been a priority, enterprise ORS shops received only a fraction of what they needed. One engineering works had enough food to provide each of its 1,200 employees just 4 grams of butter, 29 grams of margarine, 83 grams of meat, 16 grams of sugar, and 33 grams of fish. Needless to say it had sold out of everything in just over an hour.[9] In almost every locale where such shortages prevailed the authorities responded by retaining rationing in concealed form. Bread would be delivered directly to enterprises or organizations, or trading would be confined to specific outlets, which would in turn draw up lists of people eligible to buy there.[10]

Undoubtedly some of the shortages were exacerbated by corrupt practices on the part of trade officials. Both MVD and procuracy reports give detailed descriptions of what such actions entailed. Perhaps the most common were those officials – including bank managers, bank employees, MVD officers, and the heads of large and small trading organizations – who used their prior knowledge of the impending currency reform to move cash into their savings accounts or into commodities in order to avoid the devaluation of their cash holdings. Some of them were quite creative in the way they did this; since banks were officially not supposed to accept new deposits around the time of the changeover, they put their own money into the till receipts of their establishment and then took out an equivalent value of goods and consumer goods. Another abuse was for trade and retail shop managers and employees simply to skim off goods from their place of work. Others concealed goods in short supply for sale to their friends and cronies. In all, according to Kruglov, the head of the MVD, between 16 December 1947 and 1 May 1948 the MVD had initiated proceedings against 19,551 people. Over half of them were officials or employees in the trade network, and nearly a quarter (4,401) were members of the Communist Party.[11]

---

[7] RGASPI, f. 17, op. 125, d. 596, l. 4.   [8] GARF, f. 5457, op. 25, d. 253, l. 13.
[9] RGASPI, f. 17, op. 121, d. 584, l. 129.
[10] GARF, f. 8131, op. 37, d. 4217, l. 11–12, 52, 193, 245, 260; f. 9401, op. 2, d. 171, l. 450–3, 461–4.
[11] GARF, f. 9401, op. 2, d. 171, l. 444–7, 454–61, 499, and d. 200, l. 103–4. The most detailed reports of corruption are in the procuracy file, GARF, f. 8131, op. 37, d. 4217.

It is important to keep in mind that most of these difficulties were reported in the early weeks following the change. Much more important were the long-term developments. Serious food shortages persisted at least up until the end of 1948. Summer crops failed in a number of regions of the country that year, which left them without seed for winter sowing. Affected were Smolensk oblast', parts of Ukraine, Voronezh oblast', Bashkiriya, Yakutiya, North Ossetiya, and Khabarovsk.[12] Supplies of flour and bread continued to be extremely limited, especially in the remoter oblasti, even if they were industrial centres. Engineering plants in Sverdlovsk oblast' reported serious bread shortages in March 1948.[13] The mines of the Chelyabinskugol' coal mining combine continued to ration bread, giving 700 grams a day to underground workers and 500 grams to surface workers; but supplies were not always regular, and there were days when neither single workers nor those with families received any.[14] In April a trade union official at the Chistopol' clock factory lamented that, in order to obtain their regular bread rations, workers had to get up at four in the morning to start queuing.[15] According to *Trud* such problems with bread supplies affected most coal mining districts during the summer of 1948.[16] In August and September of that year serious flour and bread shortages hit Kemerovo, Molotov (Perm), and Irkutsk oblasti. In Kemerovo authorities warned that their cities had on hand only twenty-four hours' supply of flour and no groats whatsoever. But it was workers, clerical staff, and professionals, such as doctors and teachers, living outside the big towns who suffered the most. In Kabardino, a small autonomous republic in the Caucasus, urban residents, including workers at its engineering works and tungsten-molybdenum combine, were allocated only 430 grams of bread a day; workers and professional staff on state farms had to make do with half that amount. Even these supplies were not regular – they might go several days with nothing at all before supplies arrived.[17] Railway workers on remote parts of the line found themselves equally disadvantaged. In early 1948 workers on the Tashkent Railway were rationed to 2 kilograms of bread issued every three days. Workers on the Amur Railway were in an even more desperate state.

One of the more interesting byproducts of the end of rationing was a huge increase in bootlegging, because sugar, potatoes, and bread were now cheaper than vodka. Most of it took place in rural oblasti of Ukraine, Belorussia, and Kazakhstan, as well as in Central Russia. During the first five months of 1948 the MVD broke up over 31,000 stills. Much of the moonshine was allegedly being brewed for sale through official trading organizations (GARF, f. 9401, op. 2, d. 199, l. 427–8, and d. 200, l. 352–3).

[12] RGASPI, f. 17, op. 121, d. 669, l. 5, 24, 26, 29, 39.
[13] GARF, f. 7676, op. 16, d. 490, l. 46–46ob.   [14] GARF, f. 7416, op. 4, d. 268, l. 5–6.
[15] GARF, f. 7676, op. 16, d. 490, l. 64.   [16] *Trud*, 31 July 1948.
[17] RGASPI, f. 17, op. 121, d. 669, l. 13–14, 37, 46, 52–52ob.

According to their trade union, the stores were totally devoid of any food other than bread; railway workers were being rationed between 500 grams and 1 kilogram of bread a day, but without any allowance being made for the size of their families. Discontent among the workers had reached such a state that they had begun staging 'massive' work stoppages.[18] Even those whose job it was to collect and store grain suffered, and insofar as some of them quit their jobs in desperation this must have added to the bottlenecks in supplying grain and flour to the towns.[19] The fact was that in all of these areas *de facto* bread rationing persisted at least through the end of 1948, and in some rural industries right up until the time that Stalin died.[20]

The shortages affected other foods besides flour. The fact that outlying oblasti had to offer up a not-insignificant share of their potatoes and vegetables as tribute to Moscow and Leningrad certainly exacerbated their own food problems.[21] While the supplies of food available through factory Departments of Workers' Supply undoubtedly improved compared to 1947, they were nonetheless far from adequate. ORSy in the metallurgical industry – one of the largest sectors of the economy – during the period January to October 1948 sold only about 90 per cent of the foods, consumer goods, and canteen meals that had been specified in their sales plans. This was unlikely to be because workers' demand was sufficiently sated that they shunned these stores. The stores simply did not have the wares on hand to sell.[22] The trade union organizations at a number of engineering factories complained bitterly about the shortage of general foodstuffs and consumer goods. Foods such as sugar, butter, eggs, milk, meat, and fish remained in desperately short supply. If the ORS tried to prioritize its distribution, so as to ensure that the dining rooms, child-care facilities, and Labour Reserve training schools were adequately covered, this might mean that the workers themselves did without. 'During the month of May not a single gram of foodstuffs was

---

[18] The report from Tashkent is from RGAE, f. 1884, op. 31, d. 7883, l. 59. The account from the Amur Railway is *ibid.*, op. 32, d. 7884, l. 153–5. A telegram from one of the Amur Railway's local stations cited even smaller bread rations of just 300 grams a day to town dwellers and 150 grams to those working along the rail line itself. It, too, spoke of rising disgruntlement and lost work time, but attributed this not to industrial action, but to the amount of time workers had to spend standing in bread queues (*ibid.*, op. 31, d. 7881, l. 35). The Ministry of Trade appears to have taken the reports of work stoppages quite seriously, because it ordered its regional trade departments to arrange deliveries of extra supplies of food and flour, over and above a supplemental allocation the ministry claimed already to have granted the railway (*ibid.*, d. 7884, l. 152).

[19] RGASPI, f. 17, op. 121, d. 669, l. 31.

[20] One interviewee who worked as chief engineer at a large porcelain factory in Zhitomir oblast', Ukraine, told me that the factory was still issuing bread directly to its workers when he started work there in 1950 (interview with M.Z., Baltimore, January 1997).

[21] RGASPI, f. 17, op. 121, d. 669, l. 61, 64–5.   [22] GARF, f. 7680, op. 5, d. 64, l. 1–1ob.

sold to toilers', remarked a member of the trade union committee at one engineering works.[23] A union official at the Strommashina factory, a large engineering plant in Andizhan, claimed that the availability of food and consumer articles was worse in spring 1948 than it had been under rationing, and that this was provoking discontent amongst the workforce.[24] Although such statements may have had a bit of rhetorical flourish about them, there were ample reasons why they might have been true. Workers generally suspected – often with quite good justification – that managers and workers in ORSy were setting aside food and consumer items for sale to their friends. They wanted an end to trade carried out 'behind closed doors', and queried why it was that when deliveries did come in 'nothing finds its way to the workers'.[25] Quite naturally the shortages had an especially heavy impact on enterprise catering facilities, both dining rooms and buffets. Aside from their generally slow service and lack of appropriate hygiene, meals were expensive and the fare extremely limited. Even in Leningrad, where trade union inspections claimed there had been a marked improvement in factory canteens over the course of 1948,[26] catering at some of its major enterprises remained badly deficient. [27]

One difficulty was that, with the end of rationing, Departments of Workers' Supply were subjected to capitalist-style commercial budget constraints. In order to increase revenues some ORSy opened their shops to outside customers, who bought up much if not most of the stock, not least because the workers found it hard to go there during work hours.[28] In June 1949 *Trud* complained that enterprise managers were closing unprofitable dining rooms and replacing them with more limited buffets, or snack bars.[29] Because ORSy had to operate with limited subsidies or none at all, if they ran at a loss and could not pay suppliers, the factory had a food shortage.[30] Some railway managers were charging the dining rooms

---

[23] GARF, f. 7676, op. 16, d. 488, l. 102.   [24] GARF, f. 7676, op. 16, d. 490, l. 2, 4.
[25] GARF, f. 7676, op. 16, d. 490, l. 9–10 (Komintern engineering factory, Voronezh).
[26] GARF, f. 7676, op. 16, d. 485, l. 27–8, and d. 488, l. 57–9.
[27] At the Sevkabel' works many workers ate in shop buffets; the latter, however, did not have sufficient food to feed more than a fraction of those who needed to eat. According to the factory newspaper, the menu was the same every day – boiled cod and mashed potatoes (*Kabel'shchik*, 21 April 1948). Leningrad's Elektrosila factory was in the peculiar position of having two dining rooms, each supplied by the same central source, but one of which its newspaper claimed was excellent, the other of which was awful beyond belief (*Elektrosila*, 8 May 1948).
[28] GARF, f. 7676, op. 16, d. 490, l. 50.
[29] *Trud*, 28 June 1949. V. V. Kuznetsov, the chair of VTsSPS, claimed that railway enterprises – most of which were engineering works under the authority of the Ministry of Railways – had closed 286 factory dining rooms during 1948.
[30] TsGAIPD, f. 2600, op. 3, d. 32, l. 29–32, 45. The report is from the Izhora works, one of the largest engineering works in Leningrad.

for fuel and utilities, and if they could not pay their bills the managers threatened to close them.[31] On the other hand, if they charged enough for meals to cover their costs workers could not afford to eat there. This, as noted, had already happened in the wake of the September 1946 price rises. If custom fell off too much they had to close.[32] The situation was slightly different for institutions, such as children's homes, which had budgets for food purchases that were not adjusted to take account of the rise in food prices. Since they did not charge the children for food they simply had to buy less of it, and nutrition deteriorated even further.[33]

Significantly, the move to commercial trade also provoked a change in the nature of theft. The end of rationing saw a sharp rise in the share of clerical employees and Communist Party members among those convicted of stealing state property. In 1946 and 1947 the main targets – and victims – of the laws against stealing state property had been workers and peasants (see chapter 1, pp. 28–9). The percentage of clerical employees among those convicted now leapt up, from 17 per cent in 1947, to 31 per cent in 1948, and well over one-third in each of the years from 1949 through 1952. The proportion of Communist Party members convicted also doubled, from 3.3 per cent in 1947, to 6.6 per cent in 1948, and 7.4 per cent in 1950.[34] This undoubtedly reflected the changed economic situation. The ordinary citizens had less need to steal in order to survive, while those officials strategically placed in the network of supply and distribution had greater opportunities – and incentives – to embezzle and to engage in various black-market operations. At the same time this change also mirrored the shifting attitudes of judicial officials towards enforcement of the anti-theft laws; whilst they became more and more unwilling to prosecute relatively small-scale crimes committed by people in serious material need, they were less prone to extend this liberalism to what today we would call 'white-collar crime'.[35]

The shift to commercial accounting had its most extreme consequences on the railways, where a wave of wildcat strikes broke out over the late payment of wages during the first four months of 1948. Delays in paying

---

[31] RGAE, f. 1884, op. 31, d. 7882, l. 77–9.
[32] This was the case with at least two dining rooms specially set up to cater for workers who, because of malnutrition or serious illness (such as tuberculosis), required special diets. At the Kuibyshev engineering works in Kirov oblast' the special dining room actually shut down. At the Stalin Novotrubnyi pipe works in Sverdlovsk it was kept open only because the union provided large subsidies from its social welfare fund (GARF, f. 7676, op. 9, d. 674, l. 50 (Kuibyshev works); f. 7680, op. 5, d. 58, l. 41–41ob. (Novotrubnyi)).
[33] GARF, f. 5451, op. 26, d. 848, l. 133.
[34] GARF, f. 9492, op. 6s, d. 14, l. 20. I am grateful to Peter Solomon for providing me with a copy of these data.
[35] On the judiciary's ambiguous enforcement of the 1947 anti-theft laws, see Solomon, pp. 430–7.

wages had been part of Soviet industrial reality since the First Five-Year Plan. In many, if not most cases, it was a way for enterprises to improve their balance sheet by temporarily deferring large wage outlays. In other cases it arose because the State Bank did not issue funds. We might also hazard the speculation that in the early 1930s it was also a way of indirectly cutting wages and putting extra pressure on the workforce.[36] The practice became equally common after the war in both small and large enterprises. In one of the more extreme examples from early 1947, the Serp i molot engineering plant in Khar'kov at one point went three whole months without paying any wages to its workers. Similar delays were reported from the Donbass coal mines. Given the inordinate hardship confronting workers at this time, we can imagine the distress and discontent which delays of even a few weeks, much less two to three months, must have caused.[37] The issue was still a problem as late as 1949, although the reasons varied considerably from factory to factory.[38] Where smaller enterprises were concerned, problems marketing their output and resulting shortfalls in revenue could force them into large wage arrears.[39]

Towards the end of December 1947 and throughout January 1948 trade union organizations from various parts of the national railway network began sending telegrams to the Ministry of Railways complaining that the individual railroads were weeks behind paying wages. Whilst emphasizing that this was causing workers considerable hardship, only a few reports, most notably those from the Lithuanian, Kazan', and the Amur Railways, warned that workers' inability to buy bread or other food was leading some of them to take industrial action. At one station in Lithuania thirty workers refused to show up for work. 'The failure to pay wages', warned the telegram from the trade union, 'is taking on a political character.' The situation on the Kazan' and Amur Railways was somewhat less clear. Both referred to 'massive cases of non-appearance at work', but some of their telegrams cited the food shortages as the cause, others the non-payment of wages.[40] It is doubtful, of course, that the workers

[36] Filtzer, *Soviet Workers and Stalinist Industrialization*, pp. 72–3.
[37] GARF, f. 8131, op. 37, d. 3761, l. 155, 232.
[38] I can illustrate this by citing three different enterprises in the iron and steel industry. At one, wage arrears allegedly were due to managerial neglect. At another they occurred because the State Bank did not ship bank notes on time. At a third the problem was not so much arrears as the inordinate amount of time needed to issue money to workers because of bureaucratic incompetence. All of these examples are from 1949 (GARF, f. 7680, op. 5, d. 25, l. 14; d. 152, l. 30–1; and d. 203, l. 4–5).
[39] GARF, f. 8131, op. 37, d. 5034, l. 68–9.
[40] RGAE, f. 1884, op. 31, d. 7883, l. 15, 40–40ob., 50, 56, 74ob. See also d. 7881, much of which consists of letters and telegrams complaining of excessive lateness in paying wages during January and February 1948.

gave much thought to such distinctions. All that they knew was that they and their families were hungry. The Railways Ministry, however, treated these warnings with an almost arrogant lack of concern, perhaps because at this stage there seemed little threat that the industrial unrest would become more widespread. On the contrary, it told the trade unions that the fault lay with the individual railroads, which, despite large government subsidies during 1947, had run up massive debts, were recording very large cost overruns, and were holding excessive stocks of materials. In some cases the ministry had refused the individual railroads the full amount of their subsidy because they had failed to meet their plans for carriage, and they thus found themselves in financial difficulty. The ministry ordered railroad managers to sort out their affairs and to ensure that they would be able to pay wages on time.[41] Still the telegrams kept coming in. In February the union committee for the Orenburg Railway wrote to the ministry that the wage arrears were beginning to impact on normal work, and that managers were paying out advances of between 10 and 20 rubles in order to avert work disruptions. But the ministry kept to the same line: the fault lay with the railroad's territorial administration (okrug), which it ordered to release the required funds.[42] At the same time the ministry issued a general order that all railways should ensure that they had sufficient reserves of bank notes on hand to allow them to issue wages promptly each payday.[43]

In April and May the crisis clearly escalated. Union committees from all over the country were warning that workers were so short of money that they could not buy bread or seed for planting their allotments, or pay the rent on their homes. Small-scale industrial action was clearly becoming more widespread. The Lithuanian Railway again intoned, 'The failure to pay wages is acquiring a political character.' If the authorities had imagined that Lithuania might be a special case because of the considerable anti-Soviet hostility in the Baltic republics, similar language now appeared in telegrams from the Soviet heartland. According to the trade union on the Tomsk Railroad, 50,000 of its employees had not received any wages during March. 'This situation is making it difficult to conduct the campaign to sign the collective agreement for 1948.' Telegrams reporting 'widespread discontent', 'massive absenteeism', and the refusal of engine drivers to take their locomotives out came in from the Saratov, Northern

---

[41] RGAE, f. 1884, op. 31, d. 7883, contains a raft of such telegrams and ministry replies. See in particular l. 23, 26–7, 29, 30–30ob., 31, 33, 34–34ob., 39, 40–40ob. The rules for refusing railroads their full subsidy if they did not meet their carriage plans are spelled out in d. 7882 of this *opis'*, l. 50.
[42] RGAE, f. 1884, op. 31, d. 7884, l. 146, 147–147ob.
[43] RGAE, f. 1884, op. 31, d. 7878, l. 32.

Donetsk, Perm, Kishinev, and Stalino Railroads.[44] The material situation of many workers was clearly becoming worse. Perhaps hardest hit was a group of 500 mobile track-maintenance workers who, because they were peripatetic and had no permanent base, already had to cope with very difficult living conditions. In May 1948, after not having been paid for almost two months, they appealed directly to Shvernik, the former head of VTsSPS and now chair of the USSR Supreme Soviet:

At present no one has any money. There is no one from whom we can borrow because we are constantly on the move and each of us is separated from his relatives by hundreds and thousands of kilometres. People cannot buy even a single kilogram of bread, they are coming to work hungry, and declaring that they don't have the strength to work.

The Railways Ministry ordered their parent organization to settle up with these workers, but otherwise remained unperturbed, even as more and more telegrams kept pouring in. On the contrary, up until the middle of May the ministry held to its line of strict financial discipline. Referring to a decree of the USSR Council of Ministers of 15 February 1948, its deputy head of finance chastised the unions that it was their job to assist managers to balance their books and indeed to 'expose and bring to strictest account' those managers who continued to tolerate overspending and wage arrears. It warned that no help would be forthcoming. 'The government's decree forbids the covering of losses of economic organizations, thus the railway and its economic units are obliged to take all measures not merely to make good the circulating capital which they allowed to be eaten up during 1947, but to find additional sources of accumulation and to achieve the stable financial position of their subdivisions.'[45] Within a few days of issuing this statement the ministry suddenly changed its mind. As reports of industrial action continued to arrive, it began to give railroads loans to cover April arrears and a special grant (*bronya*) to pay wages in May.[46] From this point onwards the urgent telegrams virtually disappear from the files.

This saga is interesting for a number of reasons. First of all, the higher authorities appear to have dealt with the situation very carefully. I have scoured the files of the railway procuracies on all of the railroads involved and found not a single mention of any industrial action, despite the fact that similar protests and refusals to work found their way into the regular

---

[44] RGAE, f. 1884, op. 31, d. 7882, l. 21–21ob. (Saratov); 23–23ob. (Lithuania); 26ob. (Tomsk); 39 (Northern Donetsk); 42ob. (Perm); 57 (Kishinev); and d. 7883, l. 79 (Stalino).
[45] RGAE, f. 1884, op. 31, d. 7885, l. 70–2.
[46] RGAE, f. 1884, op. 31, d. 7885, l. 7–11, 16, 17–17ob., 18–22, 22ob., 23–6, 28–30.

procuracy files. Nor is there any mention of these events in the Special Files of Stalin, Molotov, or Beria.[47] Thus there appears to have been no attempt to use violence or coercion to force the workers back to work. This can perhaps be explained by the sensitivity of the railways, which were of vital strategic importance not just for the civilian economy and the military, but also for the network of labour camps run by the Gulag. It might also be because the protests broke out more or less at the same time over widely scattered parts of Soviet territory, so that if the regime had decided to employ violence to repress the work stoppages it would have needed to do this on several different 'fronts' at once. Of course, it is possible that repression came later. It was common in the Soviet Union, especially in the post-Stalin period, for the authorities to deal with strikes first by isolating them and where necessary granting the protesters' immediate demands and then moving in afterwards to arrest the organizers and main participants. We have no way of knowing whether a similar fate befell the railway workers once the intensity of the conflict had died down.

A second notable aspect of these disputes is that the Railways Ministry – and presumably also the government – chose to ignore them for so long before the persistence of the workers' actions convinced them to make a policy U-turn and issue the additional funds needed to pay off what had become very large sums of money owed to the workers. This, in turn, raises a third issue. As chapter 5 will discuss, the response of most workers who faced conditions similar to these was highly individualized, that is, they fled their jobs, even though by doing so they ran the risk (if caught) of a long sentence in a labour camp. Illegal flight was, in fact, very low on the railways, even though housing, wages, and availability of food were comparable to, if not even worse than, those in industries like coal mining which recorded very high levels of labour turnover. Rather, railway workers appear to have been able to act collectively, at least in relatively small groups. In doing so, possibly because of the special circumstances mentioned above, they were able to win concessions, however small, for the entire workforce.

The acute food shortages persisted for most of the Soviet population through to the end of 1948. After this the situation did gradually improve, although at no point was there genuine abundance. Even in the early 1950s the improvements in real wages did not fully translate themselves into genuine buying power, since much of the decline in the consumer price index came not from increased supply, but from a succession of politically motivated annual price cuts which in no way reflected the real availability of goods. This meant that those foods and consumer goods

---

[47] Beria's Special Files are still closed, but the guide to their contents is very detailed and gives an indication of the content of each entry.

which people managed to find in the shops or the peasant markets ate up a smaller proportion of family incomes, but real demand was far from being met. It was not even the case that families were covering all of their basic necessities and simply doing without luxuries. In late 1952 the Ministry of Railways appealed to the USSR Council of Ministers for increased food allocations for 1953, since during 1952 the rail network had received only two-thirds of its planned allocation of meat, three-quarters of its salami and sausage products, and barely a third of its planned supplies of canned meats. It is unlikely that this was just special pleading by the railways: on some roads supplies were insufficient even to meet the needs of institutional catering, that is, dining rooms, child-care establishments, and hospitals, much less public sales to employees.[48]

This should not disguise the fact that, compared to the war years or the period of the food crisis workers' levels of consumption had risen significantly. We see this both from consumption surveys (which will be discussed presently) and from more qualitative signs. There is indirect evidence, for example, that already in 1948 the number of people cultivating private plots started to fall: the percentage of employees on the Central Railways growing their own food fell by about 4 per cent, although significantly enough those giving up their plots were not workers but white-collar personnel.[49] A similar phenomenon was noted among both workers and clerical staff in the machine-tool industry. Here, too, the decline was most noticeable among the better-off – in this case, however, not bureaucrats as distinct from workers, but residents of Moscow and Leningrad as opposed to the rest of the country.[50]

We can obtain a more precise picture of the extent and quality of the improvement by comparing the results of the Central Statistical Administration consumption surveys for 1950 and 1952 (table 3.1) with those from 1946 and 1947, which were presented in table 2.3. These show that by 1950 *per capita* consumption of virtually every food category had not only recovered to pre-famine levels, but began significantly to exceed them. By 1952 consumption levels had risen still further.

There was a marked and significant increase in the consumption of bread and grains, milk products, and by 1952 also of fruit and vegetables. Moreover, there was an equally marked shift to better-quality foods, in

---

[48] RGAE, f. 1884, op. 31, d. 11195, l. 173–4. Those railway workers employed in rural localities faced yet another burden. At least up until 1950 they had to pay rural prices for basic consumer goods, such as cotton, woollen, and silk cloth; shoes; knitwear; and garments. These were 10 per cent higher than prices on the same goods in the towns (which also tells us something about the regime's exploitation of the peasantry). The Railways Ministry estimated that more than 600,000 workers and clerical staff were affected by this policy, which cost each worker an average of about 83 rubles – or the equivalent of roughly half a week's wages (considerably less for locomotive drivers) (*ibid.*, d. 9244, l. 29).
[49] RGAE, f. 1884, op. 31, d. 7879, l. 158.   [50] GARF, f. 7676, op. 11, d. 346, l. 1–4.

Table 3.1. *Average daily consumption of basic food items, workers' families: grams per day per family member, third quarter 1950 and third quarter 1952*

	3rd quarter 1950		3rd quarter 1952	
Article	Total	From public catering	Total	From public catering
Bread and grains including:	*713.0*	*42.9*	*666.7*	*54.7*
Rye flour	1.9	0.2	1.5	0.1
Wheat flour	16.5	3.3	35.1	5.5
Rye bread	356.8	13.1	246.1	12.9
Wheat bread: coarse flour	78.2	2.0	50.6	3.8
Wheat bread: top-grade flour	211.6	20.1	288.8	27.5
Groats	31.5	3.0	25.2	2.9
Pasta products	16.3	1.3	19.3	2.0
Potatoes	*330.5*	*9.8*	*327.9*	*11.4*
Fruits and vegetables including:	*213.6*	*10.4*	*383.2*	*18.6*
Cabbage	45.7	3.6	53.1	4.9
Other vegetables	98.6	3.5	182.6	7.9
Gourds	31.0	1.6	77.1	3.4
Fruit and berries: fresh	36.2	1.2	67.4	1.9
Fruit and berries: dried	2.1	0.5	3.0	0.5
Milk products including:	*242.8*	*17.8*	*251.3*	*19.0*
Milk: fresh and fermented	223.1	14.5	228.6	14.9
Butter	10.5	1.4	10.3	1.4
Sour cream	2.3	0.7	3.9	1.1
Cheeses	1.2	0.3	1.5	0.4
Tvorog (curds)	5.7	0.9	7.0	1.2
Eggs (units)	*0.1*	*0.01*	*0.24*	*0.02*
Meat and fish including:	*69.0*	*4.9*	*87.1*	*9.1*
Meat and meat products	49.7	4.2	57.7	7.3
Fish and fish products	19.3	0.7	29.4	1.8
Margarine	*4.8*	*0.2*	*6.3*	*0.5*
Vegetable oil	*4.0*	*0.2*	*9.8*	*0.5*
Sugar	*33.2*	*2.3*	*48.2*	*2.5*
Candy	*15.5*	*1.3*	*10.3*	*1.4*
Jams, cookies, cakes	*trace*	*trace*	*11.3*	*1.7*

Note: Small deviations between the totals for the different food categories and the individual items are due to rounding to the nearest tenth of a gram.
Source: RGAE, f. 1562, op. 15, d. 3086, l. 170–170ob. (1950); f. 1562, op. 26, d. 25, l. 64–64ob. (1952).

particular, higher-grade white bread in place of rye bread or white bread from coarse flour, and fewer potatoes. More important, the average daily calorie intake was now roughly at the level needed to sustain reasonable health. The average member of a worker's family was consuming over 2,500 calories of food a day; the average adult worker was taking in roughly 3,800. Moreover, even workers' families in low-wage sectors, such as textiles and construction, which had suffered terribly during the food crisis years, were consuming very close to this national average. In other words, the recovery was more evenly spread, so that even low-income groups could be reasonably assured of survival.[51] Consumption levels did vary according to wage differentials, to be sure, but the variation was smaller than the variation in wages because the main limitation on consumption continued to be supply, not money. According to trade union budget surveys, the families of workers in coal mining or iron and steel spent more money on food, but their diet was not appreciably better or more varied than that of workers on lower incomes. For everyone, irrespective of the level of wages, the daily diet still consisted mainly of carbohydrates, and most protein came from dairy products. The amounts of meat and fish remained meagre; moreover, much of it was canned or dried, and not fresh.[52]

Access to basic consumer items also improved, but remained terribly inadequate. The average worker's family could now expect to acquire one pair of leather footwear each year for each member of the household, but that included everything from shoes and winter boots to leather household slippers. They could now expect to buy or receive from their workplace 3 kilograms of coarse soap and two bars of toilet soap *a year*, but with this they had to launder all their clothing as well as attend to personal hygiene. Perhaps the one significant boost was in the availability of loose cloth, the *per capita* consumption of which had grown to 12 metres a year. Only in 1952, however, did purchases of ready-made items of clothing become significant enough to register in the statistics.[53]

Housing

After food and clothing, the most important determinants of the quality of life are probably housing and health care. Urban housing conditions in tsarist Russia and the Soviet Union had never been good. They deteriorated further during the 1930s, as millions of peasants streamed into

[51] GARF, f. 5451, op. 43s, d. 996, l. 487–8.
[52] The data here are by no means consistent. Central Statistical Administration surveys showed less variation between industries in *per capita* purchases and far smaller cash surpluses at the end of the month than did the surveys of VTsSPS – a finding which may be because the families of metallurgy and coal workers in the TsSU studies had more dependants than workers' families in the same industries surveyed by VTsSPS. For VTsSPS, see GARF, f. 5451, op. 43s, d. 841, l. 175, 180–1, and d. 996, l. 486–8. For TsSU, see RGAE, f. 1562, op. 15, d. 3086, l. 172–172ob., 196, 198–198ob., 201–201ob., 204–204ob., 207–207ob.
[53] RGAE, f. 1562, op. 15, d. 3086, l. 176 (1950); op. 26, d. 25, l. 126 (1952).

the cities as workers but the regime deliberately refused to match the growth in population with commensurate investment in housing construction. Conditions were to become even worse, of course, during the war. In 1940 the total urban housing stock was 270 million square metres, enough to provide the average urban resident with just 5.1 square metres of living space. In 1945 wartime destruction had reduced the stock to 200 million square metres. By 1948 this had risen back to 260 million square metres, but this had to accommodate a much larger urban population. We do not have figures for average living space in that year, but we can gauge how cramped conditions were by the fact that in 1950 the urban housing stock had grown to 513 million square metres, a full 90 per cent more than in 1940, but this provided the average resident with only 4.67 square metres, more than 8 per cent less than before the war.[54] It was still the case in 1950 that women workers were being herded into makeshift premises living forty or even ninety-nine people in a single room.[55]

For millions of workers the housing conditions during the first postwar years were truly horrendous, and were a major cause of the labour turnover described in detail in chapter 5. The greatest suffering was undoubtedly endured by people still living in dugouts or mud huts (*zemlyanki*). We do not know the total number of people quartered in these kinds of primitive accommodation, but the coal trust Tulaugol' in Tula oblast', part of the Greater Moscow coal fields, had 1,500 workers and their families living in them in December 1945, while a further 6,500 workers slept on two-tiered plank beds.[56] The Railways Ministry claimed to have just over 4,200 families, totalling 15,750 people in mud huts, as of 1 January 1946.[57] In general it was the policy of both the regime and the industrial ministries to give people living in *zemlyanki* first priority when it came to rehousing, and the numbers appear to have fallen rapidly, although it obviously took some years for the phenomenon to be totally eliminated, especially in areas badly damaged by fighting. Towards the end of 1947 it was still the case, for example, that a sizeable proportion of workers and staff on the Southern Railways network, which included large parts of Ukraine, were living in cellars or, in the words of their trade union, 'semi-cellars'.[58]

The extent of the housing crisis was so great that the regime made little attempt to deny it. Indeed, the trade union newspaper *Trud* carried numerous articles giving quite accurate descriptions of conditions in dormitories and the myriad problems which were holding up construction

---

[54] Zaleski, pp. 592–3, 608, 630–1, 633.
[55] GARF, f. 8131, op. 28, d. 310, l. 3, and d. 311, l. 3.
[56] RGASPI, f. 17, op. 125, d. 421, l. 3.   [57] RGAE, f. 1884, op. 31, d. 6585, l. 112.
[58] RGAE, f. 1884, op. 31, d. 7203, l. 221.

(it did not, however, point out that state investment in house-building was in any case woefully inadequate). Both *Trud* and factory newspapers also openly admitted the connection between bad housing and high labour turnover, something which we might expect them to have denied, given that quitting was still a criminal offence and the regime had little interest in admitting that it was taking place on a massive scale.[59] However, the problem went far beyond labour turnover *per se*. Certainly in the first postwar years the housing shortage made it very difficult for enterprises to make good their labour shortages. Factories in Leningrad during 1946 and Bryansk oblast' in 1947 had to call a temporary halt to the recruitment of new workers because they had nowhere to house them.[60] The housing shortage even manifested its own perverse dialectic: because the building materials industry had a housing deficit, its enterprises found it hard to recruit and retain workers – a phenomenon which, by compromising production in this sector, threatened the entire construction industry, including, of course, house-building.[61]

As with food supplies, housing conditions varied considerably from industry to industry and region to region. Cities which had suffered extreme damage during the war obviously were in the worst position, but this was partially compensated by the fact that they received top priority for reconstruction, and so were able to restore housing stock more quickly than cities which had suffered no damage, but with housing stock that had deteriorated over the years for lack of repair and was now being overwhelmed by the influx of new workers. Workers in coal mining, construction, and rural industries, such as building materials, were especially badly off because they relied heavily on dormitories or, worse still, barracks. These were mainly but not exclusively occupied by young workers, and the special problems these workers faced with accommodation I discuss in more detail in the next chapter.

The conditions in the dormitories almost defy description. A procuracy inspection of the Greater Moscow coal fields in 1947 found that the average worker living in a flat had less than 4 square metres of living space; those in dormitories had less than 3 square metres. The Moskovugol' combine had at its disposal 3,057 rooms, each with approximately five beds in them. But these 15,560 beds had to accommodate 26,000 single workers and a further 3,600 workers with families. Nearly

---

[59] See, for example, the editorial in *Trud* of 5 June 1948, and *Za sovetskuyu malolitrazhku*, 15 April 1946 and 1 June 1946.

[60] *Elektrosila*, 17 August 1946; *Kabel'shchik*, 16 February, 6 June, 14 June, 12 July 1946. The Bryansk case, which concerned an engineering works under the Ministry of Construction and Road Building Equipment, also involved a shortage of ration cards (TsKhDMO, f. 1, op. 8, d. 454, l. 49).

[61] RGAE, f. 8248, op. 21, d. 274, l. 234–6; d. 275, l. 91–2; and d. 699, l. 88–9, 93–4, 113.

half of these workers slept on planks or trestle beds. There was a chronic lack of furniture: the dormitories had an average of one table for every ten workers, one stool for every three, one bedside table for every five, one wardrobe for every twenty-one, and only one wash basin for every seven rooms – that is, roughly one for every seventy people. The 257 dormitories had between them just 84 drying rooms (which meant that most workers had nowhere to dry out wet work clothes or street clothes); 58 storage rooms in which to keep private belongings (so that workers had to keep all of their possessions, including coats and clothes, around their beds); and 143 kitchens. The latter represented a critical hardship at a time when food was scarce and many workers, especially young workers, found it prohibitively expensive to eat in enterprise dining rooms. There were not enough blankets for everybody, and many workers slept in their dirty street clothes. Even more striking, according to the report, was that housing conditions had actually deteriorated, rather than improved, over the course of 1947.[62]

It is true that the Moscow coal fields, primarily the area around Tula oblast', had some of the worst working and living conditions in the country, but the above account is by no means atypical. It would be possible to reproduce similar reports from almost any industry in virtually any part of the USSR. Workers in the oil fields of Tatariya and Bashkiriya lived in dormitories where lice and bed bug infestation was so bad that many allegedly chose to sleep out in the streets or in the nearby woods.[63] A trade union inspection of the Urals turbine factory in Sverdlovsk from early 1947 found that the dormitories lacked almost every basic amenity: wash basins, tanks for boiling drinking water, storage rooms, drying rooms, kitchen areas for preparing food, even taps for the water cisterns. The sleeping areas were infested with bugs and rats. There were no laundry rooms in either the factory or the dormitories, so workers had to wash clothes in their already crowded rooms, often in makeshift tubs which they had fashioned out of metal pilfered from work and had to hide from the authorities.[64] The archive and press reports tended to focus especially on the conditions of young workers because they made up the majority of new arrivals and showed the highest turnover, but significantly the dormitories at the Urals turbine factory were occupied almost solely by older workers. Thus age, experience, or seniority did not necessarily guarantee better housing. Workers mobilized during the war to work at the Gor'kii motor vehicle factory (GAZ) inundated the factory administration with requests to be sent home, not just because they had been separated from their families (in most such cases families had the right, and indeed were encouraged to join a mobilized worker), but because they were simply fed up living in such cramped and ill-equipped quarters. Even experienced workers who had been at the plant since the early 1930s were still living in barracks, together with their wives, children, and parents.[65] In early 1948 large railway junctions in Siberia reported that they each had several hundred families who still had nowhere to live.[66] Nor were workers in Moscow exempt: they suffered the same overcrowding and lack of basic amenities as people elsewhere.[67]

The problems of overcrowding were exacerbated by a general lack of amenities, the most serious of which was a shortage of fuel for keeping premises warm during the winter. *Trud* noted with irony that a number of Donbass miners had spent a good part of the winter of 1947/8 without any coal to heat their flats.[68] The refusal of the Railways Ministry to issue adequate fuel rations to workers in rural areas was a running source of conflict between the trade unions and management. In late 1947 the ministry cut the fuel allocation of workers on the Southern Railways by 75 per cent. The union made a direct appeal to Zhdanov to have the action reversed, but we do not know how this came out.[69] A year later the same union complained of inadequate fuel supplies to workers of the Stalino Railroad, part of the Southern Railways network. The union claimed that the allocation, which had been set in 1944 when the railroad had a third of its then-current number of employees, now met only about 30 per cent of actual need, leaving the 'overwhelming majority' of workers facing the coming winter without fuel.[70] In these, as in other cases, the affected workers lived in areas with few forests, and were thus wholly reliant on what the ministry gave them. The ministry, however, would not relent, claiming that fuel was scarce and it could not increase existing allowances, even for disabled former workers who had been forced to retire because of accidents suffered while on duty.[71]

---

[65] RGASPI, f. 17, op. 121, d. 575, l. 97–8.   [66] RGAE, f. 1884, op. 31, d. 7884, l. 61.
[67] Workers at one Moscow engineering works were housed in a settlement which had no water supplies, not even a well, and where the cesspits had gone years without being emptied (GARF, f. 5451, op. 26, d. 1128, l. 164). I have already noted the case of women textile workers in Moscow who lived in dormitories with over forty people, including children, all sleeping in one room (*ibid.*, f. 8131, op. 28, d. 310, l. 3 – see n. 55, above). Significantly, both of these reports are from 1950, when conditions should have started to improve.
[68] *Trud*, 10 December 1947.   [69] RGAE, f. 1884, op. 31, d. 7203, l. 221.
[70] RGAE, f. 1884, op. 31, d. 7887, l. 2–2ob.
[71] RGAE, f. 1884, op. 31, d. 7888, l. 10–12. For similar conflicts on the Krasnoyarsk Railway and in railway engineering factories, see *ibid.*, d. 7887, l. 6–6ob., and d. 7886, l. 17–17ob. respectively.

The regime attempted to accelerate house-building through various campaigns, most notably by urging workers to build their own private homes. One objective of this approach was to cut labour turnover, on the quite reasonable assumption that workers living in their own homes would be unlikely to abandon them by moving to another job.[72] On the basis of this philosophy, some enterprises used the promise of a house to lure workers from other areas to come work there, but in at least some cases this was merely a ruse and the houses did not exist.[73] In general, however, the individual house-building campaign did enjoy some notable, if limited, successes. Even if everything had run smoothly the amount of such housing which could be erected would meet only an insignificant proportion of the overall need.[74] But everything did not run smoothly. Instead the campaign was hampered by lack of funds, materials shortages, managerial reluctance to provide workers with the necessary technical assistance, and massive amounts of bureaucratic red tape.[75] Funds for the construction had to be approved by the Communal Bank, a process which could take several months, during which time not a single foundation could be laid, even if all the building materials had been gathered and the designs were finished. The latter could themselves contain some rather peculiar specifications, for example, fitting houses in the coal mining regions of the Kuzbass with wood-burning stoves or failing to provide for the installation of electric wiring.[76] This same report noted that, if the actual building costs exceeded the price at which the state allowed the contractors to sell the houses, the workers would have to make up the difference. We know that this became a serious obstacle in the iron and steel industry, where workers grew reluctant to participate in the scheme.[77]

---

[72] *Trud*, 6 July 1948.

[73] This was the case at Magnitostroi, which did construction work in Magnitogorsk. The construction trust housed the newly recruited workers, but did not give them the private accommodation it had promised. Nor did it fulfil its pledges to give each family a loan to buy livestock. The procuracy became involved when it turned out that the trust had doctored the contracts to prevent the deceived workers from suing it (GARF, f. 8131, op. 37, d. 3747, l. 257ob., 258).

[74] By way of example, the workers and clerical staff at eight engineering and toolmaking enterprises in Leningrad oblast' built just twenty-nine units during 1946–7, and another forty-one families began building homes in 1948 (GARF, f. 7676, op. 16, d. 485, l. 26). The Stalin metalworks in Leningrad city had a plan to build just nine private homes during 1947 (*ibid.*, op. 9, d. 697, l. 27). When we consider how critical the housing shortage was in Leningrad and its surrounding oblast' after the war, these figures are truly risible.

[75] *Trud*, 27 December 1946; *Stalinets* (Rostsel'mash), 22 August 1947; RGASPI, f. 17, op. 116, d. 237, l. 42–3; GARF, f. 7676, op. 9, d. 697, l. 27; op. 16, d. 485, l. 26.

[76] *Trud*, 27 March 1947. *Trud* commented wryly that when workers knocked down the wood-burning stoves they could use the space for storing vegetables, since the architects had also failed to provide for cellars.

[77] GARF, f. 7680, op. 5, d. 152, l. 7, and d. 203, l. 1–3.

There is no reason to suspect that this same problem did not arise elsewhere.

The regime also employed less public measures to accelerate construction, namely the use of prisoners of war and MVD prisoners on civilian housing construction. Given the above-cited problems with the individual house-building campaign in the Kuzbass, it is perhaps no accident that during 1947 MVD prisoners built 2,048 individual houses for the region's coal miners, and were planned to put up another 1,800 units during 1948. Overall prisoner involvement in housing construction was by no means negligible. The total housing stock erected by prisoners during 1947 was 556,000 square metres, a not inconsiderable amount when we consider that this would have accommodated over 100,000 people given then current norms of occupancy. But it was a tiny proportion of the average of 20 million square metres put up each year between 1945 and 1948. Prisoners of war, despite their use on some of the better-constructed buildings in Moscow after the war, made an even smaller contribution. Of the 1,065,000 prisoners of war still in the Soviet Union during 1947, only 17,700 were allocated to civilian housing construction.[78]

The responsibility for most house-building fell to the individual industrial ministries or equivalent non-industrial economic organizations. This proved a major source of delays and of the poor quality of the housing that was actually completed, for the ministries found the temptation to divert resources from housing to what they considered the more pressing needs of industrial construction and reconstruction almost irresistible. This was not as straightforward a calculus as it might seem. Admittedly, the logic of the Stalinist system was to accord production, and heavy industrial production in particular, absolute priority over all areas of consumption. This imperative was particularly strong in the postwar period, as the regime sought to complete the reconstruction as rapidly as possible. There were, however, pressures pulling in the other direction, since ministries also knew that they could not stem labour turnover or elicit the full commitment of those workers who did not change jobs if they did not solve, or at least attenuate, the housing problem.

Yet virtually everywhere house-building plans, as modest as they were, remained badly underfulfilled. One reason was the typical Soviet practice of dispersing construction activity over a large number of projects simultaneously, and this affected industrial construction and housing construction alike. There was a certain budgetary logic to this, since managers calculated that a project once started would receive further funding from

[78] GARF, f. 9401, op. 2, d. 199, l. 41–5, 73–4.

the centre, even if the year's construction budget had been used up. Where housing was concerned, at least in the late Stalin era, managers reinforced this tendency by withdrawing workers and materials from housing projects and using them elsewhere within the enterprise. Thus we see some rather curious statistics. The Ministry of the Engineering and Toolmaking Industry, for example, managed during the first nine months of 1948 to spend just over a quarter of its house-building budget, but it actually completed less than 10 per cent of the work this budget was supposed to pay for. The results at some of its individual factories were quite spectacular. The engineering factories in Klimovsk and Podol'sk, both located in Moscow oblast', spent nearly 40 per cent of their house-building budgets in this period but completed not a single square metre of actual living space. The same was true of the compressor factory in Penza and the clock factory in Chelyabinsk. Other factories in the engineering industry did slightly better, but not appreciably so. I should point out that this was not a statistical artefact of the construction calendar, that is, it was not the case that the buildings in question were near to completion and that by year's end everything would be finished. At all of these factories housing construction was virtually dormant, and in some cases actually suspended, because management had taken all but a handful of the workers off the sites and/or the parent ministry had failed to provide building materials.[79] Exactly this same pattern was repeated on the railways: work would be started and then either slow to a snail's pace or be abandoned altogether because the workers were moved to other projects which management deemed of higher priority. This trend was exacerbated by a tendency for the heads of some construction organizations to hire out their workers to outside organizations, or even to sell off their building materials, because this brought in additional revenue.[80] This abandonment of projects once underway was so chronic that, during 1946, most housing construction on the railways was actually completed not by the construction administrations responsible for it, but by the housing repair offices of the different railroads' communal services departments. In theory the latter were supposed to look after the day-to-day maintenance of existing housing stock only, and accordingly received low budgets and equally low priority in the allocation of building materials, yet they managed to outperform the construction organizations by a considerable margin.[81]

[79] GARF, f. 7676, op. 16, d. 485, l. 1–6.
[80] GARF, f. 5475, op. 21, d. 744, l. 7–7ob., 8–8ob., 9; RGAE, f. 1884, op. 31, d. 7204, l. 107–8.
[81] GARF, f. 5475, op. 21, d. 548, l. 5–6. We do not know how long these repair departments continued to assume a major responsibility for housing construction. What is

The situation was exacerbated by the fact that much of what was built was substandard. It was quite common for brand new buildings to have leaky roofs, plaster falling off the walls, door frames and floor boards which warped because they were made from raw wood, and rooms which filled up with smoke because the heating stoves had not been properly ventilated. The press and archive reports contain more than one reference to buildings being completed without the installation of gas or electric wiring.[82] Such defects had no single cause, but arose from a combination of factors: a rush to complete the work; the use of poor-quality building materials; and careless work by the builders themselves. The latter becomes more understandable when we consider that at least some projects tried to compensate for the shortage of a permanent core of skilled building workers by drafting in prisoners or 'special contingents'. The skills and motivation and hence also the productivity of these supplemental workers were all extremely low, and this must necessarily have taken its toll on the quality of the work. This was not helped by the fact that building workers themselves were generally very badly paid and lived in horrendous conditions, and this, too, told on their performance.[83]

The pace of housing construction continued to lag behind plans right up until Stalin's death, although the gap between plan and performance seems to have improved considerably when compared with the period 1946–9. Thus the Ministry of Construction of Enterprises in Heavy Industry managed to meet nearly three-quarters of its plan in 1950; the Ministry of Railways fulfilled just over two-thirds of its housing plan in 1952.[84] Although it is questionable just how relevant such plan fulfilment figures are – the real issue was the total volume of housing built – the urban housing stock, as noted, did nearly double between the end of the war and Stalin's death in 1953. Overcrowding, however, remained the norm, partly because the regime accorded housing – and consumption in general – low priority, and partly because the achievements which were eventually made were overwhelmed by the rapid expansion of the urban population and the industrial workforce. Any serious attempt to address the housing problem had to wait for the next generation of political leaders, in particular the rapid, if clumsily executed, housing campaigns of Nikita Khrushchev.

clear from the other sources, however, is that the Administration for Construction and Reconstruction Works continued to treat house-building as an unwanted stepchild.
[82] TsGAIPD, f. 1012, op. 8, d. 111, l. 17, 22; RGAE, f. 1884, op. 31, d. 7888, l. 58; *Trud*, 26 May 1948, 14 January, 19 August, 10 September 1949; GARF, f. 7680, op. 5, d. 152, l. 7. Once again, workers in Moscow were by no means exempt from such problems, even as late as 1952 (RGAE, f. 8592, op. 2, d. 909, l. 155–6).
[83] GARF, f. 7676, op. 9, d. 697, l. 32, 35–6.
[84] RGAE, f. 8592, op. 2, d. 601, l. 29 (Construction of Enterprises in Heavy Industry); GARF, f. 5474, op. 20, d. 2643, l. 1 (Railways Ministry).

Health care

Until recently there has been little systematic research into public health in the late Stalin period, save discussions or inferences contained in more general studies on Soviet health care, almost none of which were historical or made use of archives. More recently the Canadian scholar, Chris Burton, has produced a very detailed account of public health policy and its role in the postwar system of social welfare, thanks to which we now know a great deal about the structure of the USSR Ministry of Health, the evolution of health policy, expansion of medical training and facilities, and the myriad contradictions and stresses which occurred at all of the system's different levels.[85] Knowledge about the actual state of people's health during these years, however, still remains vague, save what Zima has told us about the outbreak of epidemics during the famine.

The war, of course, took a terrible toll on the nation's health. Even when people did not starve to death, sustained shortfalls in nutrition inevitably compromised immunity to disease and affected the development of the stature of children. Medical facilities, by no means outstanding even before the war, suffered further neglect, especially in small towns and rural areas. Thus the potential dangers of the food crisis of 1946 were bound to have an exaggerated effect on an already-weakened population. At the same time the regime made a major effort to expand the system and extend its coverage to all regions and sectors of the population. The number of practising doctors grew by nearly two-thirds between 1947 and 1952, much of the increase in rural areas.[86] The government also had an ambitious programme of mass vaccination against the major infectious diseases, such as smallpox, diphtheria, and typhoid; the latter programme in particular almost certainly kept down the death rate during the famine, especially in affected areas of Ukraine.[87] There

---

[85] I am extremely grateful to Chris Burton for the advice and criticism he has given me in my attempt to develop the material in this section, especially for his generosity in directing me to the recently declassified reports on factory medical facilities in the files of the Ministry of Health of the RSFSR. To the best of my knowledge he is the first person to have looked at this material and I would never have found it had he not given me quite precise instructions on what it contained and how to locate it.

[86] Burton, p. 65.

[87] During 1947 the health authorities in Ukraine administered 7.9 million vaccinations against typhoid, and another 7.5 million against dysentery, although it is difficult to see what impact the latter could have had, given that there is no vaccine against the Shigella bacterium which causes the disease. They also gave over 1.1 million inoculations against typhus, primarily in the epicentres of the outbreak in L'vov, Drogobych, Vinnitsa, and Chernovtsy oblasti. The Western allies had developed a typhus vaccine during World War II which virtually eliminated mortality and reduced morbidity but did not prevent infection. I have not as yet been able to find out what the Soviet vaccine was made from, or how effective it might have been (GARF, f. 8009, op. 3, d. 607, l. 27). The amount of effort and money which must have gone into these vaccination programmes stands

were long-term signs of this shift as well, most notably a fall in both overall and infant mortality, which by 1950 were probably around half of what they had been in 1940.[88]

By the same token, Soviet health care under Stalin had always had a strong punitive dimension, and this was retained alongside the improvements in care. During the industrialization drive of the 1930s the prevailing philosophy of medical care, at least in urban areas, had been to keep workers sufficiently healthy to allow them to carry on producing on the shop floor, and to this end the delivery of medical care became centred on the workplace. Doctors were expected to improve workers' attendance, on the one hand, by reducing the real incidence of disease and, on the other hand, by being extremely stringent when deciding whether or not to grant a sick note. Doctors were not always as ruthless in this regard as the regime would have liked, and many were willing to grant sick notes in order to protect workers who fell foul of the labour discipline laws. These enterprise-based structures underwent some change after the war, but the philosophy on which they were based stayed the same.[89]

What I want to examine here, however, is a different aspect of the question, namely how workers experienced health care in their day-to-day lives, and what the impact of this experience was on what we could call their quality of life. A major difficulty here is the availability of data. Many of the files in the archives of the USSR Ministry of Health are still closed. The statistics in the open files, as well as those in the formerly secret files of the RSFSR Ministry of Health and various trade unions, present different and not easily combinable categories. Some give figures on infectious diseases, such as tuberculosis, malaria, typhoid fever, gastrointestinal ailments, and major childhood diseases such as measles and whooping cough. Others give the nature of ailments not by causative agent, but by the nature of the complaint and doctors' diagnoses, for example, heart disease, diseases of the central and peripheral nervous systems, gynaecological problems, or stomach ulcers. The reports by factory doctors use still other criteria, that is, the major reasons why

---

in sharp contrast to the regime's refusal to release the food supplies which could have prevented the famine in the first place.

[88] According to varying sets of figures provided by G. F. Konstantinov, head of the USSR Ministry of Health's Department of Medical Statistics, overall mortality fell from just over 18 per 1,000 population in 1940 to just under 10 in 1950. During the same period infant mortality – which the Soviets defined as deaths within the first year after birth – declined from between 180 and 190 per 1,000 live births to around 80 per 1,000 live births. The data are from two different sources, one public, the other secret, and differ slightly; hence I have only given the range. They are from G. F. Konstantinov, ed., *Zdravookhranenie v SSSR (Statisticheskii spravochnik)* (Moscow, 1957), p. 40; and GARF, f. 8009, op. 32s, d. 1372, l. 65. I owe thanks to Chris Burton, who provided me with both of these references and the data they contained.

[89] Filtzer, *Soviet Workers and Stalinist Industrialization*, pp. 239–40; Burton, ch. 5.

workers had to be signed off work; these tend to cite both infectious diseases, primarily influenza and gastrointestinal infections, and chronic or acute conditions, such as heart disease, skin infections, gynaecological ailments, and workplace and domestic accidents. The factory reports also contain a large and unmeasurable arbitrary element, because they recorded only those illnesses and conditions which were severe enough for a worker to receive a sick note excusing her or him from work for three days or longer; they excluded illnesses which warranted a shorter absence or for which either the worker did not seek a sick note or the sick note was refused. Thus if two different factories had widely varying sickness rates, this did not necessarily mean that the workers at one were healthier than the workers at the other; the differences might have been because the one factory's doctors were more readily disposed to grant workers sick leave.[90]

All of these different types of files withhold vital pieces of information. Tables on infectious diseases in 1947, for example, deliberately leave out typhus (data for which can be found in the Central Statistical Administration, however). Tables for 1947 which list doctors' diagnoses or causes of lost work time exclude malnutrition, even though (as we saw in chapter 2) individual factory or hospital reports sometimes cite it and most reports from urban health authorities cite numbers of workers who needed to be put on supplemental diets. None of the tables give figures for diseases like cancer, hepatitis, diabetes, or cirrhosis, nor do they always give major medical causes of death.[91] This is not to say that the data do not exist. Undoubtedly they do and detective work by future researchers will build up a much better epidemiological picture than we have now.

What then can we say about workers' health in this period? Let us look first at the potential effect of the food crisis and famine. We know that the famine encouraged the spread of serious epidemics, in particular typhoid, dysentery, and influenza. It also aggravated, or made people more susceptible to, other diseases and conditions, such as tuberculosis, severe gastrointestinal ailments, and coronary-artery disease. The statistical picture, however, is by no means clear. Reports from the coal mining

---

[90] GARF-RSFSR, f. A-482, op. 52s, d. 222, l. 27.
[91] The factory medical reports always include a huge and unspecified category of 'other illnesses'. Some of these may have been diseases which occurred in small numbers of cases and would have appeared insignificant if listed on their own in the tables. Others, however, were clearly serious conditions which the regime wished to conceal, even in its secret reports. Thus the Sverdlovsk Institute of Labour Hygiene and Occupational Diseases complained that a February 1950 circular from the USSR Ministry of Health removed the diagnostic category 'deficient nutrition' from forms on which doctors listed the causes of retarded physical development among teenage workers and Labour Reserve students (GARF-RSFSR, f. A-482, op. 52s, d. 285, l. 40ob.).

areas of the Greater Moscow region, the Russian Donbass around Rostov-on-Don, and the Ukrainian Donbass, and from the huge Uralmash engineering works in Sverdlovsk, do not show any appreciable deterioration in workers' sickness rates which could be directly attributed to the food shortages.[92] Obviously further research may refute this impression, but we can suggest a number of reasons why this picture may prove accurate. First, the state of public health in 1944 and 1945 was extremely bad and undoubtedly began to improve during 1946 as sewerage systems were reconstructed, vaccination programmes were extended, some of the housing stock began to be restored, and food supplies increased. Although the food situation worsened again in 1947, this may have been more or less cancelled out by the other factors which lessened susceptibility to disease. This, of course, is quite speculative, but there is a second factor which is not. Chapter 2 described how, when factory doctors discovered cases of workers with severe malnutrition, they were able to put them on special high-calorie diets. Aside from indirectly proving that the regime did have the food supplies on hand to block the worst effects of the famine, it also would help explain why disease rates did not shoot up out of control, even in industries located in famine regions.[93] Thirdly, and working in the other direction, there were so many other, largely environmental factors which so badly compromised workers' general health that changes in the food supply may not have had a statistically measurable effect.

The fact remains that, irrespective of causes, sickness rates among workers in 1947 were high and remained so during the ensuing years. At the Komintern iron and steel works in Ukraine, the average worker lost thirteen days during 1947 for medical reasons, with injury accounting for less than 10 per cent of the total. At the Petrovskii iron and steel works in Dnepropetrovsk, the figure was eleven days. The situation improved only slightly during 1948 and 1949.[94] Workers in the major engineering plants of Khar'kov in 1947 were signed off work for periods averaging between ten and fourteen days per person.[95] A larger survey of fifty-five machine-tool factories carried out in 1949 showed that even then workers lost on average ten days a year, most of it due to illness.[96] Other industries, such as shipbuilding and means of communications, showed a similar pattern: 1946 and 1947 were the worst years, but even in 1948 and 1949 the average worker lost over nine days a year, although in these two cases

[92] GARF, f. 7416, op. 3, d. 165, l. 9–11; f. 7676, op. 9, d. 837, l. 65.
[93] This is not the same as saying that the malnutrition caused no increase in days lost to illness. We know this was not the case, and that many of those put on special diets had to be signed off work for several weeks. See above, ch. 2, pp. 67–8.
[94] GARF, f. 7680, op. 5, d. 402, l. 28, 49.
[95] GARF, f. 7676, op. 9, d. 837, l. 61.   [96] GARF, f. 7676, op. 11, d. 718, l. 1.

we do not know what percentage was due to accidents.[97] Considering that these data do not include time lost due to very short illnesses, they suggest a serious problem in maintaining a healthy working population. Surprisingly, given the rise in the standard of living after 1948, data assembled by VTsSPS during 1951 and 1952 show that the situation had hardly changed. Of thirty-five branches of industry, construction, and transport, in only five (sugar, peat, housing construction, railways, and water transport) were workers losing fewer than eight days per year to illness. Sixty per cent had sickness rates of over ten days a year. Thus the overwhelming majority of industries were losing nearly as many days to illness at the end of the period as they were right after the war.[98] What little improvement had occurred was by no means commensurate either with the rising standard of living or with the expansion of health care. How can we explain this? One possible reason is that infectious diseases were not necessarily the main causes of ill health. There were many chronic conditions, such as heart disease, gynaecological problems, hypertension, and diseases of the central nervous system, which accounted for a far larger percentage of patient visits to doctors than did infectious diseases,[99] and which had their causes in longer-term factors associated with the stresses and deprivations of the war and environmental factors other than the food supply. A second, related reason is that the severity and frequency of infections themselves were also largely influenced by environmental factors, such as housing, urban sanitation, and working conditions, which did not improve as rapidly as did food supplies and which better medical care could not always influence.

There were at least two infectious diseases – tuberculosis and malaria – which tended to manifest themselves as chronic, rather than acute conditions, with which most sufferers were able to carry on working even though they were unwell. The number of adult tuberculosis cases which received hospitalization was not, in fact, very large. Between January and August 1948 the country's network of sanatoria treated 308,000 patients (compared to 229,000 during the comparable period in 1939), 183,000 of whom were children.[100] Most TB sufferers of working age took treatment not in a sanatorium or hospital, but at their enterprise, in

---

[97] RGASPI, f. 17, op. 131, d. 112, l. 5 (means of communications) and l. 124 (shipbuilding).

[98] The constancy of these figures was not due to an increase in days lost to accidents, which stayed relatively unchanged at an average of roughly one day per worker each year. We can therefore conclude that rates of actual illness also stayed the same. For the problems of industrial accidents, see ch. 6, pp. 203–13.

[99] I base this on the tables for visits to urban polyclinics and doctors' house calls made in urban areas during 1949 in GARF, f. 8009, op. 6, d. 2069. They show that taking all age groups together, coronary-artery disease and gynaecological ailments were far and away the largest causes of people seeking medical care.

[100] RGASPI, f. 17, op. 121, d. 680, l. 133.

the form of special meals and on-the-job rest periods in what were called 'night sanatoria'. Like so many other aspects of public health in this period, however, such data badly understate the real seriousness of the situation. Tuberculosis was not just endemic; it was widespread, highly costly to the economy, and a cause of real tragedy to the people and families whom it affected. We can gain some impression of its scale from the fact that in Leningrad in 1947 and in Sverdlovsk oblast' as late as 1949 and 1950, tuberculosis accounted for 5 per cent of all days lost due to sickness.[101] In Moscow during 1947, roughly 30 per cent of all clinic visits were by tuberculosis patients, up from just 20 per cent ten years earlier. In fact, in the cities, towns, and workers' settlements of the RSFSR during 1948, tuberculosis was the leading cause of death among adults of either sex aged between twenty and thirty-nine, and of men between the ages of twenty and forty-nine, being responsible for approximately a third of all male deaths in that age range.[102]

Malaria was another endemic problem, although it tended to cause high morbidity, rather than mortality. In 1947, 2.5 million people sought treatment for malaria, and 900,000 of them were new cases. Two years later there were still 800,000 new cases, but the disease declined radically after that.[103] As we would expect, malaria affected mainly rural areas and the smaller urban communities, rather than the big cities. But there were certain groups of workers who were especially vulnerable to catching it. Workers on railway construction, for example, were particularly susceptible. Much of the work they did was in mosquito-infested regions of Ukraine and Siberia. Bridge builders along the Dnepr river outside Kiev were said to run a 50 per cent risk of contracting malaria during the summer months.[104] On the Dnepropetrovsk Railroad 19 per cent of all its construction workers suffered from malaria in 1945; although this fell to just under 10 per cent by 1947, this was still an extraordinarily high percentage who were either catching the disease or suffering relapses.[105]

Virtually all illnesses, whether chronic or acute, were closely associated with a complex of social problems: working and housing conditions, difficulties maintaining basic hygiene, dire shortages of soap and proper

---

[101] GARF-RSFSR, f. A-482, op. 52s, d. 222, l. 47, and d. 285, l. 288.
[102] GARF-RSFSR, f. A-482, op. 52s, d. 245, l. 156, 159. I have not yet found comparable data for the whole of the USSR. The RSFSR figures also show that coronary-artery disease was setting in at an alarmingly early age. It was the leading cause of death of women over the age of forty, and of men over fifty, far outstripping either tuberculosis or cancers (*ibid.*, l. 156).
[103] GARF, f. 8009, op. 3, d. 607, l. 12–13, 15, 30, 46ob., 47ob., 58, 61, 81–2, 105, 107–9, 119–20, 138–9, 160–1, 171–2, 188, 193; RGAE, f. 1562, op. 18, d. 509, l. 1; d. 580, l. 2; d. 717, l. 24.
[104] RGAE, f. 1884, op. 31, d. 7888, l. 14.
[105] GARF, 5475, op. 21, d. 483, l. 29. For similar problems on railway construction in Siberia, see RGAE, f. 1884, op. 31, d. 7882, l. 97–9.

protective clothing at work, and a lack of warm street clothes and decent shoes during the winter. Making matters worse was the fact that when workers did become ill they found it difficult to receive proper treatment because the medical facilities were simply inadequate.

Hygiene was incredibly difficult to maintain. One obvious cause was the overcrowded and generally filthy barracks and dormitories in which so many workers lived. Besides provoking labour turnover they were a major health hazard, not the least during the famine when lice infestations threatened to spread and sustain the typhus epidemic. The main worry, of course, was food poisoning and the spread of diarrhoea and dysentery. At one Donbass mine well over half of all underground workers came down sick because of the total lack of sanitation.[106] Under such circumstances it was understandable, but also somewhat ironic, that during virtually the whole of the postwar period factory medical personnel spent no small amount of their time promoting public hygiene through shop-floor lectures, articles in factory newspapers, and broadcasts over local and factory radio stations.[107] Factory newspapers ran regular articles on the need to observe personal cleanliness at home and at work. They explained in quite simple terms the relationship between hygiene and dysentery and typhoid, and counselled workers on the need to 'use the toilet in a civilized fashion', to wash their hands after using the toilet, after work, and before meals, to boil drinking water and milk, to rinse vegetables with boiled water before cooking, and to cook foods thoroughly. They even advocated 'a merciless struggle' against flies.[108] Conditions in the factories and dormitories did not always permit the observance of even these basic rules. Enterprises could not always guarantee supplies of safe drinking water either at work or in the dormitories. Many enterprises, especially but not exclusively in outlying cities, were not hooked up to municipal drinking water. In such cases they were obliged to provide safe water to shops in special tanks. This they often failed to do, and many workers became ill because they resorted to drinking water used for industrial purposes or because the tanks containing 'clean' water had become contaminated.[109] Factory dining rooms lacked sufficient refrigeration equipment, which led to an increase in gastrointestinal disorders

[106] At the mine in question the drinking water was stored in dirty tanks, the grounds were strewn with garbage, the toilets were never cleaned, and many of the young workers living in its dormitories were infested with lice. It was hardly surprising that, during the first half of 1947, 38 per cent of its total workforce illegally ran away (GARF, f. 8131, op. 37, d. 149–51).

[107] GARF-RSFSR, f. A-482, op. 52s, d. 222, l. 26.

[108] *Golos Dzerzhintsa*, 7 March 1946, 24 June 1948; *Stalinets* (Kuibyshev), 2 August 1950, 6 September 1951.

[109] GARF-RSFSR, f. A-482, op. 52s, d. 285, l. 150–1; d. 309, l. 15–16, 195.

during the summer. Not all workers had somewhere to shower after work, or even to wash their hands.[110] The Novotrubnyi iron and steel works in Sverdlovsk proudly reported that it had cut the incidence of both intestinal sickness and influenza simply by boiling the spoons in dining rooms. Yet even here the factory found it hard to provide clean drinking water, especially in winter, because factories and ore mines were polluting the local water supplies with their wastes.[111] There is, however, evidence that hygiene alone was not the culprit here. Catering establishments were trying to cope with the food shortages by using spoiled foods or food substitutes unfit for human consumption.[112]

The other major health problem arising from poor hygiene was skin infections. It is easy to forget how important the public bathhouse was in the control of disease, especially in the wake of the destruction or dilapidation of the housing stock.[113] The rapid growth of railway settlements, especially in the eastern half of the USSR, also put pressure on these resources, as towns with populations of several thousand people were having to cope with bathhouses which could hold only a few dozen people, or even with no bathhouse at all.[114] Workers on railway construction were even worse off, because they were living temporarily in isolated areas (often billeted in disused railway carriages or peasant barns) and might have no access to a bathhouse for months at a time.[115] The main cause of skin diseases, however, was the almost universal absence of soap. Large amounts of work time were lost because of abscesses and other skin infections. Factory after factory reported serious and protracted shortages of soap, which made a mockery of the regime's health education campaigns. Throughout 1946, 1947, and 1948 heavy engineering factories complained about their inability to obtain soap, the production of which had fallen catastrophically during the war and immediate postwar period. At one point in 1946, the Kuibyshev factory in Irkutsk had received no soap at all for three months, and it had a shortfall of 2.5 tons.

---

[110] *Golos Dzerzhintsa*, 14 March 1946; GARF, f. 7676, op. 9, d. 488, l. 12–13; d. 674, l. 45–6, 48, 50, 123, 143–4; and d. 837, l. 12; RGAE, f. 1884, op. 31, d. 7885, l. 111.
[111] GARF, f. 7680, op. 5, d. 58, l. 42–42ob.
[112] In an effort to curb the incidence of gastrointestinal illness, not so much among its workers as among the general public, the Ministry of Railways in early 1947 introduced stringent controls over public catering, including a 'categorical ban' on the use of 'new types of raw produce in food preparation or issuing any kind of food substitutes or surrogates, without clearance of the railways' hygiene inspectors'. Similarly, the ministry banned suppliers from sending catering establishments or trade outlets food products the quality of which was suspect, or shops from selling such products without prior approval of a food hygiene inspector (GARF, f. 5475, op. 21, d. 728, l. 8ob.).
[113] RGAE, f. 1884, op. 31, d. 7880, l. 173.
[114] RGAE, f. 1884, op. 31, d. 7884, l. 60, 64–5, 67.
[115] RGAE, f. 1884, op. 31, d. 7880, l. 170; d. 7888, l. 60–1.

At one shipbuilding yard in Ukraine young workers had not received any soap for an entire year.[116] During the fourth quarter of 1947 the city of Sverdlovsk was allocated 235 tons of soap, but received only 15.[117] The problems were compounded by the general lack of protective clothing and, especially for young workers, even a change of underwear. Under these conditions a simple scratch or cut at work could easily turn into a major illness.

If workers did fall ill or have an accident, enterprises and local authorities were ill prepared to treat them. By and large medical facilities were poorly equipped, suffered from a shortage of drugs and medical supplies, and were staffed by too few doctors, many of whom were badly trained. Not all of this could be blamed on the damage inflicted by World War II. The regime gave medical care the same low priority as it did consumption and housing. Throughout the country, including Moscow, there was a serious shortage of drugs. During World War II the Soviet Union had relied heavily on imports of basic medicines: aspirin, codeine, sulfanilamides, aminopyrine. At the end of the war these imports fell back sharply, or were stopped altogether. Yet rather than rearrange the overall distribution of resources to allow domestic production to make up the gap, in almost all cases it actually fell in 1947, compared to 1945 and 1946. Even such essentials as glucose, boric acid, castor oil, and medicine bottles were available in a fraction of the required quantities; there were forty drugs or medical preparations that were not being manufactured at all.[118]

Another obstacle was bureaucratic empire-building. Responsibility for providing health care was divided up among a dizzying array of

---

[116] GARF, f. 7676, op. 9, d. 488, l. 8, 30; d. 674, l. 48–9, 100; d. 837, l. 3ob., 49 (engineering); TsKhDMO, f. 1, op. 4, d. 843, l. 109 (shipbuilding).

[117] Zima, p. 174. For similar reports throughout the railway network, which in general received only between 8 and 20 per cent of planned allocations of soap, see RGAE, f. 1884, op. 31, d. 7884, l. 14, 32, 178; d. 7885, l. 5, 6–6ob.; d. 7886, l. 17–17ob., 34; d. 7887, l. 160. If anything railway workers were even worse off than those in regular factories, since part of any soap consignments actually delivered was immediately taken to launder bed linen for sleeper cars. At one point the Railway Ministry's Chief Administration of Material-Technical Supply proposed to offer workers monetary compensation for the soap they had not received, since the ministry saw no prospect of making good the shortage (*ibid.*, d. 7885, l. 159–60).

[118] RGASPI, f. 17, op. 121, d. 575, l. 119, 121–4, 127–9, 131–3, 134–8; d. 680, l. 70–6, 80. The crisis in the pharmaceutical industry led to the Ministry of the Medical Industry being abolished in March 1948. There is perhaps more to this story than meets the eye, since there was a simultaneous purge of medical research institutes, and other – political, rather than medical – issues may have been involved. As for the drugs shortage, one paediatrician whom I interviewed claimed that she personally was able to prescribe whatever medicines she needed. Aside from possible regional variations and/or priority given to children, this might also be explained by the testimony of another doctor, who said pharmaceuticals were generally unobtainable, and that they used mainly herbal and natural preparations, of which there was a plentiful supply.

organizations. At the pinnacle of the system were the USSR Ministry of Health and the Ministries of Health of the separate republics, which, through their oblast' and district departments of health, were in charge of most public hospitals, polyclinics, and clinics for outpatients, including the facilities at industrial enterprises. After the war there was a policy of shifting enterprise health systems from factory budgets – where the level of care was at the mercy of enterprise directors – on to the budgets of the districts.[119] In theory enterprises were to have a full range of medical provision, ranging from first aid stations in the shops, to outpatient clinics, special 'hygiene rooms' for women workers, and polyclinics. Some enterprises had their own hospitals; others referred their workers to the local district or oblast' hospital. However, the Ministry of Health and local health departments did not control all facilities. Some care was still provided by the individual ministries and the trade unions. The most important of these were the Ministry of Railways, which had its own, completely separate health-care network, including hospitals, and the trade unions, which controlled a large proportion of the country's sanatoria and rest homes.

The system was plagued by overlapping competencies and localism, exemplified in part by the network of sanatoria and rest homes. These were an important part of the Soviet health system. The rest homes provided workers with short-term treatment for relatively minor conditions (including exhaustion due to malnutrition), as well as somewhere to take a much-needed holiday. The sanatoria dealt with many chronic and long-term illnesses, most notably tuberculosis, but also heart disease, serious gastrointestinal disorders, and diseases of the nervous system, and were an important supplement to the hospitals. In August 1948 the country had 1,974 sanatoria, with 242,200 beds, plus 876 rest homes, with 114,000 beds. There was also a separate system of children's sanatoria with 93,000 beds, three-quarters of which were for children with TB. Looking first at the sanatoria, the USSR Ministry of Health and its local bodies controlled 63 per cent of the beds; VTsSPS and the local trade unions managed 24 per cent; the railways 4 per cent; and all of the other ministries together 9 per cent. The rest homes, in contrast, were run mostly by the trade unions: 70 per cent of the beds belonged to them, and another 29.7 per cent belonged to various ministries, with the Ministry of Health providing only a trivial proportion (0.3 per cent).[120]

Because the Stalinist ministerial system was so intensely competitive, the splintering of health-care provision among so many different

---

[119] GARF-RSFSR, f. A-482, op. 52s, d. 205, l. 37.
[120] RGASPI, f. 17, op. 121, d. 680, l. 131–2.

authorities made it highly vulnerable to bureaucratic parochialism. The chief of the Tambov oblast' Department of Health summarized the problem honestly and succinctly in a February 1948 report to Zhdanov:

Having worked for fourteen years in the field of organizing Soviet medical care, and having a certain amount of experience, in recent years I have begun to come to a rather sad conclusion: that each of the large collectives of organizers in our ministries, split up into tens of special administrations, departments, and sectors, devotes all of its thought and effort solely to increasing its own network, to 'prying loose' additional posts and personnel [stavki i kadry] only 'for itself', showing not the least bit of concern for the overall coordination of the business of health care, for the *integrated singleness of purpose* of the entire business of protecting public health.[121]

It was inevitable that some sectors of this bureaucratic leviathan would be more successful than others and produce a system rampant with inequalities. The most obvious was that between the special doctors, hospitals, and clinics which served the elite, and those for the rest of the population. Our concern here, however, is not with this but with the inequalities within the system of mass provision. Perhaps the worst gap was between urban and rural areas. Moscow, Leningrad, and other large cities had medical schools and teaching hospitals, and a range of specialist clinics. Rural facilities – which catered not just for the agricultural population but also for a large number of workers and clerical personnel – were far inferior. Here the lack of resources was crippling. According to the above report from Tambov, only 7 or 8 per cent of rural health budgets went on medicines, supplies, instruments, and equipment, the shortages of which had become so bad that doctors could not do their jobs. Bureaucratic infighting meant that hospitals could not even obtain timber to carry out repairs: the Ministry of Health and the local executive committees were too busy arguing over whose responsibility it was to supply it. Hospitals and clinics which had switched from kerosene lamps to electric lighting worked in darkness because local power stations could not obtain enough fuel; doctors had to go out and track down their own fuel supplies, some of which went to the power stations and some of which went to hospitals for their internal use. In Tambov oblast' the hospitals were idle a third of the year because of the fuel shortage, causing the report's author to marvel, 'We are surprised how, with our planned economy, such methods of supply are still possible.'[122]

We see these same inequalities of provision and access within industry – not just between the different branches of the economy, but even within

---

121 RGASPI, f. 17, op. 121, d. 680, l. 24 (emphasis in the original).
122 RGASPI, f. 17, op. 121, d. 680, l. 25–30.

one and the same ministry. One of the best illustrations of this was the
health system on the railways, for which the documentation is relatively
extensive. The quality of medical care for railway workers had suffered
badly during World War II. Many medical buildings had been commandeered for use by other organizations, and clinics found it difficult to
reclaim them.[123] A large number of clinic buildings were crumbling, yet
their heads found it nearly impossible to compel railway managers to give
them materials with which to carry out repairs. Even such basic instruments as syringes and needles were in short supply. Not all clinics or
hospitals had autoclaves for sterilizing instruments and bandages. There
was a terrible shortage of doctors, especially in such core specialities
as ear, nose, and throat, tuberculosis, paediatrics, ophthalmology, and
venereology and dermatology. Clinics were so overcrowded that nurses
could not carry out proper hearing tests for new engine drivers, a fact
which trade union inspectors claimed could compromise safety. In some
localities the facilities were so bad that railway workers would not use
them, but would travel to the nearest town to use the local polyclinic.[124]

As the postwar recovery proceeded facilities clearly improved, at least
for some workers. The Union of Workers on Construction of Railways
and the Metropolitan claimed that, by 1947, the two-thirds of its members who were actually railway employees, rather than those employed on
construction *per se*, were served by a network of well-equipped and well-
staffed polyclinics, outpatient clinics, and hospitals, complete with laboratories and x-ray and physiotherapy departments. Even more privileged
were construction workers and associated clerical staff on the Moscow
Metro, who received medical care not from the Railways Ministry, but
in closed treatment centres run by the USSR Ministry of Health. Not
only did they have access to the closed polyclinic and outpatient clinic
in Cherkizovo in north-east Moscow, but each factory and underground
shaft had its own medical station run by a doctor, or in a minority of cases
by a doctor's assistant. Construction workers outside the Moscow Metro,
by contrast, were not so lucky: their clinics had little equipment and few

[123] The seriousness of this problem nationwide can be judged from the fact that the USSR
Council of Ministers felt compelled to issue a decree on 16 November 1947, ordering all
organizations which had requisitioned medical buildings during the war to return them
to health authorities. Enforcement of the decree was patchy at best, even in Moscow. The
women's clinic in the city's Lenin district, which had a female population of 200,000,
had been taken over during the war by a factory belonging to the Ministry of Means of
Communications, yet despite this decree (not to mention a 1944 order of the Moscow
City Executive Committee) the factory was still occupying it in 1948.
[124] GARF, f. 5475, op. 21, d. 542, l. 2–2ob., 3–3ob. This report covers medical facilities
on the Kalinin Railroad, much of which serviced regions around Moscow and some
of whose depots were within Moscow itself. It was unlikely, therefore, to have been
atypical.

bandages or medicines; because they did not have enough doctors most treatment was dispensed by paramedics.[125] Perhaps a better illustration of the progress that could be achieved was the North Caucasus Railroad, which serviced the region around Rostov-on-Don, including the heavy industry centres of Taganrog, Novocherkassk, and Novorossiisk. This area had suffered phenomenal devastation during the war, and although medical institutions still faced daunting problems, the improvement made since the war's end was indisputable.[126]

Such advances were not, however, universal. They may even have been an exception. Railway workers in the city of Gor'kii – like Rostov also a major industrial centre – faced conditions which differed little from those described on the Kalinin Railroad right after the war, namely hospitals and clinics which were overcrowded, understaffed, and so badly equipped that the entire Gor'kii Railroad (and not just the railyards in Gor'kii) possessed not a single electrocardiograph or piece of radiotherapy equipment, and this for a health-care system which had to cater for 155,000 employees and their families, that is, a population equivalent to that of a medium-sized city.[127]

The railway documentation is almost unique in that it shows that shortages and underfunding were compounded by the poor competence of many doctors, nurses, and ancillary staff. Logic dictates that much of this was itself due to the pressures of working in a badly underresourced system. Be that as it may, medical practice was in many cases truly horrifying. A review of the large regional hospital at Perovo, a rail junction on the Gor'kii Railroad which was also the site of a carriage-repair factory, shows this only too well. Misdiagnoses, the failure to keep proper case notes, and chaotic admissions and discharge records meant that patients received treatment only after long and sometimes critical or even fatal delays; often the wrong treatment was prescribed or it was administered incorrectly. Babies were delivered using 'absolutely primitive' methods, and some babies even suffered broken bones as a result. The clinical laboratories lacked basic reagents, equipment, and even running water, and the hospital could not do its own pathology or histology analyses. The medical commission in charge of overseeing the issue of sick notes was so overworked that it merely rubber-stamped requests for extensions, and patients with quite serious conditions escaped diagnosis and treatment.[128] As serious as these problems were, they were dwarfed by the

---

[125] GARF, f. 5475, op. 21, d. 482, l. 1–3.
[126] GARF, f. 5474, op. 20, d. 538, l. 22–4. The report is from 1949.
[127] GARF, f. 5475, op. 20, d. 534, l. 151–3.
[128] It is interesting that from the 1930s onwards Soviet discussions of doctors' casual attitude to issuing and renewing sick notes almost always focused on the role this played in

state of the hospital's sanitation. The hospital had a bad record of patients contracting infections (in March 1950 the entire maternity wing had to close after one outbreak), but in fact it is a miracle that everyone did not just simply die. The dining room observed not even the most basic rules of hygiene. Toilets were never cleaned and in the maternity wing even had faeces on the walls. Courtyards were littered with garbage, including faecal matter. Dirty linen was not disinfected and was sorted in the same room as the linen being laundered. Clean linen was dried in the hospital's boiler room right next to the boilers. The polyclinic did not have a sewage system; waste water was collected in barrels which overflowed in the courtyards, including in an area which adjoined a bakery.[129] It is doubtful that the Perovo hospital was an extreme case. An inspection of the tuberculosis hospital in L'vov (also from 1950) described almost identical conditions, most alarmingly the practice of pouring the sputum from patients directly into the main sewer.[130]

The question, of course, is how representative of the rest of the country the railway medical system was. Its network of facilities was independent of the Ministry of Health, and so extrapolation from the railway reports may be methodologically risky. We know, however, that the situation in coal mining regions was roughly comparable. They had so few doctors that many clinics had to be staffed by paramedics; in Moscow oblast', doctors who had been recruited could not take up their posts because there was nowhere for them to live. Clinic buildings were dilapidated, dirty, and unheated; staff lacked basic medicines – and in some cases did not even have soap or bed linen.[131] The machine-tool workers' trade union gave a more mixed report about conditions in its industry in 1950. Some of the factory treatment facilities were very well equipped and could provide not only general medical care but also specialist treatment. Others, however, were clearly inadequate, including those in large cities.[132] In Sverdlovsk, probably the most important industrial centre in the USSR after Moscow and Leningrad, the city's only medical laboratory

allowing workers to malinger or to 'legalize' absenteeism. This is the first report I have seen from the 1920s right up to 1991 which pointed out the medical dangers that could also result.

[129] GARF, f. 5474, op. 20, d. 1234, l. 10–32.
[130] GARF, f. 5474, op. 20, d. 1234, l. 47–50. See also the report in this same file on the railway hospital in Stanislav, Western Ukraine (l. 64–7). The boast that this hospital had made significant improvements during the course of 1950 is itself alarming, given the state of affairs which prevailed afterwards. Needless to say conditions were even worse in the isolated communities on the Eastern and Far Eastern Railways (RGAE, f. 1884, op. 31, d. 784, l. 60, 62–3, 67).
[131] GARF, f. 7416, op. 3, d. 165, l. 17, 49; op. 4, d. 129, l. 2–2ob.; and d. 214, l. 21–5, 44; RGASPI, f. 17, op. 121, d. 680, l. 10–11, 17–19.
[132] GARF, f. 7676, op. 11, d. 931, l. 8–14.

had no microscope until 1948 and could not carry out any medical analyses.[133] As late as 1951, one large defence enterprise in Molotov, which we might have expected to have received preferential allocation of resources, complained that it was badly understaffed, lacked essential equipment, and was even short of basic supplies such as syringes and needles. Moreover, the lack of beds in the local hospitals had made it difficult to control an outbreak of dysentery in the summer of that year because they had not been able to isolate the sick workers from those who were still healthy.[134]

There was one other important area of workers' health care which was almost totally neglected in this period, namely occupational diseases caused by exposure to toxic or hazardous substances. Whether or not this reflected the political ideology of the regime, which did not wish to acknowledge just how bad conditions were in its factories, we do not know. The problem had always been officially acknowledged, insofar as local health authorities issued yearly reports on occupational illnesses, and any serious incidents of industrial poisoning, especially if they led to a fatality, had to have a special investigation. Beyond the paperwork, little was actually done in practice. In August 1950, Marchenko, the chief of the Department of Industrial Medicine of the RSFSR Ministry of Health, issued a scathing attack exposing failures right across the system.[135] Factory physicians, he complained, were 'semi-literate' on questions of occupational pathologies, as a result of which workers were not properly diagnosed or treated. Recording of illnesses was so bad that he assumed that official data on the incidence of such diseases were but a fraction of the real total. In theory workers in at-risk enterprises and trades were supposed to receive regular medical checks, but these were not always carried out, partly because doctors did not actually know which workers required them. Even when they were, doctors did not have the necessary instruments or access to laboratories to allow them to make accurate diagnoses: in fact, the entire RSFSR had only forty-seven laboratories which could carry out such tests, and they lacked basic equipment and reagents. Even when problems were detected, the workers could not always receive treatment, because enterprises either lacked specialized infirmaries capable of dealing with their illness, or just lacked treatment facilities

[133] GARF, f. 7680, op. 5, d. 58, l. 43ob. This is part of a report on the hospital which served the Novotrubnyi iron and steel works in the city. This was not a closed factory facility, but a general hospital which served the entire community. Like the other reports discussed here, it had difficulty obtaining bandages, glucose, sulfamide preparations, and even alcohol.
[134] GARF-RSFSR, f. A-482, op. 52s, d. 309, l. 194, 201 (Molotov aviation factory, Molotov city, 1951).
[135] GARF-RSFSR, f. A-482, op. 52s, d. 287, l. 187–93.

in general.[136] It appears that serious progress began to be made in this area only in 1952, but even then there were major occupational hazards which continued to go unrecognized.[137]

Conclusion

I have labelled the period from 1948 to 1953 as one of 'attenuated recovery'. By this I mean that the main determinants of the quality of life improved slowly yet palpably, but in the end still could not cover more than the most essential needs of most urban citizens. On the eve of Stalin's death the average worker, even outside Moscow and Leningrad, lived not nearly as precariously as he or she had between 1945 and 1948. Having said this, there is equally no question but that life was still basically a struggle to survive. People had food, but shortages, rather than abundance, were the general rule, and the quality of nutrition remained poor. People were housed, but for most this meant living in cramped and barely habitable quarters. People did not die of starvation or hunger-related diseases, but the diseases of poverty were still endemic and medical treatment was highly variable in quality, and for most of the urban population inadequate to deal with all but the simplest illnesses or injuries.

The improvements were nonetheless sufficient to allow for a stabilization of society and its relationship with the regime. One consequence of the desperation of the food crisis years was that people were grateful for the small steps forward and for the calming of the turmoil. This trend was strengthened by the signs of a tentative political relaxation, at least where the repression of ordinary workers was concerned, and was felt most notably in the easing of criminal sanctions against job-changing and the decriminalization of absenteeism, which are discussed in chapters 5 and 6 respectively. Gratitude, however, is not the same as positive, much less enthusiastic, support. In the absence of total social and political breakdown and without institutions through which people can articulate and act on their grievances, poverty tends to wear down a population, to force people to retreat into the family or extremely narrow circles of relatives and friends, and to adopt a docile public profile. If people placed

---

[136] In Magnitogorsk, for example, only the iron and steel combine had a proper medical treatment facility. Those in the other large metalworks in the city were staffed only by paramedics (GARF-RSFSR, f. A-482, op. 52s, d. 287, l. 189).

[137] GARF-RSFSR, f. A-482, op. 52s, d. 342, l. 89–96. This is a report on hazards in the defence industry, and notes that even in 1952 the country's Scientific Research Institutes of Labour Hygiene and Occupational Diseases had not a single laboratory or specialist investigating the impact of vibration and noise, despite the fact that these were a known cause of deafness among workers (*ibid.*, l. 95).

few active demands on the regime it was because they saw no safe way to do it.

There were cracks in this facade. The brief but no less remarkable actions of railway workers in protest against wage arrears, the widespread defiance of the criminal penalties against job-changing which chapter 5 examines, and the outright hostility with which at least some middle-ranking trade union organizations saw their relations with their parent ministries – all give evidence for the fact that the workforce was less than perfectly integrated into the postwar Stalinist system, a discussion to which I return in more detail in this book's conclusion. Nowhere was this more evident than among the young, the new generation of workers upon whom the regime relied to rebuild the workforce which had been partially destroyed during the war. This was the generation from whom the regime had to make the new 'Soviet' worker, whom it sought to socialize as Stalinist citizens. Here, too, the elite came up against inordinate obstacles, most of which were of its own making. This is the subject of the next chapter.

4   'Socializing' the next generation: the position of young workers

Why was I brought into this world,
Oh, Mama, why was I born?
Why this wretched fate as reward,
To be handed a miner's uniform?
They spy on the miner from front and behind,
They call the miner a drunken swine,
They allow the miner no peace to find.

From the diary of a young coal miner, 1949[1]

Setting the stage: an unhappy *komandirovka*

At the end of May 1946, the Minsk tractor factory (MTZ) despatched a contingent of 714 young workers to the Stalingrad tractor factory (STZ) for training. Minsk, of course, had been occupied during the war, and the Stalingrad factory was itself still completing restoration. Nearly three-quarters of the group were aged sixteen to eighteen; just under a quarter were between eighteen and twenty-five. Their education levels were not high: 23 were illiterate; 336 (47 per cent) had finished primary school; 337 had completed grades 5 to 7; just 18 had gone beyond grade 7. Well over 90 per cent of them were from the countryside. In all respects the group was fairly typical of the young workers coming into Soviet industry during the postwar period. Unfortunately, so too was their experience. From the very outset the Minsk factory had lied to them about what they would encounter at STZ. Their training was to last from four to eight months, but they were told they would be away for only three months and would leave Stalingrad before the cold weather arrived in late September and October. It also told them that STZ would provide them with housing, bedding, clothes, shoes, and decent food, as a result of which they took nothing with them. It should be said that many of them had no choice in this, since they did not own any spare clothing or footwear.

[1] TsKhDMO, f. 1, op. 4, d. 1172, l. 239.

When they arrived in Stalingrad the group received nothing of what they had been promised, since under the terms of the training contract it was the Minsk factory that was to have provided it. STZ did not even have dormitories for them and had to house them in tents. Nor did it give them any bedding, work clothes, shoes, warm clothing, or even underwear. The reaction of the Minsk workers was to desert *en masse*. Over a quarter fled during the first two months. Those who stayed endured terrible squalor. Nearly half the group had no change of underwear or outer clothing; many refused to go to the public baths to wash, embarrassed because they had no change of clothes. Many were infested with lice. The cold weather came in late September and they were still living in tents with no warm blankets. Even after STZ rehoused most of them in hastily repaired dormitories during October, their lack of warm clothing made it almost impossible to go out to work or, if they did, to remain in the unheated factory for more than a couple of hours each day. Eventually STZ gave the most deprived workers an emergency issue of underwear and clothing. It also advanced them a subsistence wage, even though this was actually the responsibility of MTZ. Although the amount was comparable to what young workers were earning in other industries at the time, it was not enough to allow them to eat in the factory dining rooms, and many sold off what few belongings they owned in order to survive. For its part, MTZ ignored repeated pleas to send material relief to its trainees. Its only response had been in August, when it sent its deputy director and a Minsk public prosecutor to conduct a show trial of one of the 'labour deserters', who received six years in a labour camp for unlawfully quitting his job.

The incident had one further consequence, this time political. Because most of these workers had been recruited for this *komandirovka*, or temporary posting, by their local Komsomol district committees, they 'cursed' the Komsomol for their misfortune.[2]

What happened to these MTZ trainees may have been extreme, but in almost every respect it typifies the experiences of the millions of young workers who entered industry and construction in the aftermath of World War II. Almost everywhere young people entered the world of work with inadequate education and vocational training, earned low (often little better than starvation) wages, and had to cope with living and working conditions which were barely tolerable. A large minority manifested their discontent by running away from their jobs, even though this was a criminal offence which, up until the spring of 1948, could earn workers in key industries many years in a labour camp. Their alienation, which began

[2] TsKhDMO, f. 1, op. 3, d. 479, l. 131–46.

its incubation when they were still in the Labour Reserve schools, was marked by a deep political apathy which proved almost impervious to the attempts at 'political education' carried out (or rather in most cases, not carried out, as we shall see later) by the Komsomol and trade unions.

It could be argued that most of the hardships which vocational trainees and young workers encountered were the logical result of the economic and social damage caused by the war. This is no doubt true, but it was little comfort to those who had to cope with them. We might equally argue, especially in light of the evidence presented in chapters 2 and 3, that the young were not alone in experiencing harsh and at times almost unendurable living and working conditions, especially during 1946 and 1947. This, too, is undeniably true. Yet what happened to these workers acquired an exaggerated significance in the context of the postwar reconstruction for a number of reasons. First, most young workers were indentured workers, and in this respect their status and conditions were significantly worse than those of older workers, despite the fact that the latter still faced severe restrictions on their freedom and mobility. Secondly, the recovery in living standards between 1948 and 1953 led to far smaller improvements for the young than it did for workers who were even slightly older. Although the lives of adult workers were extremely hard when Stalin died, they were still considerably better off than they had been during the late war years and the postwar famine. To a lesser extent the same could be said of the teenage workers of 1946 and 1947, most of whom by 1952 had begun to earn an average wage or even better. The new wave of teenage workers of the late 1940s and early 1950s, on the other hand, found themselves in conditions far closer to those of their predecessors in terms of wages, professional advancement, housing, and leisure opportunities. Finally, because the regime relied disproportionately on the young to replenish its badly depleted workforce, the disenchantments and resentments which their conditions provoked had potentially serious consequences for the regime's ability to instil in this generation a strong sense of identification with the Stalinist system.

In this chapter I examine the special position of young workers, in particular those aspects of their recruitment, training, and work experience which made them distinct from the adult workforce. I begin by looking at the Labour Reserve system: its methods of conscription; conditions in the vocational training schools; and the students' responses to these conditions. I then discuss the experiences of young workers when they moved into the factories, focusing on wages, housing, and their position in the workplace's occupational hierarchy. From there I examine the difficulties the regime encountered in its attempts to socialize young workers into pliable, if not model, Stalinist citizens. Finally, I provide a brief discussion of what we might call the shadow side, or alter ego, of the youthful work-force, that is, the homeless, abandoned, or simply delinquent children who were socially marginalized by the system and lived either under the direct tutelage of the MVD or on the borders of its universe.

The Labour Reserve system and Young Workers' Schools

In chapter 1 we discussed the role which the Labour Reserve system played in reconstituting the workforce in industry, construction, and transport. There I noted that its system of vocational education was ac-tually bifurcated into two parallel sets of institutions, the factory training schools, or FZO, which fed workers in so-called mass trades into industry, mining, and construction; and the trade schools (RU and ZhU), which prepared skilled workers. The FZO relied heavily on conscription, over-whelmingly from rural areas; the RU relied less heavily on agricultural youth and were able to fill their ranks by and large with volunteers. It was, therefore, with the FZO that the regime had its greatest problems. These manifested themselves at two key moments in the recruitment and training process: the call-up, through which teenagers were conscripted into the schools, and the retention of students in the FZO themselves. As discussed further in chapter 5, running away from a school was a crim-inal offence, governed by a law of 28 December 1940, and anyone who absconded and was caught faced incarceration in a labour camp for a period of one year.

The implementation of the call-up for the schools was not very dissim-ilar to the way in which the tsars had raised their armies. Once a year for the RU and twice a year for the FZO (later temporarily modified for coal mining to four times per year), the USSR Council of Ministers would issue a decree specifying the numbers to be mobilized or recruited for the different types of school for each industry. On the basis of these figures the Ministry of Labour Reserves would issue targets to its oblast' administra-tions, which were given legal status by joint decrees of the oblast' executive committees and the oblast' committees of the Communist Party. These latter decrees devolved targets further down the ladder to the oblast' dis-tricts, which through local call-up commissions (prizyvnye komissii) then issued quotas to the village soviets, which informed each collective farm how many youths it had to surrender. It is here that the problems arose.

In theory the call-up was supposed to be voluntary, and it was the responsibility of the local Party, Komsomol, and soviet authorities to carry out 'mass educational' work to try to persuade local youth that they should sign up. A number of district organizations undoubtedly took this task seriously, especially right after the war. They used radio broadcasts and articles in the local newspapers to publicize the schools and the call-up. They put on social events for prospective recruits or draftees and their parents, including meetings with school staff and with current and former students.[3] Some of these activities would be perfectly familiar to anyone involved in recruiting students to a British further education college or university today. Success, however, was mixed, and even in 1944 and 1945 we see discernible patterns which were to emerge very starkly by 1947. The urban areas, for example, had far less trouble recruiting than did the countryside, and in some cases it was only over-recruitment in the towns which allowed oblast′ authorities to meet their overall plans.[4] More ominously, the state of dormitories and teaching blocks and supplies of food and clothing were so inadequate right after the war that some schools refused to accept their planned intake of students or were barred from doing so by local executive committees.[5] In the end, as the statistical data show, filling the ranks of the FZO voluntarily became virtually impossible.

This left only conscription. In and of itself this need not have caused problems, but the truth was that large numbers of young people did everything in their power to avoid it. Much depended on the industries for which they were being recruited and the regions in which they were located. Like labour turnover among workers, which I discuss in detail in the next chapter, FZO 'draft dodging' affected mainly coal mining, ferrous and non-ferrous metallurgy, and construction, most notably in the Donbass area of Ukraine, Chelyabinsk, Molotov, and Sverdlovsk oblasti in the Urals, and the coal and metallurgical centres of the Kuzbass in Western Siberia. The problem was that these were the sectors which relied most heavily on the FZO for their supplies of labour power, so much so, in fact, that, as noted in chapter 1, in 1948 they accounted for 88 per cent of the entire planned FZO intake.

The Ministry of Labour Reserve statistics make it very easy to assess this phenomenon by two different measures. The first is the extent to which the FZO for the major recipient industries failed to meet their enrolment targets. We do not have data for this for 1947, the worst turnover year, but the 1948 data show the problems quite unmistakably. These are presented in table 4.1, which shows that coal mining, construction, and metallurgy badly under-recruited and underconscripted.

The second measure is the extent to which unpopular regions, primarily the coal and metallurgical centres of the Donbass, the Urals, and

---

[3] TsKhDMO, f. 1, op. 8, d. 355, l. 7–11 (Kirov oblast′); d. 408, l. 54–6 (Kaluga oblast′), l. 57–9 (Moscow city), l. 71–71ob., 72 (Poltava oblast′), l. 73–5 (Chelyabinsk oblast′).
[4] TsKhDMO, f. 1, op. 8, d. 355, l. 15–17 (Omsk oblast′).
[5] TsKhDMO, f. 1, op. 8, d. 355, l. 26–32, 39–43. For examples of schools still refusing to accept students during 1947, see *ibid.*, d. 454, l. 51 (Kherson oblast′, Ukraine), and RGAE, f. 8248, op. 21, d. 275, l. 93 (building materials industry).

Table 4.1. *FZO recruitment by major industry, 1948*

Ministry	FZO plan	FZO actually enrolled	% plan fulfilled
USSR total	*781,500*	*608,938*	*77.9*
Coal Industry	517,800	332,006	64.1
Metallurgical Industry	58,650	39,646	67.6
Construction of Enterprises in Heavy Industry	88,000	71,593	81.4
Construction of Military and Naval Enterprises	21,670	21,003	96.9
Other ministries	95,380	144,690	151.7

Source: GARF, f. 9507, op. 2, d. 420, l. 9.

Western Siberia, found it difficult to meet their targets for students mobilized from other oblasti. This was an important issue, because the insistence of the authorities on mobilizing FZO trainees and young workers for employment far away from their homes badly aggravated labour turnover, a fact which did not escape the notice of either the procuracy or the industrial ministries.[6] In many ways, however, the authorities felt they had no choice, since the supply of local youth in the relevant age groups was simply inadequate to meet the demand for labour power.[7] Just how problematic these mobilizations were we can see clearly from the Ministry of Labour Reserves data. In 1947, for example, Penza oblast' was supposed to have mobilized nearly 6,000 youth for FZO in Sverdlovsk oblast', but sent only 1,300. Of the 2,000 rural youth it was told to send to Primorskii territory in the Far East it managed only 429. In that same year the Chuvash republic was to have recruited 2,000 students for coal mining FZO in Molotov oblast' and another 2,000 for FZO in Sverdlovsk oblast'; in fact, it mobilized only 1,000 and 840 respectively. In 1948 the Chuvash republic was to provide 3,800 students for Chelyabinsk oblast', but despatched only 1,100.[8] According to a Komsomol report, young people in the republic who were subject to mobilization would flee to other districts, hide in the woods, or otherwise 'use every means possible to

[6] GARF, f. 8131, op. 37, d. 3543, l. 69; RGAE, f. 8875, op. 46, d. 235, l. 171. In 1948 the iron and steel workers' trade union called for an outright ban on the practice of recruiting FZO students from far-away locations (GARF, f. 7680, op. 5, d. 15, l. 16).

[7] Stalino oblast' in the Donbass, for example, found that in late 1944 most of the teenagers of call-up age residing in the oblast' were either students or were already employed in iron and steel, coal mining, or defence industry factories; there was simply no way the oblast' could fill its FZO without relying on young people mobilized from other regions of the USSR (TsKhDMO, f. 1, op. 8, d. 355, l. 115).

[8] GARF, f. 9507, op. 2, d. 418, l. 19–21 (1947), and d. 420, l. 38 (1948).

Table 4.2. *Mobilization of FZO students from other oblasti, 1948*

Target oblast' or republic	Planned intake from other oblasti	Actual intake from other oblasti	%
USSR total	*502,105*	*320,214*	*63.8*
Chelyabinsk oblast'	27,500	19,170	69.7
Karaganda oblast'	26,445	21,527	81.4
Kemerovo oblast'	72,500	44,492	61.4
Molotov oblast'	26,800	15,721	58.7
Moscow oblast'	11,050	7,327	66.3
Rostov oblast'	16,200	13,354	82.4
Sverdlovsk oblast'	14,300	11,842	82.8
Tula oblast'	10,500	7,074	67.4
Ukraine total	*329,390*	*212,055*	*64.4*
Stalino oblast'	152,450	90,015	59.0
Voroshilovgrad oblast'	98,700	49,945	50.6

Source: GARF, f. 9507, op. 2, d. 420, l. 31, 33–8.

evade the call-up'.[9] Lest there be any suspicion that either Penza oblast' or the Chuvash republic were somehow exceptional, the Ministry of Labour Reserves' own data show that they were representative of a general trend. Table 4.2 lists those oblasti which, during 1948, had the greatest difficulties recruiting or mobilizing students to their FZO from other regions, together with the shortfall between their planned and actual intake. The figures are quite expressive, and reveal the extent to which young people in other oblasti already knew about the conditions that would await them in the Urals, Kemerovo, and most strikingly in the Donbass, and took steps to avoid being sent there. The scale on which they succeeded in this is also striking: throughout the USSR many tens of thousands of young people, overwhelmingly from the countryside, escaped mobilization, even after the introduction of a special military call-up for coal mining and related construction.

With evasion of the call-up so widespread, village soviets found themselves in a contradictory position. On the one hand, they needed to meet their Labour Reserve quotas. On the other hand, they also wished to retain their best young labour power in the villages and collective farms. They resolved the contradiction in typical Soviet fashion, by doing both at once, using violence and coercion when they deemed it necessary, but at the same time helping other youngsters to escape. The procuracy reports cite instances where local officials (heads of village soviets, the police, and local party representatives) dealt with refusals to report

[9] TsKhDMO, f. 1, op. 8, d. 500, l. 7.

for the call-up with beatings, holding parents hostage, fining parents or confiscating their property, and organizing vigilante groups to go house to house (sometimes waiting until the night) and drag out the unwilling youngsters. One district in Stalino oblast′ formed armed brigades which went through the different villages hunting down teenagers who had failed to report. Another district used similar methods and then held the draftees under armed guard until they could be despatched.[10]

This, however, is only part of the story. Many of those 'mobilized' had been conscripted illegally. This was by no means accidental. If the mistakes were noted the schools would send the people back, sometimes on the basis of petitions filed by the very same local officials who had shipped them there in the first place;[11] if not, the village had at least limited its losses to the least productive of its teenage population. Some of those rounded up were too old for the schools. One district in Omsk oblast′ mobilized teenagers who had already done training at an FZO school and were working off their four-year indenture. At the other extreme, villages sent children who were far too young. Children as young as twelve were sent to mining schools and given false documents which purported to show that they were sixteen or seventeen years old. In the same way local call-up commissions filled their quotas with teenagers who were sick or otherwise physically incapable of doing industrial training. The reports, obviously, detail only those cases in which the ruses were uncovered, usually during a medical inspection, and the children were returned home; we have no way of knowing how many slipped through the net and wound up as child labourers working underground. Yet even these examples show that the deceptions took place on a large scale. Of the 1,770 teenagers sent to the Labour Reserve schools in Leningrad during the summer of 1946, 536 were physically unfit and 286 were underage. During the 1949 call up in Kirghizia, Control Commissions in a number of districts had to reject as many as half the conscripts because they were in obviously poor health or physically underdeveloped.[12]

---

[10] GARF, f. 8131, op. 37, d. 3529, l. 286–90, and d. 4159, l. 264–6. The latter report (l. 266) should be contrasted with a Ministry of Labour Reserves document on the spring 1948 mobilization of youth from Tambov oblast′ to work in Kemerovo and Sverdlovsk oblasti (GARF, f. 9507, op. 2, d. 421, l. 1–8). While admitting that oblast′ officials had difficulties filling their quota, it claims that abuses were relatively minor and few in number. The procuracy report paints a somewhat different picture: Tambov oblast′ met its quota only by using armed militia and night-time raids to seize conscripts and escort them to despatch points.

[11] GARF, f. 8131, op. 37, d. 4772, l. 139, citing the behaviour of call-up officials in the Tatar ASSR and Chernovtsy oblast′ in Ukraine.

[12] GARF, f. 8131, op. 37, d. 3529, l. 35–36ob., 38 (Kuibyshev oblast′), and l. 289–90 (Omsk oblast′); op. 29, d. 519, l. 39–40 (Moldavia and Kursk oblast′); op. 37, d. 3528, l. 127–8 (Leningrad); op. 37, d. 4772, l. 184–185ob. (Kirghizia). The report on Moldavia

Table 4.3. *Turnover from Labour Reserve schools, 1944–1948*

	All leavers, *less* returnees	As % of all students	'Wilful quitters', *less* returnees	As % of all students
1944 – All	165,700	12.9	89,000	6.9
Of which, FZO	89,600	13.9	55,100	8.6
Of which, RU/ZhU	76,100	11.9	33,900	5.3
1945 – All	98,200	8.2	47,000	3.9
Of which, FZO	51,100	8.8	28,900	5.0
Of which, RU/ZhU	47,100	7.6	18,100	2.9
1946 – All	72,200	5.7	31,500	2.5
Of which, FZO	42,000	6.6	20,700	3.3
Of which, RU/ZhU	30,200	4.9	10,800	1.7
1947 – All	119,900	6.1	80,700	4.1
Of which, FZO	96,600	7.8	69,200	5.6
Of which, RU/ZhU	23,300	3.2	11,500	1.6
1948 – All	75,290	3.95	46,480	2.4
Of which, FZO	61,930	5.4	41,110	3.6
Of which, RU/ZhU	13,360	1.7	5,370	0.7

Source: GARF, f. 9507, op. 2, d. 446, l. 1 (1948), 2 (1944–7).

These abuses confronted both the schools and the legal authorities with some difficult issues. In June 1947 the procurator of Kuibyshev oblast' contacted Tadevosyan, head of the USSR Procuracy's Group for Juvenile Cases, to complain that teenagers who had been illegally mobilized and despatched to the Labour Reserve schools were 'at present swelling the ranks of those who are wilfully leaving', and the schools were trying to have them prosecuted. He did not know how to proceed. 'We face the danger that if we quash these cases during investigation this will encourage the mass flight of others who have been mobilized in a similar [that is, illegal] fashion.'[13]

It was, however, the students who had been mobilized legally who constituted the biggest problem. Table 4.3 shows what we might call 'net

and Kursk oblast' shows a more sinister side to this subterfuge, noting that some of the underage children were taken out of children's homes with the promise that they would be sent to an RU, which did in fact take teenagers aged fourteen and fifteen for two-year training for a skilled trade. In fact they were sent to a mining FZO. Moreover, the children's home directors were involved in the scam, for reasons about which we can only speculate: perhaps to relieve pressure on their overstretched resources, perhaps to help out local political patrons, or possibly in exchange for bribes.

[13] GARF, f. 8131, op. 37, d. 3529, l. 36ob., 38. Tadevosyan's reply was unequivocal, if somewhat surprising: there were no legal grounds for prosecuting these runaways, since only people legally mobilized were subject to the Edict of 28 December 1940, which covered students who ran away from Labour Reserve Schools. See ch. 5, pp. 190–6.

flight' from the Labour Reserve schools, that is, the number of those who left the schools minus those caught and sent back. This gives us a more realistic picture of the actual loss of labour power from the system than do the gross figures for leavers. The table also breaks turnover down by type of school. There are several observations needed here. The first is that, as with turnover among employed workers, both total attrition and illegal flight from the schools, in absolute terms and as a percentage of students, was actually higher in 1944 than during 1947, the worst postwar year. The second is that there was a sharp distinction between the factory training schools (FZO) and the trade schools (RU/ZhU). Turnover at the latter was extremely low, a reflection of their better conditions, their more prestigious status, and perhaps also the younger age at which they took in students. Thirdly, already by 1948 turnover, especially 'wilful quitting', had dropped to quite manageable proportions. By 1950 it was negligible: illegal leavers were less than 1 per cent of the total number of students.[14]

This is not, however, the whole story. Despite the very comprehensive data in the Ministry of Labour Reserve files on intake, attrition, the oblasti from which individual regions drew their conscripted students, and the industries to which graduates were despatched, the figures contain some major distortions. The first is that school directors systematically understated the level of turnover, and in at least some cases the oblast' administrations of Labour Reserves incorporated these falsified figures into their reports from which the Ministry of Labour Reserves compiled its annual data. The techniques of concealment took a number of forms. The most obvious was out-and-out lying. Schools had an incentive to understate their losses because they earned bonuses if they had a good retention record. The levels of falsification could be quite breathtaking: one school in Georgia lost 27 per cent of all its students during the first nine months of 1948, but claimed a turnover rate of absolutely zero.[15] Another device was for directors to wait for a very long time before reporting 'deserters' in the hope that the students would return or be sent back. Sometimes this hope was justified, but often it was not. They particularly turned a blind eye to students who did not 'desert' in the sense that they disappeared altogether, but went off on extended unauthorized leave (*samovol'naya otluchka*). Although technically students who came back were still on the rolls, in reality they had missed a large part and sometimes nearly all of their training. The schools graduated them anyway and sent them on to enterprises[16] – a fact which partially explains why enterprises in turn put

[14] GARF, f. 9507, op. 2, d. 520, l. 3.
[15] GARF, f. 8131, op. 37, d. 4160, l. 46–7.
[16] GARF, f. 8131, op. 37, d. 3543, l. 25; RGASPI, f. 17, op. 121, d. 644, l. 18–19.

so many young workers on unskilled jobs rather than jobs in the trades for which they had trained. Schools also hid real levels of turnover by falsifying the documents on how many students they sent to enterprises. They claimed to have trained students who in fact had run away or simply had never existed; they equally despatched to the enterprises people who were of real flesh and blood, but had never been students in the Labour Reserve system, effectively using them to replace students who had gone missing. In at least three cases – Stalingrad, Kemerovo, and Molotov oblasti – the oblast' administrations of Labour Reserves either connived in this directly with the school directors or were happy to accept school figures without any verification.[17] Several schools, including at least one RU, developed the novel system of over-recruiting students but not entering the surplus on their rolls. They thereby created a reserve list: if a student ran away they would replace him or her with one of the reserves, thus making it appear that no one had left.[18] And of course we should not neglect the importance of greed and corruption. We know of at least one FZO where staff accepted bribes to provide absconding students with fake documents claiming they had left legally.[19]

The all-union data understate the disruptive effect of high turnover in still another important way. If we look only at the national average, the numbers absconding from the schools appear relatively modest: in 1947 the 'net' loss from FZO due to illegal flight (that is, all runaways minus those who returned) averaged 5.6 per cent for the USSR as a whole. In the problem regions, however, the flight assumed massive proportions. During 1947 it was 14.4 per cent in Chelyabinsk oblast', 14.4 per cent in Stalino oblast', and 13.2 per cent in Voroshilovgrad oblast'.[20] It was not uncommon for some schools to lose nearly half their intake. The most obvious reason, which the schools themselves openly acknowledged, was their dreadful housing and living conditions. The Molotov oblast' procurator responsible for juvenile cases noted in 1947 that 'such an intolerable level of turnover is explained by the fact that when the schools are opened they do not observe even the most elementary housing or living conditions and the instructional foundation is simply not there. The problem of creating decent living conditions is especially bad at

---

[17] GARF, f. 8131, op. 37, d. 4159, l. 115 (Stalingrad oblast'); f. 9507, op. 2, d. 482, l. 9–11, 13–14 (Molotov and Kemerovo oblasti).
[18] GARF, f. 8131, op. 37, d. 4173, l. 10; f. 9507, op. 2, d. 482, l. 5–9, 11–12, 17–18.
[19] GARF, f. 8131, op. 37, d. 4163, l. 222. The school in question was in Sverdlovsk and allegedly had 43 per cent of its students run away during 1948. The director and his staff – who were engaged in other forms of embezzlement – charged between 60 and 196 rubles for a false passport. For similar cases of factory personnel providing fake documents to workers, see ch. 5, p. 179.
[20] GARF, f. 9507, op. 2, d. 446, l. 13, 15, 19.

the schools in the coal industry. For example, at FZO School No. 23 (attached to Mine No. 6 of the Kizelugol' Trust), of a December [1947] recruitment of 200 people, 70 wilfully left.' He went on to describe other schools in which students were housed in unheated barracks, some of which had no lighting, in which the food was of terrible quality, and from which students had to walk vast distances – in one case thirteen kilometres in each direction – in order to attend the factories to which the schools were attached. The teaching staff were not properly qualified, and even half the directors in the oblast' RU and FZO did not have the required technical or pedagogical training. Moreover, the work was dangerous and the students knew it. One mine with its own FZO had seventy-eight people killed during 1947, including two FZO students. The school's director claimed that after that it was extremely difficult to persuade students to go down the pit, and 76 students of an intake of 177 ran away.[21]

This last point is of some significance, because if we read only the reports from the industrial ministries or the Party Control Commission, we assume that the main motivation for fleeing the schools was poor housing and living conditions. It would be impossible to exaggerate their influence, but the sheer terror of the coal mines, coupled with the widespread practice of deceiving recruits and conscripts with promises that they would be trained in skilled, clean trades, also played a major role. Here is how the procurator of Stavropol' oblast' described the situation of FZO students from his oblast' who had been sent to the mines in Rostov oblast' in 1947:

Upon their arrival at the schools the youngsters come face to face with the real state of affairs. It is obvious that they sent them straight down the pits without any preliminary explanatory or educational work, this frightened the students, and when they came back to the surface they fled home in batches, going back to their own collective farms. Thus, in School No. 7, according to the declaration of their representative, of 260 people called up in April only 80 are still there. It is no better at other schools. Work in the mines has so scared these juveniles that, when procurators have suggested to them that they go back to the schools, they are refusing point blank and would rather agree to bear criminal responsibility, declaring that 'I'll serve out my year but after that I'll be free and won't have to work in the mines.'[22]

The procurator of the Moldavian SSR made the same observation nearly a year later, with regard to those mobilized to coal mining FZO

---

[21] GARF, f. 8131, op. 37, d. 3529, l. 261–3.
[22] GARF, f. 8131, op. 37, d. 3529, l. 141–2. The 'year' here refers to the one-year sentence of incarceration for students running away from a Labour Reserve school.

through the military call-up. The students received a brief introduction to the 'theory' of coal mining and then were sent immediately underground:

This has the effect on them that they categorically refuse any further work and abandon their studies *en masse* and return home. When they are brought to account, they declare in court that they categorically refuse any further study and, being sentenced to deprivation of freedom of between two and five years, in the majority of cases do not appeal against the court sentence. It is even more the case that they do not object when they are tried under Part 1, Art. 56-18 of the Criminal Code of the Ukrainian SSR, since being sentenced to one year of compulsory labour they have the possibility to be near their home and, most importantly, to rid themselves of any further study and three years' work in the mines after finishing the FZO.

The scale of the 'desertion' can be judged from the fact that between the time of the military mobilization in September 1947 and March 1948, when this report was written, the Moldavian authorities had already rounded up and sent back just to Stalino oblast' 1,000 Moldavian conscripts who had fled from its FZO, and prosecuted another 200. The roundups, however, were not always effective, since many of the students simply ran away again while *en route* back to the Donbass.[23]

Another insight into the dread and foreboding with which these labour conscripts looked upon the mines can be seen in this poem, found in the diary of a young miner sometime during 1949:[24]

> They told me to report
> To Ovruch raiispolkom.
> The bosses looked me over,
> The doctor said, 'He'll do.'
>> From the trees the leaves were falling,
>> Autumn had surely come.
>> They told me, 'Pack your things,
>> It's your turn now, my son.'
> It was like I'd been hit by thunder,
> I heard not a word he'd said.

[23] GARF, f. 8131, op. 37, d. 4174, l. 230–3. The criminal code article referred to here is the law of 28 December 1940, which set penalties for those who absconded from the schools. The passage is revealing, because it shows that students were already aware of a serious loophole which the regime had left when drafting the law, namely that, after they had served their one-year sentence, there were no penalties which compelled students to return to the schools or to subsequent indenture to a coal mine. For a further discussion of this point, see ch. 5, pp. 195–6.

[24] TsKhDMO, f. 1, op. 4, d. 1172, l. 239. The little verse at the head of this chapter was found in the same diary. The author was allegedly a young FZO graduate working at a mine in Voroshilovgrad oblast', Ukraine.

When I came out of the office,
My mates could only stare.
  Right now we're being merry,
  But I know this song's my last,
  Within the hour tears will fall,
  And I'll curse what fate has done.
Friends, we're all in this together now,
One of us will soon be killed.
For me it's death, for you a cave-in,
Then send a letter to my folks.
  The letter will come with the tell-tale stamp,
  The family will read it aloud.
  Now mama's and papa's tears will fall,
  'We'll see our boy no more.'
The Sunday holiday will come,
All the lads will go out walking.
Father will look out of the window,
'I'll see my boy no more.'

Whilst coal mining might have had pride of place in the awfulness of its treatment of FZO trainees, it was worse only by degree. An October 1946 order of the USSR Ministry of Labour Reserves had required enterprises to provide RU and FZO with fuel, electricity, materials, and machinery on which to teach the students; they were also obliged to keep dormitories and teaching blocks in good repair. It is clear that many enterprises were either unable or unwilling to divert the required resources to do this. A Party Control Commission report on turnover of young workers and Labour Reserve students compiled in February 1948 found that dormitories in general were filthy, lacked bedding and furniture, and had insufficient fuel to keep them heated, so that many students had to sleep in their clothes. The dormitories had major problems with crime, including theft, 'hooliganism', brawling, and knife fights. The report also revealed that students at some FZO in Stalino oblast' had refused to attend classes or report for work in protest at the poor quality of their food and the fact that, with nowhere to dry their clothing, they had to go around in damp work clothes.[25] Occasionally a school director would be prosecuted for tolerating such conditions, but we should bear in mind that, while some school managers may have been personally culpable, many of the problems – for example, shortages of soap and food – were the result of circumstances by and large outside their control.[26]

---

[25] RGASPI, f. 17, op. 121, d. 644, l. 8–11.
[26] Thus a school director in the Donskoi district of Moscow oblast' was prosecuted in 1947 because the dormitories were dirty and lice-infested, the students had no soap

The schools could hardly claim that in mitigation for poor physical conditions they were nonetheless providing a high-quality vocational education. On the contrary, the low level of training had been a source of almost universal complaint since the Labour Reserve system's inception in 1940, and was to remain so until it was abolished under Khrushchev.[27] A Komsomol report on the Labour Reserve schools in Voroshilovgrad oblast' – which trained workers primarily for the coal industry – maintained that students were employed on tasks that had little relation to the trades for which they were allegedly being prepared. In one case students studying to become tunnellers and face workers were assigned to work in the store room. Few of the schools had proper workplaces for the students, and those that did either possessed old and outdated equipment or had no equipment at all. The foremen in charge of instruction themselves had little education, some were heavy drinkers, and others were accused of stealing.[28] Staff at some schools were physically abusive towards the students, and in exceptional cases received long sentences in a labour camp.[29] But such behaviour was by no means universal – some school directors built up considerable trust among their students, who even appealed to them for help in dealing with terrible conditions at their new places of employment.[30]

Teaching conditions in the schools in fact varied enormously, even within one and the same industry. As with living conditions, much depended on what the schools received from their parent enterprise. Shortages of teaching premises, tools, and machinery on which to train students were clearly worse in the early postwar years than later on. This did not make the problem any less serious. Machine-tool operators who had no access to machine tools, trainee joiners who had no planes or chisels, or student brick-layers who had no spirit levels, straightedges, or even string could hardly be expected to master their trades, especially if they also had no textbooks from which to study.[31] And, although supplies of tools and

and very little hot water with which to keep themselves clean, and the food was so bad that the students had felt compelled to go out and gather rotten potatoes from which to extract potato flour to bake homemade buns. Although at the very least the core of these problems lay in the famine and food shortages, the intervention of the procuracy did prompt the local authorities to mobilize resources to clean up the school, give the students medical examinations, and improve the quality of the food – again demonstrating that the government was prepared to release extra supplies in individual cases, so long as this did not compromise the sanctity of its general policy (GARF, f. 8131. op. 37, d. 3529, l. 127–127ob.).
[27] Filtzer, *Soviet Workers and De-Stalinization*, pp. 72–3.
[28] TsKhDMO, f. 1, op. 4, d. 1100, l. 72–4.
[29] GARF, f. 8131, op. 37, d. 3528, l. 105–6, and d. 4159, l. 2.
[30] RGAE, f. 8592, op. 2, d. 305, l. 44. I note this case further below, on p. 141.
[31] GARF, f. 7676, op. 11, d. 141, l. 11–13; RGAE, f. 8248, op. 21, d. 274, l. 233, and d. 275, l. 106–7; GARF, f. 8131, op. 37, d. 4163, l. 106–7.

materials clearly improved over time, even as late as 1952 the RU attached to the Kaganovich first state ball bearing factory in Moscow, one
of the USSR's major engineering works, was unable to train tool-setters
for automatic lathes since it did not own this type of equipment. The
problems of inadequate infrastructure were compounded by failures to
update school curricula in line with improvements in technology, materials, and production methods.[32] As bizarre as it may seem, RU in the
Leningrad metal trades gave pupils just twelve hours' instruction in technological processes and the use of technical documentation over the entire two years of their studies.[33] These shortcomings, combined with the
questionable competence of teaching staff, meant that enterprises simply could not rely on the students they received being able to do the
work for which they had supposedly been trained. Factories repeatedly
complained that they had to retrain FZO and even RU graduates virtually from scratch.[34] The inadequacies of the Labour Reserve system
were sufficiently transparent that the iron and steel workers' trade union
proposed, as early as 1948, that the FZO should be abolished and that
all training should take place directly in the factories. The role of the
Ministry of Labour Reserves would be reduced merely to monitoring the
quality of the teaching.[35] The plan became reality only after Stalin died,
but ministries had begun to take matters into their own hands long before
this. The Ministry of the Iron and Steel Industry claimed to have trained
284,800 new workers between 1946 and 1950, some 20,000 more than
it received from the Labour Reserve Schools during this time. During
the same period it put over 400,000 workers through various courses
to enhance their skills, three-quarters of them on the so-called technical
minimum examination.[36]

The Labour Reserve system was only one of the institutions through
which the regime attempted to train and socialize its workforce. It was
well aware that general educational levels were low, and that the war
had forced many young people to interrupt their schooling. There were
approximately 450,000 illiterates living in the RSFSR alone in 1950;
several hundred thousand more were 'semi-literate'. The Komsomol itself

---

[32] TsKhDMO, f. 1, op. 2, d. 313, l. 214.   [33] *Trud*, 17 March, 23 March 1949.
[34] TsKhDMO, f. 1, op. 2, d. 285, l. 213.   [35] GARF, f. 7680, op. 5, d. 15, l. 14, 16.
[36] The figures for internal training are from RGAE, f. 8875, op. 6, d. 279, l. 132. Labour
   Reserve intake is calculated from GARF, f. 9507, op. 2, d. 417, l. 16 (1946); d. 418,
   l. 10 (1947); d. 420, l. 9 (1948); d. 422, l. 32 (1949); and RGAE, f. 1562, op. 15, d. 3055,
   l. 25–6 (1950). The figures for 1948 and 1949 are slightly exaggerated, because they also
   include Labour Reserve graduates for non-ferrous metallurgy. Not all of the industry's
   training problems were the fault of the Labour Reserve schools. In the first postwar years
   its factories relied heavily on prisoners and semi-prison labour, who received just enough
   preparation to allow them to carry out basic production tasks.

recorded 367,000 members who did not have a primary education.[37] In April 1944 the Council of People's Commissars established Young Workers' Schools (*shkoly rabochei molodozhi*), the aim of which was to allow young workers to complete their education at least up through grade 7 and for the more able students all the way up through grade 10. In January 1946 the plan was concretized, as all industrial enterprises were instructed to set up schools and provide them with premises, heating, equipment, and lighting.[38]

The early experience of the schools was not promising. There were few textbooks. Many of the schools had no equipment and had to conduct lessons in buildings that were unheated and frequently unlit – a serious problem in the early postwar years when electricity supplies were irregular even in Moscow. To avoid at least some of these difficulties many of the classes were held at night in regular children's schools, but this meant that workers on evening shifts could not attend. Factory directors did not always cooperate, and assigned students to overtime work when they should have been attending their classes. The end result was that the schools found it difficult to recruit students and to retain those who enrolled. Drop-out rates were high: during the first year of their operation (1944/5) the schools lost nearly half their students. Moreover, the schools, at least initially, offered instruction only from grade 5 onwards; they thus ignored the very group which needed them most, those who had not finished their primary education.[39]

It is clear that at one level the schools did accomplish part of their objectives. By the school year 1948/9 they had 620,000 students spread over the different grades, and were scheduled to increase their intake in 1950/1 to over 830,000. The reality, however, was somewhat more modest. Quotas for enrolment were consistently not met. Drop-out rates stayed high. During 1948/9 for the USSR as a whole, the schools lost 264,500 students – over 40 per cent of those enrolled. Leningrad oblast' lost half its students during the first half-year alone.[40] Those who tried to stay the course did not necessarily find it easy going, for the reasons already cited. In 1948/9 a quarter of students failed and had to retake their examinations or repeat the year altogether.[41] There were factories at which attendance was so low that they had to close down a number of the classes.[42]

---

[37] TsKhDMO, f. 1, op. 2, d. 285, l. 292–3.
[38] TsKhDMO, f. 1, op. 3, d. 413, l. 18ob.
[39] TsKhDMO, f. 1, op. 3, d. 413, l. 7–12, 16.
[40] TsKhDMO, f. 1, op. 2, d. 285, l. 289–90.
[41] TsKhDMO, f. 1, op. 2, d. 285, l. 291.   [42] *Stalinets* (Rostsel'mash), 15 April 1950.

For all their weaknesses, it is clear that the Young Workers' Schools made a considerable contribution to improving overall educational levels among young workers. The problem was that the experience varied widely from region to region and enterprise to enterprise. There were some obvious successes at improving take-up and drop-out rates, especially in engineering.[43] But these results were far from universal. Iron and steel works in Southern Ukraine and engineering enterprises in Gor'kii and Siberia continued to find it difficult to fill more than a tiny fraction of their places.[44] Perhaps more telling was the fact that, even where the schools had made a marked turnaround, most notably in Leningrad engineering factories, a large proportion of young workers remained untouched by their efforts. The Komsomol estimated that even in 1952 two-thirds of the 144,000 young workers in Leningrad's large-scale industry still did not have a full basic seven-year education.[45]

Wages and living conditions of young workers

In chapter 2 I referred to the low wages of young workers and how these made them especially vulnerable to the food shortages. I must stress, however, that, whilst their poverty was made worse by the rationing restrictions and price rises of September 1946, it had long predated them. To some extent, of course, this is to be expected. In virtually any industrial economy the young will earn less than workers with more experience. In the Soviet Union of this time, however, there were quite specific factors which acted to trap a large minority of young workers into poverty even as the standard of living began to rise and most young recruits began to settle into their jobs and achieve close to average earnings.

The most striking feature of the first postwar years was the chronic cycle of indebtedness which plagued many young workers. Common practice was for an enterprise to grant an advance or loan to young workers upon their initial arrival at the factory. Council of Ministers decrees of September 1946 and January 1947 set down specific rules to govern the practice. All workers entering employment from a Labour Reserve school, whether a factory training school or a trade school, were to receive a 300-ruble advance against their first pay packet, to be repaid through deductions from their wages over the ensuing six months. In addition, Labour Reserve graduates who had been directed to enterprises

[43] TsKhDMO, f. 1, op. 2, d. 267, l. 208, 210; d. 313, l. 128, 225–7.
[44] GARF, f. 7680, op. 5, d. 152, l. 58; TsKhDMO, f. 1, op. 2, d. 313, l. 12–13, 112.
[45] TsKhDMO, f. 1, op. 2, d. 313, l. 125.

outside their parents' home district were eligible for loans to buy household articles, furniture, clothing, and shoes, up to a maximum of 2,000 rubles, depending on the extent of their need.[46]

Because the earnings of young workers were so low, however, many could not pay off these debts. Some factories tried to recoup the money by taking the repayments directly out of their wages, but this left them with almost nothing on which to live. This was a persistent problem, and one not confined to the crisis of 1946–7. On rare occasions the debts could reach truly extraordinary amounts. In 1948, for example, the textile workers' trade union interceded on behalf of a group of 400 young construction workers, who upon leaving their FZO in 1946 had been assigned to help reconstruct a linen combine in Smolensk. At various times during 1947 and 1948 the workers had been sent out for ten days at a time to do logging, but were not issued any food. This sent them into a downward spiral with tragic consequences:

This compelled the workers to wander about the countryside and to trade their clothes, shoes, and tools for bread. They then had to pay for the tools which they had exchanged, a sum equal to five times their value. The only foods made available at the logging sites were expensive ones: salami, cheese, chocolate candies, etc., and were issued against their future earnings, which the conditions on the logging works did not permit them to earn. Upon returning from logging the workers were not paid any wages, and individuals among them were forced to sell even their pillow cases and sheets, for which they again had deducted from their wages a sum equal to five times their value. Once each month the young workers were given an advance of 50 to 100 rubles against their future wages, which was enough only for bread for ten to fifteen days. But since their low wages did not cover their debts for these advances, the debt continued to mount. In addition, the young workers still had to pay off the advance given them when they finished school. The end result is that over the course of two years the young workers have run up a total debt to the Construction-Erection Administration of around 175,000 rubles. This entire situation has created difficult material conditions, [and] the young workers have fallen into extreme need: they've no clothes, no shoes, not even enough money to buy bread.

The size of this debt was almost unimaginable, even by the standards of the time: it amounted to an average of 4,375 rubles per worker, which was probably more than each of them earned in a year. So extreme was their case that the union managed to persuade the Ministry of the Textile Industry to write the debt off in its entirety.[47]

---

[46] I do not have the text of these decrees. Their contents are explained in GARF, f. 5475, op. 21, d. 478, l. 18.

[47] GARF, f. 8131, op. 37, d. 4159, l. 73–4. The union had taken the case to the procuracy because nearly half the workers had committed absenteeism at some point during their

Most young debtors owed nowhere near this amount, but the phenomenon was very widespread, especially in construction. A 1948 Komsomol report noted that the majority of young workers in coal mining construction in Rostov oblast' earned less than 350 rubles a month, under half the industry's average wage. At some construction sites the average worker was in debt to the trust for 260 to 320 rubles, and some workers owed more than twice their monthly earnings.[48] At the construction of the iron and steel works in Chkalov oblast' in late 1948, one-sixth of the site's young workers owed between them 200,000 rubles, an average of nearly 500 rubles each. This was a classical 'poverty trap'. Their earnings were so low – sometimes less than 300 rubles a month – that they could not even eat, much less pay off what they owed, and they had to keep borrowing more. There were few ways they could economize. They had given up eating in the site dining rooms, but could not buy food in the shops of the local Department of Workers' Supply (ORS) because the latter were undersupplied.[49]

By 1950 the extent of low pay had abated, at least within the priority industries. In early 1951, two-thirds of young workers in iron and steel were earning above the national average wage for unskilled workers, but this still left a large 'tail' of low earners.[50] Data for individual engineering works suggest a similar distribution, although the 'tail' (again, about one-third of young workers) was earning not just below the average industrial wage, but a true poverty wage of less than 400 rubles a month.[51] The question is why so many young workers earned so little. We can dismiss some of the more trivial explanations offered, for example, that of a factory trade union committee in Krasnodar, which claimed that young RU graduates were receiving financial help from their parents and

employment, for which the courts had sentenced them to a six months' cut in pay of between 20 and 25 per cent. This only deepened their poverty. The union claimed that they had gone truant only because of their desperation, and it wanted the sentences lifted for a small group who had not yet served them out completely. It also wanted criminal charges brought against the management of the construction administration for neglect of its workers.

[48] TsKhDMO, f. 1, op. 4, d. 895, l. 49.
[49] TsKhDMO, f. 1, op. 4, d. 961, l. 17–18, 20–2. In at least one case a factory management tried to aid young workers by lowering their rent in enterprise-owned dormitories, but then remarkably came under sharp attack from its branch trade union (GARF, f. 7676, op. 9, d. 697, l. 31 (Russkii dizel' engineering works, Leningrad)). For similar cases of poverty wages and indebtedness during 1949 and 1950, see GARF, f. 8131, op. 37, d. 3056, l. 230 (construction of the Chelyabinsk iron and steel works); f. 7676, op. 11, d. 642, l. 1 (construction of the Kolomna machine-tool factory); d. 641, l. 4–9, 73–4 (young engineering workers in the machine-tool industry); GARF, f. 5451, op. 26, d. 1128, l. 182 (construction of the Cherepovets iron and steel works).
[50] RGAE, f. 8875, op. 46, d. 279, l. 139.
[51] GARF, f. 7676, op. 11, d. 641, l. 19. The figures are from the Kramatorsk heavy machine-tool factory.

hence were under little pressure to exert themselves (in other words, they were not poor enough).[52] In one sense young workers were subject to the same problems within production as their adult counterparts. Supply shortages and equipment breakdowns could cut deeply into earnings irrespective of age or seniority. In engineering and coal mining the percentage of young workers who failed to meet their norms was not appreciably higher than the figure for workers as a whole.[53] Yet there were factors quite specific to young workers which exacerbated their difficulties. Part of the problem, already touched on in our discussion of the Labour Reserve system, was that graduates from the schools came to their first jobs inadequately trained, and were thus placed in the lowest wage and skill grades (*razryady*).[54] Engineering factories also complained that new workers were too narrowly specialized, so that if equipment broke down they could not be transferred to different pieces of machinery because they did not know how to operate them.[55] It was, however, common practice to use Labour Reserve graduates as unskilled labourers, and not in the trade for which they had been trained, irrespective of how good or bad had been their vocational preparation. The factory newspaper at the Kirov works in Leningrad reported that new turners could stay on the job for months without machining a single part; in some cases this was because their machinery was out of service and under repair, but in others shop management had simply ignored them and not given them any work to do. According to the paper some of these workers were earning as little as 30 rubles a month.[56] In the Karaganda coal fields new miners were put on hauling jobs or shovelling snow. One young tunneller complained that on some days they would sit for an entire shift with nothing to do. 'We're earning 10 kopeks a day, often we don't eat for whole days at a time.'[57] The problem was perhaps worst in construction,

---

[52] GARF, f. 7676, op. 11, d. 642, l. 9.

[53] In December 1948 roughly a third of all miners did not fulfil their norms; in December 1949 (after norms in the industry had been lowered in an effort to redress the problem of low earnings), about a quarter of young workers were still underfulfilling (GARF, f. 7416, op. 7, d. 476, l. 125; RGASPI, f. 17, op. 131, d. 53, l. 160). In engineering, an industry in which workers traditionally depended on norms being kept slack in order to permit them to earn a relatively modest wage, just over 5 per cent of workers did not fulfil their norms in mid-1947. In 1951 – after norms had been substantially raised – approximately 5 per cent of young workers in the major engineering centres such as Khar'kov and Leningrad were underfulfilling (GARF, f. 7676, op. 16, d. 170, l. 112; TsKhDMO, f. 1, op. 2, d. 313, l. 172).

[54] TsKhDMO, f. 1, op. 3, d. 509, l. 78; op. 4, d. 961, l. 41; op. 2, d. 313, l. 212.

[55] GARF, f. 7676, op. 16, d. 714, l. 6ob.

[56] *Kirovets*, 16 May 1947.

[57] TsKhDMO, f. 1, op. 4, d. 1070, l. 18. At the above-cited engineering works (n. 55) an interesting dispute broke out at a trade union meeting between a line manager, who blamed young workers' low wages on their poor discipline, and the head of the factory's

in which labour shortages and shortages of materials forced managers to move workers from job to job according to priorities and the availability of supplies. The most common complaint was that young workers allegedly trained in skilled construction trades were used as navvies; but there were also instances where they were shifted to other skilled jobs, such as carpentry or brick-laying, which they had not been trained to do. In either case earnings suffered.[58] Yet even where workers were employed at their proper trade this did not guarantee them decent pay. In 1952 the Komsomol complained that new workers coming out of Labour Reserve schools were often given old, poorly functioning equipment or poor-quality cutting tools, and were last in line when foremen and shop chiefs distributed job assignments. It is not surprising that older, more strategically placed workers should be given the best jobs, but it did mean that a certain minority of young workers could stay stuck in the lowest wage and skill grades for years.[59]

Low wages were only one dimension of young workers' plight. Equally as important, if not more so, in determining their attitudes and reactions were their general living conditions. These can only be described as gruesome and affected the vast majority of young workers, high and low earners alike. Almost all of them lived in dormitories. Those who did not were either still being housed in earthen huts or in rooms in private flats contracted by their enterprises. In both cases the conditions were even worse than in the dormitories, although that might be difficult to believe.

The conditions in young workers' dormitories were virtually identical to those described in chapter 3, when we examined the general housing situation, and in the earlier section of this chapter on Labour Reserve students. Conditions were worst in cities like Minsk, Leningrad, and Stalingrad, which had suffered huge destruction of their housing stock during the war. A Komsomol report on young workers' housing at motor vehicle factories in Minsk during late 1946 was typical. Some workers were still living in tents or directly in factory production shops because not even dormitory space was available. The dormitories themselves were crowded, had little furniture, and had not been made ready for the winter: internal window frames were not glazed; door frames had not been insulated; residents had no firewood; and in any case the stoves in many of the buildings were not working. Bed linen was dirty, and rarely laundered. There were acute shortages of clothing and shoes. Moreover, enterprises had provided no medical care, so that workers with serious diseases like

Housing and Communal Services Department, who retorted that many of them were too hungry to show up for work (GARF, f. 7676, op. 16, d. 714, l. 6ob.).
[58] *Trud*, 16 July 1949; TsGAIPD, f. 2600, op. 3, d. 6, l. 46–8.
[59] TsKhDMO, f. 1, op. 2, d. 313, l. 23, 59–60.

typhus, dysentery, and scarlatina were receiving no treatment.[60] At major factories in Leningrad dormitories lacked electric light bulbs, drying rooms for drying clothes, and even washbasins and taps (it was routine for an entire dormitory to have just one sink or tap to serve all its residents). Many buildings were unheated and windows and doors were unprotected against the winter cold. A chronic shortage of clocks and radios meant that workers did not always know when they had to wake up in the morning and leave for work.[61] At the Stalingrad tractor factory as late as November 1949 the dormitories were housing as many as ten or twenty people in a room, with single youngsters and young families all thrown in together. Residents had nowhere to prepare food, nor even to hang up their clothes. Blankets and mattresses were threadbare. For such privileged accommodation young workers would pay 38 rubles a month, which for many was probably about 10 per cent of their total earnings.[62] At every one of these enterprises workers had to cope with intense boredom during their non-working hours. Recreational facilities were minimal, and it was common for dormitory 'Red Corners' to have no books, newspapers, or musical instruments.

By 1949 the situation was clearly beginning to improve, but even then a VTsSPS report to Beria estimated that 15 per cent of young coal miners were still living in what it euphemistically called 'unsatisfactory' conditions.[63] In late 1951 a number of aviation and weapons factories in Kuibyshev and Kuibyshev oblast' (a region undergoing rapid expansion and industrial construction) were housing young Labour Reserve graduates in dormitories and barracks every bit as bad as those inhabited by young coal miners right after the war.[64] The point of this discussion is not, however, to assemble a catalogue of horror stories, but to help explain the huge problems the regime faced trying to socialize young workers. The most dramatic expression of this problem was the high rate of labour turnover, including illegal quitting, among young workers. It was most pronounced in coal mining, construction, and iron and steel, especially during 1946 and 1947, but unlike turnover among adults, showed a far less pronounced decline as wages and living conditions improved. I discuss this topic in detail in chapter 5, but I should note here that the flight of young workers made it very difficult for enterprises to develop what they called a permanent 'cadre' of experienced, skilled workers, even as late as 1950 and 1951.

---

[60] TsKhDMO, f. 1, op. 3, d. 479, l. 120–2.
[61] *Elektrosila*, 26 August 1946; *Kabel'shchik* (Sevkabel'), 20 September 1946, 14 February 1948; *Krasnyi treugol'nik*, 30 November 1946, 12 September, 3 October 1947, 9 April 1948; *Kirovets*, 21 March, 30 May 1947.
[62] TsKhDMO, f. 1, op. 2, d. 272, l. 108–9. [63] RGASPI, f. 17, op. 131, d. 53, l. 161.
[64] TsKhDMO, f. 1, op. 2, d. 313, l. 235.

Attitudes and reactions

No one has yet made a detailed analysis of workers' attitudes during the postwar period. Thanks to Elena Zubkova's studies of popular opinion, as well as other archive reports, we know that the hardships of these years provoked bitter and often quite militant expressions of discontent, but we have no way of determining how prevalent or representative these were of workers as a whole. The same is true of young workers, and of young people in general. If we are to gauge their reaction to the conditions described this has to be done indirectly, by piecing together various fragments of qualitative evidence.

The high rates of labour turnover and flight from the Labour Reserve schools tell us something of the despair which beset a large minority. There were other signs of this as well. The archives cite a few cases of suicides by young workers, at least some of which were directly related to their extreme poverty and lack of housing.[65] It is, of course, difficult to take these examples on their own as a barometer of young workers' attitudes. For one thing, we do not know how common suicide was as a social phenomenon; for another, we do not know the personal histories of the victims and whether or not they might have taken their own lives under less stressful circumstances. But it would be equally wrong to be agnostic on the subject. At one large Moscow engineering works a clutch of suicides and attempted suicides in late 1949 was a signal of more generalized discontent among the factory's young workers which the procuracy found so alarming that it recommended the immediate removal of the director.[66]

---

[65] RGASPI, f. 17, op. 125, d. 596, l. 57; Zima, pp. 85–6; TsKhDMO, f. 1, op. 4, d. 1398, l. 49, 184–5; GARF, f. 8131, op. 29, d. 207, l. 14. One of the saddest cases was that of a young woman worker at the Andreev iron and steel works in Taganrog. She and her husband had a small baby but because of the housing shortage were forced to live in separate dormitories. They had repeatedly, but unsuccessfully, petitioned the factory authorities for somewhere to live. Unable to obtain a place in the creche for the child, she tried to bring the baby to work, but was barred at the gates by the factory guards. So she developed a system whereby she would pass the baby to other women through a fence, and then herself go back around and enter through the main gate. Finally, after coming up against one brick wall after another, she killed herself. This same report cites two other suicides by young workers – both males – at the same factory (TsKhDMO, f. 1, op. 4, d. 905, l. 159–60).

[66] GARF, f. 8131, op. 37, d. 4772, l. 264–5. The enterprise was the Moscow Frezer milling-machine factory. In October 1949 two women killed themselves and a third attempted to do so by drinking solutions of potassium nitrate. All were earning barely 300 to 400 rubles a month, of which they lost so much in deductions for back rent, fines, and 'pledges' to the compulsory state loan that they had barely 100 to 200 rubles left to live on. Investigating the deaths, the Moscow Procuracy found that 40 per cent of the 4,000-strong workforce were young workers, and 10 per cent of these were earning similar below-subsistence wages. When they visited the dormitories they found the mood to be 'agitated' and the

The Komsomol made periodic complaints about discipline problems among school students, Labour Reserve school trainees, and young workers, some of which were clearly of a serious nature. A report on Moscow schools in 1949 referred to knife fights between gangs, and to pupils taking part in violent crimes.[67] At the Magnitostroi construction trust in Magnitogorsk there were mass brawls among youths living in the dormitories and violent attacks on dormitory commandants.[68] But much of the alleged indiscipline would be found in urban schools in any society with large-scale poverty. Other incidents amounted to little more than school-age pranks and a reflection of the general rebellion of the young against those in authority.[69] We should bear in mind that the concept of 'poor discipline' was also somewhat relative and would be applied to card-playing or pre-marital sex, a fact which said more about the puritanical conservatism of Stalinism than about the behaviour of the young.[70]

The responses of young workers were occasionally more organized and purposeful. In 1948 a group of FZO graduates, mobilized to work on a construction site in Georgia, struck for three days in protest at the clearly insulting behaviour of management after two members of their group were killed in an accident.[71] Other forms of protest were more passive, for example, listening to Western radio broadcasts in the dormitories.[72]

Perhaps the most telling evidence of young workers' apathy is the extraordinary difficulty which the Komsomol had recruiting and retaining members in the factories, and of persuading those who did join to take any kind of active part in Komsomol activities. One sign of this was the large number of members who did not pay their membership dues. In Khar'kov in 1947 fewer than a third of worker-members paid on time. At the Stalingrad tractor factory in late 1949 the figure was slightly better at 60 per cent. At the two large engineering works in Novosibirsk (Sibsel'mash and the V. P. Chkalov factory) in 1952 it was well under half.[73] Many of those in arrears no doubt were simply too poor to pay, as some of the reports make clear. Some of the others had actually left the enterprises in question but were still on the Komsomol books. For the majority, however, this was a sign of their basic indifference to and

workers verbally attacked the director right to his face. This prompted the procuracy to conclude that the director had lost all authority at the plant and would have to go.
[67] TsKhDMO, f. 1, op. 4, d. 1172, l. 220–2.
[68] TsKhDMO, f. 1, op. 2, d. 285, l. 345.
[69] See, for example, the report on school students and Labour Reserve trainees in Irkutsk oblast' in 1950, TsKhDMO, f. 1, op. 4, d. 1398, l. 5–10, 27–8.
[70] TsKhDMO, f. 1, op. 2, d. 313, l. 113.   [71] RGAE, f. 8592, op. 2, d. 305, l. 44.
[72] RGASPI, f. 17, op. 132, d. 114, l. 175.
[73] TsKhDMO, f. 1, op. 3, d. 509, l. 81; op. 2, d. 272, l. 97–8, 112; d. 313, l. 115–16.

disinterest in official politics and the institutions which the regime had created to 'mobilize' them.

Any doubt about this should be dispelled by looking at recruitment. Throughout heavy industry Komsomol organizations experienced a crisis of recruitment and retention at least up until 1949, if not beyond. In discussing this phenomenon we should be clear that this was something quite different from the fall in Party membership after the war, which was part of a deliberate policy by the leadership. The crisis within Komsomol ranks was not planned and was certainly not desired, since it undermined the one institution through which the regime could hope to rebuild its credibility among the young and to counter the alienation produced by their disastrous material situation. Let us look at some of the evidence in more detail.

In Kuibyshev oblast' the worker component of Komsomol membership fell from 32 per cent in January 1947 to 27 per cent two years later. Between 40 and 50 per cent of shop organizations did not recruit a single member through all of 1948; other factories recruited, but had more members leave than they took in. An almost identical picture emerged in Omsk, where the worker membership of the Komsomol fell from 44 per cent to 39 per cent in just one year; here, too, some industrial enterprises were actually losing members. In Leningrad the story was somewhat different: factory Komsomol organizations were growing, but most of the increase within each enterprise was confined to a small handful of shops or sections; growth in the majority of shops was stagnant. Officials were quite open in their explanation of this development: young workers simply did not view the Komsomol as reflecting their interests or aspirations. An even more dramatic situation was reported in Nizhnii Tagil, an iron and steel town with 10,000 young workers, a mere 240 of whom joined the Komsomol during the first ten months of 1949.[74]

The most clear-cut documentation of this trend was in Sverdlovsk and Sverdlovsk oblast'. In 1949 the oblast' had 47,000 young engineering workers, but managed to recruit just 552 new Komsomol members. Its coal enterprises showed a net growth of just ninety-two people between January and June. At Uralmash, the Komsomol membership fell by a third between January 1948 and November 1949.[75] The figures for the

[74] TsKhDMO, f. 1, op. 2, d. 267, l. 95–6, 99–101, 116, 148. The Komsomol organization at the Stalingrad tractor factory showed the same pattern. It took in a grand total of 276 people during all of 1949; between 80 and 90 per cent of its shop organizations showed no overall growth, and nearly a quarter of them recruited no one at all (TsKhDMO, f. 1, op. 2, d. 272, l. 112).
[75] TsKhDMO, f. 1, op. 2, d. 267, 66–8; d. 272, l. 46–7. The Urals coach factory (Uralvagonzavod) showed the same pattern. From 1 January 1947 to November 1949 its Komsomol membership fell from 3,701 to 2,780 (ibid., d. 272, l. 45).

oblast' as a whole are far more revealing. Its overall Komsomol membership, which included industry, agriculture, and all levels of education, fell from 18,602 in early 1945 to 8,465 at the end of 1947. It then recovered to 15,630 members at the end of 1948, before collapsing back to 9,400 members by November 1949. The percentage of workers in the Komsomol followed an identical pattern. In early 1945 workers were 42 per cent of members; this dropped steadily, to a low point of 15.6 per cent at the close of 1947. It then rose back to 24.5 per cent by November 1949. This increase was partially offset, however, by a sharp decline in membership among Labour Reserve school students. Ironically, this reached its highest level (23.5 per cent) in the second half of 1947, when factory membership was at its lowest, but then fell to a mere 11.1 per cent in November 1949.[76]

The year 1949 appears to have been the nadir of the Komsomol's fortunes. After that year we have detailed data only for the engineering industry, which shows a leap from 423,000 members in 1949 to 600,000 in 1951. There are a number of possible reasons for the recovery. The gradual improvement in the standard of living may have lessened the overt or latent hostility of young workers towards the Communist Party. Nearly half the growth in Komsomol membership in engineering occurred in just three branches of military industry – weapons, aviation, and shipbuilding – and it is possible that workers in these enterprises were put under considerable pressure to join, especially as the international situation deteriorated. However, all branches of engineering showed at least some increase, and so this speculation, even if it is correct, can explain only part of the phenomenon.

The one factor which is unlikely to have been behind the rise in Komsomol membership is the greater effectiveness of its propaganda apparatus and political education. On the contrary, these turn out to have been incredibly weak, thus presenting the regime with a serious political problem.

We need to treat 'political education' as more than just the formal efforts of agitators and activists to instruct workers in official doctrine. For young workers in particular the way they used their leisure time had an important bearing on their ideas and attitudes. Here we see a sharp contrast between the objectives of the regime and what actually took place on the ground. The goal, of course, was to monopolize leisure and cultural activities through a host of facilities. Red Corners in dormitories were supposed to be well stocked with newspapers and books. Dormitory recreation rooms were to be well equipped with board games

[76] TsKhDMO, f. 1, op. 2, d. 272, l. 66.

and musical instruments (card playing, by contrast, was severely frowned upon and taken as a sign of weak 'discipline'). Within the factory, trade union and Komsomol organizations were to organize amateur cultural circles (music, drama, literature), physical education, and sports. All the social organizations were to hold regular film showings, as well as lectures and readings on politics and current events.

The actual delivery of these activities proved far more difficult, especially in the context of the postwar economy. I have already noted the enforced boredom to which young workers were condemned in their dormitories. They found few distractions outside them either. Factories in rural areas had tremendous difficulties putting on film showings, for example. The large porcelain factory in Zhitomir oblast' in Ukraine was located in a village which even as late as 1950 had no electricity. Its weekly film showing depended on the factory being able to provide electrical current from its own makeshift sources: an old tank engine and an engine taken out of a disused locomotive.[77] Oil towns in Bashkiriya and Tatariya had problems obtaining films and spare parts for their projectors; both projectors and films were forever breaking and film screenings became an arduous process – so taxing, in fact, that the locals developed a saying, 'If you want to suffer, go to the movies.'[78] But the problems were not due simply to remoteness. The currency reform of December 1947, which also ended rationing and put state prices on a commercial basis, had the unanticipated effect of driving workers away from film showings and other recreational activities. The iron and steel workers' trade union reported that attendance at films and dances had fallen precipitously because workers now found the prices too high, while taxes imposed on workers' clubs during the war had made it impossible for many of them to stay open.[79] It appears that clubs were often the last buildings to be repaired when factories undertook expansion or reconstruction. In the Kirov district of Leningrad, which housed the Kirov works and a number of other large-scale enterprises, half the clubs were still closed for repair in the middle of 1950. Virtually the only activities they organized were dances, which given the anti-Western and anti-'cosmopolitan' (and largely anti-Semitic) campaigns of the time, put them foul of official policy. There was, however, more to this discussion than meets the eye, for the issue was not simply the lack of facilities, but the fact that even where events did take place the Komsomol played a limited role in organizing

---

[77] Interview with M.Z., a former line manager at the factory, 6 January 1997.
[78] RGASPI, f. 17, op. 125, d. 421, l. 36–8. This account is from 1946, right after the war. For a similar report on film showings in Azerbaijan in 1950, see TsKhDMO, f. 1, op. 2, d. 285, l. 451–2.
[79] RGASPI, f. 17, op. 125, d. 596, l. 57, 59.

them or controlling their content. On the contrary, young people were left to their own devices. And while the complaints about fighting, heavy drinking, and what we might call 'disorderly conduct' no doubt had some basis (as they would with any large group of young people), the authorities clearly distrusted, if not feared, the fact that the young used their own initiative to fill the gap left by the official organizations.[80]

The most serious shortcoming, however, was in the field of political education itself. The authorities were quite paranoid about young people being exposed to 'alien' political influences. The fact that enterprise managers in coal mining and construction allowed young workers to work alongside – and sometimes under the supervision of – German prisoners of war and MVD prisoners caused no small amount of consternation.[81] So, too, did the hiring of people of suspect political backgrounds, such as 'special settlers' (that is, internal exiles) or Soviet citizens repatriated from forced labour in Germany, to work in Labour Reserve schools.[82] The main cause for concern, however, was the failure of factory Komsomol and Party organizations to carry out proper instruction – itself a product of the fact that those responsible for this work themselves had a poor knowledge of the line they were supposed to put across.

The problem did not affect young workers alone, of course. Political education meetings were a rarity even in large enterprises. The Komsomol organization at the Stalingrad tractor factory, which in late 1949 employed 8,300 young workers, was said to do almost nothing by way of political education: they organized political education circles, but few young workers actually attended; agitators rarely, if ever, visited the dormitories.[83] A report to Suslov on political work in Leningrad noted, 'A significant portion of workers and clerical employees in industrial enterprises is completely untouched by any political influence and has a rather weak knowledge of current events. Political education among women and youth is especially poor.'[84] Merely holding meetings, however, did not

---

[80] TsKhDMO, f. 1, op. 2, d. 285, l. 456–8, 460, 463–4. The Kirov works itself was by way of exception credited with having a well-structured system of clubs and leisure activities, but even here the Komsomol was accused of exercising little oversight over them or not finding people to run them. The complaints about drunkenness should not be taken lightly. Violence at dance and film evenings for young railway workers appears to have been a serious problem, although in the climate of 1950 the Komsomol leadership shifted the blame for this on to club managers (whom it also accused of exaggerating the numbers involved) and on to the trade unions, which had failed to organize political education to counter such behaviour (l. 193–8).
[81] TsKhDMO, f. 1, op. 3, d. 509, l. 97, 110; op. 4, d. 961, l. 43.
[82] TsKhDMO, f. 1, op. 4, d. 1100, l. 89.
[83] TsKhDMO, f. 1, op. 2, d. 272, l. 103, 106, 109.
[84] RGASPI, f. 17, op. 132, d. 114, l. 159–60. This report has to be treated with some caution, since it was prepared in 1949, at the time of the purge of the Leningrad Party

solve the problem. Party officials were being quite candid when they cautioned against enlisting technical specialists (ITR) for educational work at Magnitogorsk, because 'their agitation among workers is unintelligible, since they earn several times more than workers'.[85] Komsomol organizations in Tatariya, Bashkiriya, and Azerbaijan came up against the problem that they conducted all of their political work in Russian, which many workers in these regions did not speak.[86] Even when language (in the broadest sense of the word) was not an obstacle, meetings were simply boring. The report just cited about Azerbaijan noted that Komsomol meetings did little more than discuss the decisions of higher bodies and attracted few non-members.[87] Meetings in Kuibyshev oblast' were said to be limited to shop superintendents making speeches about production results.[88]

Most basic of all, however, was the simple fact that the 'educators' were themselves badly educated. This was especially – but by no means exclusively – true of the Labour Reserve schools, where school heads and teachers had little or no training in pedagogy, very often only an incomplete education, and virtually no knowledge of political affairs. At one FZO school in Voroshilovgrad oblast' students could not even recognize portraits of Marx, Engels, Lenin, or Stalin. Students at another school could not find the USSR on a map. Labour Reserve students in the Kizel coal fields of Molotov oblast' had never heard of the Marshall Plan and knew nothing about Stalin's (fictitious) 'role' in overthrowing tsarism in February 1917.[89] Given that the perpetuation of such nonsense was integral to sustaining the Stalin myth, the failure to inculcate it had potentially serious consequences for the regime's legitimacy.[90] Of course not all 'miseducation' was the fault of the instructors. One lecturer at a construction site in Irkutsk was attacked in 1950 for 'committing the most heinous blunder, affirming the fabrication of the American press that the Soviet Union had exploded an atomic bomb'.[91]

organization; but its description of political work inside the factories is consistent with both earlier and later accounts from other regions. See, for example, similar reports on the lack of political education at enterprises in Kuibyshev oblast' (*ibid.*, l. 180); in the iron and steel industry (RGASPI, f. 17, op. 125, d. 596, l. 58); coal mining (*ibid.*, op. 131, d. 53, l. 162); and in Khar'kov (TsKhDMO, f. 1, op. 3, d. 509, l. 80).

[85] RGASPI, f. 17, op. 125, d. 596, l. 58.
[86] RGASPI, f. 17, op. 125, d. 421, l. 35; TsKhDMO, f. 1, op. 2, d. 285, l. 443.
[87] TsKhDMO, f. 1, op. 2, d. 285, l. 442.   [88] RGASPI, f. 17, op. 132, d. 114, l. 180.
[89] TsKhDMO, f. 1, op. 4, d. 1100, l. 67–70, 86–7.
[90] A list of the officially approved themes for political education meetings at the Stalingrad tractor factory may help explain why Komsomol activists found it so hard to persuade young workers to attend: the life and activities of Lenin and Stalin; the statutes and programme of the Komsomol; Soviet patriotism; the Communist attitude to labour; and the moral make-up of the young Soviet person (TsKhDMO, f. 17, op. 2, d. 272, l. 106).
[91] TsKhDMO, f. 1, op. 4, d. 1398, l. 48.

The deficiencies in political education were made all the more intractable by the fact that Komsomol members themselves took little part in it. The Komsomol Central Committee lamented in 1948, 'A significant proportion of Komsomol members are not drawn into political study. Many *komsomol'tsy* have repeatedly joined circles and then abandoned them, without completing the programme of study.'[92] A large minority of its industrial members did not even go through the motion of participating in study circles, but simply ignored them. In the words of the newspaper at the motor vehicle and tractor parts factory in Kuibyshev, many of the leading Komsomol activists were 'politically illiterate'.[93]

Marginalized youth

One inevitable consequence of the traumatic upheavals which periodically shook late tsarist and Soviet society – World War I, the Civil War, collectivization, the terror of 1936–8, and World War II – was the mass displacement of children. The orphans, the homeless (*besprizorniki*), or the abandoned and neglected (*beznadzornye*) together constituted an army of children and adolescents whose numbers vastly outstripped the capacity of the Soviet state to control and care for them. The categories were by no means distinct and clear cut. Children orphaned or abandoned during collectivization, when their parents were deported or shot, might be taken in by relatives or friends. Where possible, the state would try to place them in children's homes or with foster parents. But this still left a large number of children who had no parents, who had become separated from them, or whose parents could not or would not look after them. Many of them roamed the country, moving from one city to another, and lived a large part of their lives as vagabonds on the railways. They lived on petty crime and begging, sometimes on the instructions of their parents. According to Wendy Goldman, as industrialization and collectivization swelled the ranks of these displaced children the Stalinist state increasingly opted for strictly authoritarian solutions. The children were rounded up in so-called collection–distribution stations, the job of which it was to farm them out to children's homes, labour colonies, or reform schools. Because the capacity of the homes, schools, and colonies was inadequate to cope with the large numbers, the temporary reception centres themselves became more or less permanent places of imprisonment. In 1935 the government removed some of the strain on resources

---

[92] TsKhDMO, f. 1, op. 2, d. 263, l. 108.
[93] *Stalinets* (Kuibyshev), 29 March 1951. See also the reports on the Karaganda coal fields (TsKhDMO, f. 1, op. 4, d. 1070, l. 19–20) and engineering enterprises in Novosibirsk (TsKhDMO, f. 1, op. 2, d. 313, l. 110–11).

by lowering the age at which juveniles would be tried as adults, to just twelve years. Thus the surplus waifs were moved directly into the Gulag system.[94] By 1940 juveniles under the age of eighteen made up 1.2 per cent of the Gulag population.[95]

The war, of course, vastly swelled the numbers of both orphans and wandering *besprizorniki* and *beznadzornye*. In 1943 the state set up special labour colonies to deal with them and with those juveniles in the care of their own parents who had been picked up for petty crime. This system was still in place when the war ended. However, the ranks of the displaced were to grow still further during the famine, which created a new subgeneration of orphans. In addition, some foster parents and even natural parents appealed to the authorities to assume responsibility for their children since they no longer could afford to do so.[96] Many more children hit the roads spontaneously in a quest for survival.

The children's homes catered for those children who were too young to enter vocational training or employment. Unlike the reception–distribution centres and children's colonies, which were managed by the MVD, the children's homes came under the USSR Ministry of Education. Conditions in the homes were difficult at best, and in some cases catastrophic. Not all survivors of the homes would necessarily recall them that way, and for good reason; if nothing else, the homes saved them from starvation or a life on the streets, and at the very least provided them with shelter and clothing. Very probably the majority of the homes had conscientious staff who tried their best to protect the children given the extraordinarily meagre resources that were available. Especially during the early recovery years, the homes were dreadfully overcrowded and many of their buildings were unfit for habitation.[97] The famine took a terrible toll on health and mortality, since, as in the dormitories of workers and Labour Reserve students, it compounded already existing problems caused by poor sanitation and inadequate facilities. When the government cut food allocations after September 1946, the children's homes had to shoulder a share of the burden. Homes in rural districts reported receiving no bread for two to three weeks at a time, and in extreme cases sent their wards out to beg.[98]

[94] Goldman, pp. 304–27.   [95] Bacon, p. 151.   [96] Zima, pp. 81–2.
[97] The archives contain at least three comprehensive studies of the state of children's homes during 1946–8. In early 1947 Zhdanov commissioned a 'discussion' on the topic, with detailed reports from six oblasti (Stalingrad, Smolensk, Kursk, Kalinin, Dnepropetrovsk, and Kaluga) and two autonomous republics (Bashkiriya and the Chuvash republic). The reports are in RGASPI, f. 17, op. 125, d. 559. In 1948, VTsSPS sponsored a conference of personnel in pre-school establishments and children's homes, in GARF, f. 5451, op. 26, d. 848. Also in 1948 the Ministry of State Control issued a devastating report on the homes, in RGASPI, f. 17, op. 121, d. 709, l. 70–96.
[98] RGASPI, f. 17, op. 125, d. 559, l. 125.

In Saratov city, and not just the oblast', staff charged that substandard food supplies were directly responsible for the children's declining health.[99] Disease, in fact, was rife almost everywhere, with tuberculosis, trachoma, typhus, typhoid fever, fungal infections, malaria, and even syphilis frequently cited. Some homes, especially, but not exclusively, in the famine regions, reported large numbers of deaths due to malnutrition and related ailments. Baby homes in Estonia lost a third of all their babies during 1947.[100] The head of the trade union for children's home staff drew a very clear connection between the homes' difficulties and the new economic priorities: 'Executive committees feel that they have to concern themselves with grain deliveries, procurements, and economic matters, and have slackened their attention towards inspecting how the children in the children's homes are living.' In defence of her accusation she cited the case of Ryazan' oblast', where during the war district officials had been required by law to visit the homes once a month. Now they might go 'years' without making an inspection, and simply had no idea what was going on.[101]

The homes themselves were badly short of qualified staff. Shortages clearly compelled local authorities to hire directors, teachers, and medical personnel who simply were not qualified to do their jobs. The suffering this could cause was immense. One reason for high rates of illness, morbidity, and mortality was the fact that directors or other employees sometimes embezzled funds from the homes' food budgets.[102] Another was the neglect or incompetence of medical personnel. Homes in rural districts might go months without a single visit by a doctor.[103] In other cases directors passed out jobs as doctors or nurses to friends, who collected their salaries but did no work. This type of cronyism also led to reports of physical abuse, including sexual attacks or molestation of children by staff.[104]

The problems which the orphans and other wards in children's homes faced is in many ways peripheral to the topic of this chapter, and in any case requires much more research. What is most relevant here is that the homes eventually became a major supplier of labour power to the Labour

[99] GARF, f. 5451, op. 26, d. 848, l. 92.
[100] RGASPI, f. 17, op. 121, d. 709, l. 88–9, 92–6.
[101] GARF, f. 5451, op. 26, d. 848, l. 9, 11.
[102] GARF, f. 5451, op. 26, d. 848, l. 139; RGASPI, f. 17, op. 125, d. 559, l. 125.
[103] RGASPI, f. 17, op. 125, d. 559, l. 124–5.
[104] GARF, f. 5451, op. 26, d. 848, l. 36–7, 97–103. If such crimes were discovered, the penalties could be severe. One director received twenty-five years in a labour camp for raping a girl ward, although it is significant that the victim had a difficult time finding anyone to hear her complaint because of a conspiracy by the home's other staff to cover it up (*ibid.*, l. 36–7). Most reports of abuse seem to have gone unpunished, however, since the culprits managed to abscond before any action could be taken against them.

Reserve system. At first their role was very small. During 1946 and 1947 the homes supplied just under 26,000 students to the Labour Reserve schools, out of an intake during those two years of almost 2,000,000. Nearly 90 per cent went to the two-year trade schools which trained skilled workers.[105] The industrial ministries were also supposed to play a role in job placement by taking on quotas of children's home residents and even setting up homes themselves. The ministries, however, were extremely reluctant to fulfil even the meagre quotas which the USSR Council of Ministers had given them: in 1947 they offered jobs to just 11,500 teenagers, against a target of 17,000, and provided homes for another 6,900. In addition, in 1947 the Ministry of Labour Reserves was instructed to create a network of 100 trade and agricultural schools, designed specifically to train orphaned teenagers. The schools were to take in 31,000 pupils, but by mid-1948 had not achieved even a third of that target.[106] In 1949 this situation began to change markedly. As the young people orphaned by the war reached their teenage years, the children's homes began to feed ever larger numbers into the Labour Reserve schools, the overwhelming proportion into the two-year trade schools. In 1950, 1951, and 1952 they accounted for 23 per cent, 30 per cent, and 25 per cent respectively of the intake into the trade schools (RU, ZhU, and the special schools created in 1947).[107] It seems clear from these data that wards in the homes were given special priority for access to the trade schools, where they would be trained for the more skilled (and better-paying) occupations and where living conditions were immeasurably better than in the FZO. One could perhaps argue that, in light of the traumas to which the war and their postwar conditions had subjected them, they were judged to have merited some form of privileged treatment.

It may seem perverse to argue that the wards in children's homes were a favoured stratum, but compared to the overall population of children on the margins of society this may have been the case. Responsibility for dealing with the *besprizorniki* and *beznadzornye* – whom for the sake of simplicity I shall group together under a more general term of 'displaced' or abandoned – fell to the MVD, in the first instance, the local police, or militia. The latter, with the help of Party and Komsomol activists, as well as school teachers, routinely rounded up stray children from the

---

[105] GARF, f. 9507, op. 2, d. 418, l. 3, and d. 420, l. 6, 14.

[106] RGASPI, f. 17, op. 121, d. 709, l. 71, 81.

[107] The absolute figures were: 1950 – 36,828 students, of whom 33,779 went to the trade schools; 1951 – 45,993 students, of whom 42,619 went to trade schools; 1952 – 44,602 students, of whom 36,693 went to trade schools (GARF, f. 9507, op. 2, d. 423, l. 3, 47; d. 424, l. 2, 4; d. 425, l. 8). As of January 1950 there were 671,000 wards in children's homes throughout the USSR; those entering trade schools in that year therefore represented 5 per cent of the total children's home population (TsKhDMO, f. 1, op. 2, d. 285, l. 215).

streets and railway stations. Many towns had a curfew for juveniles, so that anyone caught out of doors after hours was likely to be picked up. The first port of call was the 'Children's Room' of a local police station. If the child lived locally with parents or a guardian, the latter would be summoned to take him or her away, together with a warning that if the child was picked up again in the future the adults would be fined. The fines were not small: a report from Latvia states that the average fine in 1948 was between 45 and 50 rubles. In theory the militia were to take family circumstances into account, but the Latvia survey cites cases where low-paid single mothers earning 250 rubles a month were fined as much as 100 rubles.[108]

A different fate awaited those children who had drifted in from other regions, who were homeless, or for whom a responsible guardian could not be traced. They would go to the reception–distribution centres, where in theory they were to be held on a strictly short-term basis until a permanent place for them could be found. This could be in a children's home, a Labour Reserve school, direct mobilization to a job in industry or agriculture, or to one of the two types of detention camps run by the MVD – a Children's Labour-Education Colony for those who had committed no crime or only petty offences, or to a Children's Labour Colony for juvenile criminals.

The size of this displaced or rootless juvenile population was truly enormous. Between mid-1943 and November 1947 the system processed roughly 1,380,000 children: 394,000 were returned to their parents; 506,000 were sent to children's homes; 241,000 were sent to jobs in industry or agriculture; 153,000 were sent to Labour Reserve schools; and 86,500 were sent to either Labour-Education or Labour Colonies. At least half a million of this total were orphans.[109] We can cast some doubts on the accuracy of these figures, which come from the MVD, insofar as many of these children would have been picked up several times running, each time either being released by the local militia or escaping. The claim that they despatched 153,000 teenagers to Labour Reserve schools (an average of just under 40,000 a year) also tells us something about the real procedures followed by the police, as opposed to the formal regulations. The Ministry of Labour Reserves noted in its own records (which, as we have seen, were also none too precise) that during 1947 it received just 7,880 students from reception–distribution centres.[110] The size of this discrepancy is quite startling. Although some of it may be due to the

[108] GARF, f. 8131, op. 37, d. 4787, l. 49–54.
[109] GARF, f. 9401, op. 2, d. 168, l. 68–75; d. 171, l. 228–30. The system had processed about 1 million children up through 31 December 1946, including 471,000 orphans; the 1947 report does not give a figure for orphans.
[110] GARF, f. 9507, op. 2, d. 418, l. 3.

MVD inflating its own efficiency, a more logical explanation is that the militia simply short-circuited the rules and sent these juveniles directly from the police station to an FZO without processing them through a reception–distribution centre. If so, this would not have been the only shortcut the police used. The sweeps routinely gathered in youngsters who had a legitimate reason to be out on the streets at the time (including being on their way to work); in Minsk the abuses became so common that in late 1948 the city's procurator had to intervene and place a temporary ban on any more raids.[111]

The militia were no doubt behaving here like any other police force in the world: arbitrarily, with little clear thinking and a predilection for using brute force, all tempered by a desire to minimize its workload and by the application of a modicum of common sense. The system was purely and simply overloaded. The 'children's rooms' and the reception–distribution centres obviously could not cope with the large number of waifs coming into the various urban centres from near and far. Therefore for many such children the police bypassed the entire process and a lot of the paperwork it involved, and simply made the children sign an undertaking that they would leave town within twenty-four hours. Here, too, in their haste and lack of subtlety they tended to net the innocent as well as the guilty, imposing such undertakings on teenagers who had a perfectly legal right to be where they were. The procuracy became profoundly irritated by such abuses, not so much, one suspects, because of the crass violation of legality, but because by letting the kids back out on the streets they carried on with what the USSR's deputy procurator general called 'their besprizornyi lifestyle'.[112]

For those who did not slip through the net and wound up in a Labour-Education Colony, the goal of placing them in a Labour Reserve school proved more elusive than the authorities desired. Those juveniles who had reached age fourteen were especially hard to place. They were too old to go to a children's home and too young for an FZO, but because they tended overwhelmingly to have poor education the RU or other trade schools would not take them.[113] Data from the city of Chelyabinsk suggest that the FZO were not overly anxious to have these children either. Of the 867 children who passed through the city's reception–distribution centre between January and mid-May 1948, the militia failed to place a single one in an FZO, and this in a region where the FZO were plagued by high turnover and were desperate for students.[114] It must be said that the

---

[111] GARF, f. 8131, op. 37, d. 4787, l. 118–19.
[112] GARF, f. 8131, op. 28, d. 598, l. 122. I am grateful to Peter Solomon for making this document available to me.
[113] RGASPI, f. 17, op. 25, d. 559, l. 26.
[114] GARF, f. 8131, op. 37, d. 4156, l. 28. The militia found it almost as difficult to place them directly in employment, finding work for only thirty-four of them.

government itself set up an almost insurmountable obstacle to placing the *besprizorniki* and juvenile offenders in work when it decreed that neither children's homes nor reception–distribution centres could refer children for jobs if they had not already done a course of study in either a Labour Reserve school or one of the new special trade and agricultural schools.[115]

The MVD persistently claimed that conditions in its colonies were good and that they had a thriving economy. Its 1947 report listed fifty-eight Labour-Education Colonies with 20,800 juveniles, and seventy-six Labour Colonies, with 45,300 juveniles sentenced by the People's Courts for various offences. According to the report, inmates – for that is what they were – were taught a trade, and the camps had well-equipped workshops which allowed them to take on a modest production plan and turn out goods of value to the national economy. These in the main were simple items, such as grain sorters, pumps, basic workshop tools, furniture, and shoes.[116] These assertions were a fiction. A series of investigations by the Party Central Committee and the USSR Procuracy fiercely attacked conditions in these camps. A 1946 report commissioned by Zhdanov revealed that the workshops where the children were allegedly to receive vocational training were poorly equipped and the training was so useless that only a tiny minority were able to find jobs after being let out; those with a criminal past soon reverted to crime. Living conditions were dreadful, and the general regime provoked a high number of escapes and a considerable amount of anti-Soviet feeling. Inmates at one Labour-Education Colony in Chkalov oblast' were said to have claimed that the German prisoners of war attached to it treated them better than 'the Bolshies'.[117] A 1948 procuracy investigation into the colonies described what it considered to be a very good installation for girls in Leningrad oblast'. Commenting favourably on the fact that the girls were able to wash once every ten days, it noted with regret that there were not enough shoes for every girl and many suffered injuries to their feet because they had to go around barefoot. Medical and dental provision was totally inadequate, and the colony made only the slightest pretence at providing vocational education: some of the girls did a bit of sewing and knitting, the rest just carried out domestic chores. Four girls attempted suicide and there were two organized demonstrations in which the girls refused to take meals.[118]

If this was the state of one of the better Labour-Education Colonies, conditions at the Labour Colonies for young offenders were, not surprisingly, truly barbaric. The colonies were organized on the principle of

[115] GARF, f. 8131, op. 28, d. 598, l. 66; RGASPI, f. 17, op. 121, d. 709, l. 81.
[116] GARF, f. 9401, op. 2, d. 171, l. 229–30.
[117] RGASPI, f. 17, op. 121, d. 556, l. 122–7.
[118] GARF, f. 8131, op. 37, d. 4156, l. 13–16, 103.

institutional brutality. Staff routinely humiliated and beat the inmates –
euphemistically referred to as 'wards' – and one female teacher openly
bragged, 'We've beaten them, we're still beating them, and we'll go on
beating them.' Inmates were put in solitary confinement for the slightest
violation of regulations; children sent to the colonies for petty offences
were placed together with hardened criminals. Needless to say sexual
abuse of the inmates, either by staff or by other boys, was common.[119]
To a large extent this was the inevitable outcome of the Stalinist anti-
theft laws, which saw numerous children despatched to long sentences
in the colonies for criminals for the mildest of offences – stealing a few
kilograms of onions or potatoes, a single turkey, a few chickens.[120] It
equally was built into the way the MVD managed them. Similar to the
adult labour camps, they would promote groups of inmates to the rank
of 'wards-activists', who were then given responsibility for maintaining
discipline. They 'maintained discipline' in the same way as the MVD
guards, through beatings and intimidation. It was therefore no wonder
that friction between the 'activists' and the other children was high, or
that it sometimes spilled over into open revolts.[121] On the other hand,
no one should romanticize the ordinary inmates. Many were clearly psy-
chopaths, wrecked by the brutalities of their upbringing and survival.
Attacks on other children, including murder, were extremely frequent.
The procuracy reports expressed constant alarm at the lack of leisure
activities which left the inmates little to do except to play cards. This
was not just the normal Stalinist moralizing. The 'stakes' in these card

---

[119] GARF, f. 8131, op. 37, d. 4787, l. 127, 283, 288–94; op. 28, d. 598, l. 19–20.

[120] GARF, f. 8131, op. 37, d. 4787, l. 132–6. Even the MVD recognized the intrinsic
injustice of what was happening. In October 1947, that is, just a few months after the
promulgation of the anti-theft laws, Kruglov appealed to Stalin and Beria to allow the
early release of 26,000 minors sentenced to children's Labour Colonies under these laws.
He noted that, of the 42,888 juveniles in the colonies at that point, 36,685 had been
sent there for petty theft, 29,549 of whom had no previous criminal record; moreover,
Kruglov acknowledged that many of them had been driven to theft by the difficult food
situation which followed the 1946 harvest failure (*ibid.*, f. 9401, op. 2, d. 171, l. 116–18).
We do not know the fate of this proposal, but in February 1948 the USSR Ministry
of Justice issued an instruction that juveniles should no longer be prosecuted under
these laws. This did not end convictions altogether, but the number did fall sharply,
from just under 24,000 convictions during 1947 of those under the age of fifteen, to
8,420 in 1948. Convictions of children aged sixteen and seventeen fell from 67,176 in
1947 to 29,339 in 1948 (Solomon, pp. 432, 435). I should point out that by no means
all juvenile theft was petty; some of it was well organized and involved the robbery of
thousands of rubles in cash or goods from their Labour Reserve schools or enterprises.
By the same token, many young people continued to be sent down for very small crimes
indeed, including one fifteen-year-old who received seven years for stealing eight empty
sacks from a bread factory (GARF, f. 8131, op. 37, d. 4163, l. 173, and d. 4173, l. 3,
22, 233–4).

[121] GARF, f. 8131, op. 37, d. 4156, l. 102–3, 104, 181–2, 185, 219; RGASPI, f. 17,
op. 118, d. 339, l. 65.

games might be a camp building (the winner got to burn it down), some-
body's bread rations, or even another child. In the latter case the winner
murdered the 'stake'.[122]

With conditions in the colonies so transparently appalling, the MVD's
attempts to justify its running of them had little credibility. In November
1948 Kruglov issued a lengthy reply to the procuracy's criticisms. This,
however, provoked a further document from the Central Committee's
Administrative Department (dated March 1949), which rejected
Kruglov's account. It all ended peacefully for the MVD, however. Following a more apologetic statement from the MVD's department in charge
of the 'struggle against *besprizornost'* and *beznadzornost''*, the Central
Committee acknowledged the efforts the MVD had made to improve conditions in the colonies, including the quality of the education.[123] What we
never learn, however, is whether the improvements really did take place.
Given what we know about the Gulag and the MVD's empire in general,
we could be excused for expressing a certain degree of scepticism.

Conclusion

This chapter does not pretend to be a comprehensive study of youth 'so-
cialization'. This would require an analysis of other issues, such as youth
'culture', language, family life, crime, and sexual mores, about which
we still know very little. It is nevertheless my contention that the experiences described were fundamental to the formation of these workers'
consciousness, both as youth and in later adulthood.

My essential argument has been that the environment which young
workers encountered produced a profound alienation from the regime
which the regime itself could do little to counter. It could not (or would
not) improve their living and working conditions; nor did it have any
credible ideology with which it might have neutralized this alienation and
'integrated' them into the Stalinist social system. In assessing this analysis
we have to pay attention to the unique features of this period.

First, the generation of workers about whom we are here speaking
was too young to have fought at the front during World War II. Some
participated in the war effort on the home front as juvenile workers; all
of them suffered the hardships of family separations, starvation or near-
starvation, and the death of loved ones. This is not to argue that they in
no way identified with the regime or admired Stalin once the war was
over, but it does mean that they did not have the strong psychological

---

[122] GARF, f. 8131, op. 37, d. 4156, l. 96, 103, 204–204ob.; d. 4787, l. 289; RGASPI,
f. 17, op. 118, d. 339, l. 66.
[123] These all appear in RGASPI, f. 17, op. 118, d. 339, l. 64–114.

identification with the war and the Soviet victory that their parents or grandparents had, especially the *frontoviki*. After the war they suffered immense deprivation, but were much more weakly integrated by the war experience and its attendant mythologies.

Secondly, many, and probably most, young workers had to suffer these deprivations without the emotional support of their families. While still in the mid-teens – and some as early as age fourteen – they were drafted into the Labour Reserve schools and then mobilized for compulsory labour service in construction, mines, or factories. It is no accident that many of the reports dealing with young workers' flight from Labour Reserve schools and enterprises note their desire to be reunited with their families as one of the causes. I would argue that this isolation heightened the misery, if not the terror, of what they experienced, made it more difficult to cope with, and caused it to leave a more indelible, negative impression on their attitudes and behaviour.

Thirdly, there was a sizeable group of people who did not even have the comfort of knowing that they had families 'back home'. These were the orphans, the homeless, and the abandoned: the famous *besprizorniki* and *beznadzornye*. The fate of these children warrants a much longer discussion than I have provided here, and much more research than I have yet done. Among other issues, it takes us into the much larger question of juvenile crime in the postwar years. Many of these children undoubtedly remained outside mainstream society, but insofar as they did eventually enter employment they, too, brought with them a complex legacy of their childhood years, some of it overtly anti-social or asocial behaviour, but some of it also rooted in a rebelliousness and defiance of authority which must have made it very difficult for the regime to integrate them ideologically.

Fourthly, many of the young workers discussed here came from the countryside and like the peasantry in general harboured strong resentments against Stalin and the Soviet regime. Few would have remembered collectivization or the 1932–3 famine, but they would have heard their parents speak of them. They certainly had their own direct experience of the famine of 1947 and the regime's generalized attack on the peasantry.

In all of these cases young workers were thrown back upon their own resources under the guardianship not of their families or relatives, but of officials of the state: enterprise managers, dormitory commandants, Labour Reserve school foremen, children's home directors, or MVD guards. These were people who in many if not most cases looked upon them as mere objects to be manipulated and exploited.

The question is what the long-term impact of these experiences was on Soviet society. Their affective repercussions I am not qualified to judge, but they must have been considerable. We can, however, venture some informed speculation as to their political legacy. When Stalin died, virtually the entire 'collective' leadership recognized the deep crisis of morale that was affecting Soviet society, and its role in retarding economic performance. The problem of morale affected not just young workers, of course, but everyone. However, given the demographic disruptions caused by the war, the attitudes of young workers assumed critical importance. For them the reality of Stalinism was not terror or heroic sacrifice, but despair and hopelessness. These may have eased as conditions improved, but positive identification with the system was now very difficult. Here was yet another factor blocking the creation of a Stalinist consensus.

5   Labour discipline and criminal law: the futility of repression

One of the most complicated and little-known aspects of the social history of the Soviet Union in the immediate postwar period was the mass flight of workers from enterprises in industry and construction, and of teenage labour trainees from the Labour Reserve schools. One thing that makes the phenomenon so remarkable was that workers and vocational students abandoned their jobs in the face of extraordinarily harsh penalties which had been introduced during the war: five to eight years in a corrective labour camp for workers in defence-related industry and construction; three to ten years in a camp for workers on transport; and one year in a camp for teenage trainees. Western historians writing in the period before access to the archives was possible had already deduced from oblique references by Soviet labour economists that these sanctions, imposed between 1940 and 1943, had not completely eliminated labour turnover in Soviet factories in the years after World War II.[1] However, the scale on which it occurred turns out to have been far larger than anyone had thought. Spontaneous departure was highest in those sectors of the economy – construction, coal mining, and iron and steel – which were at the core of the Stalinist leadership's programme for postwar industrial reconstruction, and threatened it with serious disruption. The other remarkable aspect of this saga is that, despite the very high numbers being caught, convicted, and sentenced to lengthy terms of corrective labour, they represented only a small fraction of all those who illegally abandoned their jobs or vocational studies. The rest found protection in an almost byzantine web of collusion on the part of local (usually rural) officials, which embraced police (militia), district public prosecutors, local soviet and Party leaders, and collective farm chairpersons. Moreover, one of the factors which sustained this collusion was the decidedly ambiguous attitude towards harsh enforcement of the anti-quitting laws on the part of top procuracy officials at all-union and republican level.

---

[1] Fitzpatrick, 'Postwar Soviet Society', p. 141; Davies, 'Reappraisal of Industry', p. 324; Filtzer, *Soviet Workers and De-Stalinization*, p. 37.

The first part of this chapter outlines the legal restrictions on job-changing and absenteeism. It traces the evolution of legal controls on workers' behaviour during the 1930s, the criminalization of job-changing and absenteeism in 1940, the sharp escalation of the criminal penalties during the war, and the eventual relaxation of the laws between 1947 and 1951. The second section analyses labour turnover among workers: its scale in different branches of industry and construction; how it changed over the course of the postwar period; its causes; and the social composition of those who absconded from their jobs. The third section examines the issue of enforcement and non-enforcement of the laws. The fourth section retraces this same discussion as it applies to teenagers in the vocational schools of the Ministry of Labour Reserves. The justification for dealing with them separately is that the laws and the prevailing legal practice governing those who illegally left the Labour Reserve schools differed in quite significant respects from those covering workers already in employment, even if the social dynamics of the process were largely the same. The conclusion draws out the main implications of this discussion for our understanding of postwar Stalinist society.

Labour discipline and the law

In the period leading up to Stalinist industrialization, Soviet industry had been characterized by relatively high levels of labour turnover, absenteeism, and extensive control by workers over the organization and use of their work time. With the collapse of the standard of living and the simultaneous emergence of a near-universal labour shortage during the First Five-Year Plan both turnover and absenteeism increased dramatically. Although the Stalinist regime always lumped the two phenomena together under the rubric of violations of 'labour discipline', the link between them is by no means direct. It is certainly true that employers in most societies which were undergoing rapid industrialization and the large-scale importation of peasants into factories and construction sites came up against the problem of inculcating in their new workers an appropriate culture of work discipline: respect for authority; accurate timekeeping; and long-term commitment to remaining in the same enterprise. In this sense the Soviet Union during Stalinist industrialization exhibited classical historical characteristics. But job-changing was also a rational response to deteriorating material conditions, irrespective of whether workers were old or young, skilled or unskilled, had substantial work experience or were newly arrived from the countryside: unless prevented by family commitments and deep local roots, workers were determined to move to wherever they thought they might find better wages,

housing, or food supplies. Absenteeism was also by no means straightforward. It could, and often did, reflect the lack of a developed industrial
work culture among peasant labourers who brought with them from the
countryside their own concepts of how to organize the workday and the
management of time. But it also reflected a breakdown of managerial
authority at a time when workers had lost their political rights to organize
and press their demands collectively through independent trade unions,
political parties, and mass industrial action. If there was a link between
turnover and absenteeism it was precisely here: that under Stalinism
Soviet workers lost their ability to engage in collective struggle and could
search only for individual solutions to their individual problems. These
'solutions' – moving from one enterprise to another, disregarding stric-
tures on attendance and timekeeping – took the specific form that they
did because of another feature of Stalinist industrialization, namely the
labour shortage, which, by increasing the demand for labour power on
the part of enterprise managers, undermined any potential sanctions they
might apply against ill-disciplined workers, in particular the sanction of
dismissal. On the contrary, if managers were too keen to punish absentees
or 'slackers', the worker could quit, leaving management in an even more
precarious position than before.[2]

During the 1930s the Stalinist regime never found a satisfactory way
of controlling job-changing, other than by waiting for it to subside spontaneously as the standard of living improved. The one major legal step
which it undertook, in November 1932, to curb absenteeism, or *progul*
in Russian, actually ran the risk of making job-changing worse, by stip-
ulating that workers who missed a single day off work were immediately
to be fired from their jobs. This was not as illogical as it might seem: for
dismissal also meant eviction from enterprise housing and loss of ration
entitlements for the worker and his or her family. The regime calculated
that at a time of impending famine access to food and housing would
be its most effective disciplinary weapon. Even in December 1938, when
labour turnover and absenteeism again began to rise, the regime merely
strengthened the November 1932 rules, most notably by redefining absenteeism to include late arrival at work of more than 20 minutes, and
restricting the rights of those dismissed to claim pensions and disability
benefits. It was not until June 1940 that it took the bold step of making both job-changing and absenteeism criminal offences. Absenteeism,
which now embraced any unauthorized loss of work time of more than
20 minutes within the working day (most notably leaving early for, or
returning late from, a meal break), condemned the offender to doing up

---

[2] For a more detailed elaboration of this argument, see Filtzer, 'Labor Discipline'.

to six months' corrective labour at his or her current enterprise at reduced pay (up to 25 per cent). The logic behind this was to close a major loophole in the old laws: workers who had requested a voluntary discharge but had been turned down would deliberately commit *progul* in order to force their managers to fire them. This was no longer possible. Meanwhile, leaving one's job without managerial permission earned a much more severe penalty: two to four months in jail (but not, significantly, in a labour camp).[3]

In the context of the times, the 1940 labour laws appeared extremely draconian. It was perhaps characteristic of their harshness that it proved very difficult to compel industrial managers and even local judges and procuracy officials to enforce them. Despite the large number of convictions – 321,000 for illegal quitting and 1.77 million for *progul* during the second half of 1940 alone[4] – circumvention of the edict was widespread. Industrial managers and local legal officials alike understood that its rigorous enforcement could jeopardize industrial relations at a time when industry was under the intense pressure of a military buildup. It was only when the regime threatened People's Court judges, prosecutors, and managers themselves with repression that enforcement became more uniform.[5]

This situation was to change radically with the war. On 26 December 1941, the government declared workers in key defence industries to have been mobilized for the war effort; a worker who left a job in a defence enterprise would face not a civilian People's Court, but a military tribunal, and if convicted would go to a labour camp for between five and eight years.[6] Quitting a job in what were deemed non-military industries, as well as all cases of absenteeism, continued to be governed by the milder

---

[3] The relevant laws are the Decree of the Central Executive Committee and the USSR Council of People's Commissars, *Trud*, 16 November 1932; Decree of the USSR Council of People's Commissars, the Central Committee of the All-Union Communist Party (Bolsheviks), and the All-Union Central Council of Trade Unions, 28 December 1938, *Izvestiya*, 29 December 1938; Edict of the Presidium of the Supreme Soviet of the USSR, 26 June 1940, *Izvestiya*, 27 June 1940. These, together with their supporting legislation, are discussed in detail, including full titles and sources, in Filtzer, *Soviet Workers and Stalinist Industrialization*, pp. 111–12, 233–5, 287–8 (nn. 192–6, 201), 310–11 (nn. 1–6, 8, 9).

[4] Zemskov, 'Ukaz ot 26 iyunya 1940 goda', pp. 44–6.

[5] See Filtzer, *Soviet Workers and Stalinist Industrialization*, pp. 232–53. A more extensive discussion, based on archive sources and which comes to similar conclusions, can be found in Solomon.

[6] Edict of the Presidium of the USSR Supreme Soviet, 'Ob otvetstvennosti rabochikh i sluzhashchikh predpriyatii voennoi promyshlennosti za samovol'nyi ukhod s predpriyatii'. The edict was unpublished but is cited in a number of documents. The most accessible public source is Zemskov, 'Ukaz ot 26 iyunya 1940 goda', p. 45. Zemskov's account, which is otherwise excellent for its succinctness and clarity, mistakenly states that violators of this edict continued to be tried by People's Courts.

penalties of the Edict of 26 June 1940, with one important proviso: absentees had their bread rations cut by between 100 and 200 grams a day; given that for most workers bread was their major source of protein at the time, this was potentially a very harsh punishment indeed.[7] I should point out that the definition of what constituted 'defence' industry was progressively broadened as the war wore on, to include not just armaments plants, but any branch of the economy which provided military supplies. Thus coal mining joined the list in June 1942; textile factories in October 1942; workers in synthetic rubber and tyre factories in July 1943; and workers in the gas industry as late as March 1944, when the war was nearly over.[8] Workers on rail and water transport faced an even harsher regime: in April and May 1943 the government declared a state of war on transport, and workers who abandoned their jobs were placed on the same footing as a soldier who deserted a military unit. This meant a labour camp sentence of from three to ten years, or worse if the worker's absence led to an accident.[9]

The terminology employed to describe illegal job-changers reflected this new legal situation. Those who left enterprises in defence industry or transport were branded as 'labour deserters'. Those who left non-defence enterprises and thus came under the June 1940 edict were known as 'wilful quitters'.

Given the harshness of the laws and the severity of wartime conditions, which made workers highly dependent on their enterprise for rations, it is surprising how many people risked violations and were subsequently convicted. As table 5.1 shows (p. 163), during the three full war years of 1942–4, military tribunals sentenced over 814,000 employees of defence enterprises and transport to labour camps under the Edict of 26 December 1941 and Article 193[7]. Yet even here circumvention was possible. Zemskov notes that 'thousands' of violators of the December 1941 edict ran away and hid. As in the postwar period, these were mainly young people drafted into mining, construction, and industrial enterprises with especially difficult working conditions. There were certainly enough of them to prompt Stalin to authorize a December 1944 law granting them an amnesty if they returned to their original place of

---

[7] Barber and Harrison, p. 173.   [8] GARF, f. 8131, op. 37, d. 4041, l. 100–1.
[9] Edicts of the Presidium of the USSR Supreme Soviet, 'O vvedenii voennogo polozheniya na vsekh zheleznykh dorogakh', 15 April 1943, and 'O vvedenii voennogo polozheniya na morskom i rechnom transporte', 9 May 1943. These laws provided for prosecution under Article 193[7] of the Criminal Code of the RSFSR, which governed military crimes, and the corresponding articles of the criminal codes of the other Soviet republics. Here, too, offenders were tried by military tribunals (Zemskov, 'Ukaz ot 26 iyunya 1940 goda', p. 46).

Table 5.1. *Convictions for illegal job-changing and absenteeism, 1940–1952*

Year	Edict of 26 June 1940 (2–4 months in prison)	Edict of 26 December 1941: 5–8 years in labour camp for workers in defence enterprises. Repealed in May 1948	Art. 193 of Criminal Code (Edicts of April and May 1943): 3–10 years in labour camp for transport employees. Repealed in March 1948	Total convictions for unauthorized job-changing	Absenteeism under Edict of 26 June 1940: Up to 6 months corrective labour at enterprise with 25% loss of pay. Relaxed in July 1951, after which only the most serious cases prosecuted
1940	321,648	not applicable (n/a)	n/a	321,648	1,769,790
1941	310,967	n/a	n/a	310,967	1,458,185
1942	297,125	121,090	n/a	418,215	1,274,644
1943	160,060	367,047	15,490	542,597	961,545
1944	167,562	275,966	35,042	478,570	893,242
1945	117,304	72,790	29,743	219,837	941,733
1946	143,600	67,532	26,575	237,707	861,340
1947	215,679	54,350	20,396	290,425	684,441
1948	249,940	24,600	6,800	281,340	564,590
1949	267,869	n/a	n/a	267,869	517,459
1950	208,962	n/a	n/a	208,962	513,891
1951	133,823	n/a	n/a	133,823	315,275
1952	179,695	n/a	n/a	179,695	147,885
Total	2,774,234	983,375	134,046	3,891,655	10,904,020

Source: Zemskov, 'Ukaz ot 26 iyunya 1940 goda', p. 45.

employment.[10] This was followed, in June 1945, by a general amnesty for those imprisoned for non-political convictions, in honour of the Soviet victory over Nazi Germany.[11]

In effect, then, in mid-1945 the slate was wiped clean. But the wartime regulations remained in force, and it is here that our story properly begins. There was a partial relaxation in March 1947, when the regime narrowed the definition of defence enterprises and removed all enterprises and construction sites in Moscow and Leningrad from the 26 December 1941 edict. Yet Moscow and Leningrad, as we shall see, had extremely low levels of labour turnover, and so this concession had little practical effect. It was not until March 1948 that the government lifted the state of war on transport and May 1948 that it repealed the Edict of 26 December 1941, in the wake of which it released from the camps 111,380 prisoners.[12] This, however, represented just over half of all those convicted under these edicts since the 1945 amnesty. Nevertheless, all new cases of illegal quitting once again came under the much milder Edict of 26 June 1940. In July 1951 absenteeism was decriminalized, except for chronic repeat offenders – of whom there were at least 150,000 in 1952; application of the anti-quitting law was also eased and, according to Zemskov, virtually immediately after Stalin's death the new collective leadership granted a broad amnesty to all those convicted under both clauses of the Edict of 26 June 1940.[13] Yet it was not until April 1956, that is, after Khrushchev's 'Secret Speech' of February of that year, that the laws were once and for all removed from the statute books.[14]

---

[10] Edict of the Presidium of the USSR Supreme Soviet, 'O predostavlenii amnistii litsam, samovolno ushedshim s predpriyatii voennoi promyshlennosti i dobrovol'no vernuvshimsya na predpriyatiya', 30 December 1944, cited in Zemskov, 'Ukaz ot 26 iyunya 1940 goda', p. 46.

[11] Edict of the Presidium of the USSR Supreme Soviet, 'Ob amnistii v svyazi s pobedoi nad gitlerovskoi Germaniei', 7 June 1945, cited in Zemskov, 'Ukaz ot 26 iyunya 1940 goda', p. 47.

[12] This is noted in a report from Kruglov, head of the MVD, to Stalin, Molotov, Beria, and Malenkov, dated 8 February 1949, GARF, f. 9401, op. 2, d. 234, l. 149.

[13] The application of the Edict of 26 December 1941 was relaxed by a decree of the USSR Council of Ministers, 7 March 1947. The edict was repealed by an Edict of the Presidium of the USSR Supreme Soviet, dated 31 May 1948. The state of war on transport was lifted by an Edict of the Presidium of the USSR Supreme Soviet, 2 May 1948. *Progul* was decriminalized on 14 July 1951, by an Edict of the Presidium of the USSR Supreme Soviet, 'O zamene sudebnoi otvetstvennosti rabochikh i sluzhashchikh za progul, krome sluchaev neodnokratnogo i dlitel'nogo progula, merami distsiplinarnogo i obshchestvennogo vozdeistviya'. All of these laws are discussed in Zemskov, 'Ukaz ot 26 iyunya 1940 goda', p. 47. I should note that these laws remained unpublished, although it is clear from the archive reports that workers knew what was in them; as I discuss in chapter 6, after the July 1951 edict, absenteeism skyrocketed.

[14] Edict of the Presidium of the USSR Supreme Soviet, 'Ob otmene sudebnoi otvetstvennosti rabochikh i sluzhashchikh za samovol'nyi ukhod s predpriyatii iz uchrezhdenii i za

This is not, however, the entire story, even from a legal point of view. In 1946 the legal authorities had proposed various relaxations of the laws, which Stalin and the political leadership rejected. In June 1946, for example, the procuracy argued strongly for an end to criminal sanctions against absenteeism. G. Safonov, at the time the acting chief procurator of the USSR, prepared a draft memorandum for Stalin (whether he sent it or not we do not know) in which he argued that since the June 1945 amnesty the courts had sentenced nearly half a million offenders for *progul*, and nearly 55,000 for illegal quitting. Citing a number of enterprises in which between 10 and 20 per cent of all workers had fallen foul of the law, he noted, 'in such a situation conviction for a crime to a significant extent loses its social-educative and preventative significance and becomes in essence a fact of everyday life. Measures for punishing *progul* – corrective labour for a period of six months – in reality are reduced to a monetary fine on the instalment plan, of up to 25 per cent of the wages of a worker or clerical employee.' He also questioned the political utility of such mass prosecutions.[15] We also know that sometime in 1946 and the beginning of 1947 there had been a discussion (by whom is not clear) of repealing the Edict of 26 December 1941, but that 'certain ministers' had requested a one-year's delay, so that the economy's continued improvement might remove some of the conditions which were encouraging workers to quit their jobs.[16] Similar pressure also came from the Ministry of Justice and the Railways Ministry, which in August 1946 pressed hard to have the government lift the state of war on transport and replace it with the Edict of 26 June 1940, together with a programme of material incentives designed to offer workers reasons to stay at their jobs. So convinced was the Railways Ministry that the government would accept its proposal that its Legal Department even printed up a new disciplinary statute 'in view of the impending repeal of the Edict of 15 April 1943'.[17]

We know, of course, that all these efforts came to nought. The laws remained in force. But here we notice something strange. Perhaps surprisingly, given the harshness with which the regime attempted to curb unwanted labour mobility, the official rhetoric was relatively understanding and showed little of the shrillness with which the regime attacked job-changers during the 1930s. In the prewar period, even before

progul bez uvazhitel'noi prichiny', 25 April 1956, *Vedemosti Verkhovnogo Soveta SSSR*, 1956, no. 10, art. 203.
[15] GARF, f. 8131, op. 37, d. 3147, l. 1–3.
[16] This is mentioned in a joint communique of May 1948 from Gorshenin, Minister of Justice of the USSR, and Safonov, by then the USSR's procurator general, to the USSR Council of Ministers, setting out the argument for the edict's ultimate repeal (GARF, f. 8131, op. 37, d. 4501, l. 3).
[17] RGAE, f. 1884, op. 31, d. 6966, l. 2, 20–4, 51–5.

the clampdown of 1938–40, those who left their jobs were branded as outcasts, 'loafers', and 'self-seekers', who, acting out of pecuniary self-interest, were sabotaging the construction of socialism and thus jeopardizing the well-being of the conscientious majority. This picture bore little relationship to reality, for even in the calmest years of the 1930s the average Soviet worker changed jobs nearly once a year.[18] Rather it reflected the antagonistic and indeed contemptuous attitude the political leadership had towards society, including the working class. But that is not what concerns us here. In the aftermath of the war, not just in the private and secret deliberations of the industrial ministries and the trade unions, but also publicly, the regime admitted that illegal job-changing was a response to harsh conditions. This is not to say that it accepted responsibility for these conditions – rather, it either treated them as outside its control or blamed them on negligent managers – or that it therefore refrained from putting violators in jail if it could catch them. Yet, as we shall see in the following sections, it did reflect the somewhat ambiguous willingness of different layers of the state system to enforce the laws with full vigour.

This leads us to another peculiarity. During 1947, 54,350 people were convicted for violating the Edict of 26 December 1941. Yet if we add up the 1947 figures for so-called 'labour deserters' reported by just eight ministries within what was still considered the defence sector, the figure comes to nearly 333,000. In other words, the number of 'deserters' in these eight ministries alone was over six times the number convicted. The detailed data are presented in table 5.2. These figures, of course, can be taken only as an orientation. Some of those who illegally left their jobs during 1947 would have been apprehended and tried during 1948. Yet, by the same token, some of the 1947 convictions represented offences committed during 1946. In general it is far more likely that the figures in table 5.2 understate the number of violators: first, because of the inaccuracy – deliberate or otherwise – of enterprise records on the number of employees who 'deserted' from their jobs; and, secondly, because there are other industries in the defence sector for which we have not found turnover data: most notably, non-ferrous metallurgy; timber and logging; motor vehicles and tractors; and armaments. But the picture table 5.2 presents is abundantly clear: even if the eight ministries listed in the table had accounted for all the 'labour deserters' in defence industry, this would still mean that five of six workers who illegally left their jobs escaped punishment. Since only a relatively small percentage of workers

---

[18] Filtzer, *Soviet Workers and De-Stalinization*, pp. 134–44. This does not, of course, mean that each worker changed jobs every single year, but it does demonstrate that turnover was a common fact of industrial life, and was a rational response by workers to an economic and political situation over which they could exercise no collective control.

Table 5.2. *'Labour desertion' in core ministries, 1947*

Ministry	Qualifying remarks	'Labour desertion' 1947
Construction of Enterprises in Heavy Industry		73,150
Coal Mining – Western Regions	Industrial workers only	87,700
Coal Mining – Eastern Regions	Industrial workers only	52,600
Oil Industry	Industrial workers only	2,500
Heavy Engineering	Industrial workers only	6,370
Building Materials	Non-seasonal workers in industrial enterprises under all-union (as opposed to local or republican) jurisdiction	8,890
Light Industry and Textiles	Only textiles was deemed a defence industry. However, the number of reporting enterprises is highly incomplete; probably only about two-thirds of factories were included in the survey	53,510
Iron and Steel		48,200
Total, eight ministries		*332,920*
Total convicted under Edict of 26 December 1941 (from table 5.1)		*54,350*
Excess of 'labour deserters' over number convicted		*278,570*

Source: See table 5.3 below.

who went before military tribunals under the Edict of 26 December 1941 were acquitted, this means that the vast majority of those who broke the law never even faced prosecution. Who were these people? Where did they go? How did they manage to avoid being caught and brought to trial?

Labour turnover: profile and composition

As in the 1930s, labour turnover in the postwar period was far more than just a question of labour economics. Illegal job-changing, and even a large proportion of that job-changing which was legally authorized, constituted spontaneous and uncontrolled movements of labour power, which had

Table 5.3. *Total turnover and illegal quitting in major branches of Soviet industry, 1947–1949, as a percentage of all workers*

	1947 All leavers	1947 Leaving illegally	1948 All leavers	1948 Leaving illegally	1949 All leavers	1949 Leaving illegally
Iron and steel	36	11	16	3.5	n/d	n/d
Construction in heavy industry	64	23	47	13	41	8.0
Coal mining, Western Region	53	22	42	16	n/d	n/d
Coal mining, Eastern Region	46	20	44	16	n/d	n/d
Coal mining, amalgamated industry	n/d	n/d	n/d	n/d	40	11.0
Oil	40	4.3	39	2.4	38	2.4
Heavy machine-building	32	9.5	21	3.7	21	2.8
Machine-tool manufacture	n/d	n/d	n/d	n/d	29	2.2
Light industry	34	8	27	2.4	24	1.1

Sources: Iron and steel: RGAE, f. 8875, op. 46, d. 227, l. 21, 51(1948 extrapolated from January and February figures). Construction: RGAE, f. 8592, op. 2, d. 586, l. 66–7. Coal mining: RGAE, f. 1562, op. 320, d. 223, l. 2–3, 29–30, 55–6, 81–2, 108–9, 134–5, 155–6, 175; op. 321, d. 416, l. 1, 15 (figures for 1948 are extrapolated from January–September. In October 1948 the Western and Eastern ministries were amalgamated into one. Figures for 1949 are extrapolated from data for January–June). Oil: RGAE, f. 1562, op. 320, d. 223, l. 4, 31, 57, 83, 110, 136, 157, 176; op. 321, d. 416, l. 40. Heavy machine-building: RGAE, f. 1562, op. 320, d. 223, l. 12, 139, 65, 91, 117, 143, 164, 181; op. 321, d. 416, l. 45. Machine-tool manufacture: GARF, f. 8131, op. 29, d. 207, l. 12. Light industry: RGAE, f. 1562, op. 320, d. 223, l. 17, 44, 70, 96, 122, 148, 169, 186; op. 321, d. 416, l. 49.

serious repercussions for the economy, for the political relationship between the regime and its industrial workforce, and for the hundreds of thousands of individuals who took the risks and fled from their enterprises. Not just the size but also the social profile of labour turnover were closely bound up with the characteristic features of these years: the dire food shortages, the lack of housing, dangerous working conditions, the political powerlessness of the workforce, and the decision of the Stalinist state to base the economic reconstruction on the massive application of slave and indentured labour. In this section we look at the available data on both legal and illegal turnover in major branches of Soviet industry and construction. Table 5.3 shows turnover in the major branches of the economy, expressed as a percentage of the average number of industrial workers in that sector. Although subject to the same caveat regarding the availability of data as table 5.2, table 5.3 suggests the following conclusions.

1. Labour turnover, and not just illegal quitting, reached a peak in 1947 and then rapidly declined as the food situation improved, the economy

stabilized, and sectors such as iron and steel began to reduce their dependence on labour conscripts.

2. Illegal job-changing was confined almost exclusively to particular branches of the economy: construction, coal mining, and, for a brief period, iron and steel. As I shall discuss momentarily, it also tended, therefore, to be highest in those geographical regions which housed these industries, in particular the Donbass area of Ukraine, the coal fields of the Moscow basin, and the coal and metallurgical centres of the Urals and Western Siberia. By contrast, it was virtually insignificant in Moscow, where the privileged allocation of supply and the presence of relatively 'clean' industries meant that even workers in very low-paid sectors and enterprises (such as textiles or the garment industry) stayed in their jobs.

3. When we look at total attrition rates, as opposed to just illegal quitting, we see that the differences between sectors were less pronounced, and that even in engineering, perhaps the most stable branch of industry, between 20 and 30 per cent of workers were still leaving their jobs in 1949. The same is true of the decline over time within each industry: total turnover fell far less dramatically than did illegal quitting.

This latter point is of some importance, because throughout the entire postwar period a relatively large minority of workers legally left their jobs under the highly ambiguous heading of 'with management permission'. In coal mining, for example, whereas 140,300 workers quit their jobs illegally during 1947, another 67,200 left with the permission of management. In industries with relatively low levels of illegal quitting, such as oil, heavy engineering, and light industry, the number of workers whom managers allowed to leave their jobs was roughly equal to the number of 'deserters' in 1947, but then began vastly to exceed them during 1948 and 1949. In light industry the pattern was quite dramatic: by 1949, just over 1 per cent of all workers quit their jobs in defiance of the law, but over 10 per cent went with management's blessing.[19] The conclusion is almost inescapable that, at least to some extent, leaving one's job with management permission was a concealed form of spontaneous quitting.

We can see the justification for this claim if we look at the Ministry of Metallurgy in 1950 (which for a brief period included both iron and steel and non-ferrous metallurgy). A survey of enterprises covering some

[19] In the oil industry roughly 12 per cent of all workers had management permission to leave their jobs each year between 1947 and 1949. In heavy engineering the figure was 10 per cent in 1947, 7 per cent in 1948, and 8 per cent in 1949. In and of themselves these represent very low levels of turnover, but nonetheless considerably exceed the numbers who quit illegally, as shown in table 5.3. Sources for the industries cited in this paragraph (coal mining, oil, heavy engineering, and light industry) are the same as for table 5.3.

380,000 industrial workers and excluding those still indentured to the system as graduates of Labour Reserve schools – that is, the group which had the highest rate of labour turnover – recorded an overall rate of turnover of 21 per cent, or 81,500 workers. Of these, two-thirds (54,000) left under the amorphous rubric, 'with management permission', a category which alone was equivalent to over 14 per cent of all industrial workers at the surveyed enterprises. What grounds did workers have to present in order to obtain their release? In the overwhelming majority of cases (in fact, three-quarters of all those with 'management permission') they cited either family reasons or reasons which were amorphous and ill-defined: 10 per cent were allowed to go because their families had moved to another part of the USSR; 27.6 per cent received permission to leave because of 'family circumstances'; and another 37.6 per cent left 'at their own desire', that is, simply by explaining that they wanted to leave.[20] Yet we can reasonably ask what the difference is between workers who 'wilfully' quit their jobs in defiance of the law, and workers who requested their release and readily received it. In the absence of concrete data we can only speculate, but part of the answer might lie in the status of the workers in question. Older, more experienced workers, who had developed reasonably strong informal relationships with management, may have found it easier to negotiate their release, especially if they could bring to bear humanitarian concerns, for example, lack of child care for their children, or geographical separation from their families. By contrast, workers who, whether because of age, lack of seniority (*stazh*), or their status as semi-free, commandeered labour, had no opportunity to engage in informal bargaining had only one route of escape: to flee.

The differences between the various industries revealed in table 5.3 allow us to draw one further, important conclusion about illegal turnover in the postwar period. It arose from a confluence of two sets of factors. The first was a large workforce of what I have termed indentured labourers, the composition of which I described in chapter 1. The second determinant was that these workers faced almost intolerable working and living conditions. Where conditions were bad but the workforce was older and settled, and thus tied to the locality and/or the enterprise, on the one hand, or better placed to receive official sanction to depart, on the other, illegal turnover tended to be lower. Conversely, where indentured labourers

[20] RGAE, f. 8875, op. 46, d. 279, l. 209, 211, 213. Managers in iron and steel were more prone to grant these requests because they were under constant pressure to rationalize production and reduce establishments. However, the trend is observable in other industries. In 1951, for example, the Ministry of the Building Materials Industry was so concerned about the number of people being released in this way that it issued an order banning anyone except an enterprise director from giving a worker a discharge (RGAE, f. 8248, op. 21, d. 603, l. 59–60).

worked in better-supplied enterprises or had the prospect of improving their position (as was the case of Labour Reserve students and graduates in Moscow) or at the very least could cope with the bad housing and low wages, turnover also was relatively small.

We can illustrate these various points by looking more closely at the composition of illegal job-changing. When presenting table 5.3, I noted that turnover was highest in specific sectors and regions. The relatively privileged urban centres of Leningrad and Moscow saw few workers leave their jobs. During the first quarter of 1947, when Leningrad and Moscow still came under the Edict of 26 December 1941, a total of 1,532 workers left jobs in defence enterprises in Moscow. Compare this with the 1,940 workers who quit enterprises in Molotov (Perm) city (roughly an eighth the size of Moscow) between April and June of 1947. For an even starker contrast, we can pose the Moscow figures against those from just a single large coal combine, Tulaugol' in the Greater Moscow coal fields, which lost 1,292 workers during the first quarter of 1947 and 2,513 during the period April through June.[21] All of this makes perfect sense: as I shall discuss in more detail below, when workers left their jobs it was generally to flee not just the enterprise but the locality; few workers were going to leave Moscow and Leningrad, the two best-supplied cities in the USSR, and run off to somewhere where life would be much more precarious; we can reasonably conjecture that, if workers in these cities did abandon their employment, most of them set themselves up with alternative employment in the same town.

It was the accepted wisdom that most job-changers were young workers who had come out of the Labour Reserve training schools. Indeed, turnover among this group was inordinately high, as indeed it was among trainees at the Labour Reserve schools themselves. Moreover, while overall turnover declined markedly after 1948, among young workers it continued to cause serious problems right up until the early 1950s, when it was still common for enterprises to lose a large proportion of new recruits within the first year of their employment, a point I discuss in more detail at the end of this section. Again, this is not surprising, since young workers had the worst housing, earned very low wages (in many cases not enough to cover minimal subsistence), and, by virtue of their lack of

---

[21] The figures for Moscow are from GARF, f. 8131, op. 37, d. 3758, l. 47; Molotov, *ibid.*, d. 3750, l. 98 (calculated from the number of unsuccessful search orders on deserters); Tulaugol', *ibid.*, d. 3753, l. 110, 130. Unfortunately the procuracy reports from Leningrad for early 1947 are based on surveys of selected enterprises. Nevertheless, they suggest that turnover in Leningrad defence plants was, as in Moscow, extremely low: during the first quarter of 1947, eighteen defence enterprises lost between them just 387 workers, which would have been an insignificant percentage of their total employment (*ibid.*, d. 3752, l. 81).

seniority, were often put on low-skilled, menial jobs even when they had been trained in a skilled trade. Yet in many ways they were simply the most numerous and perhaps most extreme manifestation of a larger group, the millions of indentured workers who were sent to the most unpleasant and gruelling industries largely against their will: 'special contingents'; camp prisoners given early release; many, if not most of the workers enlisted through *orgnabor*; and the rural youth conscripted into the Labour Reserve schools.

Analyses of the social composition of illegal job-changers show that all of these groups, and not just young workers, played a prominent role. A study of 'deserters' from coal mining and iron and steel enterprises in the Donbass during the second quarter of 1947 found that, while 30 per cent were recent graduates from Labour Reserve schools, 30 per cent were workers who had been sent to the Donbass via labour mobilization or consequent upon their repatriation back to the USSR, and another 25 per cent were workers who had been 'freely hired'.[22] Reports from Molotov oblast' told the same story. Of those who 'deserted' from the two iron and steel works in Chusovoi and Lys'va during 1946, only between 25 and 30 per cent were from the Labour Reserve system, and nearly 40 per cent had been sent there during the war, most of them via the semi-penal 'labour battalions'. At the Kospashugol' coal trust three-quarters of those who fled their jobs in 1946 were either repatriates or people mobilized during the war.[23] The situation in the Greater Moscow coal fields was equally striking: of the 1,905 people who fled the Moskvougol' coal combine during April 1947, over half were people mobilized during the war, Soviet citizens repatriated after the war, or amnestied former prisoners.[24] The Urals told an identical tale. An April 1947 report from the Chelyabinsk oblast' procurator noted that 'labour deserters' fell into four basic categories: prisoners sent on early release (who in order to make their getaway sold the bedding, ration cards, and work clothes which the coal mines had issued to them upon their arrival in the oblast'); workers mobilized during the war; young workers fresh out of factory training schools; and workers from Bashkiriya recruited via *orgnabor* who fled because they feared enterprise managers would extend their labour contracts without their agreement.[25]

[22] GARF, f. 8131, op. 37, d. 3761, l. 101–2.
[23] GARF, f. 8131, op. 37, d. 3755, l. 108–11, 114.
[24] GARF, f. 8131, op. 37, d. 3737, l. 40.
[25] GARF, f. 8131, op. 37, d. 3747, l. 158. A virtually identical analysis was offered by the secretary for propaganda and agitation of the Chelyabinsk Party *obkom* in September 1947. 'Such sentiments [to quit the region] are widespread among those workers who came to Chelyabinsk during the war and who frequently were separated from their

The key factor in illegal job-changing, therefore, was not the youth and inexperience of the workforce, but the volatile combination of an unwilling, semi-captive workforce placed in near intolerable conditions. Nevertheless, young workers presented the regime with the most serious problem, for a number of reasons. First, as discussed in chapter 1, they were far and away the largest contingent of indentured labour. During the period 1946 to 1952 some 4.2 million young people were enrolled in the Labour Reserve schools, including 3.2 million either conscripted or enlisted from the countryside. The key period was 1946–9, which accounted for three-quarters of the postwar intake, some 60 per cent of it via involuntary mobilization.[26] Secondly, during 1947 and 1948 the system was used overwhelmingly to funnel young workers precisely into the most unpopular sectors of the economy: coal mining, metallurgy, and construction (both industrial and military). Coal mining in particular became heavily dependent on the Labour Reserve system – as well as on prison labour – to compensate for its inability to recruit and retain free workers.[27] Thirdly, as already intimated, even when labour turnover declined to very low levels, enterprises still found it difficult to retain young workers. Fourthly, the vast influx of young workers, in particular from the countryside, formed the core of the replenished working class on which the economy's future development would depend. Thus their experiences during these formative years undoubtedly played a role in shaping their behaviour and attitudes within the enterprise later on.

In February 1948 the Party Control Commission prepared a report on turnover among both students at Labour Reserve schools and young workers who had completed their training and entered industry and construction. The report was based on a limited survey of nine factories in motor vehicles and engineering, five coal mining combines, and thirteen construction projects, which between them had hired 43,342 young workers during the first ten months of 1947. During this same period,

families – workers at the Kirov factory, the railway junction, among miners in mine No. 205 in Kopeisk, in the collective at Kopeisk factory no. 114, at enterprises in Zlatoust, and others. [Such] sentiments to leave the oblast's towns, albeit not always connected with problems of material provision and services, are sometimes openly expressed and supported by individual Communists. Thus, for example, from Party member comrade Astaf'ev, the superintendent of the machine workshops in the firebrick and Dinas brick shop of the Magnitogorsk iron and steel combine, one heard the following in a speech to a Party meeting: "There was the war, they kept us on a leash, it was impossible for a worker to get a discharge [from the enterprise]. It's high time to grant [the worker] freedom, so that he has the chance to work wherever he wants" (RGASPI, f. 17, op. 125, d. 518, l. 10).

[26] GARF, f. 9507, op. 2: 1940–7, d. 418, l. 1; 1948, d. 420, l. 1; 1949, d. 422, l. 2; 1950, d. 423, l. 3; 1951, d. 424, l. 4; 1952, d. 425, l. 8. See also above, ch. 1, pp. 35–7.
[27] See above, ch. 1, pp. 36–9.

24,782 young workers left their jobs, including 18,426 who quit illegally. This meant that enterprises and construction organizations were losing the equivalent of 57 per cent of all young workers hired, three-quarters of them through 'wilful quitting'.[28] In fact, at least in some branches the Control Commission report presented too optimistic a picture. In iron and steel, for example, of the 54,172 Labour Reserve graduates hired during 1947, it lost 34,088, the equivalent of 63 per cent of its intake. Most of those who left (22,323) simply ran away; a further 9,381 left with management permission. Most tellingly of all, the number of young workers who, one way or another, left their jobs in iron and steel was double the number of former Labour Reserve graduates who had stayed to complete their four years' indenture and transferred to the permanent workforce of their enterprises.[29] Worse still was the building materials industry, which during the first six months of 1947 had hired 4,453 FZO graduates and lost 3,926 – a net gain of only 527.[30] What all this shows is that, in order to achieve even modest increases in their establishments, ministries had to hire thousands, often tens of thousands of young workers. Where young workers were concerned, many branches of industry were little more than a revolving door. The reasons, of course, were not hard to find: the abysmal dormitories, low wages, lack of the most basic clothing, chronic soap shortages, and inadequate training.

Turnover among young workers fell after 1948, as it did among the workforce as a whole. But the fall was less dramatic and in many industries the number of new recruits barely exceeded departures, both legal and illegal. We should bear in mind that a certain degree of attrition was built into the system, as young workers were called up into the Soviet Army or arranged places for themselves in educational institutions. Some were discharged from their jobs each year on medical grounds. Still others were transferred to different enterprises; they still counted as 'turnover', although they remained employed in their industry.[31]

Nevertheless, there is no question that the haemorrhage of young recruits or Labour Reserve transfers continued to cause problems. As late as 1950 engineering enterprises – in which conditions were generally better and which even in the worst postwar years had relatively low rates of turnover – took in 124,711 graduates from Labour Reserve schools, but lost 91,654 – including 23,906 who illegally absconded. Hiring nearly

---

[28] RGASPI, f. 17, op. 121, d. 644, l. 20.   [29] RGAE, f. 8875, op. 46, d. 227, l. 49.
[30] RGAE, f. 8248, op. 21, d. 275, l. 94. These figures cover only non-seasonal workers, and thus are not distorted by seasonal fluctuations.
[31] However, such transfers could themselves be prompted by the same factors which drove workers to leave. In a 1952 submission to a Komsomol Central Committee Plenum, the head of the Kuibyshev oblast' Administration of Labour Reserves noted that managers at times arranged the transfer of young workers whom they could not house or employ at their proper trade (TsKhDMO, f. 1, op. 2, d. 313, l. 236).

125,000 workers in order to add just 33,000 to establishments was hardly an efficient method of creating a stable workforce. The following year, 1951, saw some improvement, but the problem of retention had hardly been solved: of 77,417 workers transferred from Labour Reserve schools, 41,777 left. One in six of the new recruits (13,358) ran away in defiance of the law.[32] Figures from the iron and steel industry show a similar pattern: during 1949 and 1950 enterprises lost roughly 37 per cent of the workers they had taken on from the Labour Reserve system due to 'wilful quitting' alone, meaning that overall attrition (the exact figure for which I have not found) would have been far higher.[33]

The industry most doggedly plagued by high turnover among new workers continued to be coal mining. In chapter 1 I noted that in June and September 1947 the regime attempted to counteract the coal industry's labour shortage – made worse by its extremely high levels of turnover – by imposing a military draft of young men between the ages of twenty and twenty-three years who had not yet been conscripted into the Soviet Army.[34] It is this special levy which very likely explains the fact that turnover among young workers in coal mining actually worsened during 1949 compared to 1948, in defiance of the pattern virtually everywhere else in the economy, including among adult coal miners. During the first six months of 1948, the coal industry – including its construction organizations – hired just over 129,000 young workers; in the same period 55,900 left, including 46,600 illegally (83.4 per cent of all leavers). The losses were equivalent to just over 18 per cent of all young workers then working in coal mining. In 1949, however, the scale of labour flight deteriorated further. In the six months from January through June of that year, coal enterprises took on 109,500 young workers, that is, fewer than in 1948; but the number who quit actually increased, to 70,600, including 56,900 'wilfully'. This was nearly 21 per cent of all its young workers. We can grasp the magnitude of what was happening if we consider that these 70,600 young workers accounted for 42.3 per cent of all those – young and old – who left their jobs in industry and construction during this six-month period.[35] Numerous reports, from the Ministry of Labour Reserves, the Komsomol, and the procuracy attributed the flight to the persistence of low pay and intolerable living conditions in coal regions. Many, it was said, had absconded before even reporting to their new jobs; others took off within weeks of arriving. Others, when caught and reminded of the penalties, simply refused to go back: they preferred to go to jail for 'draft dodging' rather than back to the mines.[36]

---

[32] TsKhDMO, f. 1, op. 2, d. 313, l. 184.   [33] RGAE, f. 8875, op. 46, d. 279, l. 136–7.
[34] See above, ch. 1, pp. 36–9.   [35] RGASPI, f. 17, op. 131, d. 53, l. 159.
[36] TsKhDMO, f. 1, op. 4, d. 1100, l. 104–11; GARF, f. 8131, op. 37, d. 4160, l. 16–17, and d. 4772, l. 238.

All this was undoubtedly true. Yet it must surely have been the case that the imposition of the military levy made things much worse; the fact that it was abandoned even while youth turnover was still quite high suggests that even the regime realized that it had been of limited utility.

Looking at the economy as a whole, what attenuated labour turnover among new workers was not so much the fact that a gradual improvement in their conditions made them more willing to stay in their jobs as the fact that the economy had simply become less dependent on young recruits: as hirings went down, so, too, did the number who quit. By 1950 and 1951 the process of re-accumulation had more or less been completed, and with it the task of reconstituting the country's industrial workforce.

Enforcement of the anti-quitting laws

The data presented in table 5.2 showed that the numbers convicted of 'labour desertion' were but a fraction of recorded offences. The questions are why this was so and how such a large number of people evaded conviction in a system with such an overdeveloped repressive apparatus as the postwar Soviet Union. We know from the experience of the laws of December 1938 and June 1940 that industrial managers and local legal officials could, where necessary, find ways to circumvent legal restrictions on workers' freedom of action if these threatened the smooth operation of the enterprise and the local economy. We also know from Peter Solomon's work that local officials were often less than diligent and enthusiastic in their implementation and enforcement of the draconian laws against the theft of state and personal property, which the Stalinist regime had imposed in June 1947 in an attempt to curb and/or forestall a rise in petty theft in the wake of the food shortages.[37] Both of these findings may seem odd, given the massive number of people convicted and incarcerated under these various laws, but there seems little doubt that this was the case. The high number of convictions does not disprove the existence of widespread circumvention; rather the two phenomena taken together give us some indication of the massive scale on which the population defied the most repressive of Stalinist laws.

In retrospect it should not be too surprising that we find the same patterns of social behaviour regarding the postwar application of the wartime laws against quitting. Like the 1947 anti-theft laws, the penalties were extraordinarily harsh. To this extent the fact that hundreds of thousands of people nonetheless broke these laws tells us something about the extreme

---

[37] Solomon, pp. 409–13, 430–44.

desperation of peasants and workers during the worst postwar years. By the same token, the very harshness of the laws no doubt helps explain the laxness and inconsistency with which officials applied them. What is especially interesting about the anti-quitting laws, however, is that they reveal a complex interaction of behaviours by different actors within the system. That workers fled their jobs was a testimony to the conditions in which they lived and worked and to the circumstances under which they had been despatched and tied to their workplace. That local officials, mostly in the countryside, hid these 'deserters' tells us something about the economic needs of the local communities, but even more about the networks of social relations that bound together political leaders, law-enforcement officials, and the local populations and that proved stronger than their loyalty to the Stalinist legal system. That some of the higher procuracy officials themselves were often less than diligent in their insistence on strict enforcement shows something about the contradictory position of the procuracy as the guarantor of legal norms in a repressive and essentially lawless system. Taking all of these 'moments' of the story together reveals something else about the nature of the Stalinist system, even in its so-called High Stalinist phase, namely the high level of institutional conflict. These conflicts existed both vertically, that is, between the different levels of power and authority, and horizontally, that is, within institutions like the procuracy and between institutions of comparable status and power within the structure, for example, urban district procuracies and rural militia.

Unlike their responses to the laws of December 1938 and June 1940, enterprise managers did not play a prominent role in hiding offenders, possibly because the penalties were too severe. The overwhelming majority of offences were referred to the local procuracy for investigation and possible prosecution by a military tribunal, if they came under the Edict of 26 December 1941, or directly to the People's Court if the enterprise was not a defence enterprise and thus came under the Edict of 26 June 1940. The asbestos industry, for example, claimed that during 1947 its managers had forwarded all violations for further action. Some – but not all – iron and steel works made similar claims.[38] If anything, managers were accused of being overzealous and sending on cases which would not stand up to further investigation or trial. In 1949, the procurator of the RSFSR complained that conviction rates for 'wilful quitting' had fallen to just over 80 per cent; the remaining cases were either acquitted or dropped at the investigative stage, allegedly because managers had failed

---

[38] RGAE, f. 8248, op. 21, d. 338, l. 44ob. (asbestos industry); f. 8875, op. 46, d. 227, l. 25 (iron and steel).

to examine the circumstances behind workers' actions.[39] Similar claims were made even in 1946 and 1947, when the attitude of the regime was much more stringent.[40] Such 'overinsuring' seems to have been especially prevalent on the railways, where a surprisingly large percentage of cases were dropped either before or during the investigative stage.[41]

Concealment of offences nevertheless did take place. In 1948, for example, procurators brought 817 prosecutions against 'people in positions of authority' for concealing cases of illegal job-changing and absenteeism, for illegally hiring 'deserters', or (significantly) for provoking violations of labour discipline by failing to provide adequate working and living conditions.[42] It is difficult to assess whether or not this figure – which would appear to be very low considering how many managerial personnel there were in the economy – demonstrates widespread compliance with the law. A procuracy report from early 1947 suggested that only a tiny minority of guilty managers were actually pursued for not reporting cases; of those who were, two-thirds received only a disciplinary reprimand instead of criminal prosecution.[43] On this principle, the 817 prosecutions in 1948 would mean that at least twice as many managers were found guilty of flouting the law but let off with a non-judicial penalty. Perhaps more to the point, there were probably many more managers who turned a blind eye to offences and were never detected.

Whether such indifference was due to basic humaneness or simple economic pragmatism is difficult to determine, at least from the procuracy reports. Some of the cases cited in the reports display large-scale defiance of the law. One coal mine manager in Chelyabinsk oblast' was accused of failing to prosecute a single one of over 100 of his workers who returned late – sometimes up to a month late – from their annual holiday, an offence which made them subject to prosecution for 'desertion'.[44] A similar

---

[39] GARF, f. 8131, op. 37, d. 4506, l. 244–5.

[40] GARF, f. 8131, op. 37, d. 3023, l. 203, 349; d. 3753, l. 131–2; and d. 5051, l. 247 (the latter file refers to Kemerovo oblast' in 1948).

[41] On the Orenburg Railway during 1946 only 415 of 929 'desertion' cases were actually sent for trial (GARF, f. 8131, op. 37, d. 3915, l. 8). On the Perm Railway between January and August 1946, 26 per cent of cases were thrown out at the pre-trial stage (*ibid.*, d. 3238, l. 74). On the Western Railway between April and December the corresponding figure was 21 per cent (*ibid.*, d. 3907, l. 53, 144, 189). A communication from the head of the Administration of Military Tribunals of MVD Troops to the USSR Procuracy, dated 29 July 1947, complained that district procurators were often negligent in rectifying unwarranted or malicious cases (*ibid.*, d. 3023, l. 279–80). This accusation was almost certainly justified. However, given the intrinsically repressive ethos of the Stalinist legal system and the almost unspoken assumption that a high proportion of people charged with offences would be convicted, this makes the relatively large percentage of cases abandoned at the investigative stage all the more impressive.

[42] GARF, f. 8131, op. 29, d. 105, l. 12.   [43] GARF, f. 8131, op. 37, d. 3023, l. 206.

[44] GARF, f. 8131, op. 37, d. 3747, l. 110.

charge was levelled at managers in light industry in L'vov oblast': some covered up illegal quitting by 'firing' the workers who had left; others quietly dropped them from the factory's rolls.[45] Factory timekeepers played a central role here, for if they failed – whether deliberately or due to negligence – to note the prolonged absence of a worker who had absconded it might not be detected for months, if at all.[46] Not all such actions arose out of noble motives. A number of staff in enterprise personnel departments were prosecuted for accepting bribes in exchange for supplying workers with false passports or documents affirming that they had been discharged with management permission.[47] If nothing else, these examples give further reason to assume that official statistics on the number of illegal job-changers significantly underestimate the true total.

Workers might escape prosecution, or at least have it delayed, for quite a different reason, namely bureaucratic carelessness on the part of managers and prosecutors when drawing up the documentation needed to activate a prosecution. When officials complained that enterprise managers were hiring people without labour books – something which in some places took place on a mass scale – this was not mere bureaucratic fussiness. If these workers ran away, management had no records to pass to the procuracy, making it almost impossible to track them down.[48] It is perhaps surprising that the military tribunals which tried cases in defence industry and on transport could at times be real sticklers for legal procedure. If investigators failed to examine the possibility of mitigating circumstances, if documents improperly listed a defendant's name, age, or enterprise, or if documents attesting to previous convictions had not been properly signed, the tribunals were very prone to dismiss the case or send it back for re-investigation. In Ukraine, where 'labour desertion' was especially high, military tribunals returned 14 per cent of cases in both July and August 1947, the period when it was at its peak.[49] The

---

[45] GARF, f. 8131, op. 37, d. 3761, l. 6–7.

[46] A timekeeper at the Enakievo iron and steel works in the Donbass received one year of corrective labour for listing forty-eight 'deserters' as being off work sick. The senior timekeeper at a mine in the Krasnoarmeiskugol' coal mining trust, also in the Donbass, was given a similar sentence for delaying the reporting of over 300 cases of absenteeism and 'desertion' (GARF, f. 8131, op. 37, d. 3761, l. 79, 167).

[47] GARF, f. 8131, op. 37, d. 3747, l. 252; d. 3751, l. 192–3; d. 3767, l. 47; d. 5051, l. 240.

[48] GARF, f. 8131, op. 37, d. 3023, l. 352. At one mine in Kopeisk (Chelyabinsk oblast') in 1946 nearly half the workers had no labour books. A factory in the city was accused of hiring 229 workers who either had no labour books or whose passports contained no record of their legal discharge from their previous employer (ibid., d. 3747, l. 112).

[49] GARF, f. 8131, op. 37, d. 3023, l. 346. This file contains several examples from various oblasti and republics: see l. 208–9, 231, 276–7, 384–6. For similar behaviour by military tribunals on the railways, see GARF, f. 8131, op. 37, d. 3908, l. 186. The careless completion of paperwork did not always work to the defendants' advantage, however. GARF, f. 8131, op. 37, d. 3023, l. 298–300, 310, cites a case in Kazakhstan in which

partial relaxation of the definition of defence enterprises in March 1947 further added to the bureaucratic logjam, as local procurators and military tribunals demanded clarification as to the status of the enterprise from which the worker had fled – if it was now a non-defence enterprise they wanted the case reclassified to come under the much milder Edict of 26 June 1940.[50]

However important these various confusions and subterfuges may have been for the workers involved, they do not, however, account for more than a tiny handful of those who escaped detection and prosecution. The first fact which confronts us is that the vast majority of those who abandoned their jobs at military enterprises were never caught. In 1945, a full 40 per cent of investigations for 'labour desertion' were suspended because the 'deserter' was never found. It is, of course, possible that these figures were distorted by the amnesty of that year, which would have led to many cases being dropped and investigations halted. But in 1946 the share of such cases grew even more: of the 488,059 new investigations undertaken in 1946, 55 per cent were suspended because of the failure to locate the person being sought.[51] The gap widened even further in 1947, as table 5.4 shows.

As striking as these results may seem, like most aggregate data they conceal what can only be described as crisis levels of non-enforcement in the regions most heavily affected by turnover. One such area was the Donbass. Two of its largest coal trusts, Stalinugol' and Artemugol', between them lost 22,331 workers during the seven-month period, January through July 1947. Of these, only 775 – just 3.5 per cent – were ever put on trial. Stalino oblast' (now Donetsk) as a whole had nearly 41,000 workers run away during the second and third quarters of 1947 (April through September), and managed to hunt down fewer than 5 per cent of them.[52] It was little different in Chelyabinsk oblast' in the Urals. During early 1947 the oblast' as a whole was able to apprehend about a quarter of its runaway workers, but this hid the fact that some of its major industrial centres were recovering almost nobody at all. Of the 311 search orders put out in February 1947 on 'deserters' from Magnitogorsk, the authorities managed to uncover just 21; of the 375 who

---

forty workers from the Karaganda coal fields were held for several months in detention because the paperwork on their cases was missing.

[50] GARF, f. 8131, op. 37, d. 3023, l. 89, 100–3, 200–1. This meant *pari passu* that such cases then had to be transferred to the People's Courts. Thus the military tribunals' insistence on strict compliance with the law may have had a more mundane purpose, insofar as it helped to lighten their workload.

[51] GARF, f. 8131, op. 37, d. 3023, l. 202–5 (1945 and 1946).

[52] GARF, f. 8131, op. 37, d. 3761, l. 147, 162.

Table 5.4. *Percentage of illegal job-changers successfully tracked down, USSR, January–September 1947*

	New search orders under Edict of 26 December 1941	Tracked down	As %	New People's Court search orders under Edict of 26 June 1940	Tracked down	As %	Tracked down on the initiative of organs of the militia
1st quarter	130,736	44,793	34.3	66,616	25,697	38.6	8,663
2nd quarter	149,949	40,916	27.3	94,883	28,449	30.0	9,420
3rd quarter	138,174	35,431	25.6	119,563	32,083	26.8	7,404

Source: GARF, f. 8131, op. 37, d. 4570, l. 1.

'deserted' their jobs in the coal mining centre of Korkino they tracked down a mere 5.[53]

One other thing table 5.4 shows is that those who abandoned work at non-defence enterprises (and thus were tried by People's Courts), despite the far larger number of them who were eventually convicted (table 5.1), appear to have been just as hard to catch as their fellow workers in defence plants.

I should point out that the number of search orders issued against 'deserters' (or People's Court orders against 'wilful quitters') is not synonymous with the number of 'deserters' leaving their jobs in the specified period. The legal procedure specified that, when a worker left his or her job, the enterprise manager would (at least in theory) forward the relevant papers to the procurator of the district in which the enterprise was located. The local procurator would then forward a search order (*rozysk*) to the local procuracy and local militia in the various districts to which the 'deserter' might have fled. This usually meant the village or rural district where the worker had formerly lived, but there might be grounds to suspect the 'deserter' might have fled somewhere else. It was then the responsibility of these district authorities to track down the 'deserter', investigate the case, and either initiate a prosecution or arrange for the person to return to their enterprise. The implications of these procedures for the workability of the system I shall deal with presently. For the moment I merely need to point out that one 'deserter' might have several

[53] GARF, f. 8131, op. 37, d. 3747, l. 161.

search orders out on him or her, and that this slightly exaggerates the number of unsolved cases. But it does not inflate it by very much: the one procuracy report which belabours this point in order to downplay its poor record of apprehending 'deserters' (that from Rostov oblast' in late 1947) admits that taking this factor into account improved its success rate by barely more than one percentage point, from 14.9 per cent to 16.1 per cent, a figure far worse than the already abysmal national average.[54]

How do we explain this phenomenon? Was it due to the sheer expanse of territory over which it might be necessary to hunt for an illegal job-changer? Here the answer is, clearly, no. In the vast majority of cases the authorities knew exactly where the person had gone, even where he or she was living, and yet they failed to arrest them. The answer lies elsewhere: first, in the unwillingness of local procurators and local militias to enforce the law; and, secondly, in the network of local protection which involved not just public prosecutors and police, but also kolkhoz chairpersons, heads of village soviets, and even local Party bosses, who were determined to prevent the arrest and imprisonment of people who were well known and part of the village community, and whose labour power in any case they sorely needed.

The indifference of district procurators and militia is extremely well documented. In early 1947, Sheinin, head of the Investigative Department of the USSR Procuracy, noted that, while 'a number of investigators take the necessary measures to find and arrest deserters from production and display initiative and efficiency [*operativnost'*]', 'individual investigators' were 'limiting themselves to a formal interrogation of one or two witnesses, in the majority of cases timekeepers and shop chiefs, without establishing where the person who wilfully left the enterprise might be found'.[55] What Sheinin claims here was the exception was, in fact, very probably the rule.

One problem was that cases were often initiated only after long delays. Enterprise managers, although they eventually forwarded almost all cases for prosecution, had an interest in delaying action in order to see if the workers returned of their own volition. This was especially true of those who had gone away for their annual leave and failed to return – a tactic which seems to have been a favourite among workers who wanted to make their getaway.[56] But the procurators in the home districts where the enterprise was located, and whose responsibility it was to initiate searches, would equally sit on cases, sometimes for as long as four or

[54] GARF, f. 8131, op. 37, d. 3750, l. 45.   [55] GARF, f. 8131, op. 37, d. 3023, l. 205.
[56] GARF, f. 8131, op. 37, d. 3751, l. 144–5.

five months.[57] What this meant in practice was that by the time a search order reached its destination the worker in question may have moved on to another locale.[58]

Most failures to act occurred not in the locality where the worker had been employed, but in the locality to which she or he had fled. A procurator from a rural district in Novgorod oblast' rejected one search order because it allegedly did not contain all of the required information, for example, proof that the worker's factory really was a defence enterprise or that the worker had genuinely 'deserted'.[59] A district procurator in Smolensk oblast' informed the authorities in Stalingrad that a woman worker who had run away from the Stalingrad tractor factory refused to go back and he was taking no further action. The Stalingrad tractor factory came up against the same kind of brick wall when it tried to pursue a woman worker who had gone home to Stavropol' oblast': there the local procuracy wrote back that the village doctor had determined that she was fit to work only as a milkmaid or poultry-hand and he was not going to prosecute her.[60] Even if the worker remained in the same district as their former enterprise the procuracy might still refuse to act. Procuracy investigators in the Kuzbass city of Leninsk-Kuznetsk took no steps to apprehend a number of 'deserters' who were living locally and whose whereabouts were openly known. In response to a complaint from one of the factories involved the investigator allegedly replied, 'You catch him and bring him in and I'll draw up the paperwork.'[61]

If anything, local offices of the militia were even less enthusiastic about hauling in 'deserters'. According to the procurator of Rostov oblast', local militias did little more than solicit certificates from village soviets or collective farms as to whether the person being sought actually lived there. If the farm or soviet said no, that was the end of the matter. The police made no effort to question parents, relatives, or neighbours, or to take any other action which might have led to discovering where the person was. Rather their aim was to be rid of the case as soon as possible and shunt it off to the authorities somewhere else. In support of his accusation, the procurator noted that one district procurator in Shakhty had received back every single search order he had sent out to militias in Zhitomir, Poltava, Dnepropetrovsk, Sumi, and other oblasti, with the simple note that the

---

[57] GARF, f. 8131, op. 37, d. 3023, l. 343. This is a report on the procuracy responsible for the Karaganda coal fields in Kazakhstan. According to the law, 'desertion' cases were to be drawn up within ten days of the offence. During the first half of 1947, however, in a third of cases the Karaganda Procuracy waited one month or more before passing the search orders to the militia.

[58] GARF, f. 8131, op. 37, d. 3750, l. 309.   [59] GARF, f. 8131, op. 37, d. 3750, l. 38.

[60] GARF, f. 8131, op. 37, d. 3751, l. 145.   [61] GARF, f. 8131, op. 37, d. 3023, l. 279.

person sought had not been 'observed' in their area.[62] The procurator
of Krasnodar territory submitted an almost identical account:

Certain officials of the organs of the MVD and City Departments of the MVD take
a formal attitude to searches, and limit themselves to obtaining a communication
on the case from the village soviet or the collective farm in the district on the
territory of which the deserter lived before being mobilized to a defence enterprise,
and take no further action on the matter.[63]

The procurator for Chelyabinsk oblast' – where, as already noted, very few
'deserters' were being picked up – was even more forthright in expressing
his frustration:

Given such massive desertion, the organs of the procuracy in the cities of Korkino
and Kopeisk have taken no serious measures whatsoever to strengthen the struggle against desertion, limiting themselves to a mere inspection of the materials
they receive, a formal inspection of the living conditions of the workers, and the
registration of the facts. Organs of the militia not only have not strengthened
their search for deserters, but have even significantly weakened it. Of the 1,815
people who have deserted from the city of Korkino, the organs of the militia
have apprehended only 25, including 3 in April, 7 in May, and 15 in June. Thus
the organs of the procuracy and militia in these cities have waged a very poor struggle against desertion, and the basic mass of deserters has remained unpunished.[64]

The question, of course, is why local legal officials should have behaved in this way. One factor was that they were simply overworked. A
highly repressive political system which criminalizes large areas of public life of necessity creates a large number of 'criminals'. Moreover, the
economic catastrophe generated a vast amount of genuine crime and
social dislocation, all of which fell to the police and local prosecutors
to deal with. This meant not only handling robberies, thefts, assaults,
and homicides, but rounding up homeless or unsupervised children from
railway stations and channelling them to the various agencies (including
MVD detention camps) that tried to assist or control them. Given these
pressures it is understandable that legal officials would be less than enthusiastic about pursuing 'labour deserters', especially if the latter found
alternative means of earning a living, either by working on a kolkhoz or
finding employment in another enterprise. These pressures became far
worse after the promulgation of the anti-theft laws of June 1947: the need
to mount two punitive and repressive campaigns at one time drove local
'law' enforcement officials to breaking point. But the problem of bureaucratic 'overload' clearly predated the anti-theft laws, and it helps explain

---

[62] GARF, f. 8131, op. 37, d. 3750, l. 46–7. The report made the same complaint about
the oblast' district procurators (l. 39).
[63] GARF, f. 8131, op. 37, d. 3745, l. 68.   [64] GARF, f. 8131, op. 37, d. 3747, l. 228.

the inordinate delays with which many procurators dealt with cases of illegal quitting, including those of former camp inmates given early release and whom we might expect them to have hunted down with greater diligence than ordinary civilians.[65] It also helps explain how, when the backlog of still-outstanding cases became too great, local procuracies and militias reduced their caseload by forwarding large numbers of them to other agencies, either to the militias in other districts or to the First Special Department of the MVD.[66]

There is, however, a further explanation: namely that, at least in rural areas, the local militia and procuracy were part of a larger network of community relations which conspired to protect those who had escaped from the factories and Labour Reserve schools and returned to their home. One of the things that emerges quite clearly from the material presented thus far is that the lines of conflict over the prosecution of 'deserters' were not necessarily between institutions, but also within them. Thus the urban district procurators who put out search orders on illegal quitters came up against opposition from the district procurators in rural areas, that is, officials within their own branch of administration. The oblast' procurators, too, experienced the frustration caused by the wayward behaviour of their rural subordinates. The main faultline, therefore, ran between town and country, and cut across the institutional affiliations and loyalties of those involved. This can be demonstrated through the experiences of three construction organizations, each located in a different part of the country and each coming up against similarly concerted resistance, including no small hint of indifference from the USSR Procuracy itself. We shall see the same phenomena at work in the next section, which discusses the fate of those who ran away from the Labour Reserve schools.

The first case involves one of the Construction-Assembly Administrations (abbreviated in Russian as SMU) of the Gosstroi Trust No. 24, which belonged to the USSR Ministry of Armaments and was located in Zlatoust, a city in Chelyabinsk oblast'. The SMU counted among its workforce Volga Germans who in 1942 had been mobilized from collective

---

[65] For the lack of urgency with which local procuracies dealt with ex-prisoners who had run away from their jobs, see the various reports in GARF, f. 8131, op. 37, d. 3023, l. 223–6, 257, 268.

[66] The number of cases shunted around in this way could total several hundred per quarter. The Chelyabinsk City Procuracy transferred 621 cases to the First Special Department of the MVD just during January 1947, nearly ten times the number of 'deserters' they actually located (GARF, f. 8131, op. 37, d. 3747, l. 102). The Stalingrad City Procuracy handed them 436 cases during the first quarter of 1947 (*ibid.*, d. 3751, l. 143). Rostov oblast' disbursed 553 cases to various 'organs of the militia' during the third quarter of 1947 (*ibid.*, d. 3750, l. 146). Krasnodar territory rid itself of 717 cases in this way during the second quarter of 1947 (*ibid.*, d. 3745, l. 140). There is no evidence whatsoever that this led to any greater number of actual arrests or convictions.

farms in Kustanai oblast' in Kazakhstan. Over the course of 1947 an unspecified number of them had returned home on leave but never came
back. The SMU drew up the necessary documentation to have these
workers tracked down and returned, and the paperwork was duly forwarded to the Kustanai oblast' procuracy, which then did nothing. The
head of the SMU described the situation in a letter to Gorshenin, at
the time still the procurator general of the USSR (he later became the
minister of justice), in a letter dated 9 December 1947:

> The local organizations in Kustanai oblast', starting with the oblast' procuracy, the
> oblast' administration of the MVD, right down to the chairs of the village soviet
> and collective farm, take in our deserters, set them up in work, and take absolutely
> no measures to return them to the construction organization to which they had
> previously been mobilized. Our letters and letters of the Nizhne-Zlatoust district
> procurator to the Kustanai oblast' procurator remain unanswered and with none
> of the appropriate measures being adopted.

The response from the USSR Procuracy displayed an air of almost total
lack of concern. M. Z. Al'tshuller, deputy head of the USSR Procuracy's
Investigative Department, wrote to the procurator of the Kazakh SSR,
asking him merely to investigate the matter and to take the measures
required to 'strengthen the struggle against deserters from production'.[67]
The case then drops out of the procuracy files.

The second example is far more graphic, and reveals the true complexi-
ties of this rural local solidarity. It arose when the head of a naval construction organization in Nikolaev, Ukraine, contacted the USSR Procuracy
towards the end of July 1947, about his experience of trying to recapture
workers who had absconded. The project drew a large proportion of its
skilled labour power from the graduates of local FZO School No. 10, the
majority of whom were running away back to their homes in Nikolaev
oblast'. His description of what happened then is worth citing at length:

> My struggle to create the most welcoming living and material conditions for young
> workers is not achieving its objective because the local organs of the procuracy
> and the chairpersons of village soviets and collective farms are violating the law
> and not only do not return deserters from military production to our construction
> project, but [also] help them to remain unpunished and often shield them [by]
> permitting them to work on the collective farms. In all, 201 people have deserted
> during 1947.
>   In the Snegirevka district of Nikolaev oblast' alone we have registered about
> 100 young workers who finished at FZO School No. 10 and fled from the project.
>   Some of them (fifteen people) who graduated in June of this year did not even
> start their jobs after their final exams, but having shot off home they are now
> calmly working in the collective farms.

---

[67] GARF, f. 8131, op. 37, d. 3023, l. 375–6.

I have personally appealed, with a letter from the oblast′ procurator, comrade Greshnov, to the procurator of Snegirevka district, comrade Pirozhok, with a request that he do everything possible to return the deserters, and to bring criminal charges against the most malicious of them.

On 12 June of this year I personally went to Snegirevka district, together with the deputy procurator of the oblast′, comrade Chepura, detailed two trucks for mustering the deserters, and, at the suggestion of the oblast′ procurator, asked the deputy chair of the Snegirevka District Executive Committee, the secretary of the District Party Committee, comrade Yurchenko, and the district procurator, comrade Pirozhok, to lend me all possible assistance in mustering the deserters.

As a result of a four-day man-hunt in the localities (in the villages) my representatives and the district procurator managed to muster twelve people, whom we sent back to the project.

Seeing that this method was yielding no results, the deputy procurator of the oblast′ and I asked the deputy chairperson of the District Executive Committee and the secretary of the District Party Committee to include on the agenda of the District Executive Committee's 17 July Plenum the question of returning workers to the project and to review the question of individual chairpersons of collective farms and village soviets who have evaded carrying out the instruction of the District Executive Committee and the procurator on the return of deserters.

On 17 July I, together with the procurator of Tsentral′nyi district, comrade Ryabin (who was there on instruction of the oblast′ procurator), went to the Plenum in Snegirevka, and once we got there we became convinced that our journey of 75 kilometres had been pointless, for not only had they not summoned to the meeting the chairpersons of the village soviets and collective farms who maliciously don't want to carry out the instruction on the return of deserters, but this question had been totally left off the agenda. Moreover, the secretary of the District Committee, comrade Yurchenko, did not even find the time to receive Procurator Ryabin and me for just 10 minutes, justifying his refusal on the grounds that he was too busy.

From what we have indicated it follows that any further struggle with deserters is impossible in this district, for the district organizations have embarked on a path not only of an irresponsible attitude towards their own obligations in this matter, but are also directly violating the existing law.[68]

Here, too, the response of the USSR Procuracy was less than animated. In early August the procuracy's General Inspectorate contacted R. A. Rudenko, Procurator of the Ukrainian SSR, and asked him 'to verify the actual state of the struggle against the desertion of young workers from the said construction organization and to take the necessary measures to eliminate violations of current labour legislation'. This apparently had no effect, because at the end of October the head of the naval construction unit once again wrote back complaining that absolutely nothing had happened. Three weeks later, on 15 November, Al′tshuller wrote to Rudenko, asking him to make a careful check of the work of the Nikolaev oblast′

[68] GARF, f. 8131, op. 37, d. 3023, l. 361–2.

procuracy in this matter and to take whatever measures were needed to eliminate 'existing inadequacies'.[69] This case, too, then disappears from the files.

Our third and final example is from the Uralkhimmashstroi construction project in Nizhne-Isetsk, Sverdlovsk oblast'. The details are almost identical to the previous two cases, except that here the organization was losing a large number of skilled workers, equivalent to 15 per cent of all the skilled specialists on the site. Most of those who quit were from various areas in Ukraine: Rovno, Tarnapol' (later redesignated as Ternopol'), Drogobych (later incorporated into L'vov oblast'), and L'vov oblasti. The management of the construction firm was especially indignant because, or so he claimed, living and working conditions at the site were very good. Workers had the right to sign a labour contract (implying that they could change their indentured status) which would entitle them to a loan to acquire a private house, and a loan for household necessities and to buy a cow, plus the opportunity to move their families and their personal belongings out to join them at the enterprise's expense. 'Under these conditions there can be only one reason for desertion', he concluded, 'the absence of a proper struggle against desertion, if we leave out of account as a reason the climatic conditions in the Urals.' Yet for all this, repeated attempts to bring these workers back came to nothing. He had heard from other workers coming back from leave that the 'deserters' were all living peacefully in their previous places of residence:

This situation has become intolerable in the extreme. The failure to punish deserters living in Rovno, Stanislav, L'vov, Drogobych, and other oblasti of Ukraine furthers the continued rise in desertion, which is having an exceptionally pernicious effect on productive activity. It will disrupt the production programme for the construction of the Uralkhimmash factory, one of the most important in the country.

And yet here, too, the USSR Procuracy responded with a tone almost of resignation, even exasperation at having to deal with such complaints. Aleksandrov, another deputy head of its Investigative Department, wrote back, 'In connection with your letter with the above reference number, the procurator of the Ukrainian SSR has been instructed to take measures to strengthen the struggle against deserters from production.' And what did this 'instruction' consist of? A note to Rudenko, 'I ask you to take the necessary measures and communicate the results to the head of the construction administration of Uralkhimmashstroi.'[70] I shall save my

---

[69] GARF, f. 8131, op. 37, d. 3023, l. 363–5.
[70] GARF, f. 8131, op. 37, d. 3023, l. 239–45.

speculation as to the procuracy's attitude to the 'struggle against deserters from production' until this chapter's conclusion.

How did the story change after the relaxation of the law in 1947 and the 'demilitarization' of industry and transport in March and May 1948? There was a sharp increase in convictions under the Edict of 26 June 1940 in both 1948 and 1949, much, if not most, of which, however, can be accounted for by the changes in the law, which now covered all cases of illegal quitting. If we add up total convictions under all anti-quitting laws we see that the aggregate number actually declined after the relaxation, but only very slightly, at least in 1948 and 1949. It was only in 1950 and 1951 that the fall-off in convictions became significant (the rise in 1952 is another question, for which I have not yet found an adequate explanation). Yet the figures are more difficult to explain than might seem to be the case. Labour turnover, including illegal quitting, fell very rapidly after 1947, but until 1950 the numbers convicted fell relatively little. This would suggest that a larger proportion of violators were arrested and prosecuted. But the procuracy data do not confirm this hypothesis. The reports do not give all-union data, but those for the RSFSR indicate that the previous trend was continuing. During the fif-teen months from April 1948 through June 1949, only about one-quarter of People's Court orders on 'wilful quitters' resulted in the offender be-ing found.[71] In addition, the reports from individual oblasti show that the only way in which local legal officials were able to keep caseloads from spiralling out of control was by shifting large numbers of search orders to other districts or agencies or by allowing search orders to lapse past their two-month period of validity.[72] The chief procurator of the RSFSR complained of a growing tendency by district and oblast' procu-rators simply to halt cases which had been lying idle for more than two months:

The procurator of Velikoluksk oblast' writes that he did not consider it necessary to protest rulings to halt suspended cases, since in reality no one carries on searching for people who have wilfully abandoned their jobs after the expiry of a two-month search, [and] if these cases aren't quashed they will remain inactive all the same, multiplying the sum of suspended cases.[73]

---

[71] GARF, f. 8131, op. 37, d. 4506, l. 199–200, 220–2, 233–4, 241–2. The specific numbers given for illegal turnover in these RSFSR quarterly reports are not consistent from one report to another; there is therefore no guarantee that the arrest figures are any more reliable. The overall trend of the relationship between court orders and the numbers actually tracked down does at least show the general orientation of events.

[72] GARF, f. 8131, op. 37, d. 4772, l. 229 (Moscow oblast'); d. 5034, l. 73, 76 (Kursk oblast'); l. 144, 174, 205 (Molotov oblast').

[73] GARF, f. 8131, op. 37, d. 4506, l. 216.

This mass of unresolved offences in turn created pressures to shortcut procedures for dealing with those whom they did manage to arrest. But this, in turn, had its own contradictions, which reached a head in 1949, when the MVD complained that its jails in Stalino oblast' in the Donbass were overflowing, as the numbers of prisoners had reached three to four times their capacity. Most of these were workers who had fled from enterprises in Stalino oblast' to other oblasti in Ukraine or to Moldavia, and were being sent back to the Donbass for trial. Legal procedures were, in fact, very clear: when a worker ran away from an enterprise and was tracked down, it was the procuracy and courts in the district where the arrest was made which were to investigate the case and bring the culprit to trial. It was precisely this procedure which had made it so easy for local officials to flout the law. So desperate were managers in areas like the Donbass (where, in exception to the national trend, turnover remained high) to recover the workers they had lost that its district procurators were flooding their counterparts in Moldavia and the rest of Ukraine with orders to return the runaways directly to Stalino. This they did, even though it meant violating the existing rules for handling these cases, no doubt because they themselves wanted to be rid of them.[74] Managers wanted these workers back at almost any price; local legal officials were only too happy to oblige, since they did not want the bother of dealing with these cases. Ironically, it was the MVD that was caught in the middle. As we shall see in the next section, runaway Labour Reserve students also became caught up in this bureaucratic battle, with sometimes tragic results.

Flight from the Labour Reserve schools

As noted in chapter 4, the mass flight of trainee workers in the Labour Reserve schools displayed a pattern almost identical to that I have described among workers. It was highest in those regions in which coal mining, construction, and iron and steel predominated, namely Ukraine, the Urals, and Western Siberia. The causes which precipitated it were also identical: bad housing, lack of clothing, and terrible working conditions. Like turnover among workers, it peaked in 1947 and then declined. And, like many workers, most of the trainees who left fled back to their homes in the countryside, where they found protection in the local community. In many ways, therefore, I am telling the same story, especially when we consider that a high proportion of the workers who absconded

[74] GARF, f. 8131, op. 37, d. 4772, l. 225–7, 233–4.

were recent graduates from the Labour Reserve schools still working off their period of indenture. Why, then, give them separate treatment? The main reason is that the laws governing flight from the schools were substantially different from those which applied to workers, as was the legal philosophy that determined the way they were treated.

Soon after creating the Labour Reserve system in October 1940, the government, in a law of 28 December 1940, had made it illegal for young people to leave a Labour Reserve school unless officially dropped from the school's rolls by the school administration or the local Labour Reserve officials. Criminal sanctions remained in force until July 1951, and were removed at the same time as the decriminalization of absenteeism. While the law remained in force, it carried a penalty of one year in a corrective labour camp, although official policy was, wherever possible, to persuade or coerce the students into going back.[75] The regime did not increase these penalties during World War II; therefore students in Labour Reserve schools could be punished only under the Edict of 28 December 1940 even if their school was attached to a defence enterprise.[76]

In keeping with this approach, cases were subject to a highly convoluted, bureaucratic procedure. To begin with, the process of initiating an investigation was exactly the reverse of that which applied to adult workers. If a student ran away, the case had to stay with the local procurator in the district where the school was located. This district procurator would then forward the case papers to the procuracy in the district where the student had come from, or wherever else they suspected he or she might have run off to. The latter then filed a formal request with the initiating procuracy to approach the school and investigate any circumstances which may have provoked the student to flee, for example, bad food or housing.[77] There was a certain logic to this system, namely the presumption that in many instances mitigating circumstances very probably existed, and that only the procuracy in the school's own district was in a position to discover them. It did, however, lead to further bureaucratic complications. Mitigating circumstances might exist, but they might not have anything to do with the school: the student might have had strong personal reasons for leaving the school, for example, if she or he was the family's only potential breadwinner and means of support. Similarly, the student might have been 'mobilized' (conscripted) into the school illegally: he or

[75] Edict of the Presidium of the USSR Supreme Soviet, 'Ob otvetstvennosti uchashchikhsya remeslennykh, zheleznodorozhnykh uchilishch i shkol FZO za narushenie distsipliny i za samovol'nyi ukhod iz uchilishcha (shkoly)', 28 December 1940. On the policy of attempting to return runaway students instead of prosecuting them, see GARF, f. 8131, op. 37, d. 3528, l. 102; and d. 4173, l. 94, 96.
[76] GARF, f. 8131, op. 37, d. 3528, l. 188–9.   [77] GARF, f. 8131, op. 37, d. 3528, l. 177.

she might have been too young or too old, or might have been physically
unfit for the type of work for which the school trained its pupils. Factors
such as these could be investigated only in the student's home district,
but this required an instruction from the originating procuracy. The outcome of these two separate investigations could then lead to clashes over
which penalties to seek: to persuade the student to sign an undertaking to
return to the school and avoid criminal proceedings; sending the student
for trial; or allowing the student to remain in his or her home district.
In theory the two procuracies were to agree on which course to follow,
but as we shall see below this was just as likely to lead to conflict as to
consensus.[78]

The idea behind this approach was to avoid filling the jails and labour
camps with young trainee workers. The assumption, however, was not
that they should escape detection and be allowed to defy the law, but
that they should be returned to the Labour Reserve schools to complete
their training and from there move to a job in industry, construction,
or transport. What tended to happen was somewhat different. No more
than half of absconders were tracked down, and most of these were returned to the schools without facing criminal prosecution. The other half,
perhaps even a slight majority, however, successfully avoided detection.
But these are only national aggregates. In the 'problem' oblasti of the
Donbass, Kuzbass, and the Urals, the percentage tracked down was far
smaller. In Stalino oblast' during the first ten months of 1948, 15,515
students ran away from its Labour Reserve schools but only 2,720 were
ever found and either sent back to their schools or brought before the
courts.[79]

[78] An excellent summary of the pitfalls inherent in these regulations is the correspondence
between Smolenskii, Procurator of Kiev Oblast', and Tadevosyan, head of the USSR
Procuracy's Group for Juvenile Cases, contained in GARF, f. 8131, op. 37, d. 3529,
l. 134–5.

[79] More specifically, the overall percentage of 'wilful quitters' who were returned to the
schools was 29 per cent in 1947; 40 per cent in 1948; 38 per cent in 1949; and 34 per cent
in 1950. It is difficult to calculate an exact figure for the total number of 'deserters' who
were eventually caught during the entire period from 1946 to 1951 (when absconding
from a school was decriminalized). This is because the 1946 data give only 'net' figures
for illegal quitting, that is, the total less returnees. However, we know that, between 1947
and 1951, 34 per cent of the 'gross' number of runaways were sent back to the schools.
If we apply this same percentage to 1946, we arrive at a rough estimate of 'gross' illegal
quitting for 1946–51 of 300,000, of whom just under 100,000 returned to the schools.
If we add to this the 70,000 who were convicted under the law of 28 December 1940,
this suggests that 56 per cent of runaways were tracked down and either prosecuted or
returned. Since the 70,000 convictions includes an unspecified number of prosecutions
for absenteeism and other discipline offences, the real number of 'deserters' who were
caught was probably closer to 50 per cent, or possibly even lower. The figures for total
numbers of students picked up and returned to the schools are from GARF, f. 9507,
op. 2, d. 446, l. 2–3 (1946–8); d. 501, l. 20 (1949); and d. 520, l. 3 (1950–1). The

It was the familiar story. Urban procurators, acting on behalf of the Labour Reserve schools, would forward case documents to district procurators in rural localities, who would do almost nothing to hunt down the missing students or to send them back. According to the head of one FZO in Kemerovo city, forty-six of whose students had gone home to Tyumen′ oblast′:

> Our representative, whom we despatched to the Tyumen′ oblast′ procuracy, in the course of twenty days achieved not a single practical measure to return the students who had wilfully run away. The procuracies make reference to the fact that they are busy with more important cases, or refer to the military tribunals of the MVD Troops, which are supposed to take measures against deserters.

When local officials did take action, the students were given suspended sentences which they were to serve out on their own collective farms. Complaints from the Leningrad city procurator expressed the same sentiments:

> Despatching to the procurators of these oblasti materials for calling [the offenders] to account has not the slightest effect, since the procurators quash these cases even in circumstances when the juveniles refuse to go back to the school.

To add insult to injury, local procurators were even refusing to sue the runaways to recover the cost of the school uniforms which they had taken with them – something they were entitled to do by law. Yet the examples cited from both the Kemerovo and Leningrad reports suggest that the local prosecutors were showing common sense, if not necessarily compassion, when refusing to take action, citing the need for the boys to stay in the village to support invalid parents or illnesses which should have barred their conscription in the first place.[80]

There is little doubt that the district procuracies were under pressure from the local village soviets to allow the youngsters to stay. The file containing the 1947 reports cites a number of claims that parents were writing to their children and encouraging them to leave the schools in order to come help with the agricultural work. Once in the village the heads of the local soviets would either provide them with false documents showing that they were part of the kolkhoz, or, if they feared that would not work, they sent the kids on *komandirovka* and denied they were in the district. One school in Voroshilovgrad oblast′ sent its 'representatives' down to Zhitomir oblast′ in Ukraine to bring back a bunch of absconders, but could not find a single one. Eventually five of them appeared and the

figures for Stalino oblast′ are from GARF, f. 8131, op. 37, d. 4160, l. 152. Convictions are from GARF, f. 9492, op. 6s, d. 14, l. 9.
[80] GARF, f. 8131, op. 37, d. 3529, l. 8–12 (Leningrad), and l. 47–47ob., 49–50 (Kemerovo).

local MVD arrested them, but then let them go, and they vanished once again. When the school's head went to the district procurator for help, the latter threw him out of his office.[81] Even allowing for the fact that the heads of the schools may have exaggerated their difficulties, there is little doubt that their basic complaints were real.

At first sight it may seem that this behaviour is inconsistent with reports cited in chapter 4, of how village officials dragooned young people into the Labour Reserve call-up in order to meet their quotas. However, these were all parts of a larger picture. The primary need was to keep labour power on the collective farms. The quota had to be filled, but I have already argued that it was no accident that they despatched large numbers who were unfit, too young, or had dependent relatives, in the knowledge that many of them would be sent back. And if those who went ran away and came back to the village, then all well and good. Local officials had fulfilled their obligation to the state when they had provided fodder for the call-up. Once that obligation was settled, they could hardly be expected to volunteer their young ones once again, especially if this might lead to their prosecution and imprisonment. Such pressures were perhaps greatest during the famine year of 1947 and its immediate aftermath. In addition to the 1–1.5 million people who died, the famine propelled large numbers of peasants to leave the land in search of food. These people had to be replaced, and one way to do this was to minimize the numbers leaving the village for the Labour Reserve system.

This nexus of local protection is extremely well documented for 1947, but less well for later years. By 1949, however, the laws themselves plunged the system of enforcement into confusion and chaos, just as they did in relation to the Edict of 26 June 1940. The potential for such a collapse was inherent in the complex procedures for investigating cases, and compounded by the legal ambiguities surrounding the military call-up for coal mining and fuel construction.

The first problem concerned the system of investigating cases of runaway students, tracking them down, and then sending them back to the district where their Labour Reserve school was located, there either to resume their training or to face prosecution. According to a May 1949 memorandum by Baranov, Procurator of the RSFSR, the red tape caused by the system of dual responsibility – the procurator in the school's district initiated the case; the procurator in the district where the runaway was caught had to send him or her back – was leading to near paralysis. There were no procedures for ensuring that a runaway was returned to the district from which he or she had fled. Knowing this, the rural procurators

---

[81] GARF, f. 8131, op. 37, d. 3529, l. 17, 46, 66, 81–2, 95, 105, 215–16, 221–2, 225.

limited themselves merely to calling the offenders in and instructing them to report to the procuracy offices in the school's district – something which quite obviously few of them were willing to do. The result was a large number of suspended cases and few actual prosecutions (although the exact number of suspended cases was disputed by the USSR Procuracy's Group for Juvenile Cases). In fact, the USSR Procuracy had already taken steps back in February of the same year, which it thought would simplify procedures and lead to more efficient treatment of offenders: it changed the rules, so that cases could now be heard either in the district where the school was located or the district where the runaway was tracked down and seized. This led to a totally unexpected result, which again focused on Ukraine, the one region of the country where flight from the Labour Reserve schools was still sizeable. The Ukrainian Procuracy and Ministry of Justice unilaterally ruled that young absconders from Donbass Labour Reserve schools who had been picked up in other districts and directed back to Ukraine were to be denied access to Ukrainian transit prisons and sent back to where they had come from, mostly to the oblasti and republics bordering Ukraine, but some as far away as Orel and Kursk. The Ukrainian officials were giving the new regulations a very selective reading. The rules had been intended to offer a choice, allowing the runaway student to be prosecuted either where he or she was caught, or returned to the locality of the school; the Ukrainian action tried to force all such students to be sent back to their home districts, to be dealt with there. Almost certainly this was due to the same pressures of prison over-crowding which prompted their refusal to take in adult workers – and in both cases what was expedient for the prison system actually went against the interests of the industrial enterprises and Labour Reserve schools in Ukraine, which wanted their runaway workers and students returned to them. This action led not just to bureaucratic confusion; for the captured students it had tragic consequences, for in reality it condemned them to long periods being shunted around to other transit prisons or on prison trains.[82]

The second issue concerned the treatment of those who had been subject to the military call-up to FZO in coal mining or to work in coal enterprises and fuel-enterprise construction. When the state imposed the call-up in 1947 it unwittingly created a bizarre legal quagmire. Young people conscripted into the FZO by their local military draft office and who refused to report could be punished only for avoiding military conscription, which carried a penalty of only three months' corrective labour – far milder than the one year's incarceration called for under the

[82] GARF, f. 8131, op. 37, d. 4772, l. 239–44, 251–2, 254, 258, 260–1ob., 273–5, 278–82.

Edict of 28 December 1940. Despite complaints from local procuracies about this anomaly, nothing was done to rectify it.[83] A third and even more glaring, if not bizarre, loophole was soon to emerge. A wartime ruling from what was then the People's Commissariat of Justice had stipulated that Labour Reserve graduates despatched to production and who were prosecuted for either quitting their jobs or for absenteeism were obliged, upon completion of their sentence, to return to their original jobs. This ruling had formed the basis for applying a similar practice to students who ran away from Labour Reserve schools: it was presumed that, after completing whatever punishment they had received under the Edict of 28 December 1940, they would return to the schools. The problem, it turned out, was that there was nothing in Soviet law which actually prescribed this; more to the point, there were no legal sanctions which could be brought to bear against anyone who refused. This explains the reactions of students who escaped from coal mining FZO, and who told local procuracy officials that they would rather do their time than go back to the school, for at least then they would avoid a future working in the mines.[84] Yet when the head of the USSR Procuracy's Group for Juvenile Cases tried to press Safonov, USSR Procurator General, to draft a new edict eliminating this anomaly, he rebuffed her efforts, saying it was unnecessary.[85]

Conclusion

How do we assess the significance of the material presented in this chapter? Is it just an interesting tale, or does it reveal (or at least suggest) issues of greater significance to our interpretation of aspects of postwar Soviet society which might force us to rethink some of the traditional assumptions about so-called late Stalinism? The flight from the factories and training schools suggests the following observations.

First, 1947 was a year in which the Stalinist regime found itself facing a genuine social crisis. It may not have feared losing power, but its control over society was certainly called into question. The overt manifestations of this crisis, however, were not uniform across all regions or all sectors of the economy. Moscow and Leningrad remained relatively stable, while the peripheral centres, most importantly the Donbass, the

---

[83] GARF, f. 8131, op. 37, d. 4160, l. 176–8. The files contain numerous references to the law on avoiding military service; the only mention I have found of the actual sentence is *ibid.*, d. 4772, l. 275.

[84] See above, ch. 4, p. 129.

[85] This equally held true of Labour Reserve graduates who quit their enterprises while still under indenture and served jail sentences under the Edict of 26 June 1940: there were no legal means to force them to go back to their former enterprise (GARF, f. 8131, op. 37, d. 4772, l. 29–31, 33).

Urals, the Greater Moscow region, and Western Siberia were thrown into turmoil. Similarly, engineering, the oil industry, and most of light industry, although they suffered from enormous difficulties, managed to establish a more or less stable workforce, largely because they had a lower reliance on indentured labour. Coal, construction, and for a brief period also iron and steel were at the other extreme: they could not retain labour power. This provoked a typically Stalinist response: if the widespread reliance on indentured labour provoked threats of labour shortage and thus jeopardized the recovery, the answer was to increase the use of indentured labour. This was not, however, a downward spiral. The situation stabilized even in these sectors, although they always remained the most precarious.

Secondly, the attempt to regulate labour mobility through criminal law was largely unsuccessful. What can only be described as the most brutal legislation did not deter workers from quitting if they perceived their situation to be sufficiently desperate, whether it be poor food supplies, bad housing, lack of clothing, or the burning desire to be reunited with their families after years of separation. People were willing to take the risk. Several tens of thousands were caught and put in labour camps, but many times that number escaped detection.

Thirdly, the problem of enforcing this legislation showed deep cracks in the political coherence of the Stalinist system. These cracks largely went along urban–rural lines, and cut across institutional loyalties. My argument, however, is that this was more than just an example of 'centre–periphery' tensions. These were not conflicts between Moscow and the oblasti, but between those responsible for seeing to the needs of industry and construction, on the one hand, and those who had to keep the rural economy from collapse, on the other. This does not mean that rural officials were acting simply out of self-interest or economic rationality. What the Russians called *zemlyachestvo*, or village ties, must also have played its part. These were small communities, in which officials from the local procuracy, militia, collective farm, village soviet, and Party organization all coexisted with peasant society – and with each other – via complex networks of dependency, influence, and shared social experience. This was shown clearly enough by the history of the anti-theft laws of June 1947. Where collective farm chairpersons and local police retained some basic sense of decency and humanity, their enforcement of the laws was highly selective and based on 'common sense'. There were, of course, plenty of collective farm chairs and judicial personnel who were far from humane and decent, and it is no doubt primarily to them that we owe the large numbers who were actually put in labour camps.

Finally, the issue of enforcement raises some interesting questions about the procuracy itself. The files relating to labour turnover suggest that this was an almost schizophrenic institution. It was responsible for ensuring the preservation of legality within an essentially lawless system. It accepted the logic of that system and the legitimacy of the use of legal repression, including the labour camps. Yet at the same time its personnel could invest countless hours of their time reviewing a handful of 'unjust' convictions and violations of what they held to be legal norms – all while sanctioning the siphoning of millions of Soviet citizens into slave labour camps. But their loyalty to their own (perhaps perverse) concept of legal norms should not be underestimated, at least when it involved laws, such as those against 'labour desertion', with which they clearly had little sympathy. Hence the insistence on investigating possible mitigating circumstances when workers, and especially young Labour Reserve students, ran away. Hence, too, the growing indifference top procuracy officials showed towards complaints from the regional centres, enterprises, and Labour Reserve schools that rural officials were subverting their attempts to round up, return, and prosecute those who had fled. Admittedly, this argument is somewhat speculative, and I re-examine it in the larger context of other institutional contradictions within the late Stalinist system in the book's conclusion.

Appendix: a note on labour discipline and the railways

One of the more interesting aspects of the story of illegal job-changing is the apparent absence of the phenomenon on the railways. Given the difficult conditions under which railway employees worked and lived, we might reasonably have suspected that illegal quitting would have been as high there as in coal mining or construction. The system had a fairly sizeable contingent of Labour Reserve students, including in the unpopular FZO, and also had relied heavily on workers involuntarily mobilized during the war, many of whom were not released and allowed to go back to their homes for several years after the end of hostilities.[86] Unfortunately, despite scouring the files of the Ministry of Railways, the railway trade unions, the railway procuracies, and the Central Statistical Administration, nowhere have I found the type of comprehensive statistics or detailed reports that exist for other sectors of the economy. No doubt this is partly due to the militarization of the railways (its minister and top personnel all held military rank, at least until 1948). The only comprehensive table on

---

[86] The Railways Ministry took in over 206,000 Labour Reserve students in 1946 and 1947, of whom some 62 per cent – 127,000 – were in FZO (GARF, f. 9507, op. 2, d. 417, l. 16, and d. 418, l. 9). For the difficulties which those mobilized during wartime had obtaining release, see RGAE, f. 1884, op. 31, d. 7885, l. 149–50, and d. 7202, l. 227–8, 229–229ob., 240–3, 253–7, 258–63, 264–6, 334–8.

turnover I have uncovered is from a 1946 report from the union of workers on the Central Railways, which at that time accounted for about two-thirds of all the ministry's employed personnel. This listed total turnover at about 1.8 per cent of the total number of employees (not just workers), and illegal quitting at approximately 0.3 per cent.[87] This seems an impossibly low figure, even given the severe legal penalties. We can approach the problem from another angle. We know that in 1947, just over 20,000 transport workers – which also includes water transport – were convicted of 'labour desertion'. If we were to assume – quite unrealistically – that all of these were railway personnel, and that those convicted represented only one-tenth of the number who actually fled their jobs, this would give us a maximum level of illegal quitting of 200,000 people, or just 6 per cent of all workers and clerical staff. By either of these measures – that suggested in the trade union report and that arrived at through what we can only term fanciful speculation – turnover on the railways was very low.

This conclusion is indirectly supported by the files from the various railway procuracies. The reports in these files, unlike the general procuracy files, do not give comprehensive figures for actual 'deserters', but only the number of cases reported each quarter. Nonetheless, they give the very strong impression that illegal turnover was indeed quite small. But they also show that those who did take the risk were very unlikely to be caught. The successive increase in the backlog of cases due to failure to track down 'deserters' shows exactly the same pattern as in industry and construction, even if on a much smaller scale. We can take by way of illustration the Kuibyshev Railway in 1947: the backlog of cases on people still at large grew from 636 in the first quarter of the year, to 713 in the second quarter, to 753 in the third, and 784 in the fourth.[88]

The other interesting feature of labour turnover was that the procuracies which investigated cases were much more likely to drop the charges than in other areas of the economy. If a case actually went before a military tribunal, however, acquittals were very rare and the sentences were harsh: taking the above-mentioned report on the Kuibyshev Railway, of those convicted during 1947, 13 per cent received a very mild penalty of corrective labour at their place of work, but at the other extreme, 76 per cent were given between five and ten years in a labour camp.[89]

This did not, however, mean that discipline on the railways was not a problem. The railways had a truly baroque system of disciplinary penalties covering a very wide array of infractions, including lateness, absenteeism, failure to carry out instructions, defective work, causing delays to rolling

[87] GARF, f. 5474, op. 21, d. 521, l. 3, 5, 8, 10.
[88] GARF, f. 8131, op. 37, d. 3911, l. 86, 200.
[89] GARF, f. 8131, op. 37, d. 3911, l. 40, 87, 139, 201. See also above, n. 49.

stock, and causing an accident. The penalties ranged from reprimands, to fines, to house arrest (the latter may or may not have allowed an employee to carry on working, depending on the circumstances). The number of personnel penalized in one way or another was quite high. In 1946, nearly 16 per cent of employees suffered some form of disciplinary punishment; however, if we look at the most important occupations, the proportion was far greater: 54 per cent of engine drivers; 38 per cent of stokers; 60 per cent of dispatchers; 47 per cent of station chiefs; and 43 per cent of station duty officers (if nothing else this shows that the infliction of punishment was relatively democratic).[90]

There is, of course, another aspect to the problem of labour discipline, which was discussed in some detail in chapter 3: that is, what appears to have been a rash of wildcat work stoppages during early 1948 in protest at the late payment of wages.

[90] RGAE, f. 1884, op. 31, d. 6669, l. 2–3, 6–7.

6   The industrial enterprise: working conditions, work organization, and wage determination

The discussion in previous chapters has centred on how events and policies affected the well-being of workers and their families: where they came from, their standard of living, housing conditions, generational problems, and their legal standing. All of these had a profound impact on the way workers internalized their experiences and developed their basic attitudes towards work, the larger society, and the regime. What of their experiences at work itself? For eight hours a day, six days a week (or sometimes even longer), they went out to the factory, construction site, or railyard. It was here that they earned the money required to live; it was here, in production, that they most directly interacted with the regime; and it was here that they fulfilled their role as labour power in the generation of the surplus product and the ongoing perpetuation of the Stalinist system – what in Marx's terminology we would term the system's reproduction.

We know from other periods of Soviet history that what happened inside the industrial enterprise was of fundamental significance to the functioning and development of the system. The Soviet enterprise, as elaborated more fully in this chapter, displayed characteristic features of work organization which were specific to the Soviet system and had long-term consequences for its historical viability. Its patterns and rhythms of production were quite different from those observed in industrialized capitalist countries. Work was plagued by chronic disruptions due to lack of supplies, the use of poor-quality inputs, and the frequent breakdown of machinery. These irregularities in turn affected the shop-floor relations between workers and line managers, in particular the informal bargaining that goes on in every factory, whether it be capitalist or Soviet-type. By this I mean the nexus of informal understandings external to the formal regulations and procedures that give the enterprise and its subdivisions the flexibility they require in order to keep production going in the face of uncertainties and unexpected developments. Part of this process involves mechanisms for sublimating workplace disputes or at the very least containing them within limits which allow production to carry on.

In the Soviet Union the contours of informal bargaining and negotiation were defined by certain political and economic limitations. Workers were not free to organize independently, either in their own trade unions or political parties. Strikes or even milder forms of industrial action were extremely dangerous: they were brutally repressed and the organizers were very likely to wind up in a labour camp or even face execution, not just during Stalin's reign, but also under Khrushchev and Brezhnev. Moreover, their trade unions were effectively arms of management, whose main task was to expedite fulfilment of the plan. In most periods of Soviet history the unions played a bifurcated role. They would often defend individual workers if the latter pursued grievances against unfair dismissal or loss of earnings, but would never defend (much less organize) workers collectively in opposition to management. The unions also played a more integrative function through their control over a large proportion of the social wage, namely pension and disability benefits, access to vacation- and rest-home facilities, or summer recreation for workers' children, all of which they used in order to dissuade workers from 'making trouble' and to persuade them that their interests lay in supporting the 'collective' – that is, enterprise management and the latter's subservience to the central plan. This quasi-corporatist role of the unions meant that, where the shop floor was concerned, to extract concessions from management, workers had to rely on whatever they could achieve either individually or in small numbers. Workers were partially able to redress this imbalance of power because, from the end of the 1920s until its demise, the Soviet economy was plagued by chronic labour shortages. This allowed workers to violate or circumvent a number of regulations and restrictions on their freedom, because management feared applying strict sanctions lest the worker quit and the factory should not find a replacement. Workers also learned that the ongoing disruptions to production – the causes of which lay ultimately in the bureaucratic methods of Stalinist economic management – had an equally contradictory impact. On the one hand, they greatly added to the strains and stress of doing their jobs; on the other hand, they compelled line managers to seek workers' cooperation to help deal with these problems and to minimize their potentially lethal impact on plan fulfilment.

These various factors defined the issues over which workers could or could not reach informal understandings with management. Wages were set not by local management, but by the centre. At a formal level workers had no possibility of negotiating wage rates or output targets. But informally they could bring pressure to bear on line managers, so that the latter might distort the official rules and find ways to guarantee workers some level of mutually agreed, customary earnings. The same was true of work speeds, which formally were laid down by rate-setters in conformity with centrally compiled handbooks. But here, too, workers found myriad opportunities to reduce the intensity of labour, either with or without managers' collusion or toleration.

During the late Stalin period this system of informal bargaining was influenced by a number of factors. First, although the laws against quitting were often weakly enforced or circumvented outright, they nonetheless significantly curtailed labour mobility. Workers could not use the threat to quit as a lever to extract concessions in the way that they had done during the 1930s and would do again after Stalin died. Secondly, partly as a legacy of the war, working conditions inside the factory were grim: factories were cold, dirty, and dangerous. Far from provoking militancy, this had a negative impact on workers' morale. Thirdly, the wartime tightening of labour discipline carried over after the war and appears to have made managers less ready to grant the types of concessions over earnings and the intensity of labour they had made before the war. At the same time, certain features of life inside the enterprise carried on unchanged. Tighter discipline did not result in improved use of work time or fewer disruptions due to shortages and breakdowns. Production continued to be plagued by poor quality. In short, the postwar enterprise was what we might call a hybrid between the ideal held by the Soviet leadership of an intimidated and thus highly disciplined workforce working at high intensity, and the reality of the 1930s and post-Stalin years, when workers enjoyed a degree of autonomy over work speeds and work organization which undermined productivity and the regime's authority.

The rest of this chapter examines these main themes in greater detail: working conditions; the organization of production; the use of work time; and wages. I then venture some conclusions about the extent to which 'normal' patterns of informal bargaining within Soviet industry were or were not transformed or attenuated during the last years of Stalin's rule.

The physical environment of the Soviet factory

The issue of labour safety is central to any understanding of the organization and execution of production within the Soviet workplace. This may seem unsurprising when dealing with the 1930s and 1940s, when the demands of rapid industrialization, the maximization of wartime production, and the equally hectic pace of postwar reconstruction all generated pressures on enterprise managements to cut corners and ignore any safety requirements which might retard plan fulfilment. Poor safety, however, was endemic to the Soviet system of production and was one of its defining features right up until the collapse of the USSR. One might

argue – with some justification – that this was unavoidable in a system
where enterprises were under continual pressure to fulfil the plan virtually
at any cost. The situation was, however, more complex than this dictum
might imply. Even in Stalin's lifetime there were parts of the system which
took safety issues extremely seriously. The labour code set down metic-
ulous rules on safety, including rules on how much overtime workers
could put in, maximum loads which workers (especially women) were
permitted to lift, the provision of protective work clothes, and standards
of lighting and ventilation. There is no doubt that the rules were inadequate and rarely were stringently enforced, but the rules did exist. So, too,
did a whole apparatus of officials whose job it was to oversee compliance
with the laws and regulations. Every trade union had a network of labour
inspectors, admittedly understaffed and overstretched, who toured workplaces, filed often damning reports, and occasionally even threatened to
close down sections of the factory if conditions did not improve. Undoubtedly some of these inspectors must have been less than diligent in
their task and turned a blind eye to violations, but there were also many
honest and conscientious inspectors who took their work seriously and
did their utmost to have the law enforced. Nor were the unions the only
body to maintain an oversight over working conditions. The Komsomol,
too, sent its inspectors out to the factories and construction sites to check
on how young workers were being treated. As we saw in chapter 4, much
of what we know about young workers comes from these inspectors' reports, many of which were even more hard-hitting than those of their
trade union colleagues. The procuracy had responsibility for overseeing
adherence to labour legislation and the maintenance of labour safety, and
much of what we know about safety conditions comes from their files.
The State Health Inspectorate under the USSR Ministry of Health carried out detailed inspections of industrial enterprises, monitoring both
safety conditions and occupational health hazards. The design bureaux
of the industrial ministries and a range of scientific research institutes devoted considerable attention and resources to safety issues, for example,
the design and installation of ventilation systems, protective guards on
machinery, and the ergonomics of equipment design. We could question
how competent they were at their jobs or how prepared the various ministries and equipment manufacturers were to implement their ideas, but
there is no denying the fact that they existed.

   If labour safety was a continual problem it was only partially due to
the imperatives of plan fulfilment and the constraints under which the
various inspection agencies operated. The patterns and rhythms of Soviet
production also played a role. Shortages of materials and tools and the
unreliability of equipment required line managers and workers constantly

to cut corners, to take risks, to leave the workplace in the search of parts, implements, or someone to give them instructions, all of which increased the danger of accidents. At a deeper level, managers found themselves subordinated to a grisly calculus which, irrespective of the motivations, sympathies, or callousness of the particular individual, pressured them to relegate safety issues to minor importance. Put crudely, labour power in the USSR was cheap, while investments to mechanize heavy or hazardous manual operations or to install safety equipment were expensive, and often yielded limited benefits even if introduced. Moreover, penalties on managers for negligence were minimal: as late as 1990 it was actually financially beneficial to an enterprise if a worker in an accident died rather than survived with a disability, since the amount of compensation was lower.[1] Workers, too, had a strong financial incentive to collude in the persistence of unsafe conditions, since they received special supplements to their wages – effectively danger money – if they worked in what were called 'hot', 'heavy', or hazardous conditions.

During the postwar period these systemic pressures were intensified by the particular conditions of recovery. First, the war had caused massive destruction to workplaces over large parts of Soviet territory. These units had to be rebuilt and restored, and until such time as the job was completed they were obviously going to be unsafe to work in. Secondly, the priorities of war production had meant that normal maintenance and replacement of equipment had been ignored in the interests of sustaining output. Thus the stock of machinery after the war was more hazardous to operate because it was in a worse state of repair. Thirdly, war production had meant that the manufacture of safety devices and installations, for example, ventilation systems, had also been neglected. The same applies to such simple items as heating fuel or glass for glazing broken windows, the postwar shortage of which meant that factories were unbearably cold in the winter. Finally, the regime's political decision to intensify the rate of accumulation at the expense not just of popular consumption but also of 'peripheral' investments such as labour safety meant that enterprises simply did not have the resources to undertake radical improvements even had they wished to. Under these circumstances it is little wonder that the Soviet factory or construction site was a very dangerous place to be.

Soviet data on accident rates concentrated on three key indicators: the number of accidents per 1,000 workers – the so-called frequency coefficient; the total number of days lost per 1,000 workers; and the

---

[1] Filtzer, *Soviet Workers and the Collapse of Perestroika*, p. 160. For a detailed discussion of the political economy of labour safety in Soviet industry, see *ibid.*, ch. 5.

number of days lost per accident – the so-called severity coefficient, which was calculated by dividing the number of accidents into the number of lost workdays. The first of these measured the probability of being involved in an accident; the second and third measured their cost to the economy (as well as to the workers who were injured). From the regime's point of view it was the first and third indicators that were most important. If it wanted to reduce the amount of work time which accidents were causing it could do this in one of two ways: either ensure that accidents happened less often, or ensure that they became less serious and removed the worker from production for a shorter period. Ideally, of course, it would have liked to do both. Official figures, however, suggest that it made progress only on the first of these fronts, and not on the second. Table 6.1 shows the frequency and severity of accidents in the more dangerous branches of industry during the period 1946–52.

If taken at face value the data suggest that the likelihood of a worker having an accident genuinely did decline over time, in most industries quite markedly. For the five industries for which we have data covering almost the entire period, the probability of injury fell by roughly a quarter in coal, the two branches of metallurgy, and woodworking, and by 40 per cent in the oil industry. This much we would have expected: workplaces were undoubtedly far more chaotic and dangerous right after the war than they were after reconstruction had neared completion and factories were both better equipped and better organized. In fact, the figures for coal mining during 1947–9 are quite daunting: if you worked as a miner you had a one in sixty chance of having a serious mishap, which if nothing else shows that young workers and draftees into that industry's Labour Reserve schools were quite right to be terrified of going underground. What might be less expected is that no matter how large the variation between the most dangerous and least dangerous industries in terms of an accident's probability, if you actually had one it was likely to be quite serious and to keep you off work for around two working weeks (Soviet industry still worked a six-day week at this time). What is more, although accidents became less frequent as the recovery progressed, they also became slightly more serious and incapacitated their victims for longer periods.

Unfortunately, as clear cut and logical as these conclusions seem to be, they do not even remotely tell the whole story. For one thing, statistics on days lost due to illness or accidents recorded only those cases in which the worker received a sick note signing her or him off work for three days or more; shorter amounts of time off work were not included. Probably more important was the fact that enterprises routinely concealed accidents when reporting to the central authorities. A construction trade union report claimed that on some large-scale projects management was

Table 6.1. *Accident rates in selected branches of Soviet industry, 1946–1952*

Columns 2–8 show the average annual number of accidents per 1,000 workers. Columns 9–15 show the average number of days lost per accident.

Branch of production	Accidents per 1,000 workers							Average days lost per accident						
	1946	1947	1948	1949	1950	1951	1952	1946	1947	1948	1949	1950	1951	1952
All workers	no data	51.3	50.4	46.4	43.5	41.2	37.2	n/d	12.7	12.8	13.0	13.4	13.6	13.7
Coal mining	n/d	171.3	161.6	162.0	148.2	139.6	124.9	n/d	11.4	11.6	11.8	13.1	12.8	14.6
Iron and steel	n/d	62.2	59.5	50.9	48.5	50.0	44.4	n/d	14.2	14.2	14.6	15.1	15.0	15.4
Non-ferrous metallurgy	n/d	69.5	68.1	n/d	62.6	61.2	53.9	n/d	12.5	13.1	n/d	13.8	13.5	13.5
Heavy engineering	44.8	46.5	45.0	41.4	n/d	n/d	n/d	12.6	12.6	12.9	13.1	n/d	n/d	n/d
Oil	n/d	53.1	46.5	40.7	37.2	35.4	31.8	n/d	11.7	12.2	12.5	13.0	13.0	12.7
Shipbuilding	58.0	46.0	42.0	38.2	n/d	n/d	n/d	10.7	16.2	15.2	14.5	13.0	13.0	12.7
Woodworking	n/d	70.9	64.3	62.1	57.0	55.3	53.6	n/d	12.1	12.4	12.1	13.6	13.9	13.9
Means of communication	25.5	24.6	23.9	21.9	n/d	n/d	n/d	13.3	13.6	12.9	13.2	n/d	n/d	n/d
Construction in heavy industry	n/d	24.4	27.0*	26.4*	n/d	n/d	n/d	n/d	13.3	12.7*	12.6*	n/d	n/d	n/d

*Data for January–September.

Sources: All workers – GARF, f. 5451, op. 43s, d. 1095, l. 41; coal – l. 9, 13, 40; iron and steel – l. 9, 13, 39; non-ferrous metallurgy – l. 9, 13, 39; heavy engineering – RGASPI, f. 17, op. 131, d. 112, l. 196; oil – GARF, f. 5451, op. 43s, d. 1095, l. 9, 13, 40; shipbuilding – RGASPI, f. 17, op. 131, d. 112, l. 111; woodworking – GARF, f. 5451, op. 43s, d. 1095, l. 9, 12, 39; means of communications – RGASPI, f. 17, op. 131, d. 112, l. 2; construction in heavy industry – RGAE, f. 8592, op. 2, d. 306, l. 113 (1947–8), GARF, f. 8131, op. 29, d. 224, l. 19 (1949). Data from GARF, f. 5451, op. 43s, d. 1095, are calculated from tables which give percentage changes in accidents over the period and absolute figures for days lost during 1952.

reporting only a tiny percentage of actual accidents.[2] Factory doctors were placed under constant pressure to 'reclassify' industrial accidents as either illnesses or domestic accidents (the blame for which would therefore fall upon the worker).[3] What this meant in real terms is illustrated by the case of a young worker at the Strommashina engineering works in Kuibyshev in 1951. The worker had gone to the factory medical room complaining that he was ill, but was sent back to work without treatment. He subsequently fell while carrying an excessively heavy load of boiler iron and badly injured his back. The factory management, however, tried to cover up the accident and refused to provide either first aid or a vehicle to take him to the hospital. Instead his friends had to carry him back to his dormitory some four kilometres away. Only five days later did they manage to get him to a hospital, but after he was discharged the factory's management fired him for no longer being able to carry out his job. And because the factory nonetheless refused to draw up any official papers on the accident, he lost all right to disability benefits.[4]

In fact, VTsSPS collected data which showed both of these distortions extremely graphically. Looking at accident records across the entire range of industry, transport, and construction between 1947 and 1952, it found that management consistently, year in, year out, reported between 25 and 30 per cent fewer accidents and between 27 and 30 per cent fewer days lost than the enterprise trade union organizations had recorded.[5] Even more dramatic, however, was that, while the number of workplace accidents and days lost seemed to go down each year, the number of accidents taking place at home or on the streets was going up. This included a wide range of mishaps: domestic accidents; an injury incurred by falling on an icy sidewalk; or being hurt in a bus or tram crash. Whatever the cause, beginning in 1950 (before that date days lost to both workplace and non-workplace injuries had been falling) the rise in their number substantially cancelled out the days allegedly being saved by making factories less dangerous. Taking industry, transport, and construction as a whole, the number of days lost per 1,000 workers because of industrial injury fell by 21.6 per cent between 1947 and 1952. During the same period, however, accidents outside work rose by nearly 9 per cent, giving a net saving in total days lost of 9.3 per cent. In some sectors, however, the variations in the categories were quite extreme. In coal mining, for example, the number of industrial accidents declined by roughly 28 per cent between 1947 and 1952, but non-work accidents went up by 68 per cent,

---

[2] RGAE, f. 8592, op. 2, d. 306, l. 129.
[3] RGASPI, f. 17, op. 118, d. 761, l. 82, on the Tashkent textile combine; interview with a former factory doctor at the Kuibyshev metallurgical factory.
[4] TsKhDMO, f. 1, op. 2, d. 313, l. 235.   [5] GARF, f. 5451, op. 43s, d. 1095, l. 43.

Table 6.2. *Days lost due to industrial and non-workplace accidents and days transferred to lighter work, workers in industry, transport, and construction, 1947–1952*

Year	Days lost per 1,000 workers: workplace accidents	Days lost per 1,000 workers: non-workplace accidents	Days transferred to lighter work per 1,000 workers	Total days
1947	652	445	59	1,156
1948	645	411	69	1,125
1949	604	397	90	1,091
1950	583	445	130	1,158
1951	561	494	192	1,247
1952	511	484	253	1,248

Source: GARF, f. 5451, op. 43s, d. 1095, l. 41.

giving a net gain of only 8 per cent in all days lost. In iron and steel, industrial accidents in the same period went down by nearly 29 per cent; but domestic and related accidents rose by 44 per cent; the overall gain in days saved was less than 5 per cent. In some industries, such as non-ferrous metallurgy, construction, and food processing, the rise in non-industrial accidents was so great that workers actually spent more time off work due to injury in 1952 than they had in 1947. Thus there is strong reason to suspect that the anecdotal evidence for the claim that factory doctors were under pressure to classify industrial injuries as 'domestic' was a broad-based phenomenon taking place across the whole of Soviet industry.[6]

This, however, was not just an attempt by industrial managers to make their safety records look better. It was part of a larger and more concerted campaign to pressure doctors to be more stingy when issuing sick notes, for, also beginning in 1950, we see a sharp rise in the number of workers who, instead of being given time off work when they took sick or suffered an injury, were transferred to lighter work instead. So pronounced was this trend that if we add up all the days lost from industrial accidents, accidents away from work, and days spent on temporary transfer to easier work, we arrive at the rather strong suspicion that the Soviet factory had become more hazardous as time wore on, not less. Table 6.2 shows the results of this exercise.

We also know that industrial managers saw certain groups of workers as more or less expendable and subjected them to especially difficult or

[6] GARF. f. 5451, op. 43s, d. 1095, l. 39–40.

hazardous conditions. A metallurgical workers' trade union report from 1949 openly admitted that managers in ore mining paid no attention whatsoever to the safety of workers assigned to them as part of special contingents.[7] Managers throughout industry violated labour legislation regulating the employment of young workers: they were made to work excessive hours, lift heavy loads, and suffer exposure to hazardous conditions.[8] Perhaps more serious, because of the greater numbers involved, was the position of women workers. Two procuracy reports from 1950 claimed a number of violations of labour protection legislation: pregnant women were working night shifts or doing physically heavy work; women were put on jobs for which they had to lift heavy loads; nursing mothers were not given breaks to feed their babies; women were given disproportionate amounts of overtime.[9] It should be noted that in mid-1949 the regime passed legislation removing women from especially hazardous trades, but the definition of these jobs was such that only infinitesimal numbers of women were affected: just over 1,200 in the building materials industry (of a total female workforce of 150,000); 400 in heavy engineering; 4,000 on the railways (of 626,000 women workers); and 3,900 in ferrous metallurgy and its associated mining and construction enterprises.[10]

If we look at the conditions under which workers had to work, it is not surprising that safety was a major problem. Workers operated within an intrinsically hazardous work environment and lacked the proper tools and equipment needed to do their jobs safely. Training in safe work methods was poor, and even where it was not both workers and managers ignored regulations in order to meet their production targets. A 1949 procuracy report on construction sites in Chelyabinsk claimed that 'not even the most elementary rules on technical safety are being observed'. Workplaces had no protective guards or railings; workers on dangerous jobs were not secured with belts or ropes; heavy objects, such as timber or armature, were thrown down from great heights instead of being lowered

---

[7] RGASPI, f. 17, op. 131, d. 112, l. 224. For the special contingents, see above, ch. 1, p. 24.
[8] RGASPI, f. 17, op. 131, d. 53, l. 155, 157–8.
[9] GARF, f. 8131, op. 28, d. 311, l. 1–4, 7–7ob., 8–10, 14, and d. 314, l. 1–3.
[10] RGAE, f. 8248, op. 21, d. 422, l. 3 (building materials); RGASPI, f. 17, op. 131, d. 112, l. 208 (heavy engineering); op. 118, d. 476, l. 37–8 (railways); op. 131, d. 112, l. 175 (metallurgy). The latter report cited 228,500 women workers in all branches of metallurgy, but the 3,900 listed as doing hazardous or heavy work for some reason does not include women in non-ferrous metallurgy. The report also notes a phenomenon that was to become common during *perestroika*: women in dangerous jobs were not always willing to give them up, since they lost the higher pay and bonuses that such jobs brought with them (RGASPI, f. 17, op. 131, d. 112, l. 176).

by ropes.[11] Accounts from other industries show that this was a general phenomenon. A trade union report on conditions in heavy engineering attributed roughly a quarter of accidents to 'incorrect work methods' and the shortage of the proper tools and attachments which workers needed in order to carry out their assigned jobs. From one-sixth to one-quarter of accidents were due to workers' own disregard for safety procedures; and a further 10 per cent were due to managerial neglect.[12] We can question the accuracy of the figures assigned to each cause, but there is no doubting the validity of the general picture.

Workplaces were almost everywhere encumbered by dirt and clutter. Passageways were blocked by abandoned parts, equipment, and uncollected litter. Sometimes the piles were so high that workers could not see the surrounding machinery.[13] The country suffered from a chronic shortage of electric light bulbs, which meant that most workplaces were badly lit.[14] Even when factories or shops had been newly constructed or refurbished the quality of the construction could be so low (falling ceilings were a frequently cited problem) that safety inspectors had to intervene and order a halt to production until the deformities had been corrected.[15]

Another factor which compromised safety was the shortage of protective clothing. Supplies of cotton goods were adequate, at least in some industries, but they offered little protection and wore out quickly. Canvas clothing, in particular gloves and gauntlets needed by workers in foundries and metallurgical shops, or by railway workers doing stoking, engine maintenance, or other jobs in which they encountered extreme temperatures, were in desperately short supply, as were rubber gloves and rubber and felt footwear. The trade union on the South-Western Railway noted in mid-1948 that its workers had just 2 per cent of the required number of canvas gauntlets, and between 10 and 40 per cent of other necessary canvas protective garments. Because most workers had to pay for work clothes themselves out of their own wages (the railways being a partial exception), they quite simply refused to waste money on

---

[11] GARF, f. 8131, op. 37, d. 5036, l. 193.
[12] RGASPI, f. 17, op. 131, d. 112, l. 200. This same file presents similar findings, with slightly different weightings for the various causes, from surveys of agricultural equipment factories (which also manufactured munitions) and the aviation industry, l. 55–8 and 260, 263–4, 268–9.
[13] *Stalinets* (Rostsel'mash), 7 December 1946; *Kabel'shchik*, 14 April 1947; GARF, f. 7680, op. 5, d. 58, l. 20 (Azov iron and steel works); RGASPI, f. 17, op. 131, d. 114, l. 92 (industrial enterprises in Krasnoyarsk).
[14] GARF, f. 7676, op. 9, d. 488, l. 11; f. 5457, op. 18, d. 213, l. 79; RGASPI, f. 17, op. 131, d. 112, l. 231.
[15] GARF, f. 7676, op. 11, d. 506, l. 56–7; RGASPI, f. 17, op. 131, d. 112, l. 205–6.

poor-quality items with a short life span, and worked without them.[16] The results could be serious: young women plasterers working on the construction of an iron and steel works in Chkalov oblast' suffered lime burns because they could not acquire rubber gloves. Other young workers on the site were working barefoot because they could not obtain protective footwear.[17]

Accidents and injuries were only one side of the picture. Workers suffered persistent ill health either because they were working in cold, unheated premises and therefore suffered from frequent infections,[18] or because of excessive exposure to toxic substances. The problem was clearly worse in iron and steel and non-ferrous metallurgy, but virtually any production process which involved the release of toxic dusts or gases posed a health hazard because of the lack of protective clothing and the inadequacy of ventilation systems.[19] Most immediately affected were workers who worked directly with abrasives, heavy metals, acids, or other poisonous compounds. In 1948 just two lead factories – one in Chimtensk, the other in Leninogorsk – had between them 542 cases of lead poisoning. Another factory in the non-ferrous metals sector listed 2,284 cases of poisoning from chromium compounds during the thirty-two months from January 1947 through August 1949. We do not know how many of these and other cases eventually proved fatal, but we do know that in ore mining during 1948 there were forty deaths attributable directly to the gases given off by a new type of explosive. Incredible as it may seem, numerous factories in non-ferrous metallurgy either had no ventilation units or had equipment which was old, underpowered, or otherwise incapable of removing lead and other harmful dusts and gases from the air.[20]

[16] The reference to the railways is from RGAE, f. 1884, op. 31, d. 7887, l. 160; but see also d. 7886, l. 33–4, and GARF, f. 5474, op. 20, d. 1145, l. 40–2 for other examples. The rest of the discussion in this paragraph is from RGASPI, f. 17, op. 131, d. 112, l. 12–14, 169–71, 211–12; GARF, f. 7680, op. 5, d. 58, l. 20ob.; f. 5457, op. 18, d. 213, l. 84. Canvas had become such a deficit good after the war that the Railways Ministry even turned down a trade union request for just ten tents for Pioneer summer camps in the Donbass (RGAE, f. 1884, op. 31, d. 7881, l. 64–5).

[17] TsKhDMO, f. 1, op. 4, d. 961, l. 18.

[18] GARF, f. 7680, op. 5, d. 152, l. 161–3; f. 7676, op. 11, d. 931, l. 16, 18.

[19] See, for example, a July 1949 procuracy report on industrial enterprises in Tomsk oblast', Siberia, which listed cases of chemical poisoning at local cable, electric motor, electrical engineering, pencil, and match factories (GARF, f. 8131, op. 37, d. 5036, l. 21).

[20] RGASPI, f. 17, op. 131, d. 112, l. 226–30. Nor was non-ferrous metallurgy alone in scoring such high rates of occupational illness. One shipbuilding yard, over the four-year period from 1945 to 1949, had to shift 70 per cent of its arc welders to different types of work because they had been poisoned by the gaseous byproducts of the welding process (ibid., l. 109–10). Bearing in mind the claim made by the RSFSR Ministry of Health, that diagnosed cases of industrial illness were a small fraction of the real incidence, we can appreciate just how serious the situation was in the industries and enterprises mentioned here. See above, ch. 3, pp. 114–15.

The problem was not solely due to ongoing underinvestment in ventilation systems. There were some branches of industry, for example, shipbuilding, which had steadily invested in new systems which, for all their expenditure and efforts, they still could not use. At Leningrad's Baltiiskii shipyard a number of newly installed ventilation units were still waiting for fans. One section of the yard had inflow ventilation but no extractive ventilation. The installation of other units was notionally complete but their impact was minimized by the fact that the yard's compressors could not supply enough air pressure.[21] Factories which manufactured lead batteries faced similar difficulties: ventilation units lacked scrubbers, filters, dust extractors, and sometimes even the electricity or steam needed to power them.[22] But ventilation was not the only source of contamination. The Soviet Union was poor at developing hermetic sealing of hazardous processes. This meant that not just workers handling hazardous materials were affected, but anyone working in the same general vicinity.[23]

As intimated at the beginning of this section, workplace safety was only one aspect – albeit an extremely important one – of the larger work environment. It both shaped that environment and was in turn shaped by it. The work regime, with its constant disruptions and crises, placed a major barrier in the way of maintaining safe working conditions; by the same token, the grim conditions under which people worked almost certainly had an impact on morale and attitudes towards work in general. It is to this topic that we now turn.

The work regime

The typical Soviet enterprise consisted of a number of factories, each divided into large workshops which were further subdivided into sections and departments. Coordination between the different units was poor. Within one and the same section workers would have to work on equipment of widely varying ages and states of repair. Equipment broke down frequently and at unpredictable intervals. Some parts of the production process were relatively highly mechanized; others, in particular auxiliary operations, such as warehousing and maintenance, were done almost completely by hand. The disparity between the two was a constant cause of bottlenecks and slowdowns. Supplies, be they raw materials or semi-finished components, arrived late and in inadequate quantities. The quality of both materials and equipment was poor, and shops had to

---

[21] RGASPI, f. 17, op. 131, d. 112, l. 107–9.
[22] RGASPI, f. 17, op. 131, d. 112, l. 8. For similar problems in the iron and steel industry, see this same file, l. 169.
[23] RGASPI, f. 17, op. 131, d. 112, l. 6, 262.

devote a great deal of time to rectifying defects. The problem was compounded by the fact that machine-building enterprises did not make spare parts for the machines they supplied, and the Soviet Union did not begin to develop a fastenings industry until the 1950s. Thus each enterprise, and indeed many large workshops had to have their own machine shops to fashion spare parts and fastenings; the cost was high and the results were invariably poor, thus leading to further equipment breakdowns and lost work time.

We should be clear that these problems were not simply the result of 'poor planning' by the centre or of excessive plan targets that outstripped available resources. Workers themselves were a central cause of these dislocations. Stalinist industrialization, as noted, had created a chronic labour shortage, which gave workers considerable scope for easing the intensity of labour and compelling line managers to attenuate the constant downward pressure on wages imposed by the centre. This was made easier by the intrinsic disorganization of Soviet production which allowed – or forced – workers to spend substantial amounts of time away from the workbench looking for parts or tools, waiting for foremen or tool-setters to adjust equipment, rectifying defects in drawings or components, and waiting in long queues at factory canteens.

The end result of all of these phenomena was to make it impossible to coordinate the different interconnected stages in the production process because work patterns were totally irregular. The best-known manifestation of this was what the Soviets called 'storming', that is, slow work during the first part of each production period, followed by a mad rush at the end to complete the plan as soon as supplies became available. In principle, had it been possible to predict delays and stoppages, central and enterprise planners might have been able to adjust their calculations in such a way as to avoid the worst of these disruptions. But the dislocations I have described were by their very nature unpredictable, so that their locus and duration could not be foreseen or anticipated and 'correctives' could not be worked into calculations.

All of this, as I have said, had emerged as a specific result of Stalinist industrialization during the 1930s. We know relatively little about the internal regime of the Soviet factory during World War II, but the following features are of particular relevance to our topic here.

1. As noted in the previous chapter, the war saw a sharp tightening of internal discipline. The overwhelming majority of workers were placed under military discipline, which meant that they were subject to compulsory mobilization to wherever the economic authorities might wish to send them, while leaving their place of employment without official authorization was punishable by a lengthy sentence to a labour

camp. Absenteeism – defined as being late to work by more than 20 minutes – meant a reduction in bread rations of 100 to 200 grams a day, a very stiff penalty in a situation in which most people, even in the hinterland, were living on the very verge of starvation.[24]

2. The war equally brought a drastic deterioration in conditions: a longer working day, including compulsory overtime; an end to leave entitlement; constant pressure to meet higher production targets; and obligatory military training or civil defence duties. Safety regulations were suspended, and workers had to cope with a chronic lack of adequate heating, lighting, and ventilation. These deprivations were partly offset by the fact that workers, especially in key industries, had privileged rations and still received social support from their factory in the form of housing (many workers actually lived in the factories, where they found at least minimal heating and lighting), medical facilities, nurseries, libraries, laundries, and baths.[25]

3. As men were drafted into the military their places in the factories were taken by women and juveniles, many, if not most, of whom had no prior experience of industrial labour. In some industries, most notably textiles, workers were given lower output quotas (known as norms in Russian) in recognition of the difficulties created by their inexperience and the need to work with poorer-quality raw materials and overtaxed and dilapidated machinery. But in other industries, for example, coal mining in the vital Kuzbass and Karaganda regions, which now had to make up for the loss of the Ukrainian coal fields to the Germans, the government refused to make such concessions; workers simply failed to meet what became impossibly high production targets.[26]

4. The war affected the work regime in somewhat contradictory ways. On the one hand, the tighter discipline imposed in factories and the concentration of resources on the relatively narrow inventory of war production acted to counter some of the tendencies towards disorganization. Workers had fewer opportunities to reduce the intensity of labour and certain operations – for example, internal transport in some machine-building factories – were rationalized or mechanized.[27] On the other hand, the destruction caused by the fighting, the accelerated depreciation of plant and equipment, the concomitant failure to carry out normal replacements and repairs, the overtaxing of railway rolling stock, and the huge population movements all acted to accentuate the disruptions and uncertainties. Some of the difficulties mentioned in

[24] See above, ch. 5, pp. 161–2.   [25] Barber and Harrison, pp. 98–9.
[26] GARF, f. 5457, op. 23, d. 604, l. 1–3 (textiles); f. 7416, op. 4, d. 110, l. 1ob., 2 (coal mining).
[27] Barber and Harrison, pp. 163–7, 173; *Trud*, 11 May 1946.

the previous section, such as the lack of light bulbs and production shops bulging with discarded parts and other industrial rubbish, were at least partially due to the deprivations and stresses of the war. For lower-priority enterprises the war also bequeathed financial burdens which made it difficult to pay suppliers, repair internal telephone systems, and even to pay wages on time.[28]

Until 1940, the legal workweek in Soviet industry had been forty-two hours, made up of six 7-hour days. In June 1940, the workday was extended to eight hours, at the same time as absenteeism and leaving one's job without official authorization were made criminal offences.[29] Discipline within the workplace, as noted earlier, was considerably tightened during the war itself. Yet for all the harshness of the formal factory regime, compounded by the disruptions which I shall detail below, the actual use of work time after the war fell far below the optimal maximum. Although officially reported losses might come to just 1 or 2 per cent of the working day, these were routinely acknowledged to be grotesque underestimates.[30] Time and motion studies revealed real losses to be far higher. A 1947 study of textile plants, for example, showed factories losing from as little as 6 per cent to as much as 25 per cent of production time.[31] Even in 1950, when the economic situation was much improved, one large excavator factory was working barely more than half the day, as opposed to officially planned downtime of just 10–12 per cent.[32] A 1950 survey of construction projects in heavy industry claimed losses of work time of 17 per cent.[33] However, even when time was officially being devoted to production, workers were not necessarily working at their proper jobs or even in their designated trades. It was common practice to move workers about from one workplace to another to cope with emergencies or to meet momentary priorities. Another survey of industrial construction, also conducted in 1950, claimed that bricklayers worked less than two-thirds of their time actually laying bricks; plasterers did slightly better, at three-quarters of their time spent on plastering; but concrete layers fared the worst, spending just over half their time mixing and laying concrete.[34]

Soviet enterprises compensated for these losses through the above-mentioned practice of 'storming'. But storming of necessity required the imposition of forced overtime, which under Soviet labour legislation was

[28] GARF, f. 7676, op. 16, d. 258, l. 106–106ob.
[29] The workday for underground jobs in coal mining and certain other especially hazardous trades was increased from six to seven hours.
[30] GARF, f. 7676, op. 16, d. 894, l. 1.   [31] GARF, f. 5457, op. 23, d. 729, l. 25.
[32] GARF, f. 7676, op. 16, d. 987, l. 72–72ob.
[33] RGAE, f. 8592, op. 2, d. 596, l. 41.   [34] RGAE, f. 8592, op. 2, d. 596, l. 42.

highly restricted and technically required the prior consent of the factory trade union – consent which was rarely denied.[35] Although the amounts of overtime worked were relatively low by Western standards – officially reported overtime in heavy engineering came to just 1.3 or 1.4 per cent of total person-hours in that branch between 1947 and 1949[36] – the practice was a constant source of resentment among Soviet workers, in contrast to their Western counterparts who often rely on the availability of extra hours to boost their earnings. Moreover, the amounts factories recorded were far below the overtime actually imposed. There were various ways in which management could do this. The simplest was simply to hide the overtime, for example, by keeping workers at their jobs until the day's production quotas had been filled and recording it as a normal shift.[37] One of the most common and most frequently abused practices was to cancel official days off. Sometimes workers were given time off in lieu – on occasion even in advance – but usually management forced them simply to put in the extra days without compensation.[38]

The lengths to which such abuses could go are illustrated by the Vtorchermet iron and steel works in Voronezh in May 1952. On 3 May the factory director, with the collusion of the factory trade union, called the workers to a meeting and had them vote to declare the following day, their routinely scheduled day off, a working day. He promised the workers an extra day off in lieu, but only at the discretion of each individual worker's line manager. A week later the director repeated the stunt. No minutes of these meetings were kept and there was no written record of the management order to cancel workers' rest days. Then, on 26 May management summoned the workers to yet another meeting – again with the connivance of the trade union – this time 'asking' them to put in an extra two hours a day for the final five days of the month, so that the factory could meet its production plan. The workers were never paid for the overtime. Finally the workers had had enough: they filed an official complaint with the national trade union, claiming that they had worked virtually every off day during 1952 and were putting in ten- or eleven-hour shifts. 'In what law is it stated that workers work more than eight hours?', they wrote in their letter. 'Our fathers and brothers won this right for us with their own blood . . . All these machinations they carry out under the guise of a decision of a general meeting. But at the meeting the factory's director, the pot-bellied Pavlov, convinced us to

[35] The law stated that each worker could work no more than 120 hours of overtime a year and no more than four hours over two successive days (*Za sovetskuyu malolitrazhku*, 17 April 1946).
[36] RGASPI, f. 17, op. 131, d. 112, l. 204.   [37] RGASPI, f. 17, op. 131, d. 112, l. 15.
[38] GARF, f. 7680, op. 5, d. 152, l. 171–2; RGASPI, f. 17, op. 131, d. 112, l. 67–8.

work our off days and for 10–11 hours. It was forbidden, even impossible to talk or to speak out against such outrages, because he immediately put the screws on us for any petty occurrence.'[39]

If these were the basic contours of the working day in Soviet industry, what were the causes behind them? As noted in my introductory remarks to this section, workers themselves exercised a certain degree of autonomy or control over the labour process and to this extent a proportion of lost work time arose from their own actions. This I discuss in more detail in the next section, which deals with conflicts over the regulation of work time. But there were also structural factors deeply rooted in the system of Soviet production, the most important of which we can group together under the following categories.

The unreliability of components and equipment. Even new machinery was subject to frequent breakdowns, but in the aftermath of the war factories were forced to rely on equipment that had undergone excessive depreciation and forgone regular maintenance. There were three major problems here. One was the poor quality of parts and semi-finished components which entered into machine manufacture. Machinery that was badly or carelessly assembled or manufactured from defective or substandard components was likely to break down prematurely and with excessive frequency. Defective or low-grade castings, either from within a factory's own foundry or received from an outside supplier, had an obvious, deleterious effect on parts machined from them. They required excessive time on machining, generated vast amounts of waste, and led to parts which themselves were of low quality but had nonetheless to be used in final assembly.[40] The same was true of other inputs: the Elektrosila electrical engineering works in Leningrad complained that the use of defective insulation materials, windings, and other components was causing shops to turn out defective machinery.[41] Insofar as such parts were not rejected but sent through the successive stages of manufacture and assembly, they inevitably compromised the quality of the finished product.

The second problem was the time lost rectifying defects. Sometimes the amount of defective production could be on an enormous scale: in May 1947 *Trud*, the trade union newspaper, claimed that 30 per cent of the

[39] RGASPI, f. 17, op. 131, d. 280, l. 150–1. This letter, which contains passages even more hard-hitting than those I have quoted here, is also indicative of the extent to which workers, by 1952, had regained sufficient confidence to voice such grievances, even if they knew that more direct action was still politically out of the question. I come back to this question in the book's conclusion.

[40] *Stalinets* (Kuibyshev), 30 March 1950, 1 February 1951; *Trud*, 30 May 1947.

[41] *Elektrosila*, 23 November 1946.

country's light bulbs, radio tubes, and related vacuum tube products were defective.[42] The defects themselves might arise from a whole range of factors, including low-grade raw materials or semi-finished components, the need to cut corners during storming, or outright carelessness on the part of the workers doing the manufacturing. Sometimes, of course, the cause might be a combination of all three.[43] What is relevant here is that, irrespective of the cause, this was production which then had to be either redone or sent back for the faults to be rectified, all of which ate up significant amounts of labour time. A related and perhaps more common phenomenon was the need to adapt production processes to materials that were the wrong size or specification. This is most easily illustrated through the case of machine-tool operators, who were constantly faced with the need to machine parts out of oversize and/or poor-quality castings; this not only unnecessarily extended machining times, but led to huge wastes of metal.[44] But foundries themselves also wasted metal. A 1952 Komsomol report claimed that the foundries of the Stalin metal works in Leningrad, because they lacked the correct forming materials, were using steel ingots to forge castings, nearly 60 per cent of which wound up as waste.[45]

The third main problem here was the poor quality of repairs. It was a common feature of Soviet production that machinery would be taken out of service for lengthy repairs, only to go down again as soon as the repair was completed. Illustrative in this regard is the experience of the Rostov agricultural machinery factory (Rostsel'mash) in 1950, where the rapid exit from service of newly repaired machinery was said to be a daily phenomenon. The factory newspaper complained that when equipment did break down workers would do the work by hand – with dire costs to both productivity and quality – rather than have the machinery fixed. Although this accusation was intended to demonstrate the irrational attitude of the line managers and workers in the shop in question, very probably they were responding perfectly rationally to the realities of their situation. They could either wait for mechanics to fix the broken equipment, which might then still prove to be unusable, or they could get on with the job as best they could.[46] Of course frequent breakdown of equipment

---

[42] *Trud*, 25 May 1947.
[43] For a detailed discussion of defects during the Khrushchev period, see Filtzer, *Soviet Workers and De-Stalinization*, pp. 164–7.
[44] GARF, f. 7676, op. 16, d. 894, l. 63; *Stalinets* (Kuibyshev), 1 February 1951.
[45] TsKhDMO, f. 1, op. 2, d. 313, l. 164.
[46] *Stalinets* (Rostsel'mash), 9 March, 6 May 1950. For similar reports at other enterprises see *Krasnyi treugol'nik*, 12 September 1947; *Kirovets*, 25 March 1947; and *Stalinets* (Kuibyshev), 15 March 1951.

was not always due to faulty construction or poor maintenance. Leaking roofs at Rostsel'mash in the winter of 1950 caused water to drip into machinery in the pig iron foundry and put it out of action for an entire shift.[47]

Yet such 'subjective' factors were only part of the problem. The Soviet 'planning' system, with its emphasis on maximizing gross physical output, had never made any provision for the standardization of parts and their centralized manufacture by specialist enterprises. The war had seen a small amount of improvement in the main military industries, but the experience never became generalized, and in some sectors, such as agricultural equipment, actually became worse. In the postwar period engineering factories as a matter of course had to manufacture their own tools, fastenings, and adaptations, and work out their own specifications. There was little or no standardization – and hence interchangeability – between different branches of industry or even factories within the same industry.[48] The same was true of spares. Equipment manufacturers did not produce spare parts, generally because they added little to plan fulfilment figures. If a piece of equipment broke down, it stopped, together with all subsequent stages of production which depended on it, until a mechanic could fashion a replacement.[49] If manufacturers did supply spares they suffered from the same lack of standardization as ordinary parts. The Linotip factory in Leningrad, which made typesetting equipment for the printing and publishing industry, despatched spare parts on which the threads and screws, and sprockets and pins were all of different diameters and hence unusable.[50] What did this mean in practice? Factories which required parts for broken-down machinery had to machine the parts themselves, without access to drawings or patterns. Aside from the high cost and inefficiency of such a system (all but the very smallest Soviet factories had to maintain their own separate, and often very large, machine shops), the quality of the parts was unreliable, and so it was small wonder that the machinery, once repaired, might break down again almost straightaway.

Shortages of materials and tools. Of all the characteristics of Soviet industrial production the chronic shortage of materials, both raw and

[47] *Stalinets* (Rostsel'mash), 21 March 1950.
[48] *Trud*, 18 May 1947 (Ya. Vishnyak); *Voprosy ekonomiki*, no. 6, 1948, p. 36 (K. Klimenko).
[49] *Trud*, 12 June 1946, citing problems at Moscow's Stalin motor vehicle works.
[50] GARF, f. 7676, op. 16, d. 894, l. 118. In 1947 it was still the case that two of the country's railway carriage factories cut threads in inches, while all the other factories in that branch were fully metricated (*Trud*, 18 May 1947).

semi-finished, is perhaps the most familiar to non-specialists in Soviet affairs and was the major cause of storming. The picture of factories sending out 'pushers' to suppliers in order to expedite missing orders has been well described in a number of popular sources.[51] Supply shortages permeated every aspect of Soviet industrial life: relations between industrial ministries bargaining for resources at the top of the system; relations between enterprise managers and their superordinate administrations; and shop-floor behaviour within the enterprise itself. The amount of time lost because of the non-arrival or non-availability of materials could reach staggering proportions. The Krasnyi proletarii engineering works in Moscow in 1947 found it difficult to acquire adequate quantities of almost anything made of metal – castings, ball bearings, rolled steel – even though they had multiple suppliers for many of these items. The cumulative effect was long periods of enforced idleness for a number of workers: some machine-tool operators, it was claimed, had supplies to keep them busy for only half the workday; a group of assemblers was left without work for fifteen days.[52] But losses did not stop there. From the beginnings of Stalinist industrialization until the collapse of the USSR, foremen were compelled to spend large parts of their time away from their managerial tasks, hunting down missing parts, materials, and tools.[53]

Construction was especially vulnerable to interruptions and shortfalls in supplies. The iron and steel works in Orsk-Khalilovsk in Chkalov oblast' during April and May 1948 received just 40 per cent of the bricks, 14 per cent of the timber, and 19 per cent of the crushed quarry stone needed to fulfil its house-building plan. It fared little better obtaining materials for construction of the plant itself, even though the latter would have been granted far higher priority: the coke ovens site had just 29 per cent of the required amount of cement, 30 per cent of the quarry stone, 42 per cent of the timber, 45 per cent of the lime stone, and 48 per cent of the bricks. It was this which explained why young workers on the site were constantly being moved around from one job to another, rather than working in their actual trades: there simply were not enough materials to keep them employed at one task for an entire shift.[54]

However great supply problems were at major enterprises, in lower-status rural industries they were even worse. The example of the large porcelain factory in Zhitomir oblast', Ukraine, which I have already cited

---

[51] See, for example, Kaiser's excellent account in his *Russia*, ch. 9.
[52] *Trud*, 30 May 1947.   [53] See, for example, *Kirovets*, 25 March 1947.
[54] TsKhDMO, f. 1, op. 4, d. 961, l. 14–15.

in other contexts, shows the extremes to which supplies shortages determined both the work routine and family life. Because the factory made
consumer goods it received no allocation of coal; instead, it had to fire
its kilns with peat, which had a high but variable moisture content. As
the production plan allowed no time for the peat to dry out, the factory
had to use whatever was available, which meant that firing times became completely unpredictable. Workers, most of whom were women
from the surrounding countryside who had taken jobs at the factory
to escape the collective farms, would, therefore, have to load and un-
load the kilns at almost any time during the day or night. They therefore slept at the factory, and when the kiln was ready for unloading
and reloading the shop chief would go around with a flashlight waking
them up.[55]

*Lack of coordination between mechanized and unmechanized production
operations.* The frequent equipment stoppages caused by breakdowns and
lack of supplies disrupted the work not just of the workers carrying out
that particular operation, but had knock-on effects which rippled through
all subsequent stages of production. A lathe which went out of service
meant delays – sometimes long delays – for any task which had to handle
the parts which the lathe should have machined but did not, whether it
be cleaning, quality inspection, or final assembly. There was, however,
a further major factor that undermined coordination, namely the uneven mechanization of interdependent operations. The gap was greatest
between direct production operations, which received priority for investment, and auxiliary jobs. The latter, however, covered a broad range of
tasks, from foundry work to warehousing to cleaning up work areas, virtually all of which were essential to the smooth operation of a factory.
Perhaps surprisingly, engineering, which accounted for just over a quarter of all industrial workers in the immediate postwar years,[56] had one of
the highest percentages of workers doing strictly manual operations. Even
in its most highly mechanized subbranch, motor vehicle production, half
of all workers were doing manual labour.[57] Admittedly some of these were
workers in skilled occupations, such as fitters, electricians, and mechanics, who were required in excessive numbers because of the high frequency
of equipment breakdown. But the vast proportion of this unmechanized
work was heavy manual labour, especially in lifting and transporting. The
primary difficulty was that Soviet industry simply did not manufacture

[55] Interview with M.Z,, January 1997.   [56] *Trud v SSSR* (1968), pp. 84–5.
[57] *Voprosy ekonomiki*, no. 6, 1948, p. 36 (K. Klimenko).

enough lifting and conveying machinery. In 1946, admittedly still a difficult year early in the recovery period, the Ministry of Heavy Engineering, which had responsibility for producing this equipment, could fill fewer than a tenth of its orders for basic conveyors; more specialized conveyors, or transporting machinery needed for only certain branches of industry, it did not produce at all. Moreover, much of what it did manufacture was of poor quality. This in turn had two effects. The first and most obvious was that Soviet industry simply went without warehousing machinery. The second was that each individual ministry set about instructing its own factories – which did not have the specialized know-how or capacity – to make the equipment themselves. This was expensive, deepened the problems of standardization and quality, and diverted scarce resources away from the lines of production these ministries were supposed to produce.[58]

The fact was, however, that in this area Soviet industry, from central ministries down to factory directors, worked according to that same macabre calculus which dictated attitudes towards the mechanization of unsafe production processes. Labour power, especially that of women and teenagers, was cheap, while investment in the mechanization of auxiliary operations was expensive. Stalinist 'planning' operated according to a strict hierarchy of priorities, with heavy industry – that is, coal, iron and steel, non-ferrous metallurgy, engineering, and industrial construction – receiving the lion's share of investment; within these sectors and their constituent enterprises investment went first and foremost to 'direct production', leaving auxiliary operations neglected, no matter how essential they were to the smooth working of the enterprise.

The use of work time

The discussion in the previous two sections allows us to construct a general picture of the 'typical' Soviet industrial enterprise. Workers and managers had to operate within a hazardous environment, where basic safety features were lacking and the absence of safety equipment, the shortages of basic tools and materials, and the pressures of plan fulfilment compelled them to cut corners and ignore what were to a large extent unenforceable regulations – at enormous cost to their health. The factory was also a highly uncertain terrain which threw up countless obstacles to meeting the centre's relentless demands for increased production. Factories were dirty, badly lit, cold in winter, and unbearably hot in summer.

[58] *Trud*, 11 May 1946 (L. Kifer, A. Spivakovskii); *Trud*, 12 June 1946.

Most lacked basic amenities, such as decent showers and locker rooms, not to mention clean facilities for women workers. Workers and line managers faced virtually permanent frustration having to cope with shortages of raw materials, fuel, metal, tools, and reliable machinery, all of which made a mockery of production schedules and plans.

Yet this is only one dimension of the reality of industrial life. Such conditions necessitated ongoing efforts by workers and managers not just to adapt themselves to the system, but to adapt the system to them. And so, as under capitalism, we see under Stalinism an intricate set of informal relationships develop on the shop floor. We can loosely present this as a matrix of vectors, some of which moved in the same direction, others of which were in conflict. At the centre was the regime, which pressured both workers and managers to boost production, irrespective of the human and economic cost. Within the enterprise, managers and workers sometimes acted in concert to resist this pressure, in order to ease the strains of the work regime and to utilize what resources were on hand in order to make the plans more 'fulfillable'. At other times, however, management, usually supported by the enterprise trade union organization, acted as the enforcer of central policy, and in these situations workers found themselves trying to cope with – and to circumvent – not just the intense pressures coming from the centre, but those from management as well.

The factory, therefore, became a contested field in which specific groups of people pursued their own interests, sometimes in tandem, sometimes in opposition to one another. The main area of contestation was the use of work time. The regime attempted to assert its control over work time partially through direct regulation – in the postwar period still linked to criminal penalties – of attendance, timekeeping, and behaviour on the job, and partially through a highly coercive wages system.

The Stalinist regime was obsessed with the question of what it called 'labour discipline'. This proved to be an extremely sweeping category. It included forms of behaviour which we would associate with discipline issues at a Western enterprise, such as insubordination, disobedience, time wasting, drinking on the job, or absenteeism; but, as we saw in chapter 5, it also embraced job-changing, which, from the First Five-Year Plan until Khrushchev's 'Secret Speech' of February 1956, the regime tried to control through a mixture of administrative, economic, and criminal sanctions.

The issue that, after job-changing, most preoccupied official attention was absenteeism, which from 1940 to 1951 was also a criminal offence, punishable by corrective labour at one's place of employment at reduced pay. There are no good data on absenteeism, even of an indicative nature, for the early postwar period. We know that each year up until its decriminalization in mid-1951, between 500,000 and 900,000 people were convicted for it under the Edict of 26 June 1940. The penalties were relatively minor, insofar as they did not involve imprisonment, but instead imposed up to six months of corrective labour at the worker's ordinary enterprise, subject to a cut in pay of up to 25 per cent. Given the hardships of postwar conditions, however, the latter could in and of itself be a severe sanction. The bits and pieces of anecdotal evidence mentioned in factory newspapers and ministerial files suggest, however, that absenteeism was really very low. The Ministry of Construction of Enterprises in Heavy Industry reported that during 1948 the equivalent of 18 per cent of its workers committed absenteeism during 1948, and roughly 14 per cent during 1949. This may seem a significant percentage, but the costs to production were in fact small: total time lost because of truancy accounted for only about 0.5 per cent of all work time, a quite trivial figure when compared to the amounts of time lost because of equipment stoppages, shortages of tools, non-arrival of supplies, or any of the other difficulties which routinely plagued Soviet production.[59]

This contention is, of course, somewhat conditional because the officially recorded data were extremely unreliable, probably even more unreliable than the reports from the Labour Reserve schools on the numbers of students who ran away. There is ample evidence to suggest that even the archive reports on absenteeism were a gross underestimate. Timekeeping in Soviet enterprises was notoriously lax. Some factory entrances did not even have timekeeping boards. Many timekeepers paid little attention to who came and went, and the number of tallies hanging up at any given time might have little or no relation to the actual number of people on the premises. Punctuality and good attendance even among timekeepers was also a problem.[60] Adding to the confusion was the extremely poor record-keeping of enterprise establishments. Managers sometimes did not know how many people were actually working for them or who these people were. In such situations accurate reporting of absenteeism became simply a pipe dream. A report from the procurator of Karaganda oblast' on labour discipline in coal mining construction during late 1949 sums up the problem with extraordinary eloquence. Referring to the official information which the construction organizations were submitting on labour discipline violations, he noted:

[59] GARF, f. 8131, op. 29, d. 224, l. 4. The data cover the first nine months of each year; I have estimated annual rates from these.
[60] GARF, f. 8131, op. 37, d. 3747, l. 109, 145, and d. 3761, l. 141–3.

The figures produced in this report on the number of cases of absenteeism and wilfully abandoning production during the fourth quarter of 1948 and the three quarters of 1949 are of little reliability, although they have been obtained from the *glavk* with the appropriate signatures. An inspection carried out in November of this year established that, just as one year ago, the data from personnel departments of the construction organizations do not correspond to the data from timekeepers, the data of the administrations do not correspond to the data of the *glavk*, etc., and all this because on this question a total muddle reigns inside the construction administrations, the section chiefs and timekeepers do not know which cases of *progul* to consider justified and which unjustified, the information sent to the personnel departments is arrived at 'by eye', and then this confusion goes to the *glavk*.

On the construction of the Kostenko mine the chiefs of certain sites have no idea how many workers they have on their assigned establishment. In addition, the heads of construction transfer workers from one site to another without the knowledge of the site superintendents, which makes the confusion on this matter even greater, and as a result the superintendents of individual sites record certain workers as truants or even as having wilfully abandoned their jobs, when in fact they are working on the very same construction project, but on different sites.[61]

The data on *progul* were also questionable for another reason: managers and timekeepers deliberately covered it up. The line managers in the machine-tool industry, for example, granted their workers nearly four times as many days off to tend to personal business than the industry officially lost due to absenteeism.[62] Obviously some, even much, of this might have been totally warranted, but there is ample other evidence that a great deal of absenteeism was simply concealed, over and above those truants who slipped through the net because of slovenly timekeeping on the part of shops and work sites.[63] We also know that at least some managers minimized the need to refer cases to court by handling absenteeism as a matter of internal discipline.[64]

There were, however, other factors involved, especially during the terrible shortages of food and clothing in the first postwar years. As I noted in chapter 4, the extreme poverty of young workers led at least some

---

[61] GARF, f. 8131, op. 37, d. 5038, l. 119–20. The somewhat torturous punctuation is in the original.

[62] GARF, f. 8131, op. 29, d. 207, l. 12. The data are for 1949.

[63] References are too numerous to list in full. For illustrative examples, see *Trud*, 30 May 1947; GARF, f. 8131, op. 37, d. 3747, l. 109, 145; d. 3761, l. 141–3; and d. 5036, l. 207.

[64] *Elektrosila*, 30 August 1947; GARF, f. 8131, op. 37, d. 3747, l. 70–2, and d. 5036, l. 227–8. The Karaganda oblast' procurator alleged that mines in his region were allowing truants to make up the time lost by working on their days off, as an alternative to prosecution (*ibid.*, op. 29, l. 266, l. 5).

of them to fail to report for work because they did not have adequate clothing, or shoes, or on occasion even sufficient food.[65] In at least one such case their actions were supported by the trade union.[66] However, young workers were not the only ones affected in this way. We know of cases in which older workers on railway construction were so poor that they, too, survived by selling off their bedding, clothing, and work boots, and, according to their trade union, could not work because they had no money to buy bread.[67] Possibly more significant from a political point of view were those instances in which workers used *progul* as a way of staging *de facto* strikes. I have already described the most important of these incidents in chapter 3, in discussing the protests of railway workers against wage arrears. Similar but smaller-scale protests occurred in other industries. Thus in 1948, the coal mining trade union reported the refusal of between seventy and eighty young workers to report to work at a mine in Korkino (Chelyabinsk oblast') because they had not been paid for two months. The union placed the blame fully on the management for using the courts as a substitute for creating decent working and living conditions.[68] Another case of *progul*-as-strike was in Latvia in 1946, when a group of railway construction workers were commandeered to do logging work at wages far below those they had been earning. Eventually they had had enough and simply refused to report for work, demanding their return to their parent construction organization. The inspector from the workers' trade union defended them, noting with a certain degree of understatement that whatever administrative measures were taken against them had best take account of the 'reasonableness' of their motives.[69]

Peter Solomon has already documented the pressures which led the regime to decriminalize *progul* in its Edict of 14 July 1951, in particular the huge backlog of cases which by the end of the 1940s were clogging up the courts.[70] Under the new law, all but the most serious cases of flagrant absenteeism became matters of internal discipline, to be dealt with by Comrades' Courts – workplace tribunals at which workers were allegedly judged by their peers and which could impose only minor, non-criminal penalties. If the regime thought that this liberalization was the mere legal recognition of the docility of its workforce it was quite mistaken. Almost

[65] TsKhDMO, f. 1, op. 4, d. 1100, l. 106; RGAE, f. 8592, op. 2, d. 25, l. 4; GARF, f. 8131, op. 37, d. 3747, l. 50ob., 251.
[66] See above, ch. 4, pp. 134–5 (citing GARF, f. 8131, op. 37, d. 4159, l. 73–4).
[67] RGAE, f. 1884, op. 31, d. 7888, l. 60.   [68] GARF, f. 7416, op. 4, d. 268, l. 4.
[69] GARF, f. 5475, op. 21, d. 356, l. 8–10.   [70] Solomon, pp. 423–5.

everywhere there occurred a huge leap in the number of offences.[71] An internal Communist Party report, dated 18 March 1952, noted with alarm that absenteeism during the second half of 1951 had nearly tripled in coal mining, doubled in chemicals and cotton textiles, and gone up by 50 per cent in the oil industry.[72] In non-ferrous metallurgy absenteeism during the first three months of 1952 was nearly three times what it had been during the three months before the law was relaxed.[73] Data from the Ministry for Construction of Enterprises in Heavy Industry (Mintyazhprom) show an identical trend: absenteeism leapt from 112,689 days lost during the period January–June 1951 to 178,562 days during July–November, which extrapolates out to over 214,000 days for the half-year July to December – that is, a rise of virtually 100 per cent. This trend continued through the first half of 1952, and started to show a decline only towards the end of that year.[74] Young workers appear to have been the most eager to take advantage of the new regulations, at least according to Komsomol reports from the engineering industry. Absenteeism among this group during the second half of 1951 compared to the first half rose five-fold at the Stalingrad tractor factory; six-fold at the Stalin factory in Nizhnii Tagil and the Chelyabinsk tractor factory; and ten-fold at the Rostov agricultural machinery factory (Rostsel'mash).[75]

It is possible, of course, that some of this increase was due to a greater willingness by enterprise directors and line managers to report violations, since they no longer needed to protect workers from criminal penalties.

[71] It is possible – although not overly probable – that the regime and/or its legal advisors were lulled into a false sense of complacency by the experience following the demilitarization of transport in the spring of 1948. Here, too, there was a large increase in the number of cases of absenteeism, but most of these were due to the reclassification of offences under the new law. Under the Edicts of April and May 1943 lateness of up to two hours was dealt with as a violation of internal discipline and handled by local managers. With demilitarization, absenteeism now came under the Edict of 26 June 1940, which classified as truancy any lateness of more than 20 minutes. In the same way, prolonged periods of absenteeism (*otluchka*) had been prosecuted as desertion, but after April 1948 were treated as *progul*. However, even allowing for this fact the reports from the railway procurators make it clear that absenteeism had gone up, and that much of it was now being concealed by local management. See, for example, GARF, f. 8131, op. 37, d. 4581, l. 230–1; d. 4585, l. 119; and d. 4592, l. 64, 64ob.

[72] RGASPI, f. 17, op. 131, d. 279, l. 24.   [73] GARF, f. 8131, op. 28, d. 1152, l. 11.

[74] RGAE, f. 8592, op. 2, d. 899, l. 84–7, and d. 915, l. 74. Iron and steel also showed a fall in *progul* at the end of 1952, but we do not have figures for the period immediately following decriminalization, and so cannot assess whether this had been preceded by an upward trend (RGAE, f. 8875, op. 46, d. 279, l. 87).

[75] TsKhDMO, f. 1, op. 2, d. 313, l. 273–5. Similar figures were cited for engineering works in Gor'kii, Kramatorsk, Novosibirsk, and Khar'kov. Perhaps the most spectacular increase was among young workers at the Lipetsk tractor factory: from 37 cases of *progul* in July 1951 to a monthly average of 1,200 cases during October through December (*ibid.*, l. 272).

This was not, however, the view of either VTsSPS or the above-mentioned internal Party report, both of which complained in early 1952 that managers were continuing to use various ruses to conceal absenteeism, often on a massive scale.[76] Even if such charges were exaggerated, they at least suggest that the huge leap in violations was more than just a statistical artefact of more accurate reporting. It seems equally evident that the Comrades' Courts were somewhat less than successful. Enterprise Party and trade union organizations were slow to organize them, and once they were set up there were long delays in hearing cases. More seriously, from the regime's point of view, they inspired a resounding apathy among workers, few of whom bothered to attend sessions. In this, however, they apparently were merely imitating the behaviour of management, Party, and trade union officials, who also showed little interest. The courts tended to be dominated by Party functionaries, which, according to one report for the Central Committee Secretariat, undermined their legitimacy in the eyes of ordinary workers.[77]

However, even if we take all of these factors into account, it is clear that the damage absenteeism did to production did not even remotely approach that caused by factors within production itself, whether it be equipment stoppages, supply shortages, incompetent scheduling, or deliberate slacking by workers themselves. Figures for construction suggest that, even after the steep rise in absenteeism after mid-1951, the amount of work time lost in this way continued to be very small.[78] Examples from the engineering industry suggest a similar pattern: the machine shop of one large excavator factory incorporated into its calculations *planned* downtime of machinery of between 35 and 40 per cent.[79] In its own way the regime acknowledged this fact through incessant campaigns to intensify the use of the working day and to limit the amount of time workers spent away from their assigned tasks. Because the regime could

[76] RGASPI, f. 17, op. 131, d. 278, l. 65–6, and d. 279, l. 25–6. The latter backed up its claim with a few quite spectacular examples. Management at the Metallurgstroi construction trust in Sverdlovsk oblast' levied penalties on only 7 of 656 truants during the second half of 1951. While it fired thirty-four of the truants during this time, it did not enter this in their labour books, thus allowing them to retain their record of uninterrupted service, without which workers could not claim full pension or disability benefits.

[77] RGASPI, f. 17, op. 131, d. 279, l. 26–30, 32–5.

[78] Although absenteeism in industrial construction tripled between the first half of 1951 and the end of the first half of 1952, even then it cost enterprises well under 1 per cent of work time, a trivial amount compared to what was lost because of routine stoppages (RGAE, f. 8592, op. 2, d. 915, l. 74).

[79] GARF, f. 7676, op. 16, d. 894, l. 72–72ob. The factory was the Kovrov excavator factory in Vladimir oblast'; the data are from December 1949 through February 1950.

not acknowledge that the huge losses of work time stemmed from the bureaucratic system itself, it was prone to explain them as the consequence of poor management and/or the negligent attitudes of workers. In reality there is no clear dividing line between the losses due to 'structural' factors and those caused by the deliberate actions of factory personnel. Disruptions to the smooth organization and flow of production undoubtedly created occasions during which workers could, and perhaps even had to, spend significant amounts of time partially or even completely idle. By the same token, the deliberately lax use of work time by workers in one stage of production caused, or at least helped to cause, the dislocations which then imposed enforced idleness on workers further along the production cycle. This is extremely well documented for the prewar period and from Stalin's death onward.[80] Evidence for the period we are dealing with here is less abundant. Factory newspapers and archive reports certainly do cite cases of workers arriving late, abandoning work before the end of their shifts, unilaterally extending their meal breaks, being drunk on the job, and even sleeping on the job.[81] Control over the amount of time workers spent trying to obtain food was especially difficult to impose, given the sorry state of factory dining rooms and buffets. Cramped premises, irregular food deliveries, shortages of plates and cutlery, and understaffing made it extremely difficult, if not impossible, for workers to eat within the standard half-hour allotted for meal breaks. The main coal trust in Chelyabinsk oblast' estimated in 1948 that its workers needed anywhere between one hour and two and a half hours to obtain lunch,[82] thus making a mockery of official regulations. By the same token, it was equally hard for timekeepers or line managers to determine how much of the extra time taken was unavoidable, and how much workers may have taken advantage of the situation to extend their break even further.

[80] Filtzer, *Soviet Workers and Stalinist Industrialization*, ch. 6; Filtzer, *Soviet Workers and De-Stalinization*, pp. 139–45; Filtzer, *Soviet Workers and the Collapse of Perestroika*, ch. 6.
[81] *Elektrosila*, 30 August 1947; *Stalinets* (Rostsel'mash), 12 March 1948; *Stalinets* (Kuibyshev), 11 October 1950; *Stalinskaya vakhta*, 28 March 1951; RGASPI, f. 17, op. 131, d. 278, l. 67; GARF, f. 7676, op. 16, d. 1203, l. 51–2.
[82] GARF, f. 7416, op. 4, d. 268, l. 5–6. According to *Trud*, 31 July 1948, the dining rooms in other coal trusts were so badly equipped that 'knives, glasses, and forks are a great rarity'. This phenomenon is documented even more strikingly in the files and factory newspapers of the engineering industry. See GARF, f. 7676, op. 16, d. 488, l. 41–3; d. 490, l. 20–1, 26ob.–27, 28ob.–29, 46; *Elektrosila*, 21 March, 24 September 1947; *Kabel'shchik*, 21 April 1948; *Krasnyi treugol'nik*, 9 April 1948; TsGAIPD, f. 2600, op. 3, d. 32, l. 24–5. During 1947 and 1948 some enterprise canteens were put under even greater pressure because they allowed members of the public to eat there, making it yet more difficult for their own employees to eat and get back to work on time.

Compared to other periods in Soviet history, however, references to deliberate slacking or time wasting are surprisingly scarce. The question is why. One possible explanation is that the tighter discipline imposed during World War II had made such overt disregard of work regulations less frequent and this carried over into the postwar period, when conditions were nearly as stringent. We know that this was certainly the case in rural industry, in which workers saw factory employment as the only thing keeping them from having to work on the dreaded collective farms, and only skilled male workers in scarce trades, such as fitters or tool-setters, could afford to violate discipline with any kind of impunity.[83] Although jobs in the major urban centres may not have been seen as a direct salvation from the kolkhoz, it was still the case that the lack of labour mobility took away from workers a powerful bargaining tool, namely the threat to quit. To this extent we could argue that workers simply had less power on the shop floor. On the other hand, given what we know about the relatively widespread circumvention of the laws against job-changing, it is equally possible that minor discipline infractions were more common than the sources suggest, and that managers simply covered them up or did not report them. An even more important consideration is that lax discipline, in particular the slack use of work time, could be an opportunistic and even logical response to the irregular rhythms of Soviet production: if workers wandered away from the work bench to look for scarce tools or parts they were also likely to stop along the way for a smoke or to chat with a mate. In such instances, as with extended meal breaks, no one may have bothered to differentiate between losses of work time which were the workers' 'fault' and those which were part and parcel of the Soviet working day.

What levers did the regime have at its disposal to control workers' behaviour? As in other periods of Soviet history, dismissal and the threat of unemployment were not an option. Even allowing that towards the end of the recovery period some industries actually shed labour, most workers still enjoyed the *de facto* protection of the labour shortage, although the fact that most of the postwar deficit in labour power was made good by either indentured or slave labour undoubtedly weakened its impact. The heavy criminal penalties against job-changing and absenteeism were equally not relevant. If anything, managers were prone to conceal or ignore those cases of sloppy timekeeping which might render a worker liable to prosecution for truancy. This left two main levers of control: political mobilization and ideological appeals, on the one hand, and speedup campaigns, on the other. The former had little efficacy, as I discuss in this book's conclusion. The main instrument, therefore, was the

[83] Interview with M.Z., January 1997.

intensification of labour. And the primary method of intensifying labour was the system of wages and norm-setting.

Wage determination

During the 1930s the Stalinist elite had utilized a range of policies to extract more surplus product from labour power. Broadly speaking these fell into two categories: the encouragement of rate-busters, whose production records were used to push up output quotas for all workers; and periodic – usually annual – increases in output quotas (norms) and a corresponding cut in piece rates. Rate-busting was both collective and individual, and was by no means always voluntary. Under so-called socialist competition, groups of workers would pledge to outproduce each other or achieve some other major indicator of production, for example, a reduction in production costs. The competition might be between entire enterprises, or between different shops within an enterprise, or even between individual workers. By and large it was a phoney system, and workers had little choice over whether or not to participate. Resolutions to challenge another factory or another work team in competition were proposed and carried at carefully orchestrated meetings. Workers often did not know that they had signed up to compete. By the same token, the patent fakery of socialist competition meant it played a rather questionable role in motivating workers to improve their performance. Much more effective were appeals to individual rate-busting, first through the system of so-called shock work, and later through its successor campaign, Stakhanovism. Both operated on the same principle. Individual workers were given material incentives to overfulfil their production targets, and their achievements were then used to ratchet up the production quotas for everybody else. Although there is no doubt that some shock workers participated out of pride or ideological enthusiasm, the fact was that given the dire hardships of the 1930s most took part out of desperation to improve their meagre standard of living. Both shock work and Stakhanovism engendered considerable resentment among rank-and-file workers and had more or less ceased to have any great importance from late 1937 onwards. Although Stakhanovism maintained a formal existence throughout the postwar period, it had little practical impact on work practices or worker behaviour and, I would argue, even received only token resonance in the press. Socialist competition was taken rather more seriously by the industrial ministries and the official trade unions, but there is ample evidence to suggest that at factory level management and the enterprise union organizations implemented it in an even more formalistic and mechanical fashion than they had in the 1930s.[84]

The main vehicle for exerting pressure on workers was the system of wages and norm-setting. This, too, since the 1930s had become a more or less permanent area of contestation between the regime, workers, and industrial managers. The basic premise was quite simple: the overwhelming majority of industrial workers worked on piece rates, and production quotas were set in such a way that workers needed to overfulfil them by quite substantial amounts in order to earn what by Soviet standards would be a living wage. Each year the regime, on the pretext of upgrading quotas to bring them into line with technological improvements, raised norms and reduced job prices, so that workers would have to produce even more in order to maintain earnings at their previous level. There is no question that this system imposed considerable hardship on workers, but as a method of disciplining them, it was far from perfect. Management, forced by the intrinsic disorganization of production and the fear of losing workers to enterprises offering higher wages, often refused to impose the full rises. When this was not possible, they might collude in other ruses to maintain workers' customary earnings, for example, by allowing them to inflate their production results or paying them spurious bonuses. Norm-setting itself was bedevilled by numerous structural impediments. Norm-setters were badly trained and underpaid. On most operations it was extremely difficult to set quotas and rates in conformity with those set down in nationwide handbooks since the conditions of production varied enormously from one factory to another, depending on the age of equipment, the rate of breakdown, and the accessibility of raw materials, fuel, and spare parts. While the Soviet regime struggled throughout its entire existence to impose so-called technically based norms, that is, norms calculated on the assumption that equipment would be used at its optimal technological capacity, the overwhelming majority of norms continued to be set 'empirically', that is, calculated on the basis of actual equipment utilization within the given enterprise and taking account of all of the ordinary disruptions to work rhythms. There were also wide variations between workers in more mechanized operations, for which rates were easier to set, and those in manual, usually auxiliary operations, in which workers had greater control over how they organized and carried

---

[84] On shock work and Stakhanovism, see Filtzer, *Soviet Workers and Stalinist Industrialization*, chs. 3 and 7; and Siegelbaum. On the formalistic application of socialist competition in the postwar era, see RGASPI, f. 17, op. 132, d. 114, l. 95–6; TsKhDMO, f. 1, op. 2, d. 272, l. 98–102, and d. 313, l. 56–7, 61–3, 65, 106–8, 109, 243; and op. 3, d. 509, l. 78.

out their jobs. During most of the Soviet era these various tendencies – that is, the structural barriers to accurate rate-setting and the informal intervention of line managers to protect customary earnings – created a situation in which workers in most industries were substantially overfulfilling their norms, even if plans were only barely being met. It was not uncommon for norms to lag so far behind actual productivity that if an enterprise's workers fulfilled them by only 100 per cent, that enterprise would substantially *underfulfil* its plan. The other side of this, of course, was that mere 100 per cent norm fulfilment would not earn workers a living wage.[85]

Norm-setting in the immediate postwar years did not fully conform to this pattern. There were a number of factors – discussed more fully in previous chapters – which, as with the use of work time, would have acted to weaken workers' ability to extract concessions from management in the so-called effort bargain on the shop floor. First of all, informal negotiation over norms and piece rates needs to be seen in the general context of the catastrophic fall in the standard of living imposed first by the war and then by the 1946–7 famine, in response to which the Stalinist leadership imposed further ruthless restrictions on consumption. As during the First Five-Year Plan, dearth undoubtedly had a disciplining effect insofar as it compelled workers to maximize earnings by maximizing output. Secondly, that large proportion of the labour force which was semi-free, in particular young workers (I leave out of account here the slave labour sector), had extremely limited bargaining power on the shop floor. Occupying the least skilled and worst-paid jobs, the strongest sanction they could bring to bear on management was to run away. This was indeed a serious problem, but the attitude of management seems to have been that such young recruits were expendable; they could be easily replaced by further labour conscription, if not by prisoners. It is noteworthy that the most strident calls for enterprises to improve conditions for young workers came from the trade unions, the Komsomol, and the industrial ministries, while concrete measures taken by managers themselves were very modest.

The picture that we see, therefore, is one of almost universally low wages, with a large minority of workers not even managing to maintain basic levels of subsistence. The amount that workers earned depended on a range of circumstances: the importance or unimportance of the industry in which they worked; the region in which they lived; trade; skill levels; gender; age; and their bargaining power with line management on the shop floor. For some of these determinants, for example, discrepancies

---

[85] On the history of Soviet wages and norm-setting policies, see Filtzer, *Soviet Workers and Stalinist Industrialization*, ch. 8; Filtzer, *Soviet Workers and De-Stalinization*, ch. 4; and Filtzer, *Soviet Workers and the Collapse of Perestroika*, ch. 2.

Table 6.3. *Average monthly wages, major branches of Soviet industry, December 1946 and September 1950, in rubles*

Industry	Average money wage, December 1946	Average money wage, September 1950
All industry	626	687
Coal	1,255	1,223
Metallurgy	846	1,104
Metalworking	633	735
Oil	750	731
Cotton textiles	574	608
Building materials	n/d	591
Construction	n/d	565
Food processing	n/d	512
Footwear	n/d	462
Garment	n/d	433

Note: Metallurgy figure is for March 1950.
Source: 1946 – RGAE, f. 1562, op. 15, d. 2129, l. 80 and d. 2130, l. 32–6. 1950 – RGAE, f. 1562, op. 15, d. 3086, l. 172, 196, 198, 201, 204, 207 (oil, metallurgy, coal, and metalworking); *Trud v SSSR* (Moscow, 1968), pp. 140–4 (all industry, cotton textiles, building materials, construction, food processing, footwear, and garment industries).

between the different branches of industry, the disadvantages suffered by young workers, and the importance of informal bargaining, we have a fair amount of information about the postwar years; for others, most notably gender discrimination, we still know relatively little, although we can draw some inferences regarding horizontal gender segregation from table 6.3, which shows the average wage in the major branches of industry.

We see from table 6.3 that coal mining and iron and steel were the most privileged industries in terms of wages, a fact which reflected the priority the regime attached to them, as well as the difficulties they had retaining and recruiting workers, given their unfavourable locations and harsh working conditions. Textiles and other sectors of light industry were, by contrast, the worst paid and politically the most vulnerable. Their ministries had the lowest priority in the regime's economic plans and their workers had relatively little bargaining power within their factories. A possible exception to this pattern was construction, which despite its strategic importance nonetheless paid extremely low wages.[86] But even

[86] Wages in railway construction were even lower. The average monthly wage of skilled carpenters and erectors ranged between 410 and 430 rubles in late 1949; unskilled workers averaged as little as 290 rubles a month. These earnings were well below the

within a given industry earnings could fluctuate considerably, not just between factories, but even between workers in the same occupation or skill
grade (*razryad*). Such fluctuations or disparities depended on a number
of factors, many of which workers were unable to influence: the ease
or difficulty with which workers could fulfil their norms; the number of
stoppages suffered due to lack of supplies or equipment breakdowns; the
amount of overtime worked; and the myriad informal bargaining arrangements which evolved at shop level between workers and line managers,
and through which workers in a relatively strong position could extract
various concessions, for example, being put on jobs in which the norms
were easy to fulfil.

In certain industries, such as textiles, norms and bonus systems had
been relaxed during the war because of the large influx of inexperienced
and low-skilled workers, mostly women and young teenagers, who without such adjustments could not have earned enough to survive. The same
was true on the railways, where basic wage rates for engine drivers were
supplemented by various bonuses which when added together made up
over half their monthly earnings.[87] Whereas the locomotive drivers earned
relatively high wages, even while failing to meet their performance targets, in most other industries the situation was quite the opposite: high
norm fulfilment did not guarantee workers anything remotely resembling
'customary' earnings, and at many enterprises workers were not even
earning the wages called for by the central plan. The most extreme case
was the knitwear industry, in which wages ranked near the bottom of
light industry: in 1947 and early 1948 average norm fulfilment was considerably above 100 per cent, yet average earnings were only around 500
rubles, roughly three-quarters of what was then the average industrial
wage, and well below the average wage even in cotton textiles. The picture was very similar in the building materials industry, another low-wage
sector with high average norm fulfilment. But even in engineering and
iron and steel wages did not come up to planned levels at least until the
end of the 1940s.[88] Part – but only part – of these disparities can be
explained by the large 'tail' of low earners, primarily young workers, in
almost every industry, workers whose inexperience and lack of bargaining power allowed management to put them on the lowest-paid jobs with
the worst conditions, in which they found it extremely difficult to fulfil

already quite miserable *planned* wages set by the Railways Ministry of just 458 rubles a
month, a fact that prompted the ministry to petition the USSR Council of Ministers to
allow it to raise wages along the lines proposed for workers in industrial construction,
discussed below (RGAE, f. 1884, op. 31, d. 8315, l. 37–8, 41).
[87] For the railways, see GARF, f. 5475, op. 21, d. 520, l. 101–101ob., 102–102ob., 103.
[88] GARF, f. 5457, op. 22, d. 707, l. 2 and d. 708, l. 26–7, 46 (knitwear); RGAE, f. 8248,
op. 21, d. 162, l. 5 (building materials); GARF, f. 7676, op. 16, d. 170, l. 110ob., 112
(engineering); RGAE, f. 8875, op. 46, d. 210, l. 9–10 (iron and steel).

their norms. Again we can cite the example of the building materials industry, in which in December 1946 one in five workers and in December 1947 one in six workers could not meet their targets, while average fulfilment remained quite high.[89] Even more dramatic was the situation in coal mining, in which as late as December 1948 one-third – and in some trades nearly one-half – of workers were not fulfilling their norms, although I need to stress that this disparity was perhaps the most extreme in Soviet industry.[90]

It seems almost extraordinary, but in the face of such massive poverty and low earnings, from 1947 onwards the regime imposed substantial annual norm rises. The norm revisions should be seen in concert with other measures the Stalinist leadership adopted to force down consumption in the wake of the famine of 1946–7 and its determination to restore war-damaged industry through accelerated accumulation. The large increase in norms – with a corresponding cut in piece rates – for industrial and construction workers acted to limit consumption further. In most branches of light industry norms in 1948 were put up by approximately 10 to 14 per cent for production workers and 20 to 30 per cent for auxiliary workers.[91] In engineering they were raised by about 30 per cent in 1947 and 1948, and by between 20 and 30 per cent in 1950, although as throughout industry the actual rises varied considerably between one factory and another and between different trades within each enterprise.[92] In building materials in 1949 norms rose by an average of 23 per cent.[93] In all cases the pretext given was the high average norm fulfilment which most workers were achieving, together with the continued poor application of so-called technical norms. The latter argument was adduced to show that factories were operating well below their technological capacities, an issue on which I shall comment in a moment. Given the reality of low wages and low consumption levels such norm increases were little more than attempts at naked speedup.[94]

---

[89] RGAE, f. 8248, op. 21, d. 162, l. 5, and d. 213, l. 3. Even as late as 1951–2, when real wages and norm fulfilment had improved considerably compared to the period 1945–7, a large percentage of young workers in engineering – a relatively favoured sector – could not meet their output targets (TsKhDMO, f. 1, op. 2, d. 313, l. 171–2, 242–3).

[90] GARF, f. 7416, op. 7, d. 476, l. 125.   [91] GARF, f. 5457, op. 22, d. 708, l. 35–7.

[92] I have deduced the rises in 1947 and 1948 from individual factory reports: *Stalinets* (Rostsel'mash), 28 June, 5 July 1947; GARF, f. 7676, op. 16, d. 170, l. 101; d. 396, l. 15, 77; d. 397, l. 40, 121; d. 403, l. 71, 78. In 1949 machine-tool manufacture, which at the time was separate from engineering, put up norms by an average of 20 per cent (GARF, f. 7676, op. 11, d. 445, l. 10). The rises cited for 1950 are for engineering and toolmaking, and are an industry average (*ibid.*, op. 16, d. 959, l. 8–9).

[93] RGAE, f. 8248, op. 21, d. 360, l. 240.

[94] I can illustrate this general principle with a simple example, taken from the norm rises in industrial enterprises of the Railways Ministry in 1951. Norms for piece workers were put up by around 15 per cent and piece rates cut by about 14 per cent. If workers had

There is strong indirect evidence that workers' relative defenceless-
ness had prompted the regime to such an open attack. In two sectors
in which, despite the ruthless penalties for unauthorized job-changing,
labour turnover was exceptionally high, the government actually lowered
norms in order to push wages back up and in this way stem the haemorrhage of workers. In 1947 it decreed a reduction in norms for coal miners
in the Kuzbass coal fields in Western Siberia; in 1949 it decreed a similar
cut for workers in industrial construction.[95]

As in other periods of Soviet history, the mere declaration of norm rises
and rate cuts did not guarantee their universal or uniform application at
plant level. Norms, and in fact earnings in general, were always subject
to informal negotiation, even in a period such as the postwar years, when
workers' bargaining power appears to have been very weak. It is clear,
for example, that in a number of industries management retarded the introduction of new norms or found other ways to compensate workers for
the increases. The 1950 norm increases in locomotive repair factories, for
example, had virtually no impact on earnings whatsoever. The norms had
been raised in April of that year, following which both average fulfilment
and earnings momentarily dipped; but by the end of 1950 workers were
overfulfilling their norms by the same margins as before, while earnings
had either made up the lost ground or actually increased.[96] An absolutely identical pattern emerged in iron and steel, in which between 1950
and 1952 norms went up annually by an average of 15 to 17 per cent, yet
average rates of fulfilment remained virtually unchanged. What is more,
the industry also showed a long-term trend for the norms to become more
manageable. If around 14 per cent of iron and steel workers could not
meet their targets in 1945, and just under 13 per cent in 1946, by 1950
this was down to around 5 per cent, and fell to 3 per cent in 1951.[97] We
should be clear that such persistently high rates of norm overfulfilment
did not mean that workers were earning large amounts of money. On the

worked the same number of hours as before and at the same level of productivity, hourly
and therefore monthly earnings would have fallen by just under 14 per cent. Therefore,
for workers to have maintained earnings at their previous level, they would have had to
increase either their hourly productivity or the total number of hours they worked. Put
another way, they either had to work more intensively or to reduce the amount of time
during which they were idled by materials shortages or equipment stoppages. In reality
the regime used norm rises to coerce workers into doing both (GARF, f. 5474, op. 20,
d. 1858, l. 16).

[95] For coal mining, see GARF, f. 7416, op. 4, d. 110, l. 2. Norms in heavy industry
construction were reduced by a decree of the USSR Council of Ministers, No. 2892,
3 July 1949. Its impact was extensively discussed at a January 1950 Board of the Ministry
of Construction of Enterprises in Heavy Industry, RGAE, f. 8592, op. 2, d. 568, l. 74–81.

[96] GARF, f. 5474, op. 20, d. 1858, l. 23.

[97] RGAE, f. 8875, op. 46, d. 235, l. 197–8, and d. 279, l. 74–5, 144–5.

contrary, it was precisely because earnings were so precarious that many managers were willing to intervene and keep norms attainable. Moreover, the regime was operating to two different standards here. It routinely put up norms in response to perceived high average levels of overfulfilment, while ignoring the fact that such levels had become necessary to allow workers to earn merely planned – rather than above-plan – wages. This point can be illustrated through the example of the USSR's eight excavator factories in late 1951. Between September and November of that year average wages hovered just slightly above the average for engineering and metalworking workers as a whole (735 rubles in 1950; see table 6.3). However, to earn what was in effect the standard wage for their sector, these workers had to fulfil their norms by approximately 200 per cent. Looked at the other way, had they fulfilled their targets by just 100 per cent they would have earned just barely enough to ensure basic subsistence.[98]

There were, in fact, a number of ways in which managers, especially line managers at shop-floor level, could intervene to regulate earnings. In so doing they were not merely countering the harshest effects of government wage cuts, but also buffering workers against the often-devastating impact which equipment stoppages and shortages could have on earnings.[99] Norms could be lowered *de facto* by including overtime or stoppages in the calculations, thus effectively claiming that the job in question required more time to complete than allowed for in official handbooks.[100] Line managers exercised little oversight over the accurate completion of job sheets, the documents which workers filled out when finishing an assignment and which were used to calculate their output for the day. In some cases this was just a product of poor organization and sloppy management, and workers could lose money just as easily as they might come out ahead; but in other instances it was a conscious practice and had the effect, in the words of one factory trade union official, of convincing workers that their earnings were for all intents and purposes guaranteed, irrespective of how little or how much they produced.[101]

The norm-setting system itself also acted as a curb on speedup. I have already commented on what was in effect a sixty-year campaign to harangue managers and norm-setters into calculating norms on the basis of technically optimum output, rather than what was possible under real

---

[98] GARF, f. 5451, op. 26, d. 1163, l. 114.
[99] Stoppages could be so massive in scale that even skilled workers could find themselves earning less than 200 rubles a month. See the example of the Sverdlovsk turbo-motor factory – a large engineering works in one of the country's most important machine-building centres – from April 1950, GARF, f. 5451, op. 26, d. 1128, l. 42–3.
[100] GARF, f. 7676, op. 11, d. 642, l. 16–17, 39, 52–3.
[101] GARF, f. 7676, op. 11, d. 446, l. 37; d. 642, l. 52.

Soviet conditions. The fact was that norm-setters, aside from in many cases being badly trained and not very good at their jobs, were beset by endless problems and would have been unable to impose such norms even if they had wanted to and even if shop chiefs would have tolerated it. A lot of equipment lacked essential documentation listing its technical specifications. As incredible as it may seem, rate-setters lacked such basic items as clocks and stop watches. Moreover, the Soviet system of splintering jobs into myriad small-scale operations, each of which had to have its separate rate calculations, meant that the sheer volume of norm revisions required each year was simply beyond the reach of most factory rate-setting departments.[102]

These devices, which in essence were inherent to the whole structure of informal bargaining on the Soviet shop floor, were supplemented by more arbitrary concessions, some of which were tied to corruption or personal favouritism on the part of managerial personnel. We know of at least two instances in which managers were disciplined or even prosecuted for allowing favoured workers to earn vast sums through so-called contract work, in which workers were paid a set (and often very generous) price for the job. Since the price was fixed irrespective of the amount of time taken to do it, such arrangements totally undermined the coercive principles behind piece rates and norm-setting.[103]

These various examples notwithstanding, we must be clear that not all workers benefited from such arrangements and far from all managers were prepared to intervene to ensure that workers were guaranteed at least a minimal level of earnings. Skilled workers were in a far stronger position than the unskilled; older workers were more favoured than the young; men had greater leverage than did women. There is some evidence that the skilled and older workers had a strong sense of customary practice and earnings, and reacted vocally when the authorities tried to infringe them.[104] At the other extreme, the files also cite cases in which managers systematically cheated workers of their rightful pay. These were mainly in coal mining and on the railways during the early postwar years, although there is little reason to believe that similar abuses did not go on in other industries and on a more or less permanent basis. In the coal mines of both the Donbass and the Urals, managers imposed heavy and quite arbitrary fines for trivial violations of internal regulations. In some cases they refused to pay any wages to workers who had put in a full shift but had forgotten to hang up their tally, and even went so

---

[102] GARF, f. 7676, op. 16, d. 396, l. 8, 28–28ob., 33ob.; d. 397, l. 5–5ob., 19–20, 88–88ob.; *Trud*, 14 June 1949.
[103] RGAE, f. 1884, op. 31, d. 7879, l. 113–16; GARF, f. 8131, op. 29, d. 207, l. 18–19.
[104] GARF, f. 5451, op. 26, d. 966, l. 181–2, and d. 1136, l. 166–8.

far as to take away not just their money, but also their daily bread allowances and use of colliery dining rooms (an incredibly severe sanction
during the famine year of 1947). They withheld excessive amounts from
workers' wages for minor damages to equipment, as well as for rent, work
clothes, and bedding.[105] The railway trade unions complained of virtually
identical practices affecting their workers: arbitrary fines, depriving workers of customary bonuses, and large deductions for minor damages to
equipment.[106]

Conclusion

In the introductory remarks to this chapter I ventured the idea that the industrial enterprise during the postwar years was a kind of hybrid between
the type of disciplined, high-productivity workplace that the Stalinist
regime had always sought as its ideal, and the reality that emerged during
the 1930s, which deviated from this ideal rather radically. The discussion
in the preceding section might seem at odds with this characterization.
On what basis is it therefore justified? One problem is the sources of our
information. Extensive perusal of the archives of VTsSPS, the most important individual trade unions, the main industrial ministries, and the
procuracy gives us examples which show that some accommodation between workers and line management obviously took place, primarily over
norm-setting, and perhaps to a lesser degree over the use of work time.
Yet the number of detailed accounts of how this worked in practice are
surprisingly few. If we contrast this with the 1930s, we see, even without
consulting a single archive document, that the published sources, namely
the newspapers and specialized journals, give us a very detailed understanding of the give and take that went on over wages and earnings, the
intensity of the working day, and the enforcement of laws and regulations
on labour discipline. How is it that the internal postwar documents and
correspondence, most of which are highly detailed and were absolutely
secret, offer only a glimpse of this picture? One conjecture might be that
the process of informal bargaining had in fact been substantially weakened, that workers were less able to extract concessions from management
and managers were less willing to grant them.
    If we look at other aspects of the postwar period, we can cite various
pieces of circumstantial evidence that would seem to support this conclusion. First, we have the wartime controls over labour mobility and the

---

[105] GARF, f. 8131, op. 29, d. 234, l. 7; op. 37, d. 3747, l. 110, 113; op. 37, d. 3761, l. 80,
157.
[106] GARF, f. 5475, op. 21, d. 520, l. 35–6, 39, 43; d. 679, l. 53–53ob., 63; op. 25, d. 225,
l. 1–3.

violation of internal regulations. Granted that in chapter 5 I noted massive circumvention of the laws against quitting, but turnover nonetheless differed fundamentally from what had gone on before the war. Then not only were workers free to quit their jobs and move to another enterprise, but factories openly competed with each other to attract workers, even going so far as to poach them from neighbouring enterprises. The picture in the postwar period was very different. There was no 'free market' in labour power. Those who quit their jobs did so by stealth; most went back to the countryside, not to another factory or construction site. In terms of scale, turnover was far lower than in the 1930s, and was confined to a few core sectors. For them it presented a major problem, but the managers in these sectors knew that they could compensate for the loss of these workers by replacing them with prisoners or a new wave of labour conscripts. In short, workers were far less able to use the threat of leaving a job in order to extract concessions from management.

A second factor was the extreme hardships of this period, which left most of the population engaged in a simple struggle to survive, a struggle which, in sharp distinction from the 1930s, they could not pursue through strikes and mass demonstrations, as happened frequently during the First Five-Year Plan, or by the less risky and confrontational route of leaving their jobs and looking for better conditions at another enterprise. We see repeatedly in the history of both capitalist and Stalinist industry that, when workers are fearful for their basic survival, their morale falls, and with it their willingness and indeed their ability to engage even in limited forms of struggle with management. During most of Soviet history workers exercised what limited power they possessed partly by threatening to leave their jobs, but also by restricting output and threatening to withdraw cooperation with management in helping overcome the ongoing disruptions to production, for managers well knew that without such cooperation they could not fulfil their plans. It is plausible, perhaps probable, that during the early postwar period morale was so undermined by the food crisis that workers suspended even such attenuated forms of action. In effect, the balance of power had shifted even more strongly against them than under 'normal' circumstances, and management almost certainly sensed this and took advantage of it.

Thirdly, the social composition of the workforce meant that it was disproportionately made up of those who were in the weakest position to exercise any leverage with management: young workers, women, the semi-skilled, and the indentured workers still answerable to the MVD. We know from our discussion of young workers that many managers (but by no means all) treated them in an authoritarian, negligent, and at times abusive manner.

Fourthly, although I have argued throughout this book that the conditions workers encountered would have tended to undermine or negate their positive identification with the regime and the Soviet system brought about by the war, such identification was by no means irrelevant. Even if many people felt that their hopes had been dashed or even betrayed, they nonetheless accepted the need to make sacrifices in order to rebuild the country. Given all of the other factors that weakened their position on the shop floor, this may well have strengthened their docility.

Against all of these considerations we need to set the basic observation that the core features of the Soviet enterprise persisted. The use of work time was erratic at best, and poor at worst, and we simply have no way to assess whether workers saw this more as a burden on them or more as an opportunity to reduce their work effort. We also know that managers, irrespective of their attitudes, accepted that there was a level of customary earnings below which they would not allow wages to sink. If we had to characterize this situation, we might say that during the postwar period the industrial environment which made possible and even necessitated the informal bargaining so readily observed in other periods of Soviet history persisted, while the mechanisms of this bargaining were substantially, if only temporarily, weakened.

If this is correct it leads us to a perhaps unanticipated conclusion. One of the defining characteristics of Soviet industry was that the social antagonisms inherent within the system were sublimated at a political level, where workers had no collective or organizational means to influence events, and were transposed to other arenas within which the individual could assert a certain degree of autonomous action, even if only of a negative, individualistic kind. This manifested itself in a number of ways: high labour turnover; absenteeism; slowing down the pace of work; lack of diligence; endemic petty theft of enterprise property; and alcoholism. To the extent that during the postwar period there was less pressure on managers to reach accommodation with workers, this carried with it certain risks. One was the danger that workers would be more prone to see the division of power within the enterprise as 'them versus us' and less susceptible to any integrative, corporatist rhetoric or ideology concerning the 'collective' striving towards a common purpose. We have some evidence of this, for example, the work stoppages noted in chapters 2 and 3. Such overt manifestations of collective action were rare, however. Nevertheless, the undermining of the bargain still did not necessarily work to the advantage of the regime, because it negated one of the mechanisms through which incipient conflict could be regulated. While this may have reduced the extent to which workers actively impeded production, it equally removed the 'positive' aspect of informal bargaining, namely management's ability to enlist workers' cooperation in reducing the disruptions to production coming from other quarters. To the regime it may have appeared that it had suppressed those tendencies within the enterprise which acted as constraints upon output, but this was only an illusion. Neither the culture of informal bargaining nor the underlying need for it had disappeared. It could be contained for a time but, like most of the other pressures which the Stalinist regime had placed upon society, not indefinitely. When Khrushchev began to roll back the most repressive aspects of Stalin's rule the Soviet enterprise very quickly reassumed the patterns of shop-floor interaction which had arisen during the 1930s; these then further evolved to manifest all of those features which I outlined at the beginning of this chapter, and which played a major role in the decline of the Soviet economy under Brezhnev and Gorbachev.

Conclusion: labour and the 'renormalization' of Stalinist social relations

Let us begin by summarizing the book's main arguments. From there I move on to address some of the conceptual implications they have for my interpretation of postwar Stalinism and the legacy it bequeathed to Stalin's successors.

The nature of the postwar labour force. The Stalinist regime pursued a policy of rapid industrial recovery, which in turn demanded high rates of accumulation. Although the main shortage was in 'capital', that is, plant, equipment, fuel, and materials, there was a serious shortage of labour power in critical areas, most importantly, coal mining, construction, metallurgy, and transport. To satisfy their demand the regime had to mobilize millions of new workers. Many of them were slave labourers under the control of the MVD, but the regime relied even more heavily on semi-free or indentured labour. These workers came mainly from two sources: the Labour Reserve vocational schools, which conscripted most of its students from the countryside; and workers enlisted through so-called organized recruitment. They formed the core of the workforce in coal mining and construction, and for a brief period also iron and steel. These were key sectors of the economic recovery, yet they were also the sectors with the worst conditions and were heavily reliant on an unwilling workforce. All workers, however, faced severe restrictions on their freedom of action and movement. Leaving one's job without official sanction warranted a long sentence in a labour camp.

The postwar food crisis. Any hope on the regime's part that it might be able to relax its use of coercion suffered a setback with the harvest failure of 1946. The standard of living in early 1946 was already extremely low. In the wake of the harvest failure and ensuing famine, the regime chose not to release food from its reserves, but instead ruthlessly suppressed consumption in both the countryside and the towns.

245

Millions of workers lost their entitlements to rations and millions more saw their access to food sharply reduced. While there were relatively few deaths among workers from hunger, the decline in nutrition was pronounced, especially among young workers, many of whose wages were below subsistence level. And, although the regime had not planned on this crisis, it nonetheless played an important role in dampening down popular expectations and helping to render society politically passive.

The recovery in the standard of living. The food crisis reached its nadir in 1947, and during 1948 there was a gradual improvement. By the end of 1947 the regime felt sufficiently in control of events to end rationing, but outside Moscow and perhaps Leningrad this did not bring noticeable short-term improvement in standards of living. On the contrary, in small centres, more outlying industrial regions, and on the railways, the food situation continued to be extremely harsh throughout 1948. There is evidence that many railway workers even engaged in industrial action to force the payment of wage arrears which were driving them deeper into poverty. Only towards the end of 1948 did real improvement set in. Yet even by 1952, although probably no workers were on the verge of starvation, the diet remained very spartan, and workers could lay hold of only small quantities of even basic consumer goods, such as shoes and clothing. Moreover, in two other areas the improvement in the quality of life remained slow and uneven, namely housing and health care.

The position of young workers. Within the group of indentured labourers young workers played a prominent role. Numerically they were central to the recovery plan, but of all indentured workers they probably endured the very worst conditions of appalling housing, low pay, and very frequently discrimination at work at the hands of factory managers. In theory it was the task of the Komsomol to oversee improvements in their conditions and more generally to attempt to socialize them into good 'Soviet citizens'. This proved an almost impossible task. Enthusiasm for the Komsomol was low, even in industries such as engineering, which enjoyed better conditions.

Criminal law and labour turnover. For a significant minority of workers their conditions were sufficiently desperate that they risked heavy criminal penalties and ran away from their jobs or the Labour Reserve training schools into which they had been conscripted. Most of the turnover was in a few sectors – coal mining, construction, and iron and steel – but these were precisely the industries on which the regime had placed highest economic priority. Yet deeper examination shows that most of those who fled were never caught. In fact, the judicial authorities made only half-hearted attempts to pursue them. What emerged was a complex network of collusion: workers and Labour Reserve students fled back to the village, where local police, public prosecutors, Party officials, and heads of collective farms concealed their whereabouts and protected them from capture. Unable to retain a workforce in its core industries the regime tried to make good the losses by drafting yet more young villagers into these industries. Turnover did, in fact, begin to decline as the standard of living started to improve from 1948 onwards. From about 1950 the regime also began to reduce its dependence on indentured labourers, partly because the industrial ministries recognized that they were an inefficient workforce.

Inside the industrial enterprise. Finally, we examined life inside the industrial enterprise. Not surprisingly, given the rundown of plant and equipment during the war, combined with the regime's general neglect of its citizens' welfare, working conditions in Soviet factories were harsh and hazardous. Some of the strains this imposed on workers were exacerbated by the typically Soviet patterns of work organization, which were dictated by chronic shortages of parts and materials, the unreliability of equipment, and poor quality of repairs. Such patterns of work were discernible in the 1930s, and the war, despite the harshness of internal discipline regulations, had done nothing to transform them. After the war losses of work time were considerable, partly because of the rise in absenteeism after criminal penalties against it were lifted in 1951, but mostly because of the chronic disruptions to production which plagued almost every factory. The postwar period does, however, suggest that one important aspect of Soviet industrial relations had been at least partially, if only temporarily, undermined. Workers appear to have had less bargaining power on the shop floor, and thus were less able to exert informal pressure on line managers to modify the intensity of labour and centrally decreed downward pressures on earnings.

By the time of Stalin's death the Soviet economy had made good its war losses and resumed a path of economic growth. With the process of accumulation completed and social tensions having eased, the regime showed signs of relaxing its reliance on coercion and repression, at least among industrial workers, and probably against most other sectors of society. To what extent, then, had Stalin achieved a political victory over the Soviet population? I assess this question in the final two sections.

The limits of coercion in the postwar recovery

As I discussed in the introduction, in the aftermath of the war diverse groups within Soviet society had harboured a number of desires and demands. It is a reasonable guess that most people felt that what they sought was compatible with the professed goals and the existing political structures of the Stalinist version of Soviet power; others, such as those peasants who entertained a fantasy about the liquidation of the collective farms, clearly were not so sure. What most more or less shared in common was the hope that the mild political and ideological relaxations of the war years would continue and that they would be left in peace to get on with the process of rebuilding their country and their lives. As one interviewee told me, the returning soldiers approached the tasks of reconstruction 'with enthusiasm, but it was a joyless enthusiasm . . . We did everything that we had to do, but not gladly.' The Stalinist elite soon disabused the population of any illusions. From a political standpoint, the elite had to show that, following the concessions made in order to prose-cute the war, the Stalinist political system would be fully restored. It is true that, unlike the social turbulence of the first prewar five-year plans, the elite faced no concerted mass threats to its domination. There were no mass protests (if we ignore the vexations of banditry in the Western territories) and no threats of rebellion. Nonetheless, the elite under-stood that it was absolutely essential to demonstrate to society that it was firmly in control, and that it, and it alone, would set the polit-ical, ideological, economic, and social agenda for the USSR's future development.

The main argument of this book is that this political imperative was accompanied by, and indeed completely bound up with, an economic one. The reconstruction of the postwar economy meant far more than repairing buildings, putting machinery back into service, and bringing production and investment back up to prewar levels. No economy ex-ists in isolation from its political and social context. The reconstruction of Soviet industry meant above all else the reconstruction of the entire Stalinist economic system, including its top-down decision-making struc-tures and power relations. Without this the perpetuation of the Stalinist political system would have been impossible. The very essence of Stalin-ist industrialization of the 1930s was that the elite's power, the source of its privileges, and indeed the driving force behind the entire economy lay in heavy industry. It was therefore essential that in the immediate post-war period the restoration of heavy industry should proceed at breakneck speed and at all costs. This would have been the case even if the leadership had not wished to bolster the USSR's military capacity in the face of a deteriorating international situation.

Once this decision had been made it meant that the elite would seek a maximal rate of accumulation and the forcible suppression of popular consumption at a time when the population was desperate for an improvement in the standard of living. All resources – both human and non-human – were to be marshalled to this end. It is beyond dispute that the 1946 harvest failure and the ensuing famine made the consumption crisis sharper and led to social tensions and upheavals which the elite had neither anticipated nor wanted. But the fact is that the coercive subordination of consumption to the interests of accumulation would have taken place even without it. We should keep in mind that the hardships here were not confined just to food. The wretched housing stock, the painstakingly slow restoration in most cities of basic amenities like sewerage and supplies of clean water, and pervasive ill health all weighed heavily on popular morale. For the elite, this forcible acceleration of accumulation required more than harnessing a despairing and exhausted society to the task. It meant exercising an unprecedented degree of control over the toiling population, far more than the regime had attempted to impose during the 1930s. Granted, those peasants who remembered collectivization, the August 1932 law against theft of socialist property, and the famine of 1932–3 may not have perceived much difference, but workers certainly did. Not only was their freedom of movement sharply curtailed and violations punished by long sentences in a labour camp, but the regime subjected millions of workers, predominantly the young (but not only them) to forced mobilization. This part of the workforce – and it was a sizeable minority, equivalent to the entire net addition of workers to industry, transport, and construction between 1945 and Stalin's death – was in effect semi-enserfed.

By suppressing consumption in this way the drive for accumulation necessarily provoked counterreactions from many of those who suffered. Unlike the First Five-Year Plan, which saw countless outbreaks of strikes, angry meetings, and street demonstrations, the responses now were muted and overwhelmingly individual. Those in the most dire circumstances and without families ran away from their job or training school; others stole; still others, on the evidence we have, fell increasingly into passivity. Only a relatively small handful appear to have engaged in any kind of collective action. Because of the regime's intrinsic contempt for both workers and peasants, it could conceive of no way to control what it saw as refractory behaviour other than to criminalize it. It thus made criminals of a sizeable minority of the population. This, however, revealed another basic truth of Stalinist society, what we might call the 'psychology of circumvention'.

This aspect of Stalinism had already become well entrenched before the war. The almost impossible demands which the plans had placed upon managers, workers, and collective farmers had virtually compelled them to break the rules, circumvent restrictions, lie about their activities, and then conceal any and all of their transgressions from the centre. Many of these were discussed in chapter 6: managers would produce one type of good and say they had produced another; line managers would refuse to impose higher output norms and conceal violations of labour discipline; workers would inflate output figures. To the extent that these various economic actors succeeded in this, their actions tended to undermine the centre's control over the economy, the results of which never conformed to the centre's expectations. At another level, however, the perpetual circumvention of orders gave the system a degree of flexibility it never would have possessed if its economic managers and toilers had simply tried to carry out the formal dictates of the central plans. Partly because the planning authorities were divorced from the day-to-day realities of production, and partly because the plans were a vehicle for realizing the goals of the elite, which were inimical to the goals of the bulk of society, the plans in their formal versions were always unrealistic and unrealizable. As I also discussed in chapter 6, unless managers and workers had made their own 'adjustments' on the shop floor – for example, by changing the product mix when the required materials were lacking, or altering product specifications when centrally approved designs were clearly faulty – the bottlenecks and shortages endemic to the system would have brought production almost to a standstill. Seen from this perspective, the 'psychology of circumvention' revealed a high level of contradiction within the Stalinist system. It tended to undermine the centre's control over society but at the same time became a condition of the system's survival and reproduction *as a system*. What is more, it became so integral to the inner workings of the economy that it became one of its defining features right up until its ultimate collapse.

How did the postwar years differ in this regard from what was to happen after Stalin's death? What differentiated them was not that society was more malleable, more compliant, or more prone to identify with the politics and ideology of the regime in one period as opposed to another, but that under Stalin the elite was more willing to use repression to bring society to heel. We should at least consider the possibility that this readiness to employ force reflected not just the personal pathologies of Stalin and his entourage, nor even their particular views on human nature, but also perhaps a more realistic assessment (compared to their successors) of the fundamental antagonism which existed between the elite and Soviet society. But this dependence on state violence equally reveals the largely reactive nature of Stalinist governance. The centre commanded in the full expectation that people would do what they were told; when the population behaved differently the centre tried *post factum* to recapture its control over events by applying coercion. If that proved inadequate, the centre had few options but to increase the level of coercion even further, although this, too, usually produced counterresponses from below, either because people devised yet more sophisticated methods of evasion, or because sections of society were sufficiently desperate to run the risks of falling victim to the repressive apparatus. In theory the regime had myriad institutions through which it should have been able to render 'anti-social' behaviour minimal and harmless, most importantly the trade unions and the Komsomol. Insofar as they failed in this task – and I have suggested in chapter 4 some of the reasons why this was so – this, too, narrowed the elite's range of options.

   It is in this context that we should analyse the major pieces of repressive legislation that were applied after the war. Clearly the anti-theft laws of 1947 were the most important in terms of the numbers arrested and coerced, but, as we have seen in chapter 5, the laws against quitting equally fall into this category. It is worth reprising the argument I presented there in order to draw out some of its larger significance. Enforcement of these laws broke down at every level. Most of those who fled were from the countryside and when they ran away they went back to their villages. There the village soviets, local Party officials, the local procurators, and even the local militia conspired to prevent their identification, capture, and return.

   This was not simply a conflict between metropolis and countryside. Something of far greater societal significance was at work here. The imperatives of rapid accumulation and restoration had required the regime to criminalize millions of its citizens and reduce millions more to a state of indenture. The leadership felt that it had no other way to carry out the massive tasks of construction and restoration of core sectors, in particular coal mining and iron and steel. When hundreds of thousands of indentured labourers rebelled against their wretched conditions by running away (note, *not* by organizing mass protests or strikes), this left these core sectors short of labour power, which they then tried to solve by petitioning the authorities to provide them with yet more slaves and more indentured labourers, thus setting the entire process in motion anew. In theory the conscientious enforcement of the laws should have reduced these pressures, but there were other institutions within the system which, either out of their own self-interest or because of principled objections, refused to cooperate. This aspect of regime policy therefore broke down. I should stress that this vicious circle would have reproduced itself virtually indefinitely had it not been for an eventual improvement in the standard of living after 1948. It was this that brought labour turnover down to manageable levels, and not institutional conformity or compliance with the goals and policies of the leadership.

With the benefit of hindsight this web of collusion might not seem quite so striking as I have claimed. It certainly fits more or less comfortably into the larger picture historians have built up over the years of Stalinist society as a 'recalcitrant society'. Yet in these early postwar years something more was going on. The social turmoil engendered by the attack on consumption created fissures both between and within the institutions of the regime itself – fissures which, I would maintain, went far beyond the types of institutional conflicts upon which historians have usually concentrated, for example, between centre and periphery, between managers and central planners, between industrial ministries, or bloodletting at the top of the hierarchy itself.

One of the clearest examples of this is procuracy's reaction to the wartime laws on labour discipline. The procuracy did not like these laws, and in fact had tried to have both quitting and absenteeism decriminalized right after the war. When the procuracy lost this battle it continued to carry out all of the formal procedures needed to enforce the legislation, as bureaucratic and costly as they were. District and oblast' procurators had to file detailed quarterly reports on how many had run away, how many had been searched for and located, how thoroughly investigators had conducted case investigations – including, I should stress, seeking mitigating circumstances which would justify leniency (such mitigating circumstances were not hard to find: bad housing, food shortages, appalling working conditions, and general neglect by factory or vocational school management). By the same token, local procurators would appeal with equal conscientiousness against what they considered to be unjust convictions, on the one hand, and overly lenient acquittals or sentences, on the other. Overriding all of this was the exasperation and indeed near indifference with which the highest procuracy officials, most notably but not exclusively Safonov, USSR Procurator General, treated complaints from enterprise managers and Ministry of Labour Reserve officials that the law was not being enforced. There were no hysterical reproaches of subordinates for 'sabotage', no pressure exerted on oblast' or district procuracies to clean up their act. On the contrary, the documents reveal an insistence on the observance of legal procedures and a resistance to pressure for tighter enforcement, even when such pressures came from inside the organization, that is, from other sections of the procuracy itself. Time and again Safonov was approached with requests to tighten up various loopholes which were allowing offenders to go unpunished, and he consistently refused.

We need to be careful how we interpret this. We know from Peter Solomon's study of how the procuracy enforced the anti-theft laws that there, too, they found the whole matter somewhat distasteful. In a letter to Zhdanov, dated 19 June 1948, Safonov noted, 'The court must hand down a penalty of no less than seven years' deprivation of freedom for the theft of a pair of galoshes, for the theft of three metres of satin, etc. Sometimes such sentences are totally incomprehensible to citizens, and create the impression that the severity of the penalty does not match the severity of the crime, since penalties for other serious crimes are clearly lower than those for theft.' A murderer, he noted, received a maximum penalty of eight years, or ten years if there were aggravating circumstances involved. An official convicted of bribery received only two years' deprivation of freedom. 'Thus for petty theft from production the court must by law fix a sentence of between seven and ten years, for premeditated murder, from one to eight years, and for accepting a bribe, up to two years' deprivation of freedom.'[1] These reservations notwithstanding, the procuracy oversaw the enforcement of these edicts and, as I have noted, at least 2 million people were convicted under them. Like the labour laws, however, local networks of officials, including kolkhoz chairs and local prosecutors, judges, and militia, allowed a lot of offenders to slip through the net.

The anti-theft laws and the laws against labour turnover both show the procuracy as an almost schizophrenic organization. Because it accepted the basic principles and foundations of the Stalinist system, it supervised the application of the most brutal and inhumane laws and willingly presided over the despatch of several million Soviet citizens into labour camps. At the same time it was in charge of inspecting the state of the camps and was not averse to launching heated attacks on the MVD when, in its view, conditions had sunk below tolerable levels.[2] More broadly, the procuracy saw itself as the system's guarantor of rationality and the defender of legal norms. When it thought the laws were bad its insistence on the norms effectively condoned massive law-breaking. When it

---

[1] GARF, f. 8131, op. 37, d. 4041, l. 372–5.

[2] I have not made a special study of this regarding camps for adult prisoners, but examples can be found in GARF, f. 8131, op. 29, d. 480, l. 89–90, and d. 476, l. 40, 42, 44. We also have the well-documented conflict between the procuracy and the MVD over the children's Labour Colonies, discussed in ch. 4 (see above, pp. 153–4).

accepted the laws it had no difficulty, ideological or practical, enforcing them. The core of the problem was that the procuracy was operating as a guarantor of legality within a system with political rules and power relations that expressly denied any role to legal norms.

The desperate social situation equally threw into disarray those institutions nominally responsible for monitoring workers' welfare, most notably the trade unions and to some extent also the Komsomol. The numerous reports (some of which I cited in chapter 4) filed by Komsomol inspectors on the conditions of Labour Reserve students and young workers bristle with genuine anger at the circumstances in which they had to work and live: filthy, unheated, lice-ridden barracks; workers with no shoes or underwear; managerial indifference towards their pay, health, and safety. The reports of the trade union inspectors – whose job it was to monitor working and living conditions and enforce regulations on safety and hours – were at times equally scathing, and there were even occasions when they did not just threaten to close down sections of a factory but actually did so.[3] We should not exaggerate the frequency of such actions, which were no doubt the exception and not the rule. But they are noteworthy for two reasons. First, the unions were here encroaching upon the prerogatives of management and, secondly, in doing this they were endangering the process of accumulation.

Even more graphic, however, is the crisis into which all of these institutions were thrown by the price rises and ration cuts of September 1946. Then, as discussed in detail in chapter 2, unions, local procurators, and local Party organizations reacted with dismay and disbelief. They flooded the centre with a barrage of appeals, pleas, and on occasion quite forthright expressions of indignation in what were largely futile attempts to have these measures relaxed, if not actually reversed. Yet for all their protests none of these organizations and institutions grasped the essential fact that this massive hardship was a deliberate policy of the regime. Like loyal Communists arrested during the Terror of the mid-1930s, they were convinced there had been some mistake.

At least some workers appear to have adopted a different approach. They refused to report for work until their rations were restored, although we have no idea if their actions produced a positive result. Perhaps even more dramatic, because it clearly occurred on a far larger scale, was the mass protest of railway workers during early 1948 against the failure of their ministry to pay wages on time.[4] This latter incident is potentially

---

[3] RGASPI, f. 17, op. 131, d. 112, l. 107–9, 202, 205–6; *Trud*, 8 August 1946; RGAE, f. 1884, op. 31, d. 7880, l. 174–6.
[4] See above, ch. 3, pp. 85–8.

of some significance, because it suggests that, among all the cases of institutional 'schizophrenia' observed during this period, the unions were in a somewhat unique position: for in coming to the defence of their 'constituency' they on occasion went beyond merely beseeching the higher authorities for some special dispensation, and displayed some degree of militancy. This militancy was certainly muted and occurred within definite boundaries. It was directed against management and the ministries in charge of their enterprises or branches of production, and never against the Party or the Stalinist leadership, to which the unions remained steadfastly loyal.

The most striking example of this attitude is that of the railway unions, the reactions of which we are able to trace in detail thanks to the presence in the archives of some thirteen volumes of correspondence between the rail unions and USSR Ministry of Railways during 1948. Their overt or implicit defence of the work stoppages against wage arrears may be the most obvious instance of their adversarial stance towards their parent ministry, but it is not the only one. The different union authorities, from local committees, to oblast' committees, and even the union central committees, constantly pestered and harassed the Railways Ministry over medical facilities, shortages of soap, the state of local bathhouses, and the ministry's failure to provide adequate housing. The ministry did not usually meet their demands, but the tone of the telegrams and letters between the two suggest that the unions saw the ministry not as a partner in the race for plan fulfilment, but in terms of 'them' versus 'us', as an employer with which the unions were frequently in conflict. This would hardly sustain the traditional image of Soviet trade unions as corporatist entities which were mere appendages of management. Let us be clear here: the question is not that this image is false; on the contrary, it largely conforms to the reality of Soviet trade unions from the late 1920s until the middle of *perestroika*. The unions had disposal over a range of benefits – what we would today call the social wage – and tried to use their disbursement as a weapon to discipline the workforce. During the early five-year plans, for example, the unions attempted to make the receipt of housing, full pensions, disability benefits, and scarce consumer goods conditional on loyalty to the enterprise and fulfilment of production targets. More insidiously, the unions were the enforcers of the production plan, and it is not uncommon to find instances in the 1930s in which it was the factory union committees that attacked management for failing to impose norm rises and speedup. In the post-Stalin period the unions were instrumental in constructing a more paternalistic environment within the factories, the goal of which, with somewhat more subtlety than in the 1930s, was equally to dampen down dissent and bolster discipline.

Although in both periods we see evidence of enterprise unions taking up individual grievance cases, by no stretch of the imagination could we say that they saw themselves as defenders of the workforce or as opponents of management. What was out of kilter during the early postwar period, therefore, was not our understanding of the nature of Soviet trade unions, but the behaviour of some of the unions themselves. Nor were the railway unions the only examples here. Other unions expressed subdued hostility towards management over a number of specific issues, primarily abuses of the overtime laws, late payment of wages, and safety conditions. Admittedly, the picture is by no means consistent. Very often the union inspectors, central committees, or oblast' committees cast equal or even more blame on the factory union organizations for their failure to defend workers' interests. Sometimes such attacks were clearly rhetorical, but in other cases they were quite earnest.

We should not, of course, overestimate the force or power of these union responses. They were clearly far milder than those of many local union organizations during the tumult of the First Five-Year Plan, when strikes and demonstrations were common and union activists not infrequently sided openly with the workers. What is significant about the unions in the early postwar period is, first, that the unions had already been tamed and 'Stalinized' during the course of the 1930s and, secondly, that the responses observed here were not those of rank-and-file activists, but of official trade union bodies, including in several cases the middle and upper echelons of the union bureaucracy. In this regard the actions and attitudes of the branch unions at times diverged considerably from those of VTsSPS, which remained an integral organ of the Stalinist state.

These various qualifications notwithstanding, the different examples cited in this section are indicative of a larger and more basic point. The consumption crisis, which lasted right up until the end of 1948, weakened the institutional coherence of the Stalinist structures of governance, and attenuated or even nullified some of the mechanisms through which the regime sought to exercise control over society. I am not arguing that the system was in any danger of breaking up into factions. That would be absurd. Only *some* sections of *some* institutions appear to have reacted, and then only over *some* issues. By and large these were people or institutional entities which had direct, day-to-day, face-to-face contact with those who bore the brunt of the crisis: collective farm chairpersons and rural judicial and militia officials who refused to implement the anti-theft laws or the laws against illegally quitting one's job; trade union and Komsomol inspectors outraged by the conditions in which the workers (*their* constituents) had to live; individual trade unions or individual trade union committees which, like the inspectors, tried to deal with the grievances of their workers and their families and compel managers or ministries to take some action – any action – to resolve them. None of these institutions, and probably very few of the individuals within them (although without access to their inner thoughts we cannot know), saw themselves in conflict with the state, with what they understood by the concept of 'Soviet power', and certainly not with Stalin and the Party leadership. By the same token, however, these were real divergences, qualitatively different from the conflicts and internal negotiations between ministries or between leadership factions which Western observers (especially advocates of so-called interest-group theory) divined as a guiding principle of Soviet decision-making in the years following Stalin's death. These were not institutional entities jockeying for influence or a more favourable allocation of resources. These were institutions and individuals which perceived aspects of postwar Soviet reality that they found profoundly unsettling. Either they did not understand what response the regime was expecting from them or they were unwilling to play to the script exactly as they found it written. Perhaps they, too, carried over into the postwar years some of the ideas of independence and heightened expectations developed during the war, especially at the front. Such ambiguities, however, proved only temporary.

Political consolidation and historical decline

Once again, let us go back to one of the themes raised in this book's introduction. In her early articles Elena Zubkova advanced the provocative thesis that, whilst the Stalinist regime appeared to have emerged from the war politically invincible, in fact it found itself confronted by a society quite unprepared automatically to accept a return to the *status quo ante bellum*. The regime, uncertain how to proceed, required a considerable period – up until 1947, Zubkova argues – before it could begin fully to restore its authoritarian political control. This argument, in my view, is essentially correct, but it is vulnerable to the objection that Zubkova deduced it almost solely from an examination of popular opinion. No matter how provocative the examples she can cite, such studies do indeed suffer from a methodological weakness. They can establish the presence within society of particular sets of ideas and attitudes, but they cannot determine how widespread they were. Were they the vocalizations of a few isolated individuals which the Party agitators, secret police, or trade union bureaucrats chose to include in their reports, or were they indicative of ideas and opinions held by masses of people? One aim of this book has been to try to approach this problem from a different direction, namely to discern and interpret the stresses within society and within the institutional mechanisms through which the elite tried to execute its rule by looking not just at what people said, but at what they actually did.

On this basis I would agree that there was a fundamental turning point in the late Stalin period, after which the regime very clearly regained control over events and entered a period of political consolidation. I would date this turning point not in 1947, with the intensification of repression against the intelligentsia (signalled for Zubkova by the Philosophy Debate), but in 1948 or 1949. It was then that the economy began to reach prewar levels of production. This had two interconnected effects. First, the standard of living improved sufficiently to curb labour turnover and theft. From the regime's point of view this meant there were fewer incidents of potentially disruptive anti-social behaviour which had to be repressed. This helps explain what might otherwise seem a curious phenomenon of this period, namely that, while the intimidation and repression of the intelligentsia and within the hierarchy were increasing (along with anti-Semitism), the number of ordinary people being incarcerated or sentenced to corrective labour was going down.[5] Secondly, the completion of industrial recovery meant that, with the temporary exception of coal mining and related construction, the regime could decrease its dependence on the forcible conscription into the workforce of unwilling youngsters, a group among whom labour discipline (including illegal quitting) remained a problem. One clear sign of this is the contraction of the Labour Reserve system, which by 1952 was a fraction of its former size and recruited mainly through volunteers.

It is unquestionably true that this calming process took place against the backdrop of an increasingly vocal authoritarianism, and that this acted to intimidate all of society, and not just its direct victims in the intelligentsia and apparatus. To this extent the political clampdown helped to create the more tepid social atmosphere, instead of taking place despite it. But this alone does not adequately explain the decline in social ferment, for, as we have seen, repression on its own did not necessarily prevent people from violating the law or acting in ways the regime considered an obstacle to its objectives.

Certainly from 1950 until Stalin's death we see clear signs that the regime was relaxing its overt pressure on rank-and-file workers, if not on the peasantry. In July 1951 the regime decriminalized absenteeism. Workers responded by doubling or tripling the number of days they failed

---

[5] Thus the number of people sentenced to 'deprivation of freedom' fell from around 1 million in 1947 to just over half a million in 1952 (GARF, f. 9492, op. 6s, d. 14, l. 29). On the clampdown on the intelligentsia, beginning with the Philosophy Debate, see Zubkova, *Russia After the War*, pp. 123–9.

to show up for work. The regime did not react by reimposing criminal penalties. Instead it continued with the new policy, which called on managers to treat absenteeism as a breach of internal discipline regulations or brought the guilty before the now revived Comrades' Courts. Both were somewhat less than reliable solutions. Managers could not always be trusted to impose penalties and the Comrades' Courts were by and large empty institutions which barely functioned.

Workers showed a willingness to test the boundaries of what was now permissible in other ways as well. In April 1949 over a thousand coal miners in Chelyabinsk oblast' appear successfully to have refused forcible transfer to jobs in mining construction, claiming that they would suffer a drop in earnings and worse conditions in their new jobs. The Chelyabinsk oblast' procurator reported the incident to his superiors in Moscow, but no action seems to have been taken against the miners. Unable to learn from this lesson, in December 1949, the Coal Ministry ordered a nationwide mobilization of over 25,000 miners into construction, and again there were mass refusals: only 11,000 workers were actually transferred. But that is not the end of the tale. In early 1950, a group of miners in Moscow oblast' went so far as to file a suit against the Coal Ministry, arguing that the latter had tried to transfer them without their permission. In the meantime, they were refusing to work at their new jobs. In 1947 or 1948 these workers would at the very least have been committing organized absenteeism and been vulnerable to prosecution; a less charitable response by the authorities could have seen them sent to a labour camp for going on strike. Now, however, both the People's Courts and the procuracy supported them and upheld their grievance.[6]

If workers felt bolder about articulating such grievances, they also knew that their ability genuinely to influence events within their enterprise (not to mention society as a whole) was distinctly limited. A regular feature of factory life was the so-called production conferences organized at shop floor level in order to discuss problems of work organization and how they might be rectified. In theory these were supposed to serve as vehicles through which workers could be mobilized and given a feeling of

---

[6] The Chelyabinsk oblast' case is in GARF, f. 8131, op. 37, d. 5036, l. 134–6. The December 1949 mobilization and the mineworkers' suit against the Coal Ministry are *ibid.*, op. 28, d. 274, l. 3–3ob., 4–5. It is clear that once again the procuracy was acting as a force for common sense in this situation. The mobilization was undoubtedly unpopular not just with the miners but with mine managers, who had no interest in losing skilled workers. Thus the procuracy was not only defusing a potentially serious confrontation with a large number of workers; it was also siding with the mine managers against their own ministry. By the same token, it is unlikely that the workers who refused mobilization could have escaped at least some form of sanction had mine management not protected them.

genuine, if highly prescribed, participation in factory life. In reality the meetings were carefully orchestrated affairs, with a limited agenda that most workers found completely boring. Few rank-and-file workers actually spoke at them, in part because they knew they ran a high risk of being victimized by management. A 1950 report from a Party propagandist at a munitions factory in Tula oblast' summed up the difficulty:

The lack of active participation by rank-and-file workers is explained by the fact that there is no opportunity at meetings to discuss in a business-like manner vital questions of the enterprise or the shop, to develop a critique of shortcomings in [their] work. Meetings have the character of giving directives and orders[;] instead of an exchange of opinions administrative pressure often predominates.[7]

Workers at a coal mine in the same oblast' complained of management, 'The whole trouble is that they don't listen to us. There's a lot of chatter and little action. I go to the meetings, but I get angry at the time wasted for nothing.' A propman at the same pit commented, 'At one time I counted myself among the activists, but now I feel my attempts to influence any improvement at work pass by in vain, and like it or not I'm dropping it all, I've stopped going to the conferences: they don't listen to us.'[8]

Workers received an identical response when they took their complaints over the heads of management to the local city or oblast' Party authorities. This same report claimed that local Party officials had little direct contact with workers, while the workers, for their part, felt it was useless to take their complaints to them. Revealingly (and the report is probably accurate here), the only step they thought might bring results was to write directly to the Central Committee in Moscow.[9]

What emerges from these accounts is that workers had less fear of direct repression and were less desperate about their actual material survival than during the first four or five postwar years, but their actions were curbed by a realistic assessment of their political powerlessness. Another expression of this is that we find virtually no evidence of trade union 'militancy'; the unions, too, had been fully reintegrated at every level back into the bureaucratic structure. Lest anyone doubt this, they need only look at the succession of reforms which Khrushchev introduced to try to

---

[7] RGASPI, f. 17, op. 132, d. 291, l. 83–4. Elena Zubkova, *Obshchestvo i reformy*, pp. 94–5, cites this and similar meetings as evidence of worker discontent. This is certainly true, but what really emerges here is the extent of workers' atomization and how any efforts to voice their complaints were stifled by management and the local trade union and Party organizations.

[8] RGASPI, f. 17, op. 132, d. 291, l. 86. This material, too, is used by Zubkova, *Obshchestvo i reformy*, pp. 94–5.

[9] RGASPI, f. 17, op. 132, d. 291, l. 87. For similar criticisms of production conferences in the metallurgical industry, see GARF, f. 7680, op. 5, d. 152, l. 79–80 and d. 203, l. 1–3.

motivate workers to take an active part in social and political life after the moribund experience of the late Stalin years. In 1958 there was a reform of the trade unions, which accused the unions of failing to defend their members against the arbitrary actions of management, and of the bureaucratic conduct of meetings and elections. The trade union reform was backed up by other mobilizing campaigns, all of which had the same objective: to convince workers that the new leadership was 'democratizing' Soviet life and was removing the barriers to popular participation which had led to their alienation. Perhaps the two most famous of these were the twin campaigns to recruit enthusiastic young people to help settle the Virgin Lands in Kazakhstan and Western Siberia, and the newly industrializing regions of Siberia and the Far East (the so-called Social Call-up). Within industry Khrushchev launched a Movement for Communist Labour, which sought to spur productivity through moral appeals, rather than simple monetary incentives. We are not concerned here with the relative successes or failures of these various efforts. What is relevant here is that Khrushchev and those around him perceived – quite correctly – the profound estrangement which had grown up between the unions and the workforce, and that this was a major obstacle to Khrushchev's efforts to win some degree of popular legitimacy for his regime.[10]

I would argue, therefore, that in terms of the elite's relationship with its industrial workforce the period from 1950 to 1953 did not hail a process of political 'liberalization'. Any moves towards relaxation, such as they were, were symptomatic of an elite now completely self-confident about the security of its preeminence. It could allow workers greater leeway because it no longer felt itself under threat. To paraphrase Sheila Fitzpatrick, we could say that the period 1950–2 marks a normalization of Stalinist society or, perhaps more accurately, its descent into bureaucratic routinization. We see this almost everywhere: in the work of the trade unions; in the growth, under Malenkov's tutelage, of the industrial ministries into semi-autonomous mini-empires; in the tedious preoccupation with day-to-day administrative concerns which comes to dominate the documents in the ministerial, trade union, and Party archives. It is even evident in the stationery used for correspondence. In sharp distinction from the early postwar years, it is now of good quality, with bold and well-designed letterheads, and is well printed; in short, it exudes the confidence of a ruling class which expects to be around for a very long time.

One possible interpretation of these observations is that by March 1953 the system had achieved a high or at least reasonable degree of social

---

[10] For these various campaigns, see Filtzer, *Soviet Workers and De-Stalinization*, pp. 39–46, 54, 71–2, and Zubkova, *Obshchestvo i reformy*, pp. 165–7.

integration. Anyone who has read contemporary accounts of the time, or who has spoken with citizens of the former USSR old enough to recall it, will know of the mass outpourings of grief that swept the large cities when Stalin died. We should be cautious about making too much of this point, since few peasants shared these sentiments of their urban brethren, and even among the latter the intensity of their reaction was to a significant extent prompted by fear and uncertainty over the future, rather than love for the dictator. There were, however, other reasons why we might assume that the population now identified more positively with the leadership. The standard of living had improved. Most people outside the intelligentsia had less reason to fear becoming victims of repression; the intelligentsia and petty officialdom found compensation for their more precarious political position in the fact that they shared disproportionately in the improved levels of consumption. Perhaps most powerful of all, the shared experience of the war was still a strong integrating force.

There is, however, an alternative interpretation. From a political point of view there is a world of difference between a population that, whatever the real inequalities of power within the society, nonetheless sees itself as integrated into the political system, and shares the values, goals, and core aspects of the ideology of the ruling class, and a population that, while it may accept some of the more generalized values of the dominant elite, essentially recognizes its own subordinate status and reconciles itself to the fact that it has few levers or outlets for effecting any fundamental change in this power relationship. It is the latter, and not the former, formulation which most accurately characterizes Soviet society during late Stalinism. Insofar as we can find a postwar ruling class that successfully forged an ideological consensus to sustain its ascendancy, it was Western capitalism, not Stalin's USSR. The combined appeals of rising consumption and anti-Communism – coupled where necessary with the suppression of dissent – allowed the capitalist classes in the United States, Japan, and Western Europe to survive early waves of mass discontent (which gripped the United States as much as Western Europe) and even for a while to perpetuate the myth that they had finally transcended class struggles and class societies. This consensus survived for nearly twenty years. It came undone rather dramatically from the mid-1960s to the mid-1970s, under the pressure of a number of convergent forces, but even then the powerful appeal of anti-Communism, which drew sustenance from the patently visible inadequacies of the 'Soviet model', played no small role in helping capitalism to weather what was probably the most dangerous challenge to its existence during the nearly six decades since the end of World War II.

How is it that Western capitalism, so badly discredited by the rise of fascism and the devastation of World War II, could construct such a